Face-to-Face

Interpersonal Communication in the Workplace

Peter Chiaramonte
Kennesaw State College

Marco Adria
Athabasca University

Prentice Hall Canada Inc., Scarborough, Ontario

Canadian Cataloguing in Publication Data

Chiaramonte, Peter, 1951-
    Face-to-face : interpersonal communication in the workplace

ISBN: 0-13-287590-X

1. Interpersonal communication. 2. Interpersonal relations.
I. Adria, Marco, 1959-   . II.Title.

HF5549.5.C6C54 1994   302.2   C93-094349-X

Prentice-Hall, Inc., Englewood Cliffs, New Jersey
Prentice-Hall International (UK) Limited, London
Prentice-Hall of Australia, Pty. Limited, Sydney
Prentice-Hall Hispanoamericana, S.A., Mexico City
Prentice-Hall of India Private Limited, New Delhi
Prentice-Hall of Japan, Inc., Tokyo
Simon & Schuster Asia Private Limited, Singapore
Editora Prentice-Hall do Brasil, Ltda., Rio de Janeiro

ISBN 0-13-287590-X

Acquisitions Editor: Jacqueline Wood
Developmental Editor: Linda Gorman
Production Editor: Imogen Brian
Permissions/Photo Research: Robyn Craig
Cover and Internal Design: Monica Kompter
Page Layout: Hermia Chung
Cover Image: M.C. Escher, *Bond of Union* © 1956 M.C. Escher Foundation,
  Baarn, Holland. All rights reserved.

1 2 3 4 5   RRD   98 97 96 95 94

Printed and bound in the U.S.A.

Every reasonable effort has been made to obtain permissions for all articles and data
used in this edition. If errors or omissions have occurred, they will be corrected in
future editions provided written notification has been received by the publisher.

To Taryn, Michael, Dylan,
and Mia Anna

For Kathy, Laura, Joel

Table of Contents

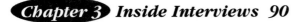 *Inside Interviews 90*

Preface

Two personal experiences illustrate the main themes of this book: face-to-face communication and personal growth.

The first experience is Marco's, and it occurred on April 28, 1987, in Toronto. Marco had arranged for an interview with Peter Gzowski, the host of CBC Radio's program *Morningside*. The interview was to take place in the splendid shabbiness of CBC's then Jarvis Street studios. This is Marco's description of what happened.

" The interview was to appear as an article in *Aurora* magazine, published by Athabasca University. I had done interviews for the magazine before, but most of them had been by telephone. This was going to be face-to-face. I was anxious about the interview and it showed. Setting up my tape recorder, I felt as if my hands were moving in slow motion as I untangled the cords. Gzowski was gracious enough to find a plug, crawl under his desk, and make my connection. What a start to the interview! Once we got going, we talked about radio in Canada, about the CBC, and about interviewing. Then I asked him about the "tricks" of interviewing. It seemed to me that Gzowski had occasionally in his career used the pacing of an interview, for example, to allow for the posing of a difficult question. In this regard, I mentioned the interview he had done in February 1974 with Prime Minister Trudeau. Gzowski agreed that there were indeed "tricks of the trade" and that Trudeau had been a particularly challenging subject. My interview with Gzowski lasted an hour and the article was published. A couple of months later, Gzowski carried out a well-publicized interview with Trudeau. It had been the first time in a long while that Trudeau had spoken publicly on the Constitution, and as a result the interview as an event became newsworthy in itself. I couldn't help thinking, of course, that by bringing up Gzowski's first interview with the prime minister I had somehow inspired him to reflect on that interview, and learn lessons from it that contributed to the planning and preparation of his next interview with Trudeau. In a way, I felt that Gzowski and I had engaged, briefly at least, in a common purpose. And I also felt that a telephone interview wouldn't have brought that point into the sharp focus for me that a face-to-face conversation did. I have done many interviews since then, but talking to Canada's most famous interviewer was a formative experience for me. It taught me about the importance of reflection and planning, and I have continued to benefit from that lesson. **"**

Peter had a similarly formative experience on a sunny afternoon while sitting on a rock overlooking the Pacific Ocean. His experience shows how reflection—which is an important part of the interpersonal communication process, as we will discuss—can lead to self-awareness.

The Esalen Institute in Big Sur, California, was founded in 1962 by Michael Murphy and Richard Price. It is a kind of administrative home for the human potential movement. The setting for the Institute is spectacular and is an important part of the "Esalen Experience." Highway One—the only road in or out of Esalen—winds along the blasted mountainside with the rocky peaks of the Santa Lucia mountains above and the blue-green swells of the Pacific Ocean below. The baths, pool, garden, falls, lodges, gazebo, children's school, and the "Big House" Conference Center are all situated on a wooded shelf of land overhanging sea cliffs and jagged low-tide outcrops. The main building, named after author and early resident Aldous Huxley, is built on a jut of land near the cliff's edge, and different meeting rooms, named after other famous writers and philosophers who have spent time there, are tucked in among the cypresses and tall mountain pines.

Since its formation, Esalen has been the site of many far-reaching developments in various contemporary interdisciplinary theories and practices. It is popularly considered to be the home base for the exploration into the relationships between philosophy, religion, education, and science. If you had visited Esalen at different times in its history, you might have spent a weekend with historian Arnold Toynbee or perhaps the psychologists Abraham Maslow and R.D. Laing. Paul Tillich, a theologian, has visited Esalen, as have the chemist Linus Pauling and popular musicians such as George Harrison and Joan Baez. People visit Esalen for all sorts of reasons. Michael Murphy once told us that the atmosphere is so amenable to contemplation that he has to keep reminding its visitors that Esalen is a center for learning, similar in purpose to a college, and that all learners eventually have to graduate. Apparently, some people just do not want to leave!

Peter visited Esalen in 1980. Here is what happened.

> ❝I was attending a week-long workshop led by anthropologist and Regent of the University of California, Gregory Bateson. The title of the workshop was "Steps Toward an Ecology of Body/Mind and Nature". Also leading a workshop of her own that same week was resident faculty member Janet Zuckerman. Janet and I were talking about the uses of making lists of goals and I decided to ask her to help me. We did a simple communication exercise where Janet would ask me "What do you want?" and I would answer with the first thought to enter my mind. Each time I answered, Janet would say, "Thank you. Write that down. Now, let me ask you: what do you want?" And I would respond again with the first thing I could think of.
>
> By the time we quit, I had a list of about 40 items that I later divided into four categories: *material items*, like a Ducati motorcycle; wishes for *family fulfillment*, *completed accomplishments*, such as a

PhD dissertation; and a whole host of *challenges and new adventures.* It was a very illuminating learning experience in itself. But let me tell you what happened to that list I made.

Ten years later, in 1990, when my family and I were packing to move to London, Canada, I found the list I had made at Esalen with Janet Zuckerman. I discovered that I had attained about eighty percent of what I said I wanted. The real surprise was that the twenty percent I didn't get, I didn't want anymore. I have found since then that the more accurately I have imagined some desired future—such as increased skill or a challenging opportunity—the more able I am to determine what I really want, and don't want. I advise all of you to sit down with someone you can talk comfortably with and make a list of your goals. Consider, in particular, those goals that you hope to achieve as a result of improving your ability to communicate face-to-face. Better interpersonal communication can lead to almost anything your heart desires. **99**

These stories illustrate the practical application of communication skills. This book is a reflection of both what we *know* about interpersonal communication and what we *understand.* It is not only an expression of theory, but of experience as well.

After attending a seminar on writing in Vancouver, B.C., we went out for dinner and found the following message in a Chinese fortune cookie:

66 The palest ink is stronger than the greatest memory. **99**

Peter immediately taped the message to his notebook. We encourage you to remember those words and to make this book your own.

For encouragement and advice, we thank Andy Higgins at the University of Toronto, Dick Hodgson and Diana Boivin at the University of Western Ontario; Julie and Albert Mills at Saint Mary's University, Stephen Murgatroyd, George Winter, and Richard Hotchkis at Athabasca University; and Linda Gorman, Jackie Wood and Imogen Brian at Prentice Hall. For reviewing the drafts, we thank Joan Condie (Sheridan College), Hal Burnham and Ken Horsman (Algonquin College), Christine Horgan and Ed Rowney (Southern Alberta Institute of Technology), Joe White (Santa Barbara City College), Dulcie Sinn (University of California), Malcolm Howe (Niagara College), Patty Lumb (University of Northern British Columbia), Mary Anne Day (Champlain Regional College), and Laurie Milton (Mount Royal College).

Peter Chiaramonte
Marco Adria

Introduction

Before we get started . . .

This book is about managing interpersonal communication at work, but it is not for managers only. Interpersonal communication is by no means the exclusive domain of managers. Everyone must learn to communicate effectively. We develop the following themes throughout this book: the importance of improving interpersonal skills at work, the centrality of the interview in the workplace, and the need for organizational members to set up coaching relationships among themselves.

Why Should I Learn More About Interpersonal Communication?

What we have sought in writing *Face-to-Face* is to access the communicative power that is available to all organizational members. We believe that individuals must include their own experience and understanding as part of the process of establishing themselves in new organizations, new cultures, and a new future. No organization can ever be entirely detached from the unique individuals who constitute it. Individuals and organizations are truly a *bond of union*—an indivisible whole. Each individual and each organization contributes to putting the puzzle together in a unique way; not like a jigsaw—more like a *hologram*, each piece adding to the clarity of the whole image. Each person is a whole body of integrated knowledge and practice. By encouraging a more dynamic relationship between and within individuals and organizations, we can expand opportunities for the mutual benefit of both. In many futuristic novels such as those that make up Isaac Asimov's *The Foundation Trilogy*, people are portrayed as having replaced face-to-face communication with videoconferences and life-size holographic images which are programmed for human interaction. Some corporate recruiters predict that videoconferencing will soon replace interpersonal face-to-face communication at work. Some say this replacement process has already begun. Entrepreneurs such as Microsoft CEO Bill Gates[1] have staked their reputations on a vision of object-oriented computer programming, multimedia, interactive television, and other projects aimed at transforming how people everywhere communicate.

It is interesting to note, however, that Mr. Gates recently chose to deliver this message—entitled "Microsoft's Vision"—*in person* to over 7200 Seattle-area staffers in the Kingdome in October 1992. We are not against technological innovation in principle. And we agree with Mr. Gates and others who foresee advances in the technology of communication as having a great role to play in the development of management skills. But we do not foresee these types of innovation having the potential to replace face-to-face interpersonal communication in the workplace. Such technological advances may, instead, increase our need for the presence of others while communicating, in order to off-set the deprivation of human contact brought about by machines. This may be why Mr. Gates spoke to his Microsoft employees face-to-face rather than face-to-screen or through videoconferencing.

There is a fundamental difference between having a conversation with a human being and talking to a machine. Despite how sophisticated and user-friendly many of these simulations are, computers, robots, magnetic tape machines, and other devices will always lack an *inner world* of emotion peculiar to human beings. Unlike any form of robotic machine, human beings possess an active inner life that affects everything we hear, feel, and say.

No matter how complex they become, there isn't ever likely to be a machine capable of assessing or revealing all of the internal factors affecting human interaction. Even we have great difficulty learning to read between the lines of our internal and external world realities. Each line of conversation conveys more than one message simultaneously. Machines must depend entirely on the efficiency of language to carry meaning. Even a few missing words can disrupt the flow of a conversation or break contact completely. In conversation only one of several messages is communicated through the actual words used; other essential messages are demonstrated or implied through signals embedded exclusively in face-to-face interpersonal communication.

Not everyone reading this book is, or plans to become, a manager of, say, a small business, or an executive in a complex organization. But we all have to perform various management tasks (planning, coordinating, organizing) which demand well-developed communication skills: a meeting here, a phone call there, lunch with so and so, a private chat on the way to or from the transit stop. All of these situations involve some aspect of face-to-face interpersonal communication. To manage each of these encounters effectively requires a concerted effort to practise specific interpersonal communication skills, and to learn where and when to apply them.

The subject matter of this book is directed to all people seeking to improve their ability to communicate in the workplace, and particularly in managerial circumstances. To perform any managerial function well, a person must first be able to communicate effectively with others. Just look at the employment section of any daily newspaper and see how often the stated job requirements for progressive positions demand a high degree of communication competence. It is difficult to think of a single job in which good interpersonal communication skills are unimportant.

It is not enough just to recognize the importance of face-to-face communication for a career in business. Awareness of this alone does not necessarily make people any better at it. Excellent communicators are also aware that all communication is constant and irreversible. Once expressed, the effect of any verbal or non-verbal message cannot be completely erased. Therefore, we must learn two things: first, how to plan carefully, and second, how to practise and hone our ability to handle particular organizational situations with strategic forethought and mastery.

Most of us take our daily face-to-face interactions and interpersonal communication for granted. We think we already know how to communicate. And to a great extent, this is true. However, with a little more awareness, planning, and practice, you may be surprised at how much room there is for improvement. *Face-to-Face: Interpersonal Communication in the Workplace* introduces the fundamental concepts and techniques of effective interpersonal communication. It invites readers to experiment with, adapt, and refine the specific skills, concepts, and guidelines presented. By actually applying these to your own workplace settings and situations, you will be teaching yourself the most valuable lessons anybody working face-to-face with people can learn.

We acquire most interpersonal communication skills quite naturally just by growing up among people. These skills are part of our natural socialization. We hardly think much about them. Yet somehow we miraculously come to understand how to talk to different kinds of people, when and where to speak, about what, and when to be silent. All of this and more gets socialized in us simply through our exposure to communication in the world-at-large.

We do not, however, always acquire a sound body of knowledge, or appropriate models and concepts to use when faced with opportunities for improving our interpersonal performance. In each of us there is room to learn. Read on.

There are at least three kinds of curricula (or domains of knowledge) which are relevant to organizational communication. First there is the *official curriculum*—consisting of subjects and courses such as interpersonal and presentation skills, writing in organizations, management communication, leadership development, and consulting.

Second there is the unofficial, or s*leeping curriculum*, taught to us in large part through our exposure to the arts and humanities. It is taught as well through our popular culture by way of music, film, literature, television, newspapers, magazines, and multi-media advertisements. Much of this knowledge is unconscious, or "sleeping" within us. Therefore it is largely unreflected upon.

A third kind of curriculum is the *hidden curriculum*, or *affective domain*, consisting of the underlying emotions, values, and beliefs that we incorporate into everything we do or say, and which are mostly taken for granted. What is missing from most learning plans or programs that set out to teach us how to become more effective interpersonal communicators is any active, deliberate, or reflective consideration of all of these domains as a whole.

In this book, we encourage you to combine all three of these curricula into a whole body of integrated knowledge and practice. The active ingredients added to this mix of learning are your, the reader's, personal communication experiences. An important objective of this book is to help you put these domains together as you reflect on your everyday interpersonal experiences.

The Centrality of Interviews in the Workplace

In this book we deal extensively with the skills and knowledge required for interviewing. The interview as a form of personal interaction can be considered more broadly than we might do in popular usage. The interview is something we do when we visit the grocery store or ask for directions. The skills of the interviewer are put into practice as much when we ask a loved one for sympathy as when we ask for advice from a colleague. In short, any time we exchange ideas or information with someone we are having an interview. Interviews have many specialized applications in the workplace. Interviews may be used for recruiting employees, assessing their performance, selling the organization's products or services, giving and receiving instructions, solving problems, and so on. In fact, we suggest that no form of interpersonal communication is used more commonly in an organization than the interview.

We have found the interview to be a challenging and rewarding aspect of our professional and personal lives. We have used the information interview, for example, which we discuss in Chapter 4, to find ways of furthering our education and to invest meaning in our relationships with family and friends. We have used media interviews as opportunities to converse with such accomplished people as Edward de Bono, Leonard Cohen, Anthony Burgess, Northrop Frye, and Peter Gzowski. As we have developed our ability to use the interview to its full potential, we have learned more about others and more about ourselves.

We consider the interview to be a metaphor for all the communication that takes place in an organization, because the interview pervades all organizational activity. Consider the first personal contact you have with an organization for which you will work: the recruitment interview. After you are hired, you are inducted into the organization through an orientation interview. Later, interviews will inform you of your progress in learning the job. You will also receive counselling and information and be promoted or disciplined, all in the context of an interview. Furthermore, you will participate in problem-solving and persuasion through the use of interviews (in our more casual sense of the word). And for many organizations, before you retire or leave, you will be invited to an exit interivew, at which you reflect on your accomplishments and your disappointments.

It is likely that your success in any organization will be determined to a significant degree by your success in interviewing and being interviewed. You may have thought of the interview as simply an opportunity for two people to sit down and talk with one another. And of course, you're right. But it takes a lot of practice to reach that "simple" stage. You must first learn how to conduct an effective interview. Furthermore, as we will emphasize in this book, an interview must be planned, even if in its execution it will be more or less unstructured, allowing both parties to improvise on the format and to discuss topics that neither had considered beforehand. So, while interviews can be very common and casual occurrences, making the most of these interview opportunities is considerably more involved.

Every Coach Needs a Coach

There is an emerging body of knowledge in organizational literature that includes the notions of counselling, mentoring, career development, and team building under the rubric of the *manager-as-coach* metaphor of organizational leadership. We will discuss this phenomenon further in Chapter 6. Some proponents, such as Roger Evered and James Selman,[2] go so far as to present a new theoretical model which claims that "managing equals creating a context for coaching." This is not just saying that coaching is *a part* of the successful manager's role. These men (Evered is a respected professor of management and Selman a busy management consultant) are saying that coaching *is central* to what management must become in order for organizations to remain competitive in the global marketplace.

Coaching in the workplace produces competitive advantages solely through the medium of communication. To improve at any task or skill, it helps to have a coach there to support your learning a new technique, or learning to better an old one. Not only does having a coach provide you with some useful descriptive feedback as to how you are doing, a coach can also help you to pick out blind spots in your performance, as well as help you to prepare for significant real-life situations all workers must face.

If you don't have a coach it may be tougher to practise communication skills, but it can still be done. Practising in front of a mirror, recording yourself on an audio tape recorder, or, better yet, videotaping your performances are ways in which you can coach yourself. Why, then, is this so rarely done? Hardly anything could be simpler or more advantageous. But most people abandon the attempt after only one try. Try again. The more you practise coaching yourself, the better you will get. The better you get, the more confidence you will gain. The more confident and comfortable you become, the more you will gain from the effort, and so on. Nobody can prescribe how to become more effective at face-to-face communication. It is something that you must learn to do by yourself, with or without the help and support of a coach. Most of the concepts, frameworks, and recommendations to be found in this book can serve as suggestive guidelines for you when you are customizing your own applications. The lasting value and effectiveness of experimenting with the ideas and exercises we suggest will depend upon the concrete experiences you bring to each assignment or activity.

How This Book Is Organized

The aim of this book is to present you with a wide range of concepts and circumstances designed to help you figure out what to do in different workplace situations involving persuading, hiring, evaluating, presenting, leading, and so on. Combining a good level of theoretical understanding with your current practice and experience will allow you to accumulate a wide body of knowledge and interpersonal expertise. For example, experienced salespeople can learn to be more persuasive when they combine careful planning with good quality listening, sensitivity to others' needs, and an honest interest in what is most important to the customer.

The overall plan of the book is structured around the most common, everyday interview settings and circumstances where we come face-to-face with other people. The text of each chapter begins by describing the central concepts and methods of communicating face-to-face in the workplace, and introduces the necessary skills and plans for accomplishing each task more effectively.

Each chapter also includes "Interpersonal Skills Clinics," which are designed to break some aspect of the interview down into its component parts for closer examination and further practice in class. The review questions, along with suggested answers, which appear near the end of each chapter, will provide you with an opportunity to summarize concepts each time you communicate face-to-face. The chapter review questions are based on the objectives which appear at the beginning of each section. Research shows that if you use an idea within 24 hours of first discovering it, you are more likely to assimilate it into your cumulative store of permanent knowledge.

The "Interpersonal Communication Scenarios" are descriptions of situations that will be similar to situations you may face in the workplace. Each one is an extended example for what has come before in the chapter. You may wish to use the scenarios as a basis for discussion, in class or in another learning situation. One way of doing this is to role-play the situation with the assistance of others. Or you may wish to use a scenario as the basis for a formal written analysis.

When we write about interviews we will usually be referring to the most common, formal or semi-formal, face-to-face interactions that occur through the course of daily work and responsibilities. But we won't stop there. From there we will show you how to design your own frameworks for applying these skills in actual interview situations that you yourself must face or participate in each day on the job.

Robert Bolton has written that:

> 66 It is one thing to read about communication skills in a book; it is quite a different matter to apply them effectively in daily life. In the realm of interpersonal communications, as in so many other matters, people's intentions tend to outrun their actions.[3] 99

So here is a book that deals with your own most fundamental and tangible workplace situations. By showing you how to reflect on your own day-to-day interpersonal communication, we hope that those of you seeking to develop your face-to-face skills and strategies will make a commitment to using them in your everyday work.

Three Ways to Get More Out of This Book

1. *Make a list* of your own objectives regarding this program. If you are reading this book as part of a course in the official curriculum, ask yourself why you decided to register for an interpersonal communication course. What is it you want to gain as a result of your commitment to study this material?

2. *Plan your time.* Keep a weekly or monthly calendar/diary in which to record your appointments, as well as your most salient recollections of the face-to-face communication events that take place each day. This will help you to understand and reflect upon your past experiences, to keep track of your present commitments, and to create a vision of what is possible for you to achieve in future. Weekly calendars can also be used to summarize a period of time in terms of (a) the opportunities you had to be more effective in face-to-face situations, and (b) the specific interpersonal skills required to accomplish each interview, task, or challenge.

3. *Take notes.* Keep a record of the learning strategies that work best for you. Make a note of them as you go. At the end of the book you will have a complete repertory of heuristics (learning strategies) you can use to improve both the planning and performance of your next interview opportunity.

And finally . . .

Each time you have to solve a problem, sell a product or idea, or convince a colleague to adopt your bold new proposals, keep track of the event and examine how you went about solving it. Speculate as to what you might have done differently—or not done at all. How might you have changed things if you could, and why?

Don't settle for abstract theories about the best ways to communicate face-to-face. Use your own good sense, experience, reflection, and intuition. Think about what works best for you and keep track of your own development. As you learn new approaches and techniques for more effective interpersonal communication, relate them to your own situation, and plan to act on them.

ENDNOTES

1 Gates' thirty percent stake in the company was valued at nearly $7.5 billion in 1993—an amount equal to the total 1991 sales of all personal computer software manufacturers.

2 Roger Evered and James Selman, "Coaching and the Art of Management," *Organizational Dynamics*, 1989.

3 Robert Bolton, *People Skills* (Englewood Cliffs, N.J.: Prentice-Hall, 1979), p. 275.

CHAPTER 1

Understanding Interpersonal Communication in Organizations

Section 1   **An Introduction to Theories of Interpersonal Communication**

- ◆ Before we get started . . . ◆ Objectives ◆ The Linear Model
- ◆ The Interactive Model ◆ The Transactive Model ◆ And finally . . .

Section 2   **Theoretical Antecedents of Organizational Communication**

- ◆ Before we get started . . . ◆ Objectives ◆ Understanding Organizational Environments ◆ Images of Organization ◆ The Classical School ◆ The Human Relations School ◆ The Contingency School ◆ The Teamwork School ◆ The Human Potential Movement ◆ The Cultural School ◆ Management by Bestseller ◆ And finally . . .

Section 3   **Managing by Wandering Around**

- ◆ Before we get started . . . ◆ Objectives ◆ A Little Touch of Harry in the Night ◆ The Double-Edged Sword of Face-to-Face Channels of Communication ◆ *Interpersonal Skills Clinic: Inside the House of Stairs* ◆ And finally . . .

Chapter Review Questions

Interpersonal Communication Scenario:
Sunset Hotel Enterprises

- - - - - - - - - - -

WORTH REPEATING

He who considers things in their origin will obtain the clearest view of them.

— Aristotle

The most exciting breakthroughs of the 21st century will occur not because of technology but because of an expanding concept of what it means to be human.

—John Naisbitt and Patricia Alburdene, *Megatrends 2000*

Management by wandering around pervades every level of the effective organization of every sort—which is to say that leaders exist at every level.

—Tom Peters and Nancy Austin, *A Passion For Excellence*

Section 1   An Introduction to Theories of Interpersonal Communication

Before we get started . . .

The first chapter of Linda McQuaig's *The Quick and the Dead: Brian Mulroney, Big Business and the Seduction of Canada*[1] begins with a description of how, over the long, unpleasant months of negotiations on the Canada-United States Free Trade Agreement in 1987, red-headed chief U.S. negotiator Peter Murphy avoided dealing with Canadian negotiator Simon Reisman's demands. According to McQuaig's depiction—"Carrot Top Meets the 800-Pound Gorilla"—the American strategy was simple: keep repeating something that irritated Reisman, or persist in saying nothing when a response was clearly called for. In the face of such imperviousness Reisman would explode, and the rest of the day's negotiations would be taken up with an outpouring of rage and hostility. This of course would leave no time for discussing the rules to ensure Canadian access to the American market.

On a typical day during the Canada-U.S. trade negotiations in 1987, just as Reisman would begin to speak, Murphy would interrupt him with a question that had already been asked and answered. While the question was being asked, Reisman would squirm in his seat, or signal his displeasure by furrowing his brow and hunching his shoulders forward—sighing and moaning throughout. Both men were constantly communicating. Then Reisman would verbally reconfirm what Murphy was concerned about, and begin again to lay Canada's demands out emphatically and insist that the American negotiators reply. While this was happening, Murphy would look uninterested, or whisper something to one of his colleagues on the American side of the table. All was happening at once. "It was all part of a disingenuous game," wrote McQuaig. Reisman's style was to be upfront, talkative, effusive. Murphy's style was to go blank, and become ever-more evasive and obscure. It would be hard to imagine two more different styles of interpersonal communication.

Because of their inability to communicate, the two sides eventually came to an agreement only after Reisman and Murphy ceased to be involved. Those early negotiations serve to illustrate the basic components of the current *transactive* theory of interpersonal communications. Both men at the heart of the trade negotiations were *simultaneously* thinking and sensing (internally as well as externally), sending (encoding), and receiving (decoding) several different messages, on several different channels (media). If we characterize interpersonal communication as a *trans-action* rather than an *inter-action* (the prefix *trans* means over or across, the prefix *inter* means between or among) we can begin to appreciate the simultaneous and continuous nature of being face-to-face. The word transaction implies the process of simultaneous sharing, rather than sequential exchanging.

Reisman and Murphy's underlying messages were a woven, complex pattern of confrontation and avoidance—a complete obstacle to effective interpersonal communication! And yet this example serves to demonstrate the processes by which all interpersonal communication is accomplished. The better you become at understanding the processes of both interpersonal and organizational communication, the more able you will be to persuade others to contribute to the effectiveness of the organization. As well, the better your understanding of the history of communication, the more capable you will become at choosing the most appropriate processes for communicating in every sector of the workplace.

In this chapter we deal with the basic theory and background you need to understand the communication process as it occurs in workplace situations. Because this chapter focuses on theory, it is more abstract than the rest of the book where we explore the practical side of interpersonal communication. In subsequent chapters, we hope the theory introduced here will aid your understanding of the "rules of the game" by which we all must operate when dealing with people face-to-face. Looking ahead to Chapter 2, for example, the theory of rhetoric provides a background for our discussion of persuasion.

The theoretical models and schools described in this chapter take a decidedly humanistic perspective. The other main perspectives that have been adopted by communication theorists have included the behavioral, sociological, and rhetorical. All of these place less importance on the construction and maintenance of the self in communication than does the humanistic perspective. Throughout this chapter, we repeatedly emphasize not only the *interpersonal* but also the *intrapersonal*. Interpersonal communication can be thought of as the "interview" component of organizational life and intrapersonal communication as the "inner view" component. While the interpersonal concerns the exchange of messages between two people, the intrapersonal concerns the processing of internal messages, or the communication that occurs within the self.

Objectives

After you complete this section, you should be able to:

1. State how the humanistic perspective on interpersonal communication differs from other perspectives, such as the behavioral, sociological, and rhetorical perspectives.

2. Discuss the following models of interpersonal communication, including reference to important written works, theoretical orientation, and key terms:
   a. linear
   b. interactive
   c. transactive

The Linear Model

An important learning device is the use of models (representations based on analogy and metaphor) to describe and explain a plan, design, pattern, or theoretical concept. We will discuss various models used to make sense of what communication is and how it works.

What might be considered the first theory of interpersonal communication comes—like so much of our thinking in western civilization—from ancient Greek philosophy. The 5th century B.C. characterized a new phase in Greek philosophy—the turning of humankind's attention from the world of things to a study of the self, and ways of being with others in the world.

Ancient Greek philosophers called *Sophists* taught that *rhetoric* (ways of communicating to persuade others) was a direct means to success in business and politics. Sophists were travelling teachers of rhetoric who tutored anyone willing

Figure 1.1: Aristotle's model

```
┌──────────┐      ┌──────────┐      ┌──────────┐      ┌──────────┐
│ Speaker  │──────│ Argument │──────│  Speech  │─────▶│ Audience │
└──────────┘      └──────────┘      └──────────┘      └──────────┘
```

to pay for their advice. Plato (427-347 B.C.) was an *idealist* generally opposed to Sophism, but he nevertheless agreed that rhetoric was a useful subject that should be studied and practised to perfection.

But it was Plato's student Aristotle (384-322 B.C.) who was the first to analyze with scientific rigor the process of rhetoric, identifying what he took to be its component parts. For Aristotle, the skill of speaking persuasively could be explained in terms of a linear model whereby a *speaker* constructs an *argument*, to be delivered in a *speech*, to an *audience* (Figure 1.1). Aristotle's principles of rhetoric, which we will discuss in more detail in Chapter 7, have remained useful, in more or less their original form, for over 2000 years.

Cicero (who lived between 106 and 43 B.C.) was a great Roman orator who, unlike many other orators, wrote about his art. Cicero's most important contribution to communication theory was his description of the five canons of rhetoric. The canons are stages or aspects of rhetoric. The first canon is *invention*, which is the gathering of information. The second is *disposition* or the organization of the information that has been gathered. Cicero had five categories for this canon (narration, partition, confirmation, refutation, and peroration) based on Aristotle's four *topics*, which we will consider further in Chapter 7. The third canon is *style*, which involves the use of figures of speech and the adoption of an appropriate tone. The fourth canon is *memory*, which in Cicero's day was a required part of public speaking. And finally, the canon of *delivery* prescribes methods of effectively controlling the voice and physical gestures.

Scholarly consideration of the topic of communication is not in great evidence between Cicero's writings and medieval times, when much of the interest in communication was in the context of religion. It wasn't until the 15th century Renaissance of classical Greek and Roman philosophy that theories of rhetoric began to reappear.

But, when the first cast metal printing presses came into existence, in about 1450, the emphasis in the study of communication had already begun to shift away from oral rhetoric, toward the arts of literature and writing. By the end of the 1800s, this emphasis on written communication was well entrenched. Most colleges and universities in Europe, Canada, and the United States had been organized into academic departments, and the subjects of rhetoric or speech were generally considered to be adjunct to departments of English literature and journalism.

In the 20th century, the rapid expansion in the social sciences advanced many new theories of interpersonal communication and widened the scope of communications to include several interdisciplinary studies. By the mid-1950s, there appeared a number of theorists, in a wide range of subjects and disciplines, who became interested in developing new theories of communication.

Practitioners in philosophy, psychology, sociology, anthropology, mathematics, linguistics, psychiatry, education, and many other fields of interest began combining research on themes related to our understanding of interpersonal communication in organizations. For example, in *The Mathematical Theory of Communication*, Claude Shannon and Warren Weaver published the results of their research for the Bell Telephone Company to study signal transmission over telephone lines. Shannon and Weaver's major contribution to the theoretical model of communication was that they introduced a new meaning for the term noise, which refers to anything that distorts or interferes with the quality of communication.[2]

Although these developments set the stage for the rapid growth of interpersonal communication as an independent field of study, the model used by Shannon and Weaver was not really much different from Aristotle's basic linear representation. It began with a **sender** at one end, who, or which, transmitted a signal or message to an audience or receiver at the other end (Figure 1.2).

A basic limitation of the linear model is that it reflects the traditional, one-way view of the communication process in organizations—the one in which the manager commands and the subordinate obeys. This model assumes that *sending* messages is all there is to communicating. For example, how often must managers think to themselves "How many times do I have to say it? Didn't you hear what I told you?" There are, of course, some instances in which one-way com-

Figure 1.2: A Linear Model of Communication

(Source: Claude Shannon and Warren Weaver, *The Mathematical Theory of Communication*, University of Illinois Press, 1949)

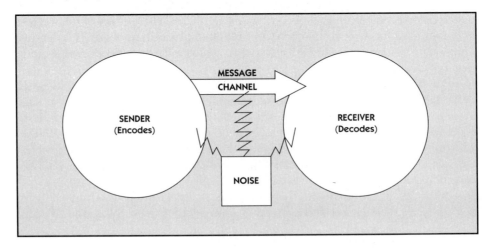

munication serves as a necessary and efficient means of relaying information in organizations. Such is the case in emergencies in which someone's welfare or safety is threatened. But effective management communicators do not simply assume that all messages sent are the same as those received. Generally, the best communicators are those who take time to assess what their audience is hearing, and adjust their messages accordingly.

In traditional hierarchies, *downward* communication flow typifies most of the organizational communication. The activities of employees are directed and controlled by supervisors, managers, and executives. Communication flowing *upward*, on the other hand, from subordinate to superior, constitutes a significant difference in an organization's focus. It implies an "open door" policy in which managers are available for casual conversation, whether related to the job or not. *Lateral* communication, like upward communication, has traditionally been discouraged by the existence of organizational hierarchies. That is, the units, divisions, and departments of an organization tend to keep messages flowing downward, rather than within or across a particular level in the organization. *Diagonal* communication allows for communication among any groups or individuals within an organization, as does *informal* communication.

The linear model does not take into account the fact that sometimes a message is acquired by retrieval rather than transmission. For example, a manager may gather documents from which she synthesizes a message, perhaps that her department has overspent its budget for the year. No one has transmitted this message, as the Shannon-Weaver model would have it; instead the "receiver" has created the message.[3]

Important Works

Aristotle, *Rhetoric* and *Poetics*
Harold Lasswell, *The Structure and Function of Communication* (1948)
Claude Shannon and Warren Weaver, *The Mathematical Theory of Communication* (1949)

Theoretical Orientation

◆ One-directional view of the communication process
◆ Assumes that *sending* messages is all there is to communicating

Key Terms

noise	message	transmission
sender	receiver	

The Interactive Model

By the 1960s, increased integration among the various disciplines produced the first books dealing specifically with *interpersonal communication*. Some early behavioral scientists, for example, influenced by research in psychology, were among the first to expand the notion of interpersonal communication to include a two-way, dynamic, and ongoing *interaction* (**feedback**) of messages between the sender (**source**) and receiver (**destination** or **effect**).

In an article published as early as 1954, titled "How Communication Works," Wilbur Schramm highlighted the importance of the sender using audience feedback to check, and adjust, his or her messages to see that they are clearly received and understood. In Schramm's two-way, *interactive model* of communication, the sender forms or **encodes** a message which is then conveyed through some channel to the receiver (Figure 1.3). A **channel** is the means, or medium, by which messages are communicated from one person to another. The receiver **decodes** the message and responds, with the use of feedback, to the source of the original message. The source, in turn, decodes the feedback and adapts new messages according to his or her new understanding. This exchange of feedback is known as a **feedback loop**; it is a control feature within the system used to regulate the interaction.

In 1965 Wilbur Schramm introduced several additional models based on the work of Canadian communications theorist Marshall McLuhan and others, who were focusing their attention on the nature of **interpretation** by different media—particularly television. All **media** represent channels through which messages are transmitted. In *The Process and Effects of Mass Communication*, Schramm attempted to unravel how feedback loops are used to inform the sender of how well messages are being received. Schramm emphasized that we do not create meaning by the messages we send; rather, we use words to awaken or share the meaning that already exists within the consciousness of the audience.[4]

Figure 1.3: An Interactive Model of Communication

(Source: Wilbur Schramm, "How Communication Works," 1954)

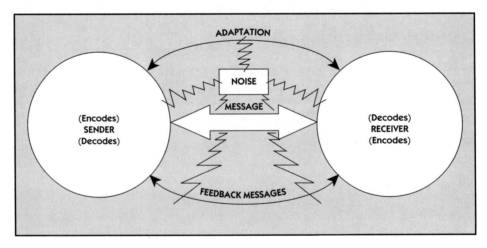

With the interactive model, feedback can be seen to occur throughout a conversation in both the sender's and receiver's verbal and nonverbal channels of communication (words and other signals). Sometimes feedback is immediate, which is the case with facial expressions, eye movement, and body posture. At other times, it may be delayed, as when a manager pauses following a speech to ask if there are any questions. Feedback is therefore an essential mechanism for managers seeking to establish or confirm whether or not the messages sent are the same, or similar, to those received.

Important Works

Bruce Westley and Malcolm MacLean, *A Conceptual Model for Communication Research* (1955)
David Berlo, *The Process of Communication* (1960)
Marshall McLuhan, *Understanding Media* (1964)
Wilbur Schramm, *The Process and Effects of Mass Communication* (1965)

Theoretical Orientation

◆ Two-directional view of the communication process
◆ Stresses the importance of *feedback* for adjusting to clearer understandings

Key Terms

feedback	encoding	interpretation
source	channel	medium (media)
destination	decoding	meaning
effect	feedback loop	

The Transactive Model

It was largely Dean Barnlund's *Interpersonal Communication* and John Wenburg and William Wilmot's "The Personal Communication Process" that led the way to more sophisticated *transactive* models of communication involving such concepts as convergence (a coming together or formation of similar opinions), communion, and intersubjectivity (being of one mind). The transactive model of interpersonal communication would have us view each participant in the process as an active communicator, continuously sending (encoding) and receiving (decoding) messages through one or more channels (media) *simultaneously*. In short, this model characterizes communication as a transaction (Figure 1.4). For example, just as a district sales manager starts to speak, a salesman might interrupt with a question. While the question is being asked, the sales manager signals agreement by nodding her head. Then she verbally confirms what the salesperson is concerned about. While this is happening, the salesperson also indicates that

Figure 1.4: A Transactive Model of Communication

(Source: Dean Barnlund, *Interpersonal Communication*, 1968)

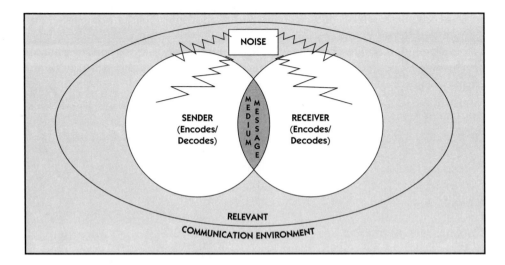

what the sales manager has begun to explain is understood and agreed upon. "I get it," he says, signalling the sales manager to continue with her next point.

Although this diagram adequately illustrates the **mutuality** of interpersonal communication, it fails to account for the affective or emotional aspect that exists in all communication. The lithograph "Bond of Union" by artist M.C. Escher (used on the cover of this book) dramatically illustrates both the simultaneous nature of effective interpersonal transactions as well as this quality of sharing which implies a joint or equal concern that is felt as much as thought. Not only does the ribbon join at the top and bottom of the image, but it also intersects at the head—serving to emphasize mutual sharing—a theme that remains overlooked in many models of face-to-face interactions and transactions in the workplace.

The transactive model of communication we have discussed did not appear in published academic or business texts and articles until the 1960s. This relatively recent theoretical development was due in large part to the rapid expansion in the social sciences throughout the 20th Century which widened the scope of communication studies to include several interdisciplinary contributions. Several, more mainstream, books and published articles on the transactional nature of communication began to appear in the 1960s and 1970s.

Important Works

Colin Cherry, *On Human Communication* (1961)
Paul Watzlavich, Janet Beavin, and Don Jackson, *Pragmatics of Human Communication* (1967)
Dean Barnlund, *Interpersonal Communication* (1968)

John Wenburg and William Wilmot, *The Personal Communication Process* (1973)

Everett Rogers and Laurence Kincaid, *Communication Networks: Toward a New Paradigm for Research* (1981)

Theoretical Orientation

◆ Transactive view of the communication process
◆ Stresses the mutual and continuous nature of shared meaning

Key Terms

convergence	intersubjectivity	sharing
communion	mutuality	

And finally . . .

As you will see in the next section, one of the basic characteristics of both interpersonal and organizational communication is that all dimensions of all human systems are continuously influencing, and being influenced by, each other. We will now use the basic interpersonal models we've discussed as tools for understanding the theoretical ties between interpersonal communication and various organizational settings.

Section 2 Theoretical Antecedents of Organizational Communication

Before we get started . . .

In this section we carry our discussion of theory a step further by suggesting links between models of communication and some relevant schools of organizational theory. Before we examine the historical development of the various schools of organizational theory, however, we discuss a general approach for understanding organizational environments.

Objectives

After you complete this section, you should be able to:

1. Discuss the systems approach to the theory of organizations.

2. Describe briefly the implications of viewing an organization as one of the following:
   a. machine
   b. organism
   c. brain
   d. culture
   e. political metaphor
   f. psychic prison
   g. flux transformation
   h. instrument of domination

3. Discuss the following schools of organizational communication theory, including references to important written works, theoretical orientation, and perspective:
   a. classical
   b. human relations
   c. contingency
   d. teamwork
   e. human potential
   f. cultural

4. Discuss, by reference to Peters and Waterman, eight ways in which "excellent" organizations can be distinguished from ordinary organizations.

5. Explain the rationale for an integrated, interdisciplinary approach to organizational communication.

Understanding Organizational Environments

All communication is bound by some context involving the integration of the individual, interpersonal relations, and the extrapersonal functioning of organizations. Taking a *systems approach* to the subject provides us with a way of viewing communication situations across boundaries normally used to isolate these aspects. All systems operate with boundaries that distinguish various subsystems within them. Organizations, as well as individuals, are continually influenced by their external environment and must be capable of adapting to the changes required for different interactions.

The term *task environment* refers to only those parts of the overall external environment that are relevant to the mission or purpose of the entire organization. Each organization must concentrate on specific matters and deliberately ignore others. James Thompson has suggested that the task environments of most organizations consist of customers or clientele, suppliers and resources, competitors, and regulatory groups—including government.[5] In addition, we would argue that many contemporary organizations also need to pay particular attention to special interest groups, the media, and the general public.

Because organizations are always embedded in larger systems, some parts of the organization must interact with other systems that are not subordinate to that organization. Thompson introduced the concept of "boundary spanning" to describe the means by which such interactions take place. Boundary spanning is a communication device that mediates the flow of information. For example, college faculty in both the English department and the Education department might boundary-span with one another when working on a joint program to improve the quality of the teaching of writing in the public schools.

By linking sources of information from within and without, organizations are able to anticipate environmental conditions and adopt strategies for dealing with them. These strategies might involve making changes between individuals, subunits of the organization, and so forth. In describing how organizations and their managers conceptualize their environment, Karl Weick further argued that particular attention should also be given to how and why individual managers focus their attention on specific aspects of an environment to the exclusion of others.[6] Weick coined the term *enacted environment* to refer to that portion of the task environment that is perceived and interpreted as relevant.

One way of "mapping" or keeping track of organizational communications regarding a particular issue or situation is to sketch the relevant aspects or units as they relate to one another. This can be done simply by listing the parties involved, drawing lines to link individuals or subunits to their common themes and issues, as is shown in Figure 1.5.

Figure 1.5: Organizational Communication Map

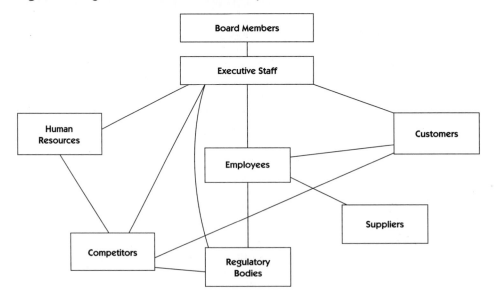

Images of Organization

Gareth Morgan provides us with an exceptionally thorough way of "reading" the situations we are attempting to analyze and manage in organizations.[7] When we theorize about, or "read," situations, says Morgan, we attempt to formulate images and explanations that help us to make sense of their fundamental nature. Instead of interpreting everything from a fixed and inflexible standpoint, he explores and develops new ways of thinking about organizations and diagnosing organizational problems. The basic premise on which his book, *Images of Organization*, is built is that our various explanations of organizational life are based on many different metaphors that lead us to see and understand organizations in distinctive ways.

What are the various metaphors or images of organizations that we use? For one, we frequently talk about organizations as if they were *machines* made up of interlocking component parts—organized to operate efficiently according to predetermined goals and objectives. This style of thought, which is fundamental to bureaucratic organization, forces human qualities into a subordinate role. Another basic, and contrasting, metaphor—that organizations are like *organisms*—focuses our attention on understanding and managing organizational needs as if organizations were living creatures. We are encouraged to understand how organizations are born, develop, decline, and die, and how they are able to adapt to changing environments in the process. What, Morgan also asks, are the implications of viewing organizations as *brains?* This metaphor draws attention to the importance of information processing, self-organization, flexibility, and learning. The idea that organizations are *cultures* leads us to a more careful examination of the ideas, values, norms, and rituals that sustain organizations as socially constructed realities. If we use a *political metaphor* to consider the different interests, conflicts, and power plays that shape organizational activities, we would focus on the principles that legitimize different kinds of rule. The idea that organizations are *psychic prisons*, where people become trapped by their own thoughts and beliefs, invites us to examine organizational life to see if we have become trapped by conscious and unconscious processes of our own creation. Taking the view that an organization is based essentially on *flux and transformation* emphasizes that organizations are self-producing systems that create themselves in their own image. And finally, in exploring the idea that organizations are *instruments of domination*, Morgan shows how some organizations use people, their communities, and the world economy to achieve their own ends—based on a process of domination where certain people impose their will on others.

After discussing all the different ways of viewing organizations, Morgan focuses on the possibility of developing an approach that builds on the transformative power people have to understand organizations differently according to specific settings and time frames. "The real challenge," he says, "is to learn to deal with this complexity . . . [and to] find new ways of organizing and new ways of approaching and solving organizational problems."[8]

Each of us has an inclination to favor certain metaphors over others. Any realistic approach to organizational analysis must recognize that organizations can be many things (at once) to many people. To apply this method of analysis in practice, one must first highlight key aspects of the situation, then make a *critical evaluation* of the different interpretations that suggest themselves.

The Classical School

The Industrial Revolution at the beginning of the 19th century was responsible for a dramatic increase in both the size of organizations and the complexity of life within them. At the same time, the growth of capitalism helped to expand the factory and transportation systems required for manufacturing. This expansion of industry brought with it the need for more efficient ways of designing production operations, as well as for more effective ways of coordinating the workforce. So it is not surprising that the classical theorists of that age focused largely on creating highly structured, mechanistic methods of production and control.

The most popular organization theory of the time was known as "Taylorism"—named after Frederick "Speedy" Taylor, father of the stopwatch-and-clipboard approach to factory life. Taylor himself called his theory "Scientific Management." His was a prescription for job design, formal divisions of labor, and formal channels of communication. Taylorism meant increasing productivity by breaking factory work down into specialized components. Each assembly worker simply followed a series of mechanical steps—such as bolting wheels to a chassis—to keep the line moving at maximum speed without wasted effort. To illustrate the apparent effectiveness of this approach, consider the fact that before Henry Ford introduced Taylor's principles of time and motion efficiency, it took an average of 12 1/2 work hours for Ford to build an automobile chassis. After creating what is believed to be the world's first moving assembly line at the Ford plant at Highland Park (outside Detroit) in 1913—the time fell to 93 minutes.[9]

Scientific management meant more accurate measures of cost accounting, and enlightened schemes for paying bonuses to employees with higher rates of production. Many of today's automation and merit pay schemes are based on scientific management concepts. On the negative side were the torrents of assembly-line products, punching a time-clock, authoritarian bosses, and the boredom that resulted from repeating simple tasks.

Another theory to join scientific management in what eventually came to be regarded as the *classical school*, was the bureaucratic tradition created by Max Weber and Henri Fayol. The writings of these "bureaucratic" theorists centred almost exclusively on the structure and rules of formal organizations, the official chain of command, and the roles or responsibilities of each functional division. This perspective came to be known as structural-functionalism—the view of organizations as objects or machines to be made more efficient and more effective, treated as though separate and detached from the personal experiences of the people who work there.

Weber and Fayol were interested in how to maintain organizational structure and control mechanisms through formal patterns of communication. In other words, they called for an official chart of who reports to whom. The classical theorists believed that an organization must have a clear division of labor and chain of command as represented by the hierarchical organization chart. Such an organization, represented in Figure 1.6, would be light on top (management) and heavy at the bottom (workers). Most formal communication was meant to flow in a one-way direction from superior to subordinate, with information generally restricted to work-related instructions, performance expectations, and so on.

Even today, many successful organizations rely on this bureaucratic, hierarchical model with each of its functional pillars and levels of formal authority.

Important Works

Frederick Taylor, *Scientific Management* (1911)
Mary Parker Follett, *The New State: Group Organization* (1918)
Max Weber, *The Theory of Social and Economic Organization* (1947)
Henri Fayol, *General and Industrial Management* (1949)

Figure 1.6: A Bureaucratic Organization

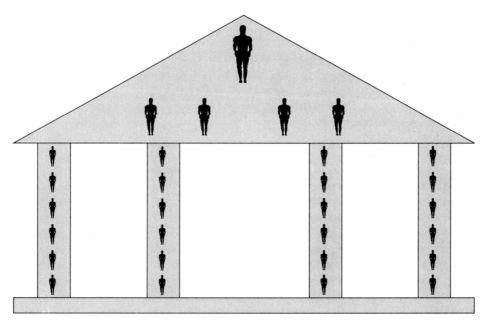

Theoretical Orientation

◆ Concern with formal management structures of control

Communication Perspective

◆ One-direction, top-down, communications restricted to instructions, rules, and procedures

The Human Relations School

By the 1930s the focus of organizational theory had begun to shift away from the classical, structural-functionalist models of organization, to ones that drew more attention to the informal, human side of enterprise. This was also the time of rising unionism in the United States. The influence of the human relations school represented a counter-response to the authoritarian, predominantly control-oriented principles of the classical school. It wasn't the classical school's theory that was opposed, so much as the drudgery it meant for those ordinary workers on whom bureaucratic management practices were imposed.

Much of this countermovement towards an emphasis on human relations in management began with research conducted at the Hawthorne Plant of the Western Electric Company in Cicero, Illinois, near Chicago. Begun in the mid-1920s, the "Hawthorne Studies," as they became known, were conducted by a team of researchers from the Harvard Graduate School of Business, under the direction of Professor Elton Mayo.

The research started out as a study to determine at what brightness and ventilation levels the workers would be most productive. As it turned out, brightness and ventilation were not as important to the workers as the researchers thought they would be. What Mayo and his colleagues discovered instead was that workers involved in friendly, informal, social environments at work tended to be more productive than those who were not—regardless of available light or ventilation.

Mayo and his associates concluded that employees' primary satisfaction from factory work stemmed from their relationships with others, and this in turn significantly influenced their levels of production. These conclusions led to an increased emphasis on group dynamics and social relations in organizations—which is still a part of organization theory and practice today.

Soon to follow the Hawthorne Studies was Chester Barnard's classic book entitled *The Functions of the Executive* (1938). Barnard, a former New Jersey Bell Telephone Company president, emphasized the importance of maintaining both formal (bureaucratic) as well as informal (social) systems of communication.[10]

For the most part, the 1940s were a period of steady growth for the human relations school. Herbert Simon (who wrote *Administrative Behavior* in 1945) was the first theorist to merge the terms "organizational" and "communication" together as fundamental concepts in managerial effectiveness. But it wasn't until the period of massive integration of knowledge from different fields and disciplines, beginning in the mid-1960s, that the term "organizational communication" was commonly used.

These and other human relations concepts continue to be useful today, since theorists continue to believe in the importance of social interaction and a less mechanistic view of human behavior. Thus, from a human relations perspective, the process of organizational communication was more than a way to pass orders down the chain of command, it was a way of accomplishing the human need for interaction. It was also a way for managers and employees to exchange valuable information with each other.

Important Works

Hugo Munsterberg, *Psychology and Industrial Efficiency* (1913)
Elton Mayo, *The Human Problems of an Industrial Civilization* (1933)
Chester Barnard, *The Functions of the Executive* (1938)
Herbert Simon, *Administrative Behavior* (1945)

Theoretical Orientation

◆ More balanced concern for formal structures and the social and psychological needs of employees

Communication Perspective

◆ Downward, linear communication is considered important, but so is informal communication up and down the organizational hierarchy

The Contingency School

The models we have examined to this point have been based on the underlying assumption that all organizations are in fact similar systems. Yet, even organizations that operate in similar industries or environments face different situations and must deal with them differently. One of the first and best known "situational" or "contingency theorists" was management psychologist Fred Fiedler.

Fiedler postulated that no one type of organizational framework for leadership is appropriate for all systems and every situation. He also stated that anyone can become a good leader, but that different people excel under different conditions. For example, the entrepreneurial, small business manager may be just great at getting new projects off the ground, but he or she may not be the right person to continue managing an established product line or service.

After Fiedler came Paul Hersey and Ken Blanchard's *situational leadership* model. Hersey and Blanchard advanced the notion that, in order to be effective, leadership strategies should be adjusted to "the subordinate's ability to take on and accomplish a job in a high quality manner through his or her own self-direction and motivation".[11] In other words, effective leadership requires that a manager encourage skill and maturity in employees and that the manager communicate in the appropriate leadership style for each situation.

A simple description of situational leadership would be the following:

1. When dealing with employees who are willing, able, and motivated to accomplish tasks, leaders should communicate with them in a "delegating style" in which workers are given all the support necessary for them to make their own decisions on the job.

2. When employees are clearly able, but unwilling or unmotivated, they should be treated with a "participatory style" in which they may become involved more in making their own decisions.

3. When employees are willing, but unable to accomplish tasks, managers should adopt a "selling style" in which they provide more guidance and direction.

4. Finally, when employees are neither willing, nor able, managers should use a "telling style" of directive communication in which there is no freedom for employees to make decisions on their own.

Contingency theory is still used in organizations. It has also become the model of choice for many successful profit-based research companies, such as those in the aerospace and chemical-pharmaceutical industries. In industries such as these, the power and influence of management relies less on the formal structure of the organization, than on high-performance project centers developed for a specific purpose. For example, in a pharmaceutical company, a center may be developed to produce a drug that will cure a disease. Such centers are linked to, or imbedded in, the larger system or organization by a matrix of communication networks (Figure 1.7).

In "matrix" organizations, communication interactions occur everywhere—at all levels of the organization—passing up and down formal channels in the hierarchy, as well as moving quickly along lateral routes that span functional boundaries. Increasingly complex and interrelated matrices of tasks and functional activities require quick and accurate communication to and from all sectors and levels of the organization.

Important Works

Robert Blake and Jane Mouton, *The Managerial Grid* (1964)
Daniel Katz and Robert Kahn, *The Social Psychology of Organizations* (1965)
Fred Fiedler, *A Theory of Leadership Effectiveness* (1967)
Paul Hersey and Ken Blanchard, *Management of Organizational Behavior* (1982)

Theoretical Orientation

◆ Concern with the organization as a whole system

Figure 1.7: A Matrix Organization

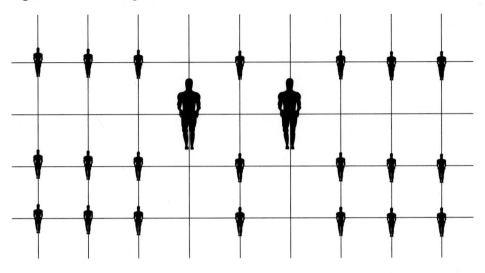

Communication Perspective

◆ Encouragement of open systems and feedback throughout the entire system

The Teamwork School

The teamwork school of organization theorists represents a variation on a theme. This school adopted the position that productivity in an organization is more readily achieved through team-building and lateral interactions than it is through top-down, vertical-linear communications through the chains of command.

The teamwork school encourages organizational communication to be informally exchanged between peers and work groups, rather than by more formal means of top-down management control. In other words, spontaneous problem-solving and decision-making among employees is encouraged along with more open face-to-face communication with management. The teamwork school continues today as a part of the movement away from autocratic leadership to a more participative leadership style. The Japanese style of management, in particular, embraces the teamwork perspective, emphasizing company loyalty, long-term planning, group decision-making, and *quality circles* (Figure 1.8).

Quality circles are regular, sanctioned (yet informal) meetings in which six to a dozen participants engage in a process of group problem-solving to accomplish "continuous improvement" on the job. The purpose of quality circles is to arrive at a solution to a problem that ultimately leads to real improvement in the quality of production.

Figure 1.8: The Quality Circle

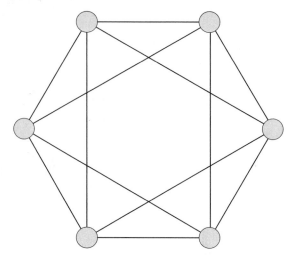

Important Works

Kurt Lewin, *Group Decision and Social Change* (1952)
William Ouchi, *Theory Z* (1981)

Theoretical Orientation

◆ Teamwork can achieve greater effects than can individuals working alone

Communication Perspective

◆ Emphasis on lateral communication and consensus decision-making

The Human Potential Movement

In addition to being responsible for much of the development of organization theory, humanistic psychologists also contributed, in a practical sense, to greater productivity results in organizations. Theorists Abraham Maslow, Rensis Likert, Chris Argyris, and others developed several important ideas about optimal performance and the fulfillment of human potential that subsequent generations of leaders and managers have incorporated into companies such as Polaroid, 3M, Honda, IBM, Apple, Sony, Mitsubishi, and Matusushita.

Abraham Maslow's *hierarchy of needs*, in particular, served as the basis for several lasting developments in subsequent organization theory. Maslow stated that people have five different kinds of needs, which may be arranged in order from the most basic through to the most elevated: physiological needs, security needs, social needs, ego needs, and the need for *self-actualization* (Figure 1.9). The

Figure 1.9: Maslow's Hierarchy of Needs

(Source: Abraham H. Maslow, *Motivation and Personality* 2nd ed.,
New York: Harper and Row, 1970.)

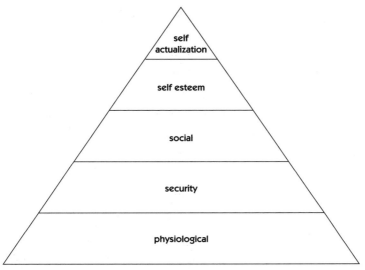

theory holds that once our most basic physiological and security needs have been met, human beings are destined to pursue the higher needs—such as the need for social interaction, greater self-esteem, and the full realization of our human potential. Traditional organizational hierarchies are designed to provide for the first three levels, but not the fourth and fifth.

Maslow's Hierarchy of Needs

Despite Maslow's humanistic intentions, his ideas can lend themselves to attempts to manipulate people's behavior. Understanding what people need and how they go about satisfying their needs can be used as a tool for controlling people in an organization or in society. In order to address these concerns, about a quarter of a century after publishing his theory of human motivation, Maslow published *The Psychology of Science*, in which he advocated the rebirth of humanistic values for those scientists working in such areas as psychology, psychiatry, and medicine. Maslow believed that human beings are governed by an instinct toward self-actualization.[12] Such a hypothesis is rooted in the religions and philosophies of many cultures.

Douglas McGregor, a management theorist, based his *Theory X* and *Theory Y* assumptions about work and human behavior on Maslow's hierarchy of needs and theories of motivation. Theory X managers, who assume that people dislike work and will generally try to avoid it, rely on the use of control and coercion. Theory Y managers, on the other hand, assume that a better way to motivate workers is to gain their commitment to doing the best job possible. This commitment arises not only out of loyalty to the team or company, but also out of each individual's need to actualize his or her potential on the job.

The psychologist Carl Rogers, in his book *On Personal Power* (1977), continues this line of thought by emphasizing an underlying flow toward "the constructive fulfilment of inherent possibilities." Rogers points to evidence in philosophy, medicine, psychology, biology, chemistry, and neurophysiology of a *natural tendency* toward complete development in human beings.

Another management theorist, Chris Argyris, and his colleagues have extended Maslow's theory. They identify the kinds of organizational dysfunctions that occur when people's personal needs are not met on the job. Argyris argues that if the individual's need and capacity for growth and self-development through work become frustrated, he or she will become apathetic toward tasks or negative toward the organization as a whole.

Summarizing decades of psychological research on the positive aspects of human experience, Mihaly Csikszentmihalyi's book, *Flow: The Psychology of Optimal Experience* explains how the best moments in life often occur when a person's body or mind is stretched to its limits in a voluntary effort to accomplish something difficult and worthwhile. Optimal experience is thus something that we ourselves can make happen. For each person, writes Csikszentmihalyi, there are thousands of opportunities and challenges to expand ourselves in the world and its institutions. His theory of optimal performance is based on organizing all experience into a meaningful pattern—a concept he calls *flow*.

Work today creates a strange inner conflict or paradox for most people, says the author of *Flow*. On the job they feel skillful, challenged, and satisfied. In their free time they feel bored, blue, and boring. Yet if you asked them, they would likely tell you that they would prefer to be at work less (where they are happy, creative, and confident in their own abilities), and spend more leisure time at home (where they feel weak, sad, and dissatisfied). Csikszentmihalyi concludes that the way to achieve mastery over one's life is through control over one's thinking, which in turn leads to control over the quality of experience. As he puts it, "Any small gain in [the direction of positive thinking] will make life more rich, more enjoyable, more meaningful. Armed with this knowledge, one can more easily achieve personal liberation."[13]

In terms of its approach to organizational communication, the human potential movement has generally stood for more open (both formal and informal) communication channels. The human potential movement is alive and well today in the businesses and professions which promote human values and potentials.

Important Works

Abraham Maslow, "A Theory of Human Motivation" (1943)
Carl Rogers, *On Personal Power* (1977)

Rensis Likert, *The Human Organization* (1967)
Chris Argyris, "Today's Problems with Tomorrow's Organizations" (1967)

Theoretical Orientation

◆ Concern for human values, autonomy, and potential
◆ Emphasis on individuals' participation in decisions that affect them

Communication Perspective

◆ More open, face-to-face, formal and informal communication channels

The Cultural School

Even though general distinctions can be drawn between each of the theoretical schools discussed up to this point, the fact is that actual teams and organizations are made up of unique blends of elements from several different models or perspectives. Each of these unique *Corporate Cultures*[14] (the title of a book by theorists Terrence Deal and Allan Kennedy) is based on a mix of particular values, beliefs, traditions, trends, and disturbances. This view of organizations allows for a variety of internal and external patterns of communication.

Several recent theorists have argued that the key to an organization's productivity and success lies in the particular communication culture that exists within that organization as it transacts with its internal and external environments. Management theorists Tom Peters and Robert Waterman claim, in their book *In Search of Excellence*, that all the "excellent" organizations they investigated actively encouraged a high degree of rich, informal communication and shared value systems.[15] Since writing this book, Tom Peters has gone even further in stating that horizontal communication within and among teams of individuals is an absolute necessity for any business that hopes to prosper in the 1990s. According to this cultural perspective, individuals are viewed as integral elements of the communication culture, and of its meanings and values.

Important Works

Terrence Deal and Allan Kennedy, *Corporate Cultures* (1982)
Tom Peters and Robert Waterman, *In Search of Excellence* (1982)
Thomas Sergiovani and John Corbally, *Leadership and Organizational Cultures* (1984)
Edgar Schein, *Organizational Culture and Leadership* (1985)

Theoretical Orientation

◆ Organizations are cultures within cultures—open to both internal and external exchange

◆ Open and direct face-to-face communication

Management by Bestseller

In what has become one of the most widely read books on management ever, Peters and Waterman distinguished "excellent" organizations from ordinary ones by idenitfying the following eight characteristics of excellence. They say that all excellent organizations:

1. Remain in close contact with customers
2. Encourage employees to be creative and self-directed.
3. Encourage managers to show respect for employee creativity.
4. Maintain strong cultures and shared values.
5. Recruit and develop the best employees.
6. Respond to challenges in the environment.
7. Maintain simultaneous "loose-tight" properties, by having a unified cultural identity, as well as decentralized decision making practices.
8. Know what business they are in, and don't take on tasks or projects they know little or nothing about.

Ever since the very beginnings of organization theory in the early part of this century, researchers and managers have been seeking ways of increasing organizational effectiveness and human development at the same time. It is therefore a bit ironic that recent theory focusing on the pursuit of excellence should be billed as "new directions." Whatever the system or theoretical model it is ascribed to, this pursuit has always been the underlying current common to all thought on the subject.

When skills learned in the workplace are transferable to home life and vice-versa, the workplace becomes a more satisfying place to be, since it is an integral part of one's life, not simply a place for "making a living." In turn, the workplace will begin to function as a means of achieving personal goals as well as career goals. The organization will be fulfilling its role as a site in which people—as opposed to workers, employees, managers—find meaning and fulfillment. The workplace will change as a result. It will become less a place of confrontation and control and more one of dialogue and consensus.

And finally . . .

After this introduction to schools of organizational theory, especially in connection to theories of communication, you may wish to consider some alternative ways of looking at organizations. For instance, you might examine the lives of distinguished men and women in organizations as models, studying their struggles and learning from their successes and failures.

In Section 3, we introduce the notion of "managing by wandering around" to help identify practical opportunities for implementing our theoretical discussion of face-to-face interpersonal communication in the situations managers encounter each day at work.

Section 3 Managing by Wandering Around

Before we get started . . .

"Managing by wandering around" (MBWA) is the "practical" aspect of communication theory that complements the material in the first two sections of the chapter. The theory in this book will only be useful if you are able to apply it to interpersonal situations.

We hope this section will stimulate you to come up with your own ideas about interpersonal communication in management. It should help you think of ways to apply theory to face-to-face encounters with others. We begin by suggesting that MBWA has roots that are at least as old as the work of Shakespeare.

Objectives

After you complete this section, you should be able to:

1. Explain briefly the notion of "managing by wandering around" (MBWA), and state its importance in the practice of interpersonal communications.

2. Describe how Shakespeare's *Henry V* successfully incorporated "the technology of the obvious" into his speech at the battle of Agincourt in 1415.

3. Discuss the MBWA approach and its merits as a communication strategy for leading contemporary organizations.

4. State briefly two opposing perspectives of MBWA as it relates to the case of Harold Geneen and ITT.

A Little Touch of Harry in the Night

Near the beginning of the fourth act in William Shakespeare's *Henry V*, King Henry conceals his royal identity and ventures—incognito—among his soldiers the night before the decisive battle in the Hundred Years' War at Agincourt in France, in 1415. In the battle of Agincourt, Claude d'Albret's French forces lost over 7000 men, while the English under Henry V lost only a few hundred. But the night before that famous battle, Shakespeare portrays the English armies as largely beaten, despondent, and ailing.

As Henry comes upon Williams, Court, and Bates—three ordinary soldiers seated morosely around a campfire—he overhears them musing on what a wretched fate awaits them in battle the next day. As Henry appears the soldiers are discussing the unbreachable gulf that exists between the king and common men such as themselves. For them, King Henry is such an elevated, unapproachable, and distant figure, that they "may as well go about to turn the sun to ice" as expect to have any influence with the king.

When King Henry—whose true identity has still not been revealed—enters into the conversation, a quarrel ensues between him and Williams. The men argue over who bears responsibility for the souls of soldiers who die in the king's cause. Williams argues that the king must bear the burden of the souls lost, and Henry argues that each man's soul is his own responsibility. The quarrel ends with King Henry and Williams so roused that they exchange their gloves and vow to fight each other to death after the battle, should they survive it. This argument with Williams causes King Henry to reflect, in a soliloquy, on the barriers to communication and understanding that isolate the king from the ordinary men who fight by his side.

As the dawn of the day of reckoning arrives, King Henry has had time to think about his encounters of the night before and, having accurately ascertained his men's state of mind, he incorporates this understanding into an inspiring St. Crispin's Day speech that strikes fire and courage into the hearts of his men. Soldiers of every rank band around him as he speaks:

> 66He which hath no stomach to this fight,
> Let him depart. His passport shall be made
> And crowns for convoy put into his purse.

We would not die in that man's company
That fears his fellowship to die with us.[16] **99**

King Henry speaks of glory, honor, and what makes them brothers:

66 This story shall the good man teach his son,
And Crispin Crispian shall ne'er go by
From this day to the ending of the world
But we in it shall be remembered,
We few, we happy few, we band of brothers.
For he today that sheds his blood with me
Shall be my brother; be he ne'er so vile,
This day shall gentle his condition.
And gentlemen in England now abed
Shall think themselves accursed they were not here,
And hold their manhoods cheap whiles any speaks
That fought with us upon Saint Crispin's Day.[17] **99**

This passage clearly shows that the notion of talking to those who are on the "front lines," those who actually do the work, is not a new one.

The Double-Edged Sword of Face-to-Face Channels of Communication

The idea of engaging in personal contact with people as a means of assessing their morale wasn't new to Henry V, or to William Shakespeare. But recently, the concept of management-by-wandering-around (MBWA) has been made famous once more, as a leadership technique advocated by management consultant Tom Peters in his immensely popular books *In Search of Excellence* (with Robert Waterman, 1982), *A Passion For Excellence* (with Nancy Austin, 1985), *Thriving On Chaos* (1987), and *Liberation Management* (1993).

Each of these bestsellers describes the activities of several prominent business executives who wander around all levels of their Fortune 500 companies *in search of excellence*. The lesson is the same today as it was for the Elizabethans: Leaders or managers must come face-to-face with the people they work with. Executives who have lost touch with their employees or their customers are at a terrible disadvantage in any competitive environment.

Tom Peters calls MBWA "the technology of the obvious." To manage by wandering around provides obvious, and necessary, contact with others. For example, a CEO who is frequently seen wandering around talking to people on the shop floor, might find out that the workers would rather take an extra 10 minutes each day to clear up their own work stations. Rather than have some outside cleaning firm come in twice a week and do a lousy job of it for them, they would rather be paid the time it takes to do this themselves. Then and there the CEO can promise to do something about it (not simply to "look into it") and later on she can get back to the person she spoke with to demonstrate what she did about it.

Managers, say Tom Peters and his associates, need to understand what their employees' and customers' interests or concerns are. The best way to keep in touch with these people is, invariably, through face-to-face interpersonal communication. When it comes to having a true understanding of something, there is no substitute for walking right up to the people involved, and finding out what's on their minds. MBWA can help us to understand the business or organization we are in, by engaging us in direct interpersonal communication with others. Face-to-face interpersonal communication in management is the primary mode by which one person or group can influence or persuade others to implement the goals of the organization. As organizations become larger and more complex, the need for personal contact becomes even greater.

Consider ITT, one of the largest and most successful corporations in the world. Harold Geneen was at the helm of ITT from 1959 to 1977. In that time his principal goal was to make ITT a truly global and unified organization, despite its huge size (over 200 subsidiaries around the world). One of his techniques was to offer managers five-year contracts and to assign and monitor demanding budget and production targets. He relied primarily on face-to-face channels of communication. For 17 years, Geneen and his senior staff went over to Europe for one week every month, to deal personally with their European counterparts. Geneen had this to say about the practice, in his book with Alvin Moscow titled *Managing*:

> ❝One of the first things I learned in those early days was that when I responded to a question or request from Europe while sitting in New York, my decision was often different from what it would have been had I been in Europe. In New York, I might read a request and say no. But in Europe, I could see the man's face, hear his voice, understand the intensity of his conviction, and the answer to the same question might be yes. So, early on, I decided that if I and my headquarters' team intended to monitor and oversee the European operations, I owed it to the European managers to be there on the spot. . . . It became our policy to deal with problems on the spot, face-to-face.[18]❞

As we shall see throughout the remainder of this book, there is no single best way to manage interpersonal communication in every organization. Furthermore, it is not always clear whether one has been successful in adopting a particular communication or management strategy. In the case of Mr. Geneen, for example, consider the following assessment, quite different than the one we just presented, provided by Marshall McLuhan. In the following passage, McLuhan refers to ITT as "Geneen University":

> 66What Geneen has done is retrieve from past forms of human commercial striving all the dissatisfactions and miseries as ends in themselves. While ostensibly striving to intensify the profit lash to stretch flagging human tendons and nerves, Geneen in effect substitutes the whiplash for the profit lash.[19]99

As you can see, we can interpret a business leader's strategy of "wandering around the organization" in very different ways. On the one hand, we can regard a person such as Mr. Geneen as being in touch, hands on, and action-oriented. On the other, we can view such a manager as being authoritarian. MBWA can be interpreted in different ways—what some see as efficient others see as cruel or meddling. It is important for managers to be aware of this double-edged sword aspect of overly aggressive MBWA.

INTERPERSONAL SKILLS CLINIC

INSIDE THE HOUSE OF STAIRS

The purpose of this clinic is to give students a chance to find out something about the culture and patterns of communication in various organizations, through the use of interviews. *Read through both exercises before you start.*

EXERCISE 1

Students should do the following:

   I. Divide into groups of three, with each person taking a turn playing the role of:
   1. interviewer
   2. respondent
   3. coach/observer.

  II. Number the corners of a blank index card 1 - 2 - 3 - 4 (Figure 1.10). Next, jot down your name (large enough so that others who may not know you can see it) in the center of the card, and fill in a few notes about:
   1. Two or three organizations to which you have belonged or would like to belong.
   2. What you believe about people: Can people be changed for the better or not? Give an example.
   3. Two or three people who have influenced you most in their accomplishments.

Figure 1.10: Index Card

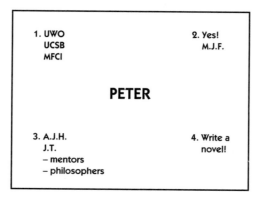

4. If you were suddenly fired from a job, what would you do before taking another position elsewhere?

III. Take turns conducting interviews with each other in each of the three roles. The interviewers should invite the respondents to describe what thoughts they had about each of the four questions, taking time to probe for relevant details. Examples of probe questions might be:

◆ What was it like working at Ace Carpets for two years?

◆ Do you really think criminals can be rehabilitated in prison-like institutions?

◆ Can you give me an example of how your mother taught you to respect the personal needs of others and how this resulted in your promotion?

IV. Leave time after each interview for the coach, who has been observing, to "process" the communication features of the interaction. Questions the coach might choose to focus on are:

◆ Were there any distortions or interferences in encoding and decoding?

◆ Was there a balance in the talking and listening, or did one person dominate the conversation?

◆ Was there any verbal feedback given and was it received and adjusted to by the sender?

◆ What was the quality or effect of any nonverbal messages?

EXERCISE 2

Students should do the following:

I. Divide one side of an index card into four sections. In each of the sections jot down a few notes to stimulate your recollection of the following people and phenomena in the organizations where you have worked, gone to school, or visited at one time or another.

1. Identify one or two *groups, cliques,* or *subunits* made up of people that tend to interact or communicate on a fairly regular basis about some interest they have in common. For instance, the softball team getting together over pizza and beer to celebrate winning a game.
2. Identify one or two *liaisons* or *gatekeepers* who connect two or more cliques or subunits, but who may not be members of either group themselves.
3. Identify one or two *opinion leaders* who have successfully influenced the attitudes and behavior of others. For example, a senior consultant in a firm who is expected to inspire and motivate junior associates or a charismatic classmate.
4. Identify either:
   — one or two *gatekeepers* who are near or who have access to those in the seats of power.
   — one or two stations on the *grapevine*—or sources of important, if informal, information about people's moods and personal backgrounds.
   — one or two *gossips* who take it upon themselves to repeat to several others, some largely unfounded rumour they may have overheard or imagined.

II. On the flip side of the card: Number three of the corners and jot down a few more notes to trigger your recollection of:

1. Any patterns of communication where you work or go to school.
   — who reports to whom?
   — who makes the decisions?
   — how do different cliques communicate with one another?
2. How would you describe the organizational culture in a past or current organization you are familiar with? scientific? bureaucratic? humanistic? beliefs? values? assumptions?
3. What kind of organization would you most like to belong to and why?
   — How would people get together face-to-face?
   — What would they talk about?
   — What formal structures would there be?
   — How would personal needs be met?

III.   Take turns conducting the interviews and processing the interactions with your coach.

● — ● — ● — ● — ● — ● — ● — ● — ● — ● — ● — ● — ●

And finally . . .

As we have discovered in this chapter, a consideration of actual interpersonal communication in the organization must include a consideration of the theoretical basis of the patterns of communication. But everyone and every organization is different and constantly changing. Theories about communication are also constantly changing—according to their usefulness in illuminating aspects of what goes on day-to-day in the organizations where we work. The purpose of this chapter has not just been to enhance an understanding of theory, but also to help us to apply this knowledge when we communicate face-to-face with others in the workplace.

CHAPTER REVIEW QUESTIONS

1. *Interpersonal* communication concerns our interactions with _____, while *intrapersonal* communication concerns our _____.
   a. the self; colleagues
   b. others; significant others
   c. others; self-conception
   d. the organization; self-conception

2. The first of the ancient Greek philosophers to analyze with scientific rigor the art of rhetoric was:
   a. Aristotle
   b. Cicero
   c. Plato
   d. Protagorus

3. Cicero's five canons of rhetoric were as follows:
   a. introduction, narrative, partition, confirmation, peroration
   b. politics, rhetoric, persuasion, poetry, semantics
   c. narration, persuasion, definition, exposition, explanation
   d. invention, disposition, style, memory, delivery

4. Aside from their restatement of the linear model of communication, what was the important contribution of Shannon and Weaver to communication theory?

5. Describe Schramm's two-way interactive model of communication.

6. In the transactive model of communication, each communicator is continuously _____ and _____ messages through one or more _____ *simultaneously.*
   a. filtering; sorting; of the human senses
   b. sending; receiving; channels
   c. collecting; revising; media
   d. channelling; coding; media

7. How can taking a systems approach help us understand organizations?

8. What are the implications of viewing the organization as a machine? a brain? a psychic prison?

9. Discuss briefly the principles of Taylorism.

10. State the importance of the writings of Max Weber and Henri Fayol in connection to classical organizational theory.

11. The theoretical orientation of the human relations school is as follows:
    a. More balanced concern for formal structures and the social and psychological needs of employees.
    b. The use of counselling sessions in the workplace.
    c. The avoidance of formal structures.
    d. The increased use of organization-sponsored day-care and spousal employment programs.

12. Fred Fiedler suggested that:
    a. Leaders were born, not made.
    b. Contingency theory was unsupported by empirical data.
    c. Leaders needed training, perhaps more than subordinates.
    d. No one type of framework for leadership is appropriate for all systems.

13. What are the principles of Hersey and Blanchard's situational leadership theory?

14. According to the teamwork school, how is productivity best achieved?

15. In progressive order of necessity, what are Maslow's hierarchy of needs?
    a. self-actualization, self-esteem, social, security, physiological
    b. security, social, physiological, self-esteem, self-actualizaton
    c. physiological, security, social, self-esteem, self-actualization
    d. security, physiological, social, self-esteem, self-actualization

16. According to Deal and Kennedy, what distinguishes one corporate culture from another?

17. List the qualities of "excellent" organizations.

18. The lesson to be drawn from the incident described from *Henry V* in connection with MBWA is as follows:
    a. The notion of talking to those who are on the "front lines" is not a new one.
    b. Even kings have to talk to their subordinates.
    c. Corporations are like armies.
    d. Strategy in the corporate world can be compared to that of the military world.

19. According to Peters, why do managers need to practise MBWA?

20. During his tenure at ITT in the 1960s and 1970s, what techniques did Harold Geneen use with his executives?

21. Who said the following?
    "While ostensibly striving to intensify the profit lash to stretch flagging human tendons and nerves, Geneen in effect substitutes the whiplash for the profit lash."

SUGGESTED ANSWERS

1. c.

2. a.

3. d.

4. Shannon and Weaver's major contribution to the theoretical model of communication was that they introduced the use of the term *noise* for anything that distorts or interferes with the quality of communication.

5. In Schramm's model, the sender forms or *encodes* a message and the message is conveyed through some *channel* to the receiver. The receiver *decodes* the message and responds, with the use of feedback, to the source of the original message. The source, in turn, decodes the feedback and adapts new messages according to his or her new understanding.

6. b.

7. Taking a systems approach to the subject provides us with a way to view communication situations across boundaries normally used to isolate these aspects.

8. The image of the organization as a *machine* will imply that it is made up of interlocking component parts—organized to operate efficiently according to predetermined goals and objectives. This style of thought, which is fundamental to bureaucratic organization, also forces human qualities into a subordinate role. The organization as *brain* draws attention to the importance of information processing, self-organization, flexibility, and learning. The idea that organizations are *psychic prisons*, where people become trapped by their own thoughts and beliefs, invites us to examine organizational life to see if we have become trapped by conscious and unconscious processes of our own creation.

9. Taylor's prescription was for job design, formal divisions of labor, and formal channels of communication. Taylorism meant increasing productivity by breaking factory work down into specialized components. Each assembly worker simply followed a series of mechanical steps to keep the line moving at maximum speed without wasted effort.

10. The writings of these "bureaucratic" theorists centered almost exclusively on the structure and rules of formal organizations, the official chain of command, and the roles or responsibilities of each functional division.

11. a.

12. d.

13. 1. When dealing with employees who are willing, able, and motivated to accomplish tasks, leaders should communicate with them in a "delegating style" in which workers are given all the support necessary for them to make their own decisions on the job.

2. When employees are clearly able, but unwilling or unmotivated, they should be treated with a "participatory style" in which they may become involved more in making their own decisions.

3. When employees are willing, but unable to accomplish tasks, managers should adopt a "selling style" in which they provide more guidance and direction.

4. And finally, when employees are neither willing, nor able, managers should use a "telling style" of directive communication in which there is no freedom for employees to make decisions on their own.

14. According to the teamwork school, productivity in an organization is more readily achieved through team-building and lateral interactions than it is through top-down, vertical-linear communications through the chains of command.

15. c.

16. Each corporate culture is based on a blend or mix of particular values, beliefs, traditions, trends, and disturbances.

17. Excellent organizations:

1. Remain in close contact with customers
2. Encourage employees to be creative and self-directed.
3. Encourage managers to show respect for employee creativity.
4. Maintain strong cultures and shared values.
5. Recruit and develop the best employees.
6. Respond to challenges in the environment.
7. Maintain simultaneous "loose-tight" properties, by having a unified cultural identity, as well as decentralized decision making practices.
8. Know what business they are in, and don't take on tasks or projects they know little or nothing about.

18. a.

19. Managers, say Tom Peters and his associates, need to understand what their employees' and customers' interests or concerns are.

20. One of his techniques was to offer managers five-year contracts and to assign and monitor demanding budget and production targets. He also relied primarily on face-to-face channels of communication. For 17 years, Geneen and his senior staff went over to Europe for one week every month, to deal personally with their people.

21. Marshall McLuhan

SUNSET HOTEL ENTERPRISES

OVERVIEW AND ASSIGNMENT QUESTIONS

In the following scenario, which is based on a situation that could well occur in an organization, you will have the opportunity to apply the principles and skills you have learned in this chapter. The scenario can be used as the basis for a written or oral analysis or for role-play.

Bob Harper, the vice-president of human resources for Sunset Hotel Enterprises faces the challenge of planning the company's acquisition of its tenth new hotel in two and a half years. The company's experienced and qualified senior managers have been working hard during this period. To impose Sunset's standards of excellence on the new property and its operations will require 20 additional senior-level managers. Therefore, Harper must implement the transition (which will take place in six months) at the management level.

1. Assume you are in the position of Bob Harper. Prepare a human resources action plan that is congruent with the corporate growth strategy of the company and with the local setting and cirumstances.

2. How should "managing by wandering around" figure in your plan?

3. How do you intend to organize and staff the Isle Vista Hotel?

4. What role will a consideration of theories and models of communication play in your plan? (For example, what kind of communication patterns seem to exist in the Sunset and Bisquaine regimes?)

5. What can you do to predict the outcomes of the changes you plan to make?

6. From where do you expect to find the number of qualified and experienced managers you will need?

7. Prepare to add a training and development program to your plan.

INTRODUCTION

Bob Harper, vice-president of human resources for Sunset Hotel Enterprises in Vancouver, looks up from his diary as the vice-president of operations, Jessica Cooke, walks in.

"We've got it!" exclaims Cooke. "Our offer for the Isle Vista Hotel in Miami has just been accepted. We take over from Bisquaine Hotels in six months."

"That's great news," says Harper. "Even though we weren't planning any more acquisitions this year, I suppose this is too good to pass up—a hotel right on the beach in Florida."

As Cooke sits down, however, Harper feels a twinge of apprehension.

"We've already stretched our managers to the limit over the past few years," says Harper. "We've opened four new hotels this year. This will be the tenth in the past two and a half years. The Isle Vista will require about 20 new managers. Where are we going to get them from?"

SUNSET HOTEL ENTERPRISES

The company is a rapidly expanding Canadian organization with high standards of service excellence and a strong customer orientation. It owns and/or operates 25 prestigious hotels throughout Canada and the United States. Yearly gross revenues exceed $500 million. Sunset manages over 7500 guest rooms and employs 10 000 people. The company's "employees per room" ratio is double that of the hotel industry.

Noted for consistent, award-winning service and amenities (European-style concierge service, 24-hour full menu room service, overnight laundry and dry cleaning, twice daily maid service, the supply of personal toiletries and bath robes, and satellite television), Sunset has been developing a preference for managing its properties rather than owning them. The company holds an equity participation of $20 million, of asset values totalling over $650 million. Along with this evolution away from ownership towards property management has come a lessening of corporate control. However, this has been compensated for by greater profitability and stability of earnings through reservation and operating fees, marketing and advertising fees, and corporate goods purchases.

Ten regional vice-presidents supervise one, two, or three hotels each in their respective regions. Each VP also serves as a general manager of one hotel. The key person in each hotel is the general manager, who is in charge of owner's assets valued up to $100 million, supervises an average of 450 employees, and administers approximately $10 million per year in payroll and benefits. Each hotel carries out almost all its own personnel recruitment.

THE VICE-PRESIDENT OF HUMAN RESOURCES TALKS ABOUT CORPORATE STRATEGY AND MANAGEMENT PRACTICES

Our strategy at Sunset is to differentiate ourselves from other hotels, primarily through our high level of services. Our guests must see our people as better than other hotel staff. They are. The quality of our service is what makes the most difference. Therefore, we must attract, train, develop, motivate, and retain the best people. We do that by caring about our people, communicating with them, and by providing good pay, strong benefits, and an exciting work environment.

We interview about 700 graduates of tourism and hospitality management programs each year for the usual 20-25 management trainee positions that will open up that year. Our managers must be strong on detail and be able to provide hands-on support at the local level. Sound "people management" skills are essential. So is a commitment to excellence.

Promotions usually come from inside the company. At the general manager level, we have only recruited outside the organization twice in the last four years. Personnel planning can be a most difficult task. Each new location presents differences of culture and locale. In addition, certain basic differences exist between operating a resort hotel and managing convention, city, or airport hotels. For example, resort guests are usually spending their own money and more time in the hotel than are business guests. Therefore, they can be more demanding, especially in affluent coastal locations such as Miami.

THE ISLE VISTA HOTEL

Housing and hotel accommodations in Miami are expensive, and the cost of living is so high that many working people hold down two jobs. For instance, it is common for hotel food servers to work in two restaurants, two shifts a day, in order to make ends meet. The community's working labor pool consists largely of Hispanic residents and university and college students.

The normal complement of Isle Vista staff totals approximately 550, consisting of 50 management staff, 300 full-time line staff, and over 200 part-time and casual employees. However, following Bisquaine Hotels' decision to sell the property, the numbers have plunged, since positions that have been vacated are not being filled. Food and beverage, front desk, and other service departments are staffed by short-term employees. Figure 1.11 is an organizational chart of Isle Vista.

Bisquaine's general manager at the Isle Vista, Shirley Bartlow, has been at the hotel for 10 years. She began as a rooms division manager and was quickly promoted for her "people and public relations" skills. A local liberal arts graduate from the University of Florida, she has a reputation for being a better than average delegator and a creative and responsible leader.

WHAT'S NEXT?

Immediately after Jessica Cooke leaves his office, Bob Harper begins working on an action plan to provide the necessary human resources for the Isle Vista property. Foremost in his mind as he works on the plan are the major differences between Sunset's philosophy and orientation and the Bisquaine system of hotel management, which is highly centralized, rigidly structured, and governed according to written procedural manuals that are intended to cover every management situation. In contrast to Sunset's management practices, the Bisquaine-run Isle Vista Hotel has had well-established corporate rules, standardized supplies and amenities, and ordinary menus with routine service restrictions. Cooke believes there are extensive changes to be made.

POINTS TO CONSIDER

Given that Harper must implement the Isle Vista transition to Sunset management in six months, the plan should include a pre- and post-takeover schedule and rationale from Bisquaine management. In addition to providing details of the steps to be taken and the corresponding time-lines, the action plan should accomplish the following:

Figure 1.11: Isle Vista Organizational Chart

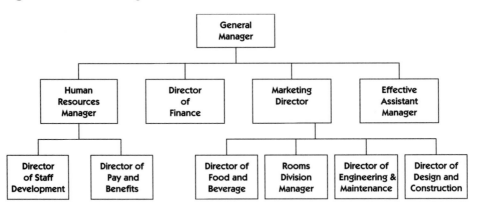

1. state the problem to be solved and the objectives of the solutions proposed
2. list alternatives to recommendations
3. explain the criteria to be used in selecting from among the alternatives
4. offer a restatement of the proposed solutions and the reasons for those decisions
5. provide evidence of a consideration of how the results will be monitored, feedback obtained, and appropriate contingency plans put in place.

● ─ ● ─ ● ─ ● ─ ● ─ ● ─ ● ─ ● ─ ● ─ ● ─ ● ─ ●

ENDNOTES

[1] Linda McQuaig, *The Quick and the Dead: Brian Mulroney, Big Business and the Seduction of Canada* (Toronto: Viking, 1991).

[2] Claude Shannon and Warren Weaver, *The Mathematical Theory of Communication* (Champaign, Illinois: University of Illinois Press, 1949).

[3] Marshall McLuhan suggested that an important weakness of the Shannon-Weaver model was that it identified "noise" as existing outside the communication system. Noise, stated McLuhan, *is* the medium, "all the unintended patterns and changes". (Quoted in Graeme Patterson, *History and Communications: Harold Innis, Marshall McLuhan, the Interpretation of History* (Toronto: University of Toronto Press, 1990), p. 100.

[4] Wilbur Schramm, *The Process and Effects of Mass Communication*, Urbana, Illinois, University of Illinois Press, 1965.

[5] James D. Thompson, *Organizations in Action* (New York: McGraw-Hill, 1967).

[6] Karl Weick, *The Social Psychology of Organizing* (Reading, MA., Addison-Wesley , 1969).

[7] The discussion of various ways of viewing organizations on page 17 has been adapted from Gareth Morgan, *Images of Organization* (Beverly Hills, Calif.: Sage Publications, 1986).

[8] Morgan, p.17.

[9] Robert Lacey, *Ford: The Men and the Machine* (Toronto: Little, Brown, & Co., 1986), p. 108.

[10] Chester Barnard, *The Functions of the Executive* (Cambridge, Mass.: Harvard University Press, 1938), p. 12.

[11] Paul Hersey and Ken Blanchard, *Management of Organizational Behavior* (Englewood Cliffs, N.J.: Prentice Hall, 1982).

[12] See Abraham Maslow, *The Psychology of Science: A Reconnaissance* (South Bend, Indiana: Gateway Editions, Ltd., 1966), especially Chapter 2, "Acquiring Knowledge of a Person as a Task for the Scientist." Data (for diagram) based on a Hierarchy of Needs from "A Theory of Human Motivation" in *Motivation and Personality*, 3rd edition, by Abraham H. Maslow, revised by Robert Frager, James Fadiman, Cynthia McReynolds, and Ruth Cox. Copyright 1954, 1987 by Harper & Row, Publishers Inc. Copyright © 1970 by Abraham Maslow. Reprinted by permission of HarperCollins, Publishers, Inc.

[13] Mihaly Csikszentmihalyi, *Flow: The Psychology of Optimal Experience* (New York: Harper and Row, 1990), page 22.

[14] Terrence Deal and Allan Kennedy, *Corporate Cultures* (Reading, MA., Addison-Wesley, 1984).

[15] Tom Peters and Robert Waterman, *In Search of Excellence* (New York: Harper and Row, 1982).

[16] *The Oxford Shakespeare: Henry V*, edited by Gary Taylor (Oxford: Clarendon Press, 1982), Act 4.3.39. and Act 4.3.67.

[17] Act 4.3.67.

[18] Geneen and Moscow, *Managing* (New York: Doubleday, 1984), p.47.

[19] Marshall McLuhan and Barrington Nevitt, *Take Today: The Executive as Dropout* (Don Mills, Ontario: Longman Canada Limited, 1972), p. 253.

CHAPTER 2

The Primacy of Persuasion

WORTH REPEATING

The wise are instructed by reason; ordinary minds by experience; the stupid by necessity; and brutes by instinct.

—Cicero (106-43 B.C.)

He that has sense knows that learning is not knowledge, but rather the art of using it.

—Sir Richard Steele

Since knowledge cannot be gained with certainty, rhetoric must aim at opinion. Since there will always be conflicting opinions, it all ultimately becomes a matter of persuasion.

—Gorgias, circa 427 B.C.

Section 1   The Art and Science of Persuasion

Before we get started . . .

Published in 1532, five years after the author's death, *The Prince*, by Niccolo Machiavelli advised leaders to use their craft, cunning, deceit, and naked power to exert their sovereign will over their humble subjects. A prince, wrote Machiavelli, must imitate the fox and the lion, for the lion cannot protect itself from traps and the fox cannot defend itself from wolves. Princes, he said, ought to murder their opponents rather than take their property, since those who have been robbed can still plot their revenge. Less so the naked dead.

Cruel advice. Yet as deadly as his views may have been, Machiavelli has countless imitators—some of whom reside in the ranks of modern management. While few of them today would emulate the master in coercion or deceit, many do seek to manage others through manipulation rather than persuasion. At the core of Machiavellianism, wrote Richard Christie and Florence Geis, is the treatment of other persons as things rather than beings. Success in getting others to do what one wishes them to do is accomplished without empathy or understanding for their point of view.[1] Worse yet, in the words of leadership scholar James MacGregor Burns, is the current vogue of "how to" manuals that treat persons "as tools to be used or objects to be stormed like a castle."[2]

Persuasion, on the other hand, engages others by wedding their needs and aspirations to our own. Persuasion involves of a mutuality between persuaders and those they seek to influence. The interaction of persuaders and the persuaded is not merely a process of exchange; rather, each becomes locked into maintaining each other's motivations and values. We must begin, then, by clarifying our personal goals and linking them with a common purpose that rises above self-interest and manipulation.

Objectives

After you complete this section, you should be able to:

1. Explain, with the use of an example, the difference between persuasion and coercion.
2. Discuss the primacy of persuasion in interpersonal communication.
3. Describe the pervasiveness of persuasion.
4. List and discuss the three factors that lead to persuasion.
5. Discuss the use of the acronyms "H3W" and "MARCS" for structuring persuasive interviews.
6. Discuss the reasons why face-to-face communication is richer than other modes of communication, especially for the purpose of persuasion.

An Offer You Can't Refuse

There is a scene near the beginning of *The Godfather* (the novel by Mario Puzo) in which the popular singer Johnny Fontane appears in the garden at the wedding of Don Corleone's daughter, Connie. The don's son Michael is seated near the garden with his girlfriend Kay Adams, who is truly impressed that Michael's father knows Johnny Fontane. Michael informs Kay that Fontane is his father's godson and says "If it wasn't for my father he might not be a big movie star today."

Michael tells the story of how, eight years before, Johnny Fontane had made an extraordinary success singing with a popular dance band that had become a top radio attraction in the early 1940s. Unfortunately, the band leader had signed Johnny to a five-year personal services contract and was pocketing most of the money.

So Don Corleone entered the negotiations personally. He offered the band leader $20 000 to release Johnny Fontane from the personal services contract.

The band leader—obviously not a man of the world outside of show business—refused. The next day Don Corleone went to see the band leader again, only this time he brought his hit man Luca Brasi along, and "made him an offer he couldn't refuse." Puzo writes:

> 66 Don Corleone persuaded (the band leader) to sign a document giving up all rights to all services from Johnny Fontane upon payment of a certified cheque to the amount of $10,000. Don Corleone did this by putting a pistol to the forehead of the band leader and assuring him with the utmost seriousness that either his signature or his brains would rest on that document in exactly one minute.[3] 99

The band leader signed the contract. Johnny Fontane went on to become the greatest singing sensation in the country. He made Hollywood musicals that earned a fortune for his studio, and his records made millions of dollars.

Although clearly intended to influence the band leader's decision, what the don did, of course, was not *persuasion* at all. When a person is influenced by force or intimidation, it is *coercion*. And coercion is a different matter altogether. **Coercion** occurs when someone is forced or manipulated into doing something against his or her will. It usually includes the threat of penalties or dire consequences, and is used to bully people into compliance, rather than to persuade them. **Persuasion** occurs when someone has been convinced by rational argument to change the way he or she acts, thinks, or feels about something.

Persuasion is largely a matter of making some choices appear more or less attractive than others. If you succeed in persuading people, they will think, feel, and do what you want because that is what *they* have decided is the right thing to do. The persuaded person has not given in to the appeals of others in an unthinking way, and should therefore feel that he or she has gained something from having made the relatively attractive choice freely.

Take My Word for It

In the most effective organizations, persuasion is a necessary and constant tool for bringing about change. Therefore, managers who have responsibility for introducing change need to develop their skill at persuading others when dealing with them face-to-face. Persuasion begins with a shared understanding of purpose and the declaration of mutual goals.

Good persuasive interviews are not usually confrontations in which categorical demands are made, or pressure applied from which there is no easy retreat. They are generally efforts at establishing common ground between the persuader and the other person. Good persuasive interviews are carefully planned so that both sides get what they want from the encounter. The *best* persuasion leads people to aspire to a "higher need" that is awakened in those who are persuaded. We will have more to say about this at the end of this chapter.

Custom Made

Change is a feature of all effective organizations. In order to facilitate change, those who have responsibility for the change need to encourage others to accept it. New ideas can't be forced. People do things because *they* decide to do them, but good persuaders can influence people so that their decisions are in line with the desired change.

Despite the practices of many large companies, good persuasive interviews are never "canned" programs designed to fit all persuaders in all situations. For the most part, people who are excellent at persuading tend to be open and resourceful when it comes to customizing their own approach to each opportunity to make a significant impact on the ideas or behavior of others.

Sales representatives are generally regarded as prime examples of people who make particular use of persuasive skills at work. Almost every major corporation involved in selling has its own sales models for training and development. However, research indicates that the kinds of sales techniques taught in sales training are substantially tailored or modified by experienced sales personnel. Later on in this chapter, in the section entitled, "How to Handle Objections," we will be learning more about how this is done. But first we need to ask ourselves not only who we want to talk with, but why, and about what, and also, who wants to talk with *us*, why, and about what?

Asking Questions to Activate Thinking

In a classic text on the techniques of persuasion, *Getting Through to People,*[4] Dr. Jesse Nirenberg, a preeminent industrial psychologist and consultant, wrote that there are no right words to use when trying to influence someone—it doesn't matter which words are used as long as your meaning is made clear. The way to do this is to get others to think about what you are saying. You must get others to fit your ideas into their scheme of looking at things. They have to visualize your ideas and the way they would use them. You can stimulate this process, says Nirenberg, by asking questions. Since a question is a request for information, in order to supply it the other person has to think. Thinking requires the use of the mind and of language. People must put ideas into words in order to respond to questions. If the question you ask someone is related to something you just said, then you are making his or her mind work on your ideas. When other people talk about your ideas, they are making them their own.

The Pervasiveness of Persuasion

It is happening all around us. Everywhere. All the time. We are bombarded with messages from every direction. Sometimes it happens so fast we don't even notice it. You watch the late night movie and are prompted to make popcorn. A sales representative shakes your hand in a shopping mall and asks you for your opinion of a new product. You hear a favorite song on the radio and the jingle that follows encourages you to take your next vacation in Venezuela. On and on it goes.

Various forms of persuasion overwhelm us through an array of media every day. Persuasion is a part of everything we think or do at work and at play. No other interpersonal communication skill is more central to organizational leadership and management success than persuasion. It has often been said the ways in which people deal with one another face-to-face make up the basis of all effective organizational functioning. At the core of most face-to-face management communication situations lies persuasion in some form or another.

Salespeople influence the choices a customer makes in essentially the same way a manager appeals to the needs of a candidate for a job. Selling is not the only place we find persuasive interviewing techniques used. Whether you are selling a product or service, hiring an employee or evaluating performance, persuading a colleague of your proposal, listening to a client, or asking the boss for a raise in salary, you must recognize the primacy of persuasion in nearly everything you do.

Why are we constantly subjected to the attempts of others to influence what we think and how we act, and vice versa? Partly because there are precious few, if any, resources available to us that can be had without the cooperation of others. Interdependent action is essential for getting things done. In addition, the communication culture or environment that surrounds us involves people who are both like us and unlike us. If everyone in society had similar needs and values, there would be little need for persuasion. As it is, we live in a pluralistic society that demands we interact with others—using persuasion to shape, alter, and elevate our goals, values, and motives.

Three Factors Leading to Persuasion

Persuasion depends on at least three major factors:

1. The credibility of the persuader.
2. Sources of evidence contained in the message.
3. A balanced presentation.

The Credibility Factor

It may seem obvious, but it bears emphasizing: People tend to be more easily influenced by those they find credible, are attracted to, and otherwise like or respect. We see examples of this fact every day in mass media advertising. Attractive personalities such as singer Whitney Houston or screen actor Michael J. Fox appear in advertisements—coaxing us to buy this or that. The assumption is that if we identify our values, tastes, and lifestyles with the person recommending the product, we can be persuaded to use it ourselves.

Those who appear to have the relevant expertise, intelligence, and credibility regarding a certain matter, will also be more persuasive to the decision maker. Other traits or behaviors that generally help to influence us positively are a sense of humor, courtesy, and flattery. One must be careful not to use excessive flattery or exaggerated praise. If it is overdone, recipients may perceive that they are being manipulated, and will react negatively rather than positively to your suggestions.

Generally speaking, credibility refers to the image we have of someone's honesty, integrity, or trustworthiness. Thus, in order to be credible, if you are ever unsure of something, you should say so and check the facts out. Having credibility means that we don't lie and that we try hard to avoid error.

People are so inundated with information from print, radio, television, and advertising that, even if the percentage of false information hasn't changed, there seems to be a lot more of it around just because there is such an overwhelming amount of information being exchanged. When you impart false information to someone once, he or she will be a lot less likely to believe you the next time. If there is a next time.

Keep in mind that everything you say and do affects your image. People don't react to the *real* you, but rather to the *image* they have created of you. And all people will have a different understanding of who you are, which is based on how they interpret these different images. For someone to be persuaded by your ideas you have to be seen as being a competent and credible individual, and to some extent you have to see what that person sees, and adjust accordingly.

Sources of Evidence

Mentioning or citing the source of evidence for your arguments can also help to persuade others—provided it is not overdone. Be selective when quoting expert sources, and determine beforehand, if you can, which references are most likely to be influential with the audience you are trying to persuade. A lot will depend on the quality or the credibility of the sources given.

When attempting to persuade someone *within* your organization, it is often better to use less extensive documentation of sources. If people need further verification they will ask you for it. *Outside* the organization, it is generally better to state your evidence first, and then cite the sources or opinion leaders that will be most credible to your listeners.

The Need for Balance

When weighing your own product or point of view against another, you must remember to discuss the possible disadvantages as well as the benefits of your proposal. As a general rule, the more aware your listeners are of the opposing side of the story, the more important it is for the persuader to take this into consideration. Experienced salespeople who know the public is aware that their company's products are more expensive than the competition's will not wait for the customer to point this fact out. Consider the following statement you might make in such a situation, followed by a statement of your evidence:

> 66While it is true brand X costs a bit more than other brands, the fact is it has proven to last twice as long as any other competing product on the market. 99

Why is it usually best to present both sides of the argument whenever your listeners are fairly knowledgeable about the topic? Because this serves to "inoculate" the listeners against opposing arguments that may be introduced later by the other side. Cheryl Hamilton writes:

> 66Inoculating a listener against opposing ideas is similar to inoculating a person against a disease. The person who has never heard any negative arguments on a certain topic will be very susceptible to opposing arguments just as the person who had lived in a germ-free environment is susceptible to catching disease. Immunity can be produced by giving a shot containing a weakened form of the disease—presenting opposing arguments with their refutation.[5] 99

The H3W and MARCS Acronyms

For those of you who find acronyms useful learning devices or reminders, Frederick Williams has proposed the H3W and MARCS formulas as planning tools for structuring persuasive interview situations.[6] The **H3W** sequence is as follows:

Hey!: here is the main issue
What?: state what it is you want
Why?: appeal to the other person's motives
When?: be as specific as possible.

To begin with, the hey! is intended to arouse the other person's attention. Before you can persuade people, you have to get their attention. One way to create interest in others is to show that you are excited about what it is you have to say. Occasionally let the other person in on how *you feel* about it.

The what? why? and when? comprise the main body of your remarks. Then a quick review of the entire sequence serves as an effective summary or conclusion. For example:

Here is the main issue, Bob. This is what you wanted. Why not do yourself a favor? Let's meet again next week at the same time and decide the next step.

The **MARCS** sequence is similar, but it is slightly more detailed and it focuses more on the person you are trying to persuade:

1. Find the **motives**.
   - Find out about those you want to persuade
   - Discover who their "significant others" are
   - Use motives that healthy people respond to
   - Appeal to the highest motives
2. **Attack** problems, not people.
   - Sidestep put-downs
   - Don't waste energy on personal hostility
   - Make the other person feel good
3. Get and give **respect**.
   - Give your credentials out front
   - Show respect for the opinions of others
   - Be friendly
4. Look for **common ground**.
   - Find value bases for common ground
   - Consider shared personal experiences
   - Read and adapt to feedback
   - Try role reversal
5. Use the persuasive **sequence**.
   - Use H3W as a planning aid
   - Use feedback to check on your H3W
   - Use plenty of hey's!
   - Use H3W on communications directed to you
   - Make your when's? especially specific

Easy Habit

A lot of persuasion is done for the purpose of encouraging habitual behavior in others. All good salespeople, for example, know that it is a lot easier to maintain a business relationship with a satisfied customer than it is to expend the energy necessary to establish one in the first place. A satisfied customer is a good prospect for further business. For one thing, if your proposal is compatible with a customer's already existing beliefs or behaviors, there will be less disruption for him or her in adopting further plans. Habits make life a little bit simpler. Use this to your advantage.

As Easy as A-B-C

Before we take a closer look at how to handle objections in Section 2, let's review some of the most salient features of persuasion we have discussed so far:

*A*rousal. Be alert to differences among customers and listeners. Make sure they understand what you are trying to convince them of, and be sure to arouse their interest in your plan or proposal.

*B*alance. Be certain to inoculate listeners against opposing ideas by making them aware of the other side of the story as well as your own.

*C*hoices. Ask yourself is there a choice to be made or will the listeners' previous habits be good enough? By making each of your points clearly, positively, and directly, you can narrow the listeners' choices down to what you want to persuade them of. Conversely, if you want to keep someone from making certain choices (in favor of others), make them sound less appealing.

*D*elivery. Once your listener has been persuaded to make the choice you wanted, be sure to deliver the benefits you promised. If at all possible, get him or her to try out the product or proposal before making a final commitment.

*E*valuation. Once the persuasion interview is over, ask yourself how well you did what you intended. How well did it go? What agreements were sought and found? How effective were your arguments? What is the next step?

*F*ollow-up. Be sure to reinforce the other person's decision by following up. Remember, it is a lot easier to obtain return business than it is to start over again from the beginning.

Face-to-Face

Managers have recently witnessed an astonishing increase in the channels of communication available to them. In addition to face-to-face discussions, telephone conversations, memos, bulletins, and written reports, new media are available such as electronic mail, voice mail, satellite teleconferencing, FAX machines, voice-activated computers, and picture telephones.

Sometimes the temptation to use this new gadgetry is triggered by its novelty as much as by its utility. Many managers fail to recognize that each channel of communication has characteristics that make it appropriate in some situations and not in others. For example, electronic mail may be a swifter way of communicating written messages, but may leave issues requiring more personal contact unresolved. The point is that the decision to send and receive information through a particular communication medium affects the meaning of the message as well as its effectiveness.

Face-to-face communication is the richest medium for persuasion because it has the capacity to handle multiple information cues simultaneously, to facilitate rapid feedback, and to establish a personal focus. Telephone conversations and interactive electronic media provide rapid feedback, but are missing the richness of nonverbal cues such as eye contact and body language. Written media such as memos, letters, and reports can be personally focused, but feedback is delayed. More impersonal media such as bulletins and brochures provide no personal focus and are limited in terms of other cues as well.

And finally . . .

In this section, we've offered some simple methods (complete with acronyms) for remembering the basic aspects of persuasion. As simple as they may seem, they are based on the rhetorical principles first articulated by Aristotle that we mentioned in Chapter 1. We will return to Aristotle in Chapter 7 when we discuss persuasion in the context of oral presentations and meetings.

Section 2 ▸ How to Handle Objections

Before we get started . . .

The critical step of a successful persuasive interview is the one devoted to acknowledging and countering the objections to your argument. In this section we offer direct suggestions for accomplishing this step.

Objectives

After you complete this section, you should be able to:

1. Describe, with the use of an example, the notion of "reading the defence" in the context of persuasion.

2. Discuss the structure and use of the social styles matrix.

3. Explain why using an "attack" approach to persuasion will not usually work.

4. Discuss the importance of using a reasoned approach and tone in a persuasive interview.

5. Discuss the 10 guidelines for persuading others.
6. Describe the process for closing a persuasive interview.
7. Discuss the "one-two punch" sales method.

INTERPERSONAL SKILLS CLINIC

PERSUADING A FRIEND

In this section we will describe some specific techniques for handling objections in persuasive interviews or presentations. This activity will help you find out how well you have learned the techniques and how effective they really are in persuasive interview situations. The activity is in two parts. You should carry out the first part before reading the rest of the section, then complete the second part after you have finished the chapter. For both parts, you will need the use of a tape recorder and the cooperation of a friend, coach, colleague, or family member.

PART 1

The first thing you will need to do is decide on a topic. The topic is what you will try to persuade your partner of. Choose a topic that you understand and that is not too complicated or broad in scope so that you can discuss it fully in 15 or 20 minutes. Try to avoid topics that are especially controversial or charged with emotion. While such topics may be important, they may cause your activity to become too personal for the purposes of learning how to improve your persuasive skills. You can move on to such topics later. The following are some possible topics:

- the advantages (or disadvantages) of leasing a vehicle over buying one, for business or personal use
- the usefulness and effectiveness of appointing committees to solve problems in an organization
- the pros and cons of instituting a smoking policy in an organization
- the need to require that municipal employees reside in the municipality for which they work

You may have to do some research on the topic, perhaps by consulting a textbook or other reference. This will especially be the case if your partner happens to be familiar with the topic. For example, with the first topic in the list, that of leasing a vehicle, if your partner is an accountant, you may need to have some facts and figures at hand. On the other hand, if your partner is simply an informed consumer, you may be able to rely on the expertise of others as evidence, rather than working out the numbers yourself.

When you have chosen a topic, convert it to a position statement. For example, if you chose the second topic in the list, that of committees in an organization, you may wish to formulate the following position:

Committees, while an important mechanism for gathering information and opinion, are not the best way of making most decisions in an organization.

Or you might take an opposing view:

If structured and managed appropriately, committees provide the best mechanism known for making balanced decisions that are supported by the greatest number of people in an organization.

When you have decided on the position you intend to role-play with your partner, ask him or her to come up with objections to your argument. Ask for enough resistance to test your ability to handle such objections. You should tape-record 10 minutes of the role-play for practice and review. You may have to provide your partner with a list of possible objections in advance, especially if he or she is not already familiar with the topic.

Afterwards, ask your partner if he or she was persuaded. Also, ask for suggestions for improvement. Then review the tape and write down an assessment. Answer the following questions about the conversation.

1. Were you overly aggressive in stating your position?
2. Did you use evidence to help persuade your partner?
3. Did you listen carefully to your partner's objections?
4. Was your topic too narrow or too broad for the time allotted?
5. How well did you incorporate your partner's objections into your argument?

It is important that you put your analysis on paper because you will need a document for reference after you complete Part 2 of the activity.

PART 2

After you finish reading through the chapter, carry out a persuasive interview again, if possible with the same partner and on the same topic. (You may find it desirable to carry out the interview some days or weeks after the first one to ensure that you have had time to consider the techniques described in this chapter.) After the interview, ask your partner what his or her impression is of the change, if any, in your persuasive style. Then answer the following questions.

1. Were you more successful in persuading your partner than the first time?
2. Did you use H3W or MARCS in the interview? Did they help?

3. Did the social styles matrix help you "read the defence"?

4. Did you state your "bottom line" at the outset?

5. Was the structure of your argument clear and appropriate?

You may find the process of self-assessment difficult at first, but it is an important part of developing your persuasive skills.

━ ━ ━ ━ ━ ━ ━ ━ ━ ━ ━ ━ ━ ━

Reading the Defence

One of the most distinguished American football players in the history of the National Football League was John Brodie, quarterback of the San Francisco 49ers. Brodie was one of the greatest passers in the history of the game, leading his team to two straight division championships. Brodie tells the story of a key passing play in the 1971 playoff game between the 49ers and the Washington Redskins.[7]

The 49ers were on their own 22-yard line late in the third quarter. The situation was third down and one yard to go. In the huddle, Brodie called a full-back-dive play up the middle of the line. But after he came up to the line of scrimmage and began his count, he noticed the Redskin cornerback shift into a position that might not happen again in the rest of the game. Seizing the opportunity right at the line, Brodie changed the call and gave an audible signal to Gene Washington, his wide receiver, to beat the defender and go long for a pass into the end-zone.

When interviewed after the game, Brodie reported *knowing*, as he faded back and threw the pass, that it was going to connect for a touchdown—so clear was his intention to complete the play. But for a moment it looked as if the pass would be intercepted. Then something inexplicable happened.

Pat Fischer, the Redskin cornerback, told reporters after the game that the ball seemed to jump right over his hands. Some of the players examining the game film later on said the wind was responsible—and maybe it was. But Brodie contends that his sense of that pass was so clear, and his *intention* so strong, that the ball was bound to get there, as he said, "come wind, cornerbacks, hell, or high water."

We mention this story with regard to persuasion because it serves as a good analogy for what happens much of the time when we are faced with objections from those we are trying to persuade. Sometimes we have a plan in mind—then, just as we are about to put our plan in play, we notice obstacles that seem sure to impede our progress. Having clear intentions is important, but we must remain flexible and be able to adjust to new circumstances along the way. We now look at techniques for developing this ability in persuasion situations.

The Social Styles Matrix

Just as the quarterback reads the defence and comes up with an alternative plan, the good persuader must also read the situation and alter the course of persuasive action. If you know your audience ahead of time, you can do a complete and careful analysis of their interests, tastes, and values. Even if you do not know them very well, or at all, you can make some quick assessments and ask some pretty good questions about their beliefs and attitudes. But even more important, and readily available for observation, are the actual behaviors of others.

One quick and easy instrument for helping us assess and analyze the attitudes, beliefs, and behaviors of those we hope to persuade, is the *social styles* approach advocated by David Merrill and Roger Reid.[8] Merrill and Reid have based their device on the proposition that all people exhibit patterns of behavior that can be identified and acted upon. In order to make the most of this instrument, it is important to know the people you are trying to influence. If we can describe and adjust to the observed behaviors in people we know, we can achieve more satisfactory results in our attempts to persuade them.

The personal and professional styles profile used by Merrill and Reid is based on how a person is perceived. It is like a snapshot of the style we observe others using most of the time. The social styles matrix allows us to identify or interpret these styles on an abstract scale measuring progression along two continuums: *assertiveness* and *responsiveness*. Those with more assertiveness are more directing. They tend to do a lot more telling than asking. Those with less assertiveness are more inquiring and tend to ask more than they tell. Those with more responsiveness are more sharing and tend to express their emotions. Those with less responsiveness are more withholding and tend to keep their emotions to themselves.

The social styles matrix is divided into four quadrants made by crossing the axes of these two continuums—one vertical and the other horizontal. The four quadrants are labelled *analytical, driving, amiable*, and *expressive*—based on the ancient Greek classification of personality types as melancholic, choleric, phlegmatic, and sanguine. The horizontal axis shows the range from least to most assertive behavior, and the vertical axis shows the range from least to most responsive (Figure 2.1).

A person exhibiting *analytical* behavior will appear less responsive and less assertive. "Analyticals" tend to be logical, thoughtful, and conservative types—fond of facts and figures, perhaps a bit cool and distant to others' attempts at persuasion.

A person exhibiting *driving* behavior will appear less responsive and more assertive. "Drivers" tend to be task-oriented, tough-minded, and disciplined—if a bit stubborn at times. They too may seem to be a bit cold and can be impatient at times.

A person exhibiting *amiable* behavior will appear less assertive and more responsive. "Amiables" tend to be friendly and supportive—cooperative team

Figure 2.1: The Social Styles Matrix

(Source: Merrill and Reid, Personal Styles and Effective Performance, Chilton Book Company, 1981).

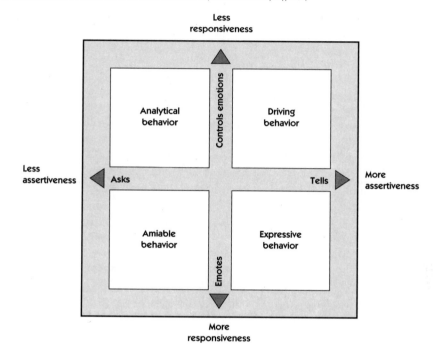

players who are generally thoughtful and caring. But they can also seem a bit slow, retiring, or cautious.

Finally, a person exhibiting *expressive* behavior will appear more assertive and more responsive. "Expressives" tend to be intuitive, creative, enthusiastic, and dramatically impulsive. Although their ideas are often stimulating and thought-provoking, they can also seem a bit too loud and flashy at times.

The following is a sample of how you might use the social styles matrix to *read the defence* or recognize the most common patterns of behavior in others as well as in yourself. Once you have identified your own social styles pattern, and that of the person you are trying to persuade, you will be able to adapt your own behavior to satisfy your goals of persuasion.

If you are a sales representative, for example, you might keep an index card folded in your pocket with a summary of approaches to use in each case when confronted with a customer's particular social style. If you are an expressive type, you would adapt your presentation to analyticals, for example, by slowing down the presentation, emphasizing facts instead of stories or opinions, and backing up the facts with credible references and sources you think customers will respect.

On the following pages you will find a sample observation summary, a blank matrix template (Figure 2.2) for you to copy and use, and four response guides that you can use to plot your own strategies for use with those you are attempting to persuade.[9]

SAMPLE OBSERVATION SUMMARY

Participant: _____ Date:_____

Instructions: For each of the following questions, select from the alternatives in *either* Column A or Column B the response that *best* describes how this person *typically* behaves. If you feel that neither choice is truly descriptive of this person, choose the description that comes closest to describing the person's behavior.

Place a tick in the appropriate column. When you have completed each section, total the ticks in each column. Subtract the smaller column from the larger one to arrive at a net total for each section. Then plot the net total on the Social Styles Matrix Template (Figure 2.2) to arrive at a summary description.

Section 1: Assertiveness Dimension

Section 1 Questions	Column A	✔ or ✔	Column B
1. Would you describe this person as:	competitive		cooperative
2.	opinionated		unopinionated
3.	decisive		indecisive
4.	direct		indirect
5.	a risk taker		a risk avoider
6.	bold		shy
7. When there is disagreement does this person tend to:	confront		conform
8. Would you say this person likes to converse more by:	telling		asking
9. When this person makes decisions, are they made:	quickly		slowly
10. Would you say this person demonstrates:	initiative		support
	Column A Total		Column B Total

If your score in Column A is greater, plot your net total on the *directing* axis. If B is greater, plot on *inquiring*.

Section 2: Responsiveness Dimension

Section 2 Questions	Column C	✔ or ✔	Column D
1. Would you describe this person as:	withdrawn		expressive
2.	formal		casual
3.	business-like		friendly
4.	logical		intuitive
5.	structured		spontaneous
6.	stiff		fluid
7.	disciplined		casual
8. When communicating with others, would you say this person is:	cautious		open
9. Would you say this person makes decisions based on:	facts		feelings
10. Would you say this person prefers to work:	alone		with others
	Column C Total		Column D Total

If your score in Column C is greater, plot your net total on the *withholding* axis. If D is greater, plot on *sharing*.

Once you have transferred your net totals to the Social Styles Matrix Template (Figure 2.2) use the guides shown in Figure 2.3 to determine how you can improve your communication skills by using the most appropriate response styles.

Figure 2.2: Social Styles Matrix Template

(Source: Merrill and Reid, 1981.)

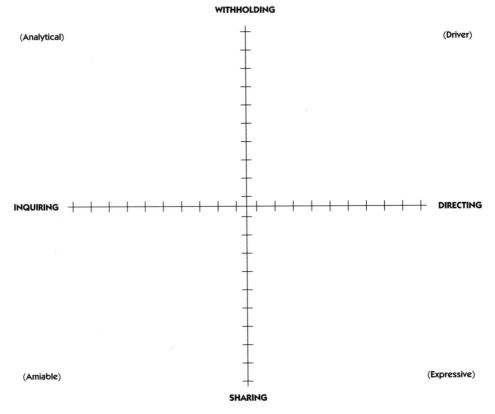

Figure 2.3 (a, b, c, d): Response Guides

(Source: Merrill and Reid, 1981.)

Response Guide (a)

RESPONSE TO ANALYTICALS

Other Analyticals	Drivers
They see you as thoughtful, wanting more facts, conservative, quiet, critical, logical, cool toward others, thorough, cooperative, distant, reserved, stern, austere, dependable, accurate. *To work better with fellow Analyticals:* Recognize the need for making timetables and for reaching decisions. Reinforcing each other's desire for more information may form a self-perpetuating cycle that doesn't bring results.	Relate to your logic, command of data, accuracy, dependability. Question your overabundance of facts, lack of decisiveness, and lack of risk-taking. *To work better with Drivers:* 1. Summarize facts with various outcomes; let them decide. 2. Depend on self-discipline rather than excessive reports, precise instructions. 3. Recognize results with monetary rewards.
Relate to your cooperative, conservative nature, accuracy, patience. Question your lack of warmth and close relationships, dependence on figures. *To work better with Amiables:* 1. Show your interest in them as people, rather than as workers. 2. Use their skills as mediators to build relationships inside the organization. 3. Help them see the big picture and how they relate to it.	Relate to your cooperativeness, dependability. Question your dependence on facts, critical, stuffy nature, impersonal approach, lack of fun. *To work better with Expressives:* 1. Spend "informal" time with time. 2. Recognize their need for package sales, incentives, contests. 3. Ask for their opinions and input on a noncritical, accepting basis. *Working with this style will require *you* to exercise *your* versatility.
Amiables	Expressives*

Response Guide (b)

Analyticals   Other Drivers

Analyticals	Other Drivers
Relate to your efficiency, logic, command of data, and task orientation. Question your haste, bossiness, decisiveness, competitiveness, risk-taking. *To work better with Analyticals:* 1. Bring them detailed facts and logic in writing. 2. Be patient while they evaluate and check the accuracy of the data. 3. Help them come to conclusions by getting them to set deadlines after you have provided time for review.	They see you as action oriented, in a hurry, bossy, commanding, efficient, stubborn, disciplined, tough, independent, secretive, logical, demanding, nonlistening, quick, decisive, unfeeling. *To work better with fellow Drivers:* 1. Agree in advance on specific goals, and provide freedom to work within these limits. An unproductive deadlock can occur when there is too much dominance and no allowance for independence and individuality.
Relate to your efficiency and discipline. Question your lack of feeling, tough-mindedness, bottom-line orientation, impatience, secretiveness. *To work better with Amiables:* 1. Show concern for them and their families, interests, etc. 2. Slow down, and provide detail and specifics on how to accomplish objectives. 3. Support efforts and accomplishments with personal attention. *Working with this style will require *you* to exercise *your* versatility.	Relate to your accomplishments, independence, decisiveness. Question your coldness, lack of playfulness, critical nature, discipline. *To work better with Expressives:* 1. Be more open about self, feelings, gossip, opinions. 2. Relax time constraints within structure, give incentives. 3. Provide public recognition for accomplishments—let them win in front of others.

Amiables*   Expressives

Response Guide (c)

Analyticals   Drivers*

Relate to your cooperative, careful, quiet, thoughtful and willing ways. Question your soft-hearted, easygoing nature, emotional responses and compliance with others. *To work better with Analyticals:* 1. Stress the need for facts and data rather than emotion, to build a case, but let them do the workup with a time limit. 2. Provide added opportunities for classwork and study in return for meeting activity standards. 3. Build confidence in the relationship through demonstrated technical competence.	Relate to your supportive, helpful, team-oriented, careful nature. Question your lack of initiative, need for detail, small thinking, responsive side. *To work better with Drivers:* 1. Be businesslike, let them tell you how to help, what they want. Don't try to build a relationship/friendship. 2. Stay on schedule, stick to the agenda, provide factual summaries. 3. Let them make decisions based on options you provide. *Working with this style will require *you* to exercise *your* versatility.
They see you as supportive, quiet, friendly, shy, retiring, team oriented, helpful, kind thoughtful, slow to act, nonthreatening, soft-hearted, easygoing, complying, responsive, open, willing, careful, cooperative. *To work better with fellow Amiables:* Being hardnosed, insistent, and directive is an uncomfortable role but a necessary one in this situation. Otherwise, it is likely that no one will take the necessary initiative and the end result will be unsatisfactory.	Relate to your supportive, friendly, responsive, helpful characteristics. Question your slowness to act, and careful, complying, non-competitive stance. *To work better with Expressives:* 1. Try to bring them definite opinions, backed by third-party endorsement—don't waver. 2. Publicly recognize and praise their accomplishments. 3. Stand your ground when challenged on rules and previously established procedures.

Other Amiables   Expressives

Response Guide (d)

RESPONSE TO EXPRESSIVES

Analyticals*   Drivers

Analyticals*	Drivers
Relate to your imaginative, stimulating, thought-provoking nature. Question your ability to perform as stated, follow-through, and loud, flashy, emotional side. *To work better with Analyticals:* 1. Talk facts, not opinions, and break down component parts, preferably in writing. 2. Back up your facts with proof from authoritative sources. 3. Be quietly patient while they discover for themselves what you already know. *Working with this style will require *you* to exercise *your* versatility.	Relate to your outgoing, imaginative, competitive and personable aspects. Question your rah-rah, demonstrative, impulsive, emotional side. *To work better with Drivers:* 1. Back up your enthusiasm with actual results; demonstrate that your ideas work. 2. Be on time, and keep wtihin agreed-upon limits, provide materials promptly. 3. Provide choices of action where possible, and let the Driver select course of action
Relate to your warmth, enthusiasm, and your stimulating and personable nature. Question your outgoing, loud, dramatic, impulsive side. *To work better with Amiables:* 1. Slow down the pace and volume, allow time to build a relationship. 2. Work on one item at a time, in detail; avoid the confusion of too many tasks or ideas at one time. 3. Encourage suggestions, participation on team activities, supportive roles.	They see you as outgoing, enthusiastic, warm, opinionated, talkative, intuitive, emotional, stimulating, imaginative, impulsive, excitable, loud, flashy, dramatic, personable, competitive, caring. *To work better with fellow Expressives:* 1. Provide the discipline in this relationship, or all the fun and creativity may accomplish nothing. Keep on track and emphasize the basics, allowing carefully limited experimentation as a reward for results.

Amiables   Other Expressives

Versatility Plus

Anytime you are trying to persuade someone who has a social style different from your own, you will have to exercise a certain amount of versatility or re- sourcefulness in adapting to the other style. This will especially be the case with social styles in the opposite (diagonal) quadrant from your own. In other words, analyticals working to persuade expressives, and vice versa; or drivers working to persuade amiables, and vice versa—will require greater versatility in adapting their style to suit those they are trying to influence.

Of course, the best approach for persuading or influencing will depend on unique circumstances in each situation—who you are, who the listeners are, and what their needs are. But the usefulness of instruments like the social styles ma- trix is that they allow you to make a quick assessment of the situation, evaluate the requirements, and adapt a suitable style according to this information.

Resisting the Urge to Conquer and Control

Often when people repel our attempts to persuade them of something, we find our- selves wanting to defeat them somehow. For the moment, they appear to be the enemy blocking our advance. So we wield our weapons of words and logic and thrust them like sabres at their defences. Forget it. This attacking actually works against our objective by making the other person even more defensive than he or she might have been to begin with.

If those we are trying to persuade are too busy defending themselves, they can- not consider the merits of our argument. None of it will make any sense. If they're too busy holding us off, or trying to prove a point, they are not in any position to be persuaded. It is much better to ask questions to find out *why* they are resist- ing. This shows the listeners that we are interested in what they have to say. This is also an opportunity for us to be seen as an ally working with them to reach the right decision.

Whenever you try to persuade someone of something, you are disturbing them in some way. For one thing, you may be introducing a new way of handling a situation when that person already has a comfortable method in place. A new way of doing something means risking that it won't work as well as the old way. The more information you provide, the better the chances the other person will understand the risk. Therefore, you will have to be patient in persuading others, in order to accommodate the resistance that is sure to be there.

Since an objection represents resistance that is likely to be at least partially un- reasonable, don't argue against it. Instead, ask for the reasoning behind it, or ask whether something you have in mind would take care of the objection. Anticipate the other person's next move and be there with a suggestion he or she might find helpful. Whatever else you do, be sure to make a conscious and deliberate effort to listen openly and to ask questions, rather than develop an opposing reaction. Acting shrewdly or smugly will only offend. If winning is all you are trying to do, you won't.

Easier Said Than Done

Enthusiasm has been called the greatest asset in the world. And most of the time it is. But enthusiasm is also a double-edged sword. It cuts both ways. Emotional excitement can sometimes lower credibility rather than enhance it. When you are making a persuasive case for something, it is often better to be calm and dispassionate about your proposal, than to be too volatile or excited. To some, attaching too much emotion to a position suggests immaturity or exaggeration. Instead of openness and consideration it may arouse suspicion and scepticism, in the same way anger does. Especially when arguing *against* something, it is best to present your argument in a reasoned tone so that the other person can follow the logic of your idea.

A lot of people ruin their credibility, writes Jesse Nirenberg in *How to Sell Your Ideas*, because their enthusiasm leads them to try selling an idea before it is fully formed or developed:

> 66 The germ of the idea is there, and it generates enough enthusiasm in its creator to propel him prematurely into the boss's office. The boss, motivated by his generalized resistance to any idea, looks for what's wrong with the idea. At this point, he isn't focusing on what's right or on how to make it work. So he raises some tough questions that our hero can't answer. He isn't prepared. His idea dies. He doesn't realize that enthusiasm isn't contagious unless you've got the answers. But he's lost more than a good idea. He's lost some credibility. He's hurt his image. From then on the boss expects this person to be unprepared. What he says is suspect. The boss looks hard for holes. And he's a little impatient because he figures that maybe he's wasting time. If he hears unsupported ideas, the boss won't listen anymore, especially when this person is enthusiastic.[10] 99

Emotional Rescue

Our emotions motivate us to act—either to take advantage of the opportunities presented or to remove tension. And our feelings are continually looking for outlets of release. One of the most common ways of releasing tension is to talk. Thus, face-to-face conversation is not only a method for communicating ideas, it is also the primary outlet for the release of emotional tension.

In every face-to-face conversation each person is being pulled in at least two directions; one is towards developing a logical line of progressive thought, and the other is towards satisfying his or her own emotional needs. A good conversationalist, especially in business and the professions, must understand the need people have to vent their feelings, bolster their egos, unleash guilt, whatever—and provide for it.

Feelings and emotions are inextricably woven into the fabric of our thinking and the ideas we express to others in conversation. Therefore, listening to what may seem irrelevant can enrich our understanding of the speaker. You can get an insight into people's personalities simply by listening to the expression of these needs. If, for example, you sense from someone a need for your approval, you might consider whether this person is suffering from a bout of low self-esteem. If so, you may decide to make him or her feel more self-confident, and act accordingly.

Guidelines for Persuading Others

To varying degrees, we all find it hard to tolerate ambiguity or missing pieces. People with a high intolerance for such things will rush ahead and jump to conclusions before they have enough information to form the whole picture. The result is that they often get it wrong. They are set up to reject your idea before they fully understand what it is all about.

Whenever we receive information, we immediately try to make sense of it—to see the whole configuration. As soon as you start talking to people they become mentally poised to grasp your point. If they can't see what you're getting at, or where you intend taking them with your idea, they will become frustrated and fill in the gaps for themselves. Here are some guidelines to help you overcome these natural tendencies when persuading:

1. *Start at the end.* The bottom line is the most motivating part of any idea. It represents the end-point of your thinking. If the person who is trying to persuade us doesn't tell us the "bottom line" right up front, we will figure something else out for ourselves, and react to that. The trouble is, without having any facts to base our conclusions on we tend to fill in the blanks with very little information and with our own prejudices, fantasies, and so forth. When people don't know your motivations, they guess at them. If you start at the end and then go back and explain how you got there you will prevent people from jumping to the wrong conclusions and reacting negatively. Tell them the bottom line right off the bat. If they object you can always ask, Why? and continue on from there.

2. *Never suggest an action without revealing its end benefit.* Whenever you want to sell an idea, you've got to answer the question of *why* you want to do it, be-

fore it's even asked. The answer is the end benefit. Before you make any suggestion, think ahead to the end benefit and reveal it with your suggestion. Others will only buy your idea if they can see that the benefit outweighs the costs by enough to justify the risks involved. So you have to make the most of your benefits right up front, and work out the relative advantages vis-a-vis other options.

3. *When people disagree with you, explore the reasons for their objection.* This is one of the hardest rules to follow, as well as one of the most important. It's hard because the natural impulse we all have is to answer the objection immediately to get it out of the way. The trouble is, people don't listen very well once they've made an objection. Instead, they may be thinking about what to say next to buttress their objection. That leaves you talking to yourself. With each of you talking and busy thinking your own thoughts, no one is in a position to listen to or comprehend what the other is saying. The important thing to remember here is to ask the other person about the objection. You have to inquire into the reasoning before you can overcome the obstacles.

4. *In forming your reply to an objection, you first have to acknowledge something in the objection that you agree with.* Whenever the other person objects, start your reply with an acknowledgment of something in his or her objection that you agree is true or worth considering. It is hard for others to resist an idea if you have first acknowledged something in their objection that can be agreed upon. Furthermore, asking a question about the objection, rather than arguing against it, makes you appear less of an adversary. Be open-minded about this. If you are, you will promote the same kind of behavior in the person you are trying to persuade. Begin by finding something in the objection that is true. Then make your point by building on this truth.

5. *Whenever you ask a question, explain why you are asking it.* The human mind can be very restless. Whenever people try to convince us of something, their motivation intrigues us. If we don't know why someone wants to know something, we fill in the gap by guessing. When your question stands alone—without any explanation—it often raises another question in the person's mind: Why are you asking? A simple rule is to think of your own question as being incomplete unless you add why you are asking it. Whenever you ask a question—unless it is perfectly obvious from the context of the conversation—add the phrase: "*The reason I ask is...*" and give the reason. This will help you to keep the argument moving forward.

6. *When you assert something, say why you think it is so.* We all have to guard against the tendency to give information without being absolutely sure of it. This tendency occurs when we have partial knowledge of something. We fill in the rest with what seems to make sense to us at the time. We forget about the difference between what we know for a fact and what seems to make sense. Giving the basis for any conclusion greatly increases its credibility. And

yet, some people are more sceptical than others about *any* information they receive. Even those who are most open and trusting about what you say will be reassured if you give them some evidence. For example, *"I say this because . . ."* Hearing this evidence will allay any scepticism others have about your motives.

7. *If you don't know the answer, say so—rather than trying to contrive one.* Listen carefully to any questions the other person has and, if you are uncertain about anything, ask for more information before you start your reply. That way your credibility is maintained. It shows that you want to help the other person make the right decision. By remaining open to the possibility that you may not know the answer, you are indicating an honest willingness to work things out for the benefit of both sides. Tell your listeners what you base your conclusions on and the sources of your information. If you don't know the answer, look into it—instead of immediately making something up just to refute their objection.

8. *Anticipate the evidence you will need through associative thinking.* A good way to figure out what evidence you will need to support your argument is to anticipate objections and questions the other person is likely to have about your idea. But trying to list all of these one after the other is not the most effective way of going about this. It is much more effective to hold a rehearsal dialogue with yourself or a friend. By allowing one idea to lead to another you will think of many more ideas than you would by trying to think of them all in advance. Having evidence on hand shows that you have done your homework. When a question is asked, you will be able to connect it to the associative tracks you have already laid down in your own mind.

9. *Link the other person's thinking to your own.* All ideas have other ideas related to them. Every idea is part of an endless landscape of interlinking ideas. In order to persuade other people, we have to make sure their thinking is linked to our own, so that each of us is creating the same mental picture. As we speak, what we say brings up all kinds of related thoughts and feelings in other people that they need to talk about. Let them. In order to keep them linked to your thinking, you have to find out what their concerns are, and respond to them. Some of the best ways to link thinking are to give plenty of examples and provide summaries of what has been said already. And don't forget to pause every now and then to let the other person say what is on his or her mind. Then you can comment on the remarks or say how they relate to your ideas. Success in persuasion depends on getting the other person to see new relationships. If he or she isn't understanding you, go over your argument again by saying, "You raise an important point. That reminds me of . . .", and run over it again.

10. *Think of those you are trying to persuade as teammates, not opponents.* Your idea looks good to you, but you have to hear the other person's evidence before

you can come to any agreement. Take the position that your own final decision is not yet entirely formed. Maybe the other person has sound reasoning against your idea. Make it clear that you want to hear it so that together you can make a wiser decision about what to do next. Giving credit to whatever is true in the other person's objection, and then inquiring in a reasonable way about whatever seems questionable, will help you maintain your objective of trying to make the right choice, even if it goes against your original idea. Adversaries don't listen well to each other because they are each too busy thinking of how to knock out the other side. Think of others as teammates. Together you are going to make a decision about the right thing to think or do. Persuasion is not achieved by defeating the other's point of view. At its best, persuasion is a kind of cooperative give and take, whereby each person plays into the other's hands, and adjusts their target so it can be met together.

Closing for Commitment

Probably the most difficult part of any persuasive interview is the closing, for it is here that the interviewee must be asked to make a commitment to your idea. There are at least four things to keep in mind at this stage. The first is *timing*.

Timing requires careful judgment. If you try to close too soon, before all necessary objections have been answered, or before the other person is ready to make a decision, the interviewee is likely to reject your proposal. Don't try to force a decision before the other person is ready to make one. On the other hand, waiting too long to close may result in making the other person impatient and frustrated.

When the time is right, you should implement the *summary*. Briefly review the points covered and the agreements reached, and then offer any additional information the interviewee might want. This signals that the interview is drawing to a close and that this is the time to deal with any unfinished business.

The final move is to *ask for a commitment*. After all, this is the point of the entire process thus far. This statement is probably the single most important thing you say and should be prepared and rehearsed well in advance. It should also state specifically what you want the other person to do, how, when, where, and/or why.

Tell your interviewee what to do about your proposal, not just what to think. In other words, restate your purpose, and ask him or her to act on it. Use a statement like the following: "I want to be elected to public office. Can I count on your vote Monday at the polls?" If the other person reacts negatively, you can continue to inquire about any remaining objections, and deal with them before attempting to close again later.

Don't expect to close with everyone the first time out. Sometimes the commitment you are asking for is simply an agreement to continue the discussion another time. The results of any particular interview may very well be the basis for establishing another interview in future. Sometimes the action step may not actually occur until a second or third time around. Perhaps you need time to follow up on an inquiry. If the person isn't ready to decide just yet, back off a little and concentrate on getting a commitment to having another go later on. Sometimes that is as much of a commitment as you are likely to come away with.

Grifters and Con Men at Your Door

The old "one-two punch" is a tactic you should watch for when would-be persuaders come calling. Some salespeople get their "foot-in-the-door" by making a small or reasonable request first, and then escalating to a larger one second, once they have gained compliance to the first. For example, a nice young man rings your doorbell and says he is conducting an "educational survey" in the area. You have kids, say, and you are interested in education, so you let him in. He takes the first few minutes to ask a few questions, then switches to a pitch for the encyclopedias he is selling. The initial request is used to get inside, the survey is a ploy to soften you up, and then he tries to hit you for the leather-bound set—all 27 volumes—with payments over two years at twenty-two percent interest.

There is also an approach known as the "door-in-the-face" technique: large request first, small request second. Here the would-be persuader starts by asking for a large favor that is almost certain to be turned down: "Can you give me and my friend a ride to Moose Jaw? We've been walking since this time yesterday and we have to be there by midnight tonight." When you say no they shift to a smaller request, such as lending them $20 for bus fare, and you start looking for your purse or wallet.

Three more persuasion tactics to consider are the *scarcity tactic*, the *social proof tactic*, and the *low-ball tactic*. With *scarcity*, the salesperson warns you against waiting to make a decision by stating that the product will soon be sold out. For *social proof*, opinion leaders (singer Celine Dion, actor Jason Priestly, or comedian John Candy, for example) are featured in sales pitches, aimed at trying to persuade an audience by appealing to their sentiments towards famous, wealthy, or powerful people. The *low-ball* tactic calls for the quotation of a low price, which is then withdrawn. ("The manager wouldn't let me sell it for that little.") In the meantime, you may have already agreed to purchase. Once a person has made a commitment to buy, it is difficult to back away from it.

As with all other types of interview we will be examining throughout this book, the persuasive interview should consist primarily of an honest exchange of information between competent individuals seeking to arrive at a worthy destination that benefits both sides. Manipulation, tricks, and clever ruses may sometimes achieve some short-term ends, but in the long run they are sure to come back to haunt their perpetrators.

PRACTISING PERSUASION

THREE RULES TO KEEP IN MIND FOR BOTH EXERCISES

1. Never suggest an action without revealing its end benefits first.

2. Whenever you ask a question, say why it is you are asking.

3. In forming your reply to an objection, first acknowledge something in the objection that you agree is worth considering.

"One Of Your Own"

1. Take a look through your favorite magazines, and write down, or cut out, two or three items of interest—either something you would like to see happen or changed; or something you would like to have or own. You don't have to restrict yourself to what you find in the magazine—just keep three things in mind that you find appealing. For example, cut out a picture of that new car you've been dreaming about. Or a beach vacation to Prince Edward Island. Or jot down a few notes on a new health care policy that you would like to see implemented.

2. Pair up with a partner and each take a turn at trying to persuade the other to want one of the things you want to advocate or possess. Sell your partner on the idea of having one of your desired objects or of supporting the changes you would like to see made. Be sure to plan a bit before you get started. Maybe run through a social styles observation summary on your partner first. Introduce the subject however you like. Take about five to ten minutes each and see if you can persuade your partner.

   (In each case the interviewee should offer as much resistance as he or she is naturally inclined to have, or role-play some objections in order to make the exercise an interesting challenge.)

"Advertisements For Myself"

1. Write an advertisement for a Personal Column describing yourself as a "communication coach" (40 words or less). *Don't* put your name or any other identifying features in the ad. Get everybody in the room to do the same.

   (List skills that would make someone want to choose you or seek your services over others.)

2. Put the ads in a hat and pass it around the room. Have someone read each ad aloud one at a time. Have people guess who wrote each ad and say *why they* guessed that person.

● — ● — ● — ● — ● — ● — ● — ● — ● — ● — ● — ● — ●

And finally . . .

In 1900, prior to an expedition to locate the magnetic South Pole which was to take place in 1908, British Antarctic explorer Ernest Shackleton placed a classified ad in several London newspapers. The ad appeared as follows:

> MEN WANTED FOR HAZARDOUS JOURNEY, SMALL WAGES, BITTER COLD, LONG MONTHS OF COMPLETE DARKNESS, CONSTANT DANGER, SAFE RETURN DOUBTFUL. HONOUR AND RECOGNITION IN CASE OF SUCCESS.

Shackleton's appeal, of course, was not to basic instincts for survival and longevity; nor did it use ploys that offered something for nothing. His appeal was to something higher. It is too confining to identify that appeal as idealism or patriotism—it was more dramatic than that. It had to do with the mysteries of passion, inspiration, deep commitment, and challenge. Leaders often tap these mysteries in their followers. We can call it the creative conscience, that which evokes some deep inner experience shared by all men and women. Such a conscience is based on the need for transcendence. Shackleton was later quoted as saying "It seemed as though all the men of Great Britain were determined to accompany me, the response was so overwhelming."

There are no foolproof formulas for persuasion. No one can teach you how to achieve success through authentic communication. The best we can do is to help you become more aware of yourself and of your communication style. Then it will be up to you to create and strive to achieve new goals for persuasion.

CHAPTER REVIEW QUESTIONS

1. What is the difference between persuasion and coercion?
   a. Persuasion is a weak form of coercion.
   b. Coercion is only used by criminals.
   c. Coercion involves force and manipulation; persuasion involves convincing someone of the desirability of change.
   d. Persuasion is based on moral appeals; coercion on material ones.

2. How are most sales models and techniques which are taught in company training programs actually used by experienced sales personnel?
   a. Successful sales personnel use the programs without substantial change; unsuccessful ones tailor the programs to their personal needs.

b. Most training programs are rarely used by sales personnel.

c. Sales techniques are substantially tailored or modified by experienced sales personnel.

d. Sales techniques are occasionally tailored slightly by experienced sales personnel.

3. Sales people influence the choices customers make in essentially the same way a manager must appeal to the needs of personnel. What are the implications for management?

a. Persuasion must be taught as part of the company's training program.

b. Managers must learn to plan carefully and prepare their persuasive acts ahead of time.

c. Managers must be flexible in their persuasive interactions.

d. Managers must recognize the pluralism of North American society.

4 What are the three major factors leading to persuasion?

a. The credibility of the persuader; sources of evidence; and a balanced presentation.

b. Attending, following, and reflecting.

c. Attention, audience, attitude.

d. The attention of the audience, the attitude of the persuader, and the atmosphere.

5. When attempting to persuade someone within your own organization, how important is it to provide extensive documentation of sources and why?

6. Why is it usually best to present both sides of the argument whenever your listeners are fairly knowledgeable about the topic?

7. How is inoculating a listener against opposing ideas similar to inoculating a person against a disease?

8. What is the H3W formula?

a. Hey! Where? Why? When?

b. Hello! Why? What? When?

c. Hi! What? Why? When?

d. Hey! What? Why? When?

9. What does the acronym "MARCS" stand for with regard to persuasion?

10. What are the "ABC's" of persuasion?

11. Which is the richest medium for persuasion?

a. video augmented by print

b. radio augmented by print

c. e-mail and video

d. face-to-face

12. What are the two continuums measured by the social styles matrix?

a. assertiveness and creativity

b. assertiveness and responsiveness

c. responsiveness and aggressiveness

d. creativity and numeracy

13. A person exhibiting *driving* behavior will appear less _____ and more _____.

14. Why is it advisable to resist the urge to conquer and control those we are trying to persuade?

15. How is enthusiasm a double-edged sword?

16. What are the 10 guidelines for persuading others?

17. What are the four things to keep in mind during the closing stage of a persuasive interview?

18. The "one-two punch" is a form of coercion. True or false?

SUGGESTED ANSWERS

1. c.

2. c.

3. b.

4. a.

5. It is not as important to provide documentation to people within the organization, because people within the organization will be more likely to ask for verification if they want it.

6. This serves to inoculate the listeners against opposing arguments that may be introduced later by the other side.

7. Immunity can be produced by giving a shot containing a weakened form of the disease, in the same way that successful persuasion is produced by presenting opposing arguments with their refutation.

8. d.

9. 1. Find the **motives**.
     ◆ Find out about other people
     ◆ Discover who their "significant others" are
     ◆ Use motives that healthy people respond to
     ◆ Appeal to the highest motives
   2. **Attack** problems, not people.
     ◆ Sidestep put-downs
     ◆ Don't waste energy on personal hostility
     ◆ Make the other person feel good

3. Get and give **respect**.
   - ◆ Give your credentials out front
   - ◆ Show respect for the opinions of others
   - ◆ Be friendly
4. Look for **common ground**.
   - ◆ Find value bases for common ground
   - ◆ Consider shared personal experiences
   - ◆ Read and adapt to feedback
   - ◆ Try role reversal
5. Use the persuasive **sequence**.
   - ◆ Use H3W as a planning aid
   - ◆ Use feedback to check on your H3W
   - ◆ Use plenty of hey's!
   - ◆ Use H3W on communications directed to you
   - ◆ Make your when's? especially specific

10. Arousal, Balance, Choices, Delivery, Evaluation, Follow-up.

11. d

12. b.

13. responsive; assertive

14. Attacking makes other people even more defensive than they might have been otherwise.

15. To some people, attaching too much emotion to a position suggests immaturity or exaggeration.

16.
1. Start at the end.
2. Never suggest an action without revealing its end benefit.
3. When people disagree with you, explore the reasons for their objection.
4. In forming your reply to an objection, acknowledge something in the objection that you agree with.
5. Whenever you ask a question, say why it is you are asking.
6. When you assert something, say why you think it is so.
7. If you don't know the answer, say so.
8. Anticipate the evidence you will need through associative thinking.
9. Link the other person's thinking to your own.
10. Think of those you are trying to persuade as teammates, not opponents.

17. Timing; summary; additional information; commitment.

18. False. The "one-two punch" is a persuasive tactic that involves making a small or reasonable request first, then escalating to a larger second request. The tactic can be manipulative and should be used with care.

ABBOTTS CANADA INC. AND SUNDAY SHOPPING

OVERVIEW AND ASSIGNMENT QUESTIONS

In the following scenario, which is based on a situation that could well occur in an organization, you will have the opportunity to apply the principles and skills you have learned in this chapter. The scenario can be used as the basis for a written or oral analysis or for role-play.

Lillian Senna, CEO of Abbotts Canada Inc., one of the country's leading merchandising companies, must decide whether or not to flout the Retail Business Holidays Act and open her stores on Sunday, in response to threats by the competition to do so. Senna has scheduled face-to-face interviews with representatives of the buying public, government officials, unionized employees, shareholders, internal management, external suppliers, and the media—all of whom are anxious to hear Abbotts' position and corporate philosophy on the matter.

1. As Lillian Senna, prepare a communication strategy for explaining your position regarding the specific issue of Sunday shopping, as well as the corporate philosophy and strategic direction Abbotts Canada Inc. intends to take.

2. How do you intend to alter or adapt your position differently for each of the special interest groups you must face? Or will your message be consistent across the board? Why or why not?

3. Whether or not your message is to be consistent in each case, how do you anticipate handling the inevitable objections which you are bound to face from certain interest groups?

4. Prepare to execute your strategy through role-play.

INTRODUCTION

Lillian Senna, chief executive officer of Abbotts Canada Inc., one of the country's leading merchandising forces since 1950, considers her morning conversation with the VP of corporate planning and public affairs. Together they have decided to schedule face-to-face interviews with representatives of the buying public, government officials, the employee union, shareholders and management, suppliers, and the media—to explain Abbotts' position on Sunday retail openings. Only two days before, Hudson's Bay Co.—a major competitor whose holdings include The Bay, Simpsons, and Zellers—announced that it will open its stores in violation of Ontario's *Retail Business Holidays Act.* Sears and Eaton's—Abbotts' most direct competitors—have not yet revealed their intent. Now Senna has to decide what Abbotts should do, and how to *persuade* the various audiences of the wisdom of her decision.

THE HISTORY OF SUNDAY SHOPPING IN CANADA

The controversy over Sunday shopping has boiled for centuries in this country. When Canada was still a collection of colonies, two British statutes, the *Sunday Observance Acts* of 1677 and 1780 prohibited "Sabbath Desecration." The *Upper Canada Act* of 1845 prohibited everything on Sundays except religious observances and works of necessity and charity, such as carrying the mail or selling medicines.

As 19th century urbanization and industrialization occurred, there were additional opportunities for businesses to open on Sundays. This was especially apparent when transportation became more readily available and increased the demand for recreation and entertainment on Sundays. The government of Ontario put the issue to a plebiscite in 1897, in which those in favor of loosening the restrictions on "whether or not streetcars should run on Sundays" won out.

A federal *Lord's Day Act* was introduced in 1907, prohibiting the sale of goods, real estate, or other personal property; and any activity connected with work, business, or service of labor on Sundays. The business community of that time successfully negotiated exemptions into the *Act*—exemptions connected with "divine mercy" or work for the relief of sickness and suffering.

When the provinces were formed, the *Upper Canada Act* in Ontario became *An Act to Prohibit the Profanation of the Lord's Day* (a snappy title to be sure!). This was followed in 1922 with the *One Day's Rest in Seven Act*, which was followed in 1950 with the *Lord's Day Act* (Ontario) similar to the federal *Act*.

The increasing number of exemptions in the legislation of each new *Act* attempted to address the increased number of retail openings that occurred during the 1960s. Changing demographics saw more women entering the workforce, who demanded more convenient shopping-related practices. Many people moved to the suburbs, resulting in the development of large suburban shopping malls that attempted to extend the traditional shopping hours both in the evenings and on Sundays. The demand for extended hours of operation coincided with experiments of "scrambled merchandising" in which drugstores sold snacks and hardware products and grocery stores offered over-the-counter drugs, cosmetics, and so on.

Special interest groups were formed to deal with the issue of extended store hours and Sunday shopping, and they subjected the government to pressure. A Provincial Commission (Ontario), headed by the Hon. George Kerr, was set up to investigate and outline legislative alternatives on the issues of Sunday shopping and uniform store hours across the province. The result of Kerr's Green Paper was the *Retail Business Holidays Act,* which became law in 1976. The intent of the legislation was to slow "growing commercialism" by regulating Sunday and holiday retail store openings.

One exemption was to give corner "convenience" stores a competitive advantage by extending hours and allowing them to stay open on Sundays, when the larger stores could not. Another exemption allowed "tourist" stores and areas—essential businesses for the maintenance or development of a tourist industry—to remain open on Sundays.

Since 1980, retailers of all sizes not only flouted the law, but some have gone so far as to challenge the legislation in the courts. In 1986, a government task force found the public adamantly opposed to Sunday shopping, and therefore recommended tighter restrictions. But more illegal openings continued to occur, in spite of the law.

SPECIAL INTEREST GROUPS

Mall Owners' Perspective

Mall owners make their revenues on a percentage of their tenants' gross sales. They view Sunday shopping as a form of leisure and recreation to be enjoyed by families. They also recognize that such excursions could result in "impulse buying," thereby increasing the total dollars to the retailers and, therefore, themselves.

Sectarian Perspective

The reactions from the religious groups to the announcements by Hudson's Bay Co. is based on two issues: the inappropriateness of the retailers' conduct in wilfully breaking the law; and the principle of a common day of rest. All denominations are unanimous in their denunciation of those retailers who announced their intentions to change the law by breaking it.

Union Employees' Perspective

The labor voice has been relatively quiet on the issue of Sunday shopping. Unions and labor federations have responded to questions on the issue, but have not mounted an active campaign against it.

Convenience Store Owners' Perspective

The corner store operators are adamantly opposed to wide-open Sunday shopping, stating that it will completely destroy their competitive advantage. The essence of their industry is the fact that the large grocery stores are not open on Sunday, and consumers have little choice of where else to shop on these days.

Hudson's Bay Co. Perspective

The executive declares that the decision to challenge the law was made "with great reluctance and only because of the chaotic state of enforcement in the Province of Ontario." The company contends that the experience of British Columbia and Alberta shows economic advantage to opening on Sundays, and also claims that there will be twelve percent more hours to be gained for the workforce by extending hours and Sunday shopping.

Media Perspective

Editorial opinion in the large city newspapers has thus far taken a position resembling the following:

There is no joy in seeing retailers flout the civil law and advertise their intent to do so. The philosophy that views the law's fines as a practical and acceptable cost of doing business is deplorable. That said, however, we repeat our long-held position that the law—outdated, flawed, and imperfectly enforced—should be repealed since there is no evidence to show that the *Act* serves the public good.

SENNA'S DECISION

Lillian Senna recognizes her dilemma: If all of Abbotts' direct competitors were to open, and Abbotts remained closed on Sunday, the company would lose a significant share of its market. On the other hand, if Abbotts were to open on Sunday, they would be violating the law of the land and the company's long-standing tradition of opposition to Sunday shopping. In fact, Senna's predecessor, Phil Horvath, had once been quoted as saying: "We at Abbotts see no merit in opening on Sunday, and will do so only if forced to by *legitimate* competition which elect to stay open."

CEO Lillian Senna has to decide what position she would take, and how she will present her position to each of the following people she is scheduled to meet with and discuss the matter:

1. the Ontario Deputy Minister for Corporate Affairs
2. representatives of the employee union
3. Abbotts' senior management team, including shareholders
4. members of the Presbyterian Church
5. reporters from the *Toronto Star* and *The Globe and Mail*.

POINTS TO CONSIDER

When planning your communications strategy for each of the various interest groups you will meet be sure to consider each of the following elements in your plan: sender, receiver, message, channel, timing, and feedback mechanisms. For example, consider these questions:

Is the CEO the best person to deliver the message to each and every audience in the schedule?

Is the message to be *exactly* the same in every case?

Can other media serve to supplement the face-to-face interview?

How important is the timing of the communication?

What environmental circumstances need to be considered, and how will they affect strategy?

What allowances have been made for checking perceptions and obtaining feedback?

ENDNOTES

1 Richard Christie and Florence Geis, *Studies in Machiavellianism* (New York: Academic Press, 1970).

2 James MacGregor Burns, *Leadership* (New York: Harper and Row, 1978), p. 447.

3 Mario Puzo, *The Godfather* (London: William Heinemann, Ltd., 1969), p. 42. Reprinted by permission of Dunadio Ashworth, Inc. Copyright © 1969 by Mario Puzo.

4 Jesse Nirenberg, *Getting Through to People* (Englewood Cliffs, N.J., Prentice-Hall, 1963).

5 Cheryl Hamilton, *Communicating for Results* (Belmont, California: Wadsworth Publishing Co., 1990).

6 Frederick Williams, *Executive Communication Power* (Englewood Cliffs, N.J.: Prentice-Hall, 1983), pp. 28 and 32.

7 John Brodie, "I Experience a Kind of Clarity," *Intellectual Digest*, January 1973, pp. 19-22.

8 David Merrill and Roger Reid, *Personal Styles and Effective Performance* (Radnor, Penn.: Chilton Book Company, 1981).

9 Merrill and Reid, pp. 140-43.

9 Jesse Nirenberg, *How to Sell Your Ideas* (Toronto: McGraw-Hill 1984), pp. 2-3. Reproduced with the permission of McGraw-Hill, Inc.

CHAPTER 3

Inside Interviews

WORTH REPEATING

A good listener is not someone who has nothing to say. A good listener is a good talker with a sore throat.

—Katharine Whitehorn

You can't learn anything when you're talking.

—Bing Crosby

There is a limit to what one can listen to with the naked eye.

—Muriel Spark

Section 1 Introducing the Interview

Before we get started . . .

In our daily lives, we use interviews to gather all kinds of information. An **interview** is any occasion where two people meet face-to-face to confer about something. Employers discussing duties with employees, reporters gathering information that is to be the subject of a published article, parents talking to their children about their report cards—these are all examples of interviews. Often the information we seek in an interview is quantifiable. For example, you might make a telephone call to your local electrical utility to try to determine why the power is out in your house. The answer you receive—alas, often from a recording machine—will inform you what the problem is, who is affected, and, perhaps, what time the power will come back on. Sometimes, on the other hand, the information we seek requires us to interpret the response we receive from the interviewee. In such cases, the approach we take to gathering the information may determine the quality of the information we receive.

Suppose you were interested in learning what kind of assistance, if any, the municipal, or federal government offers to people who renovate their homes. Your success in finding this information would be connected to your skill in making contact with the right agencies and bureaucrats, in informing people of what you want, and in eliciting from them what you need to know. In short, you would have to possess the skills of the interviewer.

We believe that interviewing skills are so important in both the workplace and everyday life that we've devoted this chapter and the next to aspects of the interview. In turn, we encourage you to practise and develop your interviewing skills in the contexts of your personal and workplace life. (Subsequent chapters will also deal with interviewing skills, albeit indirectly.) As with many aspects of this book, we don't try to draw a heavy line between the two realms. If you work in an open and creative organization, the skills you learn in one should be applicable to the other. If you don't work in such an organization, perhaps you can be the one to start the process of change.

We will discuss interviews by category. That is, we will consider the differences among various kinds of interview. In this section—and in the next three chapters—we examine each type of interview separately. However, you will find that all interviews share some features and characteristics. For example, you can apply the principles of interpersonal communication that we discussed in Chapter 2 to any interview. In fact, such principles are essential to the success of an interview. We begin by examining some interviewing techniques that apply to all interviewing situations.

Objectives

After you complete this section, you should be able to:

1. Discuss the uses and importance of the following types of interview: persuasive, employment, performance planning and appraisal, and disciplinary.
2. Given a hypothetical interview situation, devise a statement of purpose.
3. Describe the following interview strategies: highly structured, nondirective, and combined.
4. Define the following types of questions, and state their uses and importance:
   closed
   open
   hypothetical
   probes and follow-ups
   mirror statements
   leading and loaded
   neutral
   prefaced probes

5. Describe, with the aid of a diagram, the following types of question sequences: tube or tunnel, funnel, pyramid, stacked funnel, hourglass, and diamond.

6. Discuss what an interviewer can do to plan a structure for the following stages of an interview:
    before the interview begins
    the opening
    the body
    the closing

7. Discuss the use of the techniques of turn-taking, turn requesting or regulating, turn-yielding, turn-denying, turn-maintaining, making transitions, and coping with inadequate responses.

8. State the most useful techniques for dealing with the following interview problems: reluctant and compulsive talkers, irrelevant and unclear responses.

9. State and discuss the five steps for structuring an argument, and apply these to planning a persuasive interview.

10. Discuss briefly the importance of acknowledging the opponent's view in a persuasive interview.

11. State briefly the importance of notetaking in an interview.

12. Discuss some of the dos and don'ts of interviewing.

Three Categories of Organizational Interviews

For the purposes of analysis, we will consider organizational interviews as they fall under certain categories, even though when you carry out interviews in practice, you will likely find that skills you learn in one type of interview are applicable in another. Even so, we won't provide an exhaustive list of every conceivable type of interview. Instead, we will discuss briefly the following three categories: *persuasive* (an area we introduced in Chapter 2); *employment*, including recruitment, orientation, information, and disciplinary interviews (all four of which we will deal with in more detail in Chapter 4); and *performance planning and appraisal interviews* (which we will discuss more fully in Chapter 6).

Persuasive interviews. In Chapter 1, when we discussed the theoretical antecedents of communications, we mentioned the sophists, those ancient Greek philosophers who taught rhetoric. The sophists, along with Aristotle, emphasized the skill of speaking persuasively. Such a skill remains important today. In any organization, all members must persuade others, at least occasionally. For some, persuasive interviews take up much of their time and attention. For example, sales transactions, which many people have to carry out, are persuasive interviews. Other examples of persuasive interviews are proposals, presentations, and negotiations. Even if the purpose of your interview is to gather information, you will often have to persuade the person you are interviewing to give you that information. For any of these situations, the basic strategy used is to identify the values and needs of the person being interviewed and then to appeal to these values and needs. The persuader must arrange his or her claims strategically, find evidence to support the arguments, and relate the arguments to the audience's needs.

A critical—but often ignored—component of the persuader's argument is an acknowledgment of the audience's objections or criticisms; connected to this is the reconciliation of the audience's view with the persuader's view. (In Chapter 2, we used the term *inoculation* to refer to the effect this component may have on the person with whom you are speaking.) That is, a strong argument deals with the listener's views as part of its discourse. In this chapter we will provide a suggested structure for the persuasive interview to complement the principles of persuasion we discussed in Chapter 2. As you might suspect, persuasive interviewing skills may find direct expression in the performance appraisal or disciplinary interview.

Employment interviews (recruitment, orientation, information, and disciplinary). Most of us view the organization as the one making the decision in a recruitment interview. And it is probably true that it is most often the organization that declines the opportunity to continue the relationship that begins with the recruitment interview. However, we suggest that the recruitment interview can also be an opportunity for the candidate and the organization to exchange views and to determine whether the two fit. In Chapter 4 we will discuss some of the ways that this can be accomplished. We will also suggest that the orientation interview can be an opportunity not only for the new employee to adjust to a new environment, but also for other employees to learn about the organization. Such interviews provide an opportunity for managers to explain job requirements and to answer questions, but, more importantly, they provide the new employee with the first impressions of how the organization works and of how well he or she will get along in it. Therefore, the orientation interview is an opportunity for the new employee, as well as for other members of the organization, to begin to develop the organizational culture they believe is best. One of the tasks often assigned to the new employee as part of the orientation process is to gather information. We will thus begin our discussion of the information interview in connection with the orientation interview. However, information interviews may also be used in many other contexts. We will examine some of these more closely in Chapter 4.

Performance planning and appraisal interviews and disciplinary interviews. Of all the interviews performed in the organization, these are the ones that provoke the most interest and controversy. This is not surprising, since they touch on issues that members of an organization regard with personal concern: what they have done, how they did it, and what they should do in future. The performance planning and appraisal interview is used to pass along information about an employee's performance and development to the employee and to those who maintain the employee's human resources file. In such an interview, the manager, on behalf of the organization, reviews the performance objectives established for the employee in previous appraisals (if there have been any), reviews the employee's performance based on those objectives, establishes a new set of objectives for the following year, and helps the employee formulate a strategy for meeting the objectives. For some organizations, the appraisal interview may also give rise to a formal, quantified measure of performance which may, in turn, be used to determine the award of salary increments or bonuses. Disciplinary interviews are for use when other methods of planning and appraisal have failed.

Sounds Like a Plan

The two partners in an interview usually know why they have come together. Still, it's a good idea to restate the purpose of the interview so that the objectives of the interview, as well as the purpose, are clear to both parties. As one person begins speaking in a formal interview situation, the other person often thinks, "What is she getting at? What does she want?" Stating the purpose at the outset answers those questions immediately. It is true that informal conversations and interactions sometimes have underlying purposes as well, but these are usually less clearly stated or understood by the participants. In any case, these situations are usually not planned or structured in any way; they are therefore not the subject of this chapter. The first step in planning an interview, then, is to determine the *purpose* or *objective*, from which the structure and sequences will follow.

The following are some sample statements of purpose:

Persuasive:

> 66 I know you've given some thought to the strategy we might take for inviting tenders for our new building. I'd like to tell you about my own ideas. 99

Performance appraisal:

> 66 I've been looking forward to discussing your objectives for the year. It's been a good year for you, hasn't it? 99

Employment (orientation):

> 66 On your first day, I thought we could talk about what you might expect in your first few weeks here. I also have your first assignment. 99

As we will suggest, stating the purpose of the interview may be a collaborative process in which both parties contribute to formulating the statement. This is the case, for example, in interviews that are less rigidly structured.

We can imagine a continuum on which interview strategies can be placed. At either pole, we find a basic strategy; between the two are many variations. We can choose an interview type from either end of the continuum or a combination of interview types that suits our purpose. The *highly structured (or directive) strategy*, which exists at the right pole, requires the interviewer to take the initiative in determining and stating the purpose of the interview. He or she directs the interview in a manner that ensures that certain topics and issues are covered. If the goals for the meeting and the means to achieving the goals seem clear enough, the highly structured strategy may be appropriate. It may also be useful in cases in which your goal is to elicit a great deal of information. For the highly structured strategy, the questions will be specifically sequenced beforehand and the answers will most often be short and specific.

The *nondirective (or unstructured) strategy* is to be found at the left pole of the continuum. For such a strategy, the interviewer chooses the topics to be covered, but he or she allows the respondent to change the sequence of topics or to choose new or different topics. The interviewer tries to do as little of the talking as possible. He or she encouranges the respondent to offer thoughts, feelings, insights, and ideas. As you might suspect, such a strategy is most common in counselling situations. It offers respondents the opportunity to discuss topics and issues in-depth. It is less useful in most other organizational settings, since it does not allow for the attainment of tangible interview goals as quickly as do other strategies.

A caution. A nondirective interview can be unwieldy. Because the interviewer keeps his or her direction to a minimum (by definition, in fact, there is no direction), the interview may be time-consuming and involve the collection of a lot of irrelevant information. Use it with care. As well, remember that a nondirective interview strategy requires as much planning as other strategies do. In the planning stage, you may wish to set a time limit for the interview and decide how to encourage your partner to stay on topic, if possible.

Midway between the poles on our continuum we find the *combined approach*, which represents a strategy that is useful in many situations and which we recommend for most interviews. For this strategy, the interviewer determines an objective for each segment of the interview. Then, he or she adjusts the relevant strategy for reaching this objective. For example, an interviewer may try to preserve the advantages of both planning and spontaneity by writing questions, probes, and follow-ups (about which we will have more to say later in this chapter) in advance, then improvising on the plan during the interview. We suggest that the best interviews are the ones that are sufficiently structured that at the end both parties feel something has been accomplished, but are also improvisatory enough that both feel they were able to influence the direction of the interview.

The questions you ask during the interview will be the primary means of collecting information and establishing and maintaining a relationship with your partner. The structure you impose on your questions will usually consist of sequential steps. But you may also choose a *thematic* method, whereby you use themes to create a conceptual map of topics covered in the interview. We will have more to say about how to draft and organize your questions later in the chapter. For now, we suggest that you keep the questions short, that you ask them one at a time, and that you prepare more than you expect to use.

Get Them on Paper

Once you have stated the purpose of the interview and decided on a strategy, you will begin drafting the possible questions for the interview. At this point, you will not need to put them in any particular sequence. As in any writing process, it is best to draft first and revise later. What are the different kinds of questions that you may draft at this point? We will discuss eight kinds of questions to be used in interviews.

Closed questions are questions that are intended to elicit short, specific responses, and are structured accordingly. Interviewers use them when they want information only. Examples are the following:

What happened next?

How long have you been working there?

What did she say about your suggestion?

Even for in-depth interviews, in which broader questions will form the heart of the session, a series of closed questions may be required to provide the context for the interview or to allow the interviewer to help the respondent collect his or her thoughts, as we will suggest in Chapter 4.

Unlike closed questions, which require the interviewer to run through a checklist of questions, **open questions** allow for a broad range of responses. Typically, they indicate only the topic to be pursued, not a particular aspect of the topic. They impose a minimal limitation on the content that the respondent can choose to discuss or on the means by which the respondent structures that content. Such questions are an appropriate way of allowing the respondent to express his or her broadest perspectives, which may include attitudes and values. The following are examples of open questions:

What is your impression of how our project is proceeding?

Now that this recruitment interview is well along, how are you feeling about this job?

Let's discuss what you would like to accomplish this year.

How was your trip?

Hypothetical questions ask that an imaginary condition be taken for granted, in order to draw some conclusion based on that assumption. Hypothetical questions are similar to open questions, in that they encourage the respondent to come up with creative responses. The answer given to a hypothetical question may well reveal the respondent's attitudes and values, it may also indicate how well the person can solve problems. Consider the following examples of hypothetical questions:

Suppose we were to offer you the position for which you've applied. What would you do on your first day at work?

If you were involved in a conflict in your new position, how would you try to resolve it?

As our examples might suggest, hypothetical questions are especially useful in recruitment interviews, because they allow the respondent to discuss issues that may arise in an actual job situation. As a result, the interviewer can get some idea of how respondents might perform if they were offered the job.

A category of questions that is often used in association with open questions is that of probes and follow-ups. **Probes** are questions (or statements) used to allow the respondent to elaborate on a reply given to a previous question. Probes are thus helpful in connection with incomplete, inadequate, or provocative responses. When such a response occurs, the interviewer tries to initiate a discussion by formulating a probe. Similarly, **follow-ups** are used to allow the respondent to complete a thought or to provide more detailed information, but they can also lead to new topics of discussion, whereas probes tend to focus solely on topics already under discussion. Follow-ups are formulated most often as the interview progresses, whereas probes (for questions to which you expect incomplete responses) may be profitably drafted before the interview begins. A particularly useful word to employ when formulating probes or follow-ups is *when*, since it sets a scene and helps the respondent to begin a narrative or anecdote. The following are examples of probes and follow-ups. (Note that the second example uses the word *when*, as we suggested.)

You've expressed disagreement with the new policy. Could you tell me more specifically why you disagree?

A little earlier, you mentioned the events of last year connected to this project. When you were involved with these events, what were you thinking of, and why are these events so significant to you now?

Tell me more.

Why would you say that?

Probes and follow-ups can also be used to determine the intensity of feeling that the respondent has about a topic or issue. Suppose that a colleague has said that she finds her workload "heavy." You might formulate a probe by asking, "Does that cause you to have to take work home?" She might respond by saying, "Every night. And it's affecting my family life. I feel like a stranger to my own daughter." A particular type of probe—one in which something of personal significance is revealed to allow the respondent to do likewise—could also be used. In our example, you might have used the following probe instead: "I've been feeling a little overworked lately myself. And it's making me feel like my job is taking over the rest of my life." This interpersonal technique is known as reciprocity, used here in conjunction with a probe question.

As we mentioned, probes and follow-ups can be formulated during the interview itself, even though they are not part of the formal plan. Still, it may be useful to practise such questions beforehand and decide on the best way to phrase them. That way, you will be able to respond quickly and effectively to the information your partner is providing. For example, decide which of the following alternatives you prefer:

Will you elaborate?

What do you mean by that?

Discuss.

What are you saying, exactly?

All four possibilities ask the respondent for substantially the same information. Your choice of phrasing, of course, will depend on your interviewing style and, in part, on the person being interviewed and the context for the interchange. Determine beforehand which response you prefer, and then choose a couple of alternatives for variety.

Mirror statements are devices for offering constructive feedback, similar to paraphrasing (which we will discuss later in this chapter) and perception-checking (which forms part of Chapter 4). A mirror statement repeats the interviewee's comments in such a way that it encourages him or her to continue. A mirror statement does not include any personal judgment or evaluation; it is a neutral restatement, intended to help clarify and develop the interviewee's ideas.

In a persuasive interview, for example, suppose that you are trying to persuade a colleague of the merits of your proposal. When your colleague offers a criticism, you might use a mirror statement to ensure that you understand the concern. The statement might be as follows:

If I understand you correctly, you would rather that I deal with all the options at once, rather than separately.

A pair of question types that must be used with caution are leading questions and loaded questions. **Leading questions** include information that is meant to encourage the respondent to reply in a way that the questioner finds useful or desirable. You may find that such questions are occasionally helpful, but most often they are a block to the emergence of authentic communication. The following are examples of leading questions:

Aren't you being oversensitive on this issue?

I think we all know what's going on. Why don't you give us your perspective on what has happened?

When a question is prefaced by a remark that suggests the kind of answer the interviewer would like to hear, the range of possible responses is reduced. If your partner is aware of what is going on, he or she may object. You may not have realized yourself that you were asking leading questions. This is another reason to draft questions before beginning the interview; with a bit of reflection, the nature of some of the questions may become more apparent. The temptation is to use the leading question as part of a persuasive strategy. However, because leading questions presuppose something about the answer, they are more likely to result in manipulation than in persuasion.

A **loaded question** is simply an extreme form of a leading question. Through the use of emotionally charged language, loaded questions prevent respondents from making any response except one that will implicate them or reflect badly on their actions. Like leading questions, loaded questions may well be manipulative if used in an interview. The following examples, formulated at the beginning of a conversation, are loaded questions.

When did you begin to notice that you had been neglecting your duties?

Let's get to the heart of the matter. What makes you think that you're better than anyone else and that you deserve this promotion?

A **neutral question** is stated without any deliberate direction from the interviewer. In practice, whether any question can be entirely neutral is a matter for debate. However, "What is your feeling about your new job?" is certainly more neutral than "You don't like your new job, do you?" Similarly, "Where do we go from here?" is more neutral than "How do you intend to get out of this predicament?" Neutral questions allow the respondent to have a wide range of possible answers and to express more meaningful thoughts and impressions.

The most sophisticated type of question we consider is the prefaced probe. Such a question requires practice before it can be used successfully in an interview. You will have heard them used often in media interviews. In a **prefaced probe** the question is set up with a brief statement or two before the question proper. For example:

You've written often about the need for managers to have a broad interest in the humanities, as well as in the social sciences. Have you been criticized by your peers for this?

Prefaced probes give respondents time to consider the context of the question and your own views and perspective before they have to answer the question. If your respondent does not agree with your preface, allow him or her to comment on it or correct it before moving on to the question.

As we suggested earlier, you should always draft many more questions than you expect to need. Because even if you don't actually use some of them, the fact that you've thought about them and written them down can be useful. The process of putting questions on paper can lead you to other topics or issues that you might not have thought of otherwise.

Order, Order

After you have decided on your general strategy and drafted some questions, it is time to decide how you will put the questions in sequence. We identity six possible sequences. Three of these are primary types: the tube or tunnel, funnel, and pyramid. The other three are variations on the funnel and the pyramid: the stacked funnel, the hourglass, and the diamond. As shown below, the sequences can be visualized as forming different shapes (Figure 3.1).

The **tube** or **tunnel** sequence uses questions that are all of the same degree of openness. Such a sequence is useful in situations in which you are trying to gather a great deal of factual information quickly. Short, specific questions are asked in succession. For example, if you apply for a bank loan, the loan officer may well ask you a series of questions that require brief, factual responses. Similarly, market researchers or pollsters do not usually spend much time warming up to the topic through a series of open questions. Instead, they simply ask for your cooperation and then, if you agree, launch into the questions:

Have you ever used our product?

Where did you buy it?

What did you like or dislike about it?

Would you recommend the product to others?

Figure 3.1: Question Sequence Patterns

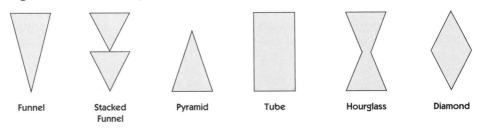

Funnel   Stacked Funnel   Pyramid   Tube   Hourglass   Diamond

Using the **funnel** sequence, you begin with general, open questions and then move gradually to questions that are more specific and closed. The sequence might be as in the following example:

What are your impressions about the potential of the field in which you work?

How did you learn about the position that is open in our organization?

Do you keep up with our organization's job postings?

What is it that appeals to you about this job?

In what ways are you qualified for this job?

The **pyramid** sequence is the opposite of the funnel; here, the opening questions are specific and closed. The interviewer then moves gradually to questions that are more open. Such a sequence is especially useful in situations in which you believe your partner will be reticent or reluctant to participate. That is, your specific questions may help the respondent to participate more fully in the interview. The following questions provide an example of a pyramid sequence:

Who are the other people working with you on the project?

Have you worked with any of them before?

Tell me about similar projects you've completed in the past.

How is this project going?

A variation on the funnel sequence is the **stacked funnel**, or compound funnel, in which an open question is followed by closed probes. This pattern is then repeated throughout the interview.

We call a combination of the funnel and the pyramid the **hourglass** sequence. This sequence begins with open questions, moves to closed questions, and then returns to open questions. Such a sequence is useful for situations in which you wish to establish some general principles, apply these principles specifically, and then examine some recommended or alternative actions to be taken. In a performance appraisal, for example, the sequence of questions might look like the following:

How many years have we been doing this?

Is the process generally acceptable to you?

What have been your successes and failures this year?

How can the organization help you meet your personal and workplace goals?

How can the appraisal process be improved for next year?

The **diamond** sequence is, like the hourglass sequence, a combination of the funnel and the pyramid sequences, but with the order reversed; it begins with closed questions, moves to open ones, and concludes with closed, specific inquiries. Such a sequence may be useful for situations in which the topic is sensitive, controversial, or difficult for one or both of the partners. The diamond sequence may be used, for example, to counsel an employee who is encountering personal difficulties that are affecting performance on the job. First, the interviewer states the purpose of the interview. Second, the two people discuss their perceptions (which may be different) of what the purpose of the interview should be. Third, the respondent discusses the problem from his or her point of view. Fourth, the two discuss what the consequences of doing nothing about the problem would be. Fifth, options are discussed. Finally, the two decide on a course of action.

These, then, are six question sequences that you should consider before the interview. Keep in mind that the process of choosing a strategy and drafting and sequencing your questions results in a plan or guide, not in a blueprint. You will have to change the plan as the actual interview progresses. Keep your options open.

Before the Opening: Getting It Together

In this chapter and the next we will use the simple but effective three-part structure of "opening-body-closing" as a framework for planning an interview. However, before we begin our discussion of the three parts of the interview, we introduce the notion of **climate control**. Controlling the climate means setting the comfort level of the situation in which the interview will take place.

Climate control is yet another aspect of the interview that must be planned, most often by the interviewer. If the climate is appropriate, both parties will be more relaxed and open. It is true that some conditions of the interview may end up being a surprise to the participants, both of whom must be able to improvise; but it is the interviewer's responsibility to ensure that disruptive or annoying influences are kept to a minimum. This can be done most effectively by anticipating such influences and acting accordingly.

Why is climate control so important? We are living in an age of mass communication. People's needs are being met increasingly by institutions. Opinion polls and market research are used by businesses and government to determine what large groups of people want or need, or say they want or need. The personal interview is important because it brings human interaction and the meeting of needs to the level of one-on-one, a level at which needs are usually best met. By controlling the climate for such an interaction, you will be reinforcing the message that you hope your partner will be receiving: that you are seeking a meaningful and free exchange of information and opinion, not just an elicitation of responses. If the physical surroundings of the interview (which are the first indication that the interviewee will have of how the interview is going to go), along with the subsequent verbal and nonverbal cues of the interview itself, have been considered with regard for human needs, the chances increase that the interview itself will follow the course of meeting human needs.

If the interview is to be carried out by telephone, you can do things such as asking others not to disturb you, closing your door, and trying to use a telephone (perhaps a speaker-phone) that has good reception and transmission sound. If you want to take notes or record the interview, mention this to your partner, and mention why you want to do so. And even if the results of the interview are to be made public later (in the case of media interviews, for example, through publication or broadcast), try to carry out the interview in private, if at all possible. This will allow the interviewee to relax. Of course, counselling and disciplinary interviews especially should be conducted privately. If you must interrupt the interview, do so after a brief explanation to your partner, taking care to make the interruption as short as possible.

Keep in mind that as you try to build rapport with your partner, nonverbal cues are as important as verbal ones. We know, for example, that two people who imitate each other's posture while talking tend to feel that they understand each other better. In addition to the aspects of making your partner feel comfortable which we have discussed, three other means of building rapport are the following:

Be clear about the purposes of the interview.

Indicate how long the interview will take.

Provide adequate opportunities for your partner to respond during the interview.

Good interviewers seek to make their respondents feel relaxed. Have you considered providing a cup of coffee or tea? It's a good idea.

The Opening: Let's Get Started

In the opening stage of the interview, you should be trying to reach the following two objectives:

1. to establish rapport with your partner
2. to state the purpose of the interview.

Thus, the opening is an effort by both people to establish "common ground" before they begin to discuss the issues at hand and, perhaps, take opposing views. The opening sets the tone for the interview. Many interviews begin with casual conversation on a topic of mutual interest. You may want to talk about something unrelated to the subject of the interview, perhaps the weather, sports, family, or common acquaintances. Throughout the interview, but especially during the opening, you should show a keen and sincere interest in the other person. Rapport is built by establishing a climate of goodwill. A smile, a handshake, an offer of coffee or tea, an expression of gratitude for coming—these all help the respondent to feel at ease. Also, if you wish to take notes or record the interview, now is the time to seek the permission of your interviewee. We will have more to say about notetaking later in the chapter.

A caution. Don't wait too long to move on to the second objective of the opening, which is to state the purpose of the interview. If you engage in too much talk about topics unrelated to the objective of the interview, your respondent may begin to feel anxious.

When you state the purpose of the interview, be sure to offer your respondent an opportunity to revise or clarify the interview's objectives. In a recruitment interview, for example, you could suggest that the interview is intended to offer an opportunity for both of you to exchange information so that you might make a decision concerning whether hiring the interviewee would be mutually rewarding. Your statement of the purpose of the interview can form a bridge to an *orientation statement.* In your orientation statement you may wish to provide an overview of the topics you plan to cover. Such an overview helps clarify the purpose of the interview. As with the building of rapport, it helps the respondent to relax.

Beyond this, the steps you take depend on the strategy you have chosen for the interview. For example, in highly structured interviews, the opening should be brief and direct, because the respondent may be deciding whether or not to participate, as is the case in information-gathering interviews for research projects. On the other hand, in nondirective interviews, the opening may be longer, allowing the respondent to participate more than is possible in highly structured interviews. Either way, be sensitive to the needs of your respondent. If he or she has questions or wants to discuss something, by all means allow him or her to do so.

The process of establishing and maintaining rapport continues with the first few questions of the interview. Often, you can use open questions to help you decide whether your strategy needs to be revised. To do this, you may want to jot down ideas for probes and follow-ups, to be used after your partner has finished speaking or later in the interview.

Consider this example of someone for whom the interview is a regular part of his job. Journalist Paul McLaughlin has worked as a producer, interviewer, and researcher for CBC Radio. In his book, *How to Interview: The Art of the Media Interview,* McLaughlin writes about the great importance he and others place on opening questions. He gives this example of how opening questions can turn a reluctant guest into a forthcoming subject:

> **"** If the right opening question is asked, it can turn a reluctant guest into an enthusiastic exponent, as Mutual Radio's Larry King discovered when he tangled with cantankerous physicist Dr. Edward Teller. Teller, who disdains most interviews, asked King, "How can you interview me if you don't know anything about physics?"

King's reply—"I'm going to learn physics from you"—didn't convince Teller that he would enjoy the experience, but, with reluctance, he agreed to talk. "I led off the interview with the question of why, when I was in high school, I recoiled at the word 'physics'," says King. "His face lit up. He said, 'Because they shouldn't call it physics. They should call it life'. Then he began to explain how it affected everyday life. We were off and running."[1] **99**

For further examples of how opening questions can set the tone for an interview, tune in to the radio. On radio, interviewers cannot rely on as many "tricks" to make an interview successful. Radio interviewers, for example, cannot grimace at or insult the leader of the house band, as television interviewers have been known to do.

After you've built rapport and stated the purpose of the interview, you're ready to move on to the next stage of the interview: the body.

The Body: The Heart of the Matter

We have discussed the kinds of questions that you may decide to use in the body of the interview. We suggested that you draft your questions before the interview and that you decide whether the interview should follow a highly structured, a nondirective, or a combined strategy. Finally, we stated that you should sequence your questions appropriately.

By the time you get to the body of the interview you will have already done most of the work required for the interview. During the interview you will revise your plan according to the needs and wishes of your partner and according to the purpose of the interview. Unfortunately, the art of improvisation is more easily modelled than taught; the best way to work on improving the body of your interviews is to listen to how others do it. However, we can offer the following description of how the interaction during an interview can be mediated through three means: turn-taking, the use of transitions, and coping with inadequate responses.

In an interview, **turn-taking** is an important process by which the participants "take the floor" and "give up the floor." It also allows either or both of the participants to change or maintain the direction of the interview. Turn-taking cues are the devices that help you determine when your partner is about to take the floor, and to let your partner know when you wish to take the floor. We identify four clusters of turn-taking cues.

If you wish to take the floor, you can use a **turn-requesting** or **regulating** cue such as voicing a word or other audible signal, holding up a hand or finger, or audibly taking a breath. Saying "mmm" or "uh-huh" or nodding your head can indicate to your partner that you wish him or her to finish the thought. If you want to indicate that your partner may take the floor, you might use a **turn-yielding** cue, which could be a pause or a drop in the pitch of your voice; or a nonverbal gesture such as exposing the palms of your hands, shrugging, or raising your eyebrows.

If, on the other hand, you wish to deny your partner the opportunity to speak, perhaps temporarily, you would use a **turn-denying** cue. Such a cue might be the exposure of the flat palm of one hand (a "stop" signal) or some other nonverbal signal such as stopping talking and raising the chin. Similarly, **turn-maintaining** cues are used to keep the floor. Examples of these cues are an increase in the volume of speech, or a physical action such as a light touch or movement of the hand as if to halt the other's speech. Verbally, you might simply say, "Allow me to complete this thought."

A caution. Turn-taking cues must be used and observed with care. If they are unnatural, aggressive, or frequent, your partner may become annoyed. If you think you would benefit from practising such cues, try them out in a non-threatening situation first. Use a tape recorder, for example, or role-play with a colleague, friend, or family member.

As for transitions between topics, the interviewer usually takes the lead. **Transitions** are devices used to smooth the move from one topic to another. They can be planned and practised ahead of time, but you will likely have to improvise during the interview. Key words that can be used to allow for transitions include the following:

now
next
so
another
second
finally
also

You can achieve a firm transition by restating the respondent's comments to provide a link to the next topic or issue. This method has the advantage of acting as a paraphrase, allowing you to check or clarify the respondent's meaning. An example might be the following:

You mentioned that you have spent several years working in similar organizations. What about your educational background?

If you use transitions effectively, your partner will understand what stage of the interview you have progressed to and will be able to provide responses based on this contextual understanding. And in the same way that you should provide appropriate transitions from topic to topic during the body of the interview, you should signal each point of transition between the opening, body, and closing.

What happens if your partner offers inadequate responses during the interview, either occasionally or consistently? Again, you may have to modify the plan you devised. For example, you might counter the answers of a reluctant respondent with a pyramid sequence of questions. You would use a few short questions that call for simple or direct, factual answers in order to encourage the respondent to answer the more general questions to which you wish to move. On the other hand, for a compulsive talker or a poor listener, you may wish to try modifying a nondirective strategy to a more highly structured one; you could use closed questions to try to limit the range of your partner's responses.

If your partner offers irrelevant responses during the interview, you may want to rephrase the question later in the interview. Using this tactic, you offer your partner an opportunity to reconsider his or her response to the question, avoiding a possibly unnecessary confrontation. Similarly, if your partner is formulating unclear responses, you may wish to allow him or her to clarify by taking the responsibility for the lack of clarity yourself. You might say, for example, "What did you mean by that last comment? I think I'm losing the thread of your argument." If the idea is still not being expressed clearly, move on and try to return to the matter later in the interview. Whatever happens, try not to make your partner feel as if he or she is not able to express an idea clearly; this will likely cause frustration or even resentment. If you need to, use a mirror statement or paraphrase repeatedly—a different one each time, if you can—to try to check on what you think your partner is saying.

With prominent or famous respondents, the opposite problem may occur. Your respondent may offer answers that are, if not rehearsed, then familiar and slightly worn. Such respondents may not even be aware that you know they are repeating themselves from other interviews. For them, responding to an interviewer is a daily grind. If you don't want your time to run out only to find that you have an interview that does not reveal anything new, you will have to treat the respondent as if he or she were offering irrelevant or unclear responses. Change the type of question or the sequence in an effort to elicit more meaningful or thoughtful responses. You may wish to indicate to the respondent that you have done a lot of research on his or her life or career and that you would like to go beyond some of the better known material. You can do this through the use of a prefaced probe question in which the preface includes specific and perhaps relatively unknown information about the person and his or her accomplishments.

These three means—turn-taking, using transitions, and coping with inadequate responses—are part of a strategy of adapting your plan to the actual interview at hand. The general rule is: plan, practise, and rehearse, but then be flexible. Before we move on to a discussion of the closing, we give some advice on the best way to organize the arguments that you'll make in the body of your interview.

Structuring a Persuasive Interview

We suggest that you use the following structure for persuasive interviews. It incorporates the principles of persuasive rhetoric that Aristotle expounded. These principles are, not surprisingly, part of the theme of this book: that authentic communication is based on empathy and active listening. Thus, in our structure for a persuasive interview, the persuader acknowledges the presence of his or her audience by addressing seriously any counterargument that the audience might advance. The steps to be taken for such a structure are as follows:

1. State the issue.
2. State your point of view, with evidence.
3. Acknowledge your opponent's point of view and its merits.
4. State the shortcomings of your opponent's point of view.
5. Resolve the issue by restating your point of view, while incorporating any qualifications introduced by your listener's arguments.

Such a structure is to be used, of course, only with what are called in rhetoric *arguable assertions*, that is, statements that can be debated. The cost of a flight from Toronto to Edmonton, for example, is not an issue that could give rise to an arguable assertion: Once you inquired at the airlines that offer service between the two cities, there would be no opportunity for argument.

On the other hand, suppose you and a colleague have to choose one airline over another for a flight. Consider the following situation. Airline A offers a flight that is $150 cheaper than the one offered by Airline B but is offered only at 4 p.m. The return flight is offered only at noon each day. You would like to use Airline B because it offers a 7 a.m. flight and a 6 p.m. return flight. You might present your argument in the following way:

State the issue: We have to decide whether to take Airline A or Airline B.

State your point of view: While Airline A offers a cheaper flight, we ought to book with Airline B because its flight is more convenient and will save us money overall.

Acknowledge your opponent's view: Airline A's flight is indeed $150 cheaper.

State the shortcomings of your opponent's view: We must consider the timing of the flights and what implications that has for our trip. With Airline A, because we would have to travel in the late afternoon and return the next day, we would incur hotel and other costs. With Airline B, we can return the same day.

Resolve the issue: If the airlines had a similar schedule of flights, the airfare would be the only cost to consider. In this case, however, we should consider other costs that would be incurred because of the different schedules. On this basis, we should fly with Airline B.

Of course, decisions are often more complex than the one in this example. However, the structure of any argument should be similar to the one we describe, even for a complex decision with many factors to be considered. The weakness in many people's persuasive communication is that it fails at steps 3 and 5. That is, it does not acknowledge the opponent's view or incorporate that view into the resolution of the issue.

In a persuasive interview you must use the strategies which we introduced in the previous section and these types and sequences of questions (about which we will have more to say later in this chapter and in the next chapter) in order to carry out the steps of the basic persuasive structure. Let's carry on with the airline example. Suppose you approach your colleague to persuade him or her to book with Airline B. Your interview might go in a manner similar to the following.

You: I've been checking into some flights for our trip on Thursday. I thought we should make a booking as soon as possible, since we've already arranged our meeting in Edmonton. *[State the issue.]*

Colleague: Glad to hear that. I hadn't given the matter much thought, but I agree that we should book right away.

You: I know that you like to fly Airline A whenever you can. Its schedules and airfare are usually competitive; in fact, for a flight to Edmonton this week, A's airfare is cheaper than B's. But this time, I think we should go with Airline B. *[State your point of view; acknowledge your opponent's view.]*

Colleague: Why's that?

You: Airline A only flies out in the afternoon and returns in the morning. We'd have to stay over in Edmonton. Aside from the inconvenience, that stay would cost us more than the difference in airfare. *[Resolve the issue.]*

To conclude our suggestion of a strategy for the persuasive interview, let's return to our debt to Aristotle. For Aristotle, the three qualities necessary to produce conviction in a listener were to be found in the speaker, not in the speech. The speaker, wrote Aristotle in *Rhetoric*, had to manifest good sense, virtue, and goodwill. This idea brings us back to the notion of authentic communication; the speaker's ability to persuade comes from self-knowledge and integrity.

The Closing: Tying Up the Loose Ends

As with the opening, the interviewer usually takes the lead in providing the transition to the closing. You will want to move to the closing when both you and your partner have reached your mutually agreed upon goals or, if both of you feel that you have failed to reach your goals, you should continue the interview at another time.

In the closing you should try to tie together what has been covered in a short summary of the key points that you and your partner have discussed. At the beginning of the closing you should clear up any loose ends from the interview. You or your partner may have some questions or comments that neither of you had the chance to articulate earlier. Check this now, before moving on to the summary portion of the closing.

You should also use the closing to ensure that you have understood as clearly as possible the meaning that your respondent has been trying to convey during the interview. You might wish to include as part of your summary a few paraphrases or mirror statements, based on notes you have made during the interview. To summarize accurately requires that you observe verbal and nonverbal cues and language. We will have more to say about this in Chapter 4.

During the last part of the interview you should thank your partner and decide what will happen after the interview. Ask one more time for further questions or comments. At this stage, the process will depend upon what kind of an interview you have been carrying out. For a recruitment interview, for example, you would indicate to the candidate when and how you will be in touch. For a performance planning and appraisal interview, you would inform the employee of the next step of the process. For a sales interview, you would try to close the sale. For any of these situations, the tone of the closing should be the same as the tone of the rest of the interview, which will have been determined by the interview's purpose.

The closing is your last opportunity to check meaning and establish authentic communication; therefore it requires care. As with the other components of the interview, the closing should be planned and, if possible, rehearsed. In some cases, feeling of the goodwill may carry you through the closing without much effort; in other cases, it won't. So take the time to plan the closing beforehand.

A final word. If the interview has a logical structure—an opening, body, and closing—it also has an emotional structure. Ideally, your interview plan can be laid over the emotional structure with little overlap. Often, however, the two will conflict. For example, your respondent may not seem ready to move from the opening to the body but you may sense that your time is slipping away and that you must move on; or your respondent will just be warming to the topic when it will be time to close the interview. You will want to do whatever is possible to make the emotional and logical structures of the interview coincide. This will be easier to do if a time limit to your discussion is not an important factor.

Take Note

Some people, perhaps not surprisingly, become uncomfortable at the sight of a tape recorder or a notebook during an interview. As a result, some veteran reporters keep their notebooks out of sight during the interview, filling them up immediately afterwards. While doing the interviews required to write *In Cold Blood* (the non-fiction novel), Truman Capote found that whenever he took notes his subjects seemed to become tense and less cooperative. Thereafter, Capote trained himself to remember details of events without taking notes during the interview, but returned to his Kansas motel room every night to make elaborate notes. If we, as perhaps less exalted notetakers than Mr. Capote, find that notetaking is inhibiting our dialogue, we should find a way to avoid it and, instead, jot things down as soon after as we can.

As you take notes you should listen not only to what is said but to the way it is said. Such a technique is well understood by media interviewers, but it can be useful in the workplace as well. The dominant impression we get from an encounter with someone else is a result of a composite of the textures, colors, setting, gestures, and verbal inflections of what is said. Here is an example of how an impression can be conveyed. It is from an article based on an interview with author and broadcaster Peter Gzowski:

> 66 Peter Gzowski puts his feet up and tips his chair back against the window of his cramped office in CBC radio's Jarvis Street headquarters in Toronto. Peter Gzowski likes to put his feet up. And he likes cigarettes. That's why a grey-blue haze of smoke surrounds him, making it difficult to know whether he's looking at me or out the door into the chaos of furniture, magazines, and typewriters that is the base of operations for his CBC radio program called *Morningside*. He is talking about laziness and about nicotine addiction.[2] 99

Unless you have an exceptionally good memory, it would be difficult to record such detail after an interview without taking notes. Even a tape recorder, which we tend to regard as an accurate record of a conversation, may not prompt you to recall visual cues. So notetaking is a means of maintaining accuracy in interpersonal communication.

Notetaking can also aid in paraphrasing, a process we discussed in Chapter 2. Often, you may want to let the interviewee express a thought without interruption. In the meantime, you can take notes to keep track of the main points. When the other person has finished speaking, your notes will help you paraphrase. Your partner will be pleased that you have taken up important points without further prompting, and this can only improve the tone and atmosphere of the interview. Paraphrasing with the aid of notetaking will thus help you maintain your interview's status as a two-way process.

A caution. If your partner indicates, no matter how subtly, that he or she would rather you did not take notes or record the conversation, discuss the matter candidly. If you think that you can get along without a running record of the interview, put down your pencil or turn off the machine. If you think the quality of the interview will almost certainly suffer without the aid of notes, ask your partner to reconsider. As components of a two-way process, such matters are always open to negotiation. Employment interviews must be characterized by authentic communication, and authentic communication cannot occur if one party is inflexible. In such a situation, the needs and aspirations of the person being interviewed would not be fulfilled.

The Dos and Don'ts of Interviewing

Before we conclude this section, we offer a short list of pitfalls for interviewers. Take this as advice. It is based on the experience of many interviewers. As well, we offer a checklist of things that you should try to do during an interview. Try using this list before and after carrying out an interview.

Don't use too many long and leading questions. The prefaced probe is a valuable and sophisticated device, but if you are boring your partner with it, try to change your tactic.

Don't wander around a topic without a purpose or focus. Try to anchor your improvised or revised questions in your plan.

Don't run out of questions, and don't run out of time. Again, the plan should provide an anchor to avoid having either to end the interview abruptly or to rush the latter part.

Don't miss important verbal and nonverbal cues from the respondent. Try to observe as much as you can during the interview and modify your strategy accordingly.

Don't read questions word for word. Have regard for natural intonation. If this requires practice, perhaps with the aid of a tape recorder before the interview, then do it.

Don't talk too much and listen too little. You should be listening more than you're talking during the interview.

Don't jump to conclusions or express biased opinions. Try to let your respondent express his or her opinions in as neutral an atmosphere as possible.

Don't neglect to make an appropriate record of the interview's proceedings. Again, deal with this in your plan.

Do have a set of back-up questions and a back-up strategy in hand. Try to have an alternative question sequence in mind and perhaps twice as many questions as you think you have time to actually use. What happens if your request to record the interview or take notes is denied? Or what if the batteries in your tape recorder fail? Try to anticipate any problems.

Do determine what you hope to accomplish in the interview. Ask yourself what problem you are trying to solve or what information you are trying to gather. As we suggested in our discussion of the opening, state the purpose of the interview at the beginning so that your partner has an opportunity to comment on it or even change it.

Do check your transitions. Using a tape recorder in a rehearsal before the interview may help you to polish your transitions and, thereby assist in achieving the objective of the interview.

Do analyze your partner. Before the interview, carry out an appropriate amount of research on the other person. In the case of a performance appraisal, you should consult the employee file. You may even try to determine beforehand whether he or she is easy to interview.

Do analyze the setting and context. We have discussed the importance of arranging an appropriate climate. You should also try to anticipate any problems that could arise. If the interview is to take place in a cafeteria, try to determine whether the background noise level is going to be acceptable.

Do plan your assessment of the interview. After the interview, you will want to determine how well it went. This assessment will help you improve your technique next time. In the case of a recruitment interview, you will also have to make a decision about whether to offer a job, which we will have more to say about in Chapter 4.

And finally . . .

As with any other activity in an organization, it is just as important to be able actually to do something as it is to know all about it. You may be a "born interviewer"; but you may not. What we have tried to do in this section is to provide some practical strategies and suggestions that will help you in either case. The advice we have provided is related mainly to the planning stage, because we believe that preparing for an interview constitutes more than half of the work that goes into the whole interview process. The rest is up to you. You will have to get as much practice as you can, because that is the only way to try out what works for you and what does not. Good luck.

Before we get started . . .

In many organizations, effective listening has come to be recognized as crucial for improved productivity as well as for other types of organizational success. As we will note in the following clinic, people spend more of their time at work listening than they do talking, reading, or writing. For their part, managers may spend half their day or more listening to people. If they are good listeners, they are not only gathering information and impressions, but conveying the message that they consider the people they are listening to important and that they respect them, even if they do not agree with them.

Many organizations are also recognizing that poor listening can lead to mistakes on important business matters or inhibit profit or success. For example, one of New England Telephone's 12 divisions discovered that twenty percent of its operator-assisted calls were being delayed by listening problems; the delays were costing the division $874 800 a year. After starting an educational program on listening and communication for its employees, the company estimated that it recovered about $500 000 of the annual loss.

Similarly, some organizations have established programs whereby employees meet customers or clients specifically to listen to what they have to say. Other organizations have begun to implement programs to help employees improve their ability to listen. The Sperry Corporation, a computer manufacturer, was one of the first companies to institute professional development courses on listening skills for its management and employees. Other corporations that have begun to implement similar programs include Xerox Canada Ltd., Pfizer, IBM Canada Ltd., Honeywell, Ford, AT&T, and General Electric.

For many people, learning to improve their listening is difficult. Perhaps the most important reason for this is that many people assume they are already listening well enough. With this assumption, they attribute the interpersonal misunderstandings in their lives to the shortcomings of others. We suggest that listening is a neglected skill, but an important one. With some study and practice, we believe you can become a better listener. But it's up to you to set your own program of improving your listening. We will suggest some activities to help you consider and refine your listening skills. We will also draw your attention to some of the points to watch for and make a series of suggestions for you to experiment with. It's up to you to make what you can out of the following clinic by coming up with your own adaptations.

Active listening, as we will define it here, comprises all types of communication. That is, listening, broadly considered, may include activities such as reading, writing, and speaking. The active listening skills you will practise in this section may be applied to many situations, including business transactions as well as personal and family activities. The emphasis is on practical application.

The structure that we suggested earlier in the chapter for a persuasive interview required that the persuader acknowledge the audience's view and even incorporate that view into the resolution of the issue. In order to do this, the persuader must know what the audience's view is. Cicero maintained that a good rhetorician (writer or speaker) had to *know*. To know we must listen. Listening requires participation. To use a term that we will introduce in the upcoming clinic, listening should be **dialogic;** that is, the listener must be not only empathetic but self-interested. But if self-reflection, a subject covered in Chapter 8, is important for interpersonal communication, knowledge of others is equally important. In this section, we demonstrate the need for listeners to engage their partners in a process of making mutual meaning.

Both people in an interpersonal situation are speakers and both are listeners. Both strive to know themselves and the other. Both try to create a shared body of meaning. It sounds simple enough. In this section we offer some practical proposals, to complement our utopian sketches.

We have placed this section after the one on interviewing because good interviewing calls for good listening. One of the first things we will discuss is the portion of our time spent listening. Perhaps because we do so much of it, we take listening for granted, assuming that we are doing a good job of it. Interviewers, on the other hand, can make no such assumption. They must continually refine their ability to absorb and process meaning by listening actively to their respondents.

Objectives

After you complete this section, you should be able to:

1. Discuss briefly the significance of the connection between listening and interviewing.
2. State a rule of thumb for a talk/listen ratio.
3. Define *reflective listening.*
4. Discuss the uses and importance of the following clusters of reflective listening skills:
   attending
   following
   reflecting
5. Define *paraphrase*, and state the two essential components of a paraphrase statement.
6. Given a hypothetical or documentary excerpt of dialogue, provide an effective paraphrase statement.
7. Define *dialogic listening*, stating its four characteristics.
8. Discuss the importance of empathy for active listening, and briefly state some methods for achieving and communicating empathetic listening.
9. Distinguish between reflective listening and dialogic listening.
10. Discuss some of the 10 items in the checklist for active listening.

INTERPERSONAL SKILLS CLINIC

LISTENING JOURNAL

As you improve your listening skills, you will find it helpful to keep a record of how your observations, knowledge, and habits are changing. To do this, you may wish to keep a listening journal. In the journal you would record interactions from your personal, academic, or organizational experience in which you listen to others. Perhaps two or three such interactions a day would be enough to get you started.

At first, you might simply write a paragraph or two about an interaction: when it happened, with whom, and your impressions about it. Your entries for a couple of days might be similar to the following ones.

January 20: Attended a meeting of the Nordic Ski Club executive tonight. Everyone on the executive was there, because we're discussing the upcoming race. I found it difficult to keep my mind on the matter at hand because I'm bored by the procedural matters: putting motions, reading minutes, and so on. I agreed to serve on the awards committee.

January 21: A customer complained about the selection of equipment our shop offers. He said that we should have more equipment for the novice. I agreed with him, but couldn't say so, because that would undermine the owner. Still, I am the manager, and I feel that it's my responsibility to make my views known to the owner.

After a few days, begin to analyze each interaction according to the techniques we present in this book, and particularly those in this clinic. The following is an example of what your annotated journal might look like.

January 24: As part of my duties on the awards committee for the ski club, I called Tony and asked him whether we could meet to discuss buying a trophy and some gift certificates. Tony seemed reluctant to get together, even though he seemed enthusiastic enough at the executive meeting.

> *[I might have paraphrased the particulars of what he was saying, since after our conversation I was not sure whether he was offering a legitimate excuse or whether he simply didn't want to help out on the committee.]*

Also today, I called the owner of the shop with the intention of asking him to reconsider ordering more inexpensive stock.

> *[He immediately began to raise objections to my proposal, which I wanted to rebut. However, I sensed that he was busy with something else when I called, so I decided to wait until we had a chance to meet personally. That way, he would be able to consider my proposal with a clearer mind, and I would be able to prepare my case beforehand. I'm not sure, though, how I sensed he was busy. Something about his voice when he's anxious.]*

Keep up the journal for two or three weeks. When you are finished, write a short essay in which you discuss whether the techniques of this clinic have helped you improve your listening. If they have, state which techniques were the most helpful and why. Also, define and discuss the two types of active listening we introduce later on in this clinic: reflective and dialogic. State which one is easier to do, which one provides the most rewards, and which one you prefer. Conclude with a statement of what role listening has in the sphere of your personal or workplace life, and how important it is relative to other areas of that same sphere. If you find keeping a journal has been a particularly valuable experience, continue to work on it as you work through the rest of this book.

● — ● — ● — ● — ● — ● — ● — ● — ● — ● — ● — ●

INTERPERSONAL SKILLS CLINIC

LISTENING TO AN INTERVIEW

The best interviewers can listen. Listening is the most important means of finding out how you can establish a relationship with your respondent. That relationship, in turn, provides the base from which both of you make meaning. To confirm for yourself the link between the topics of active listening and interviewing, we begin this clinic with an activity in which you analyze a media interview.

For this activity, you will analyze two interviews that have been carried out in the electronic or print media. You may want to tape an interview from a current affairs program broadcast on television or radio; or you may want to clip an interview from a magazine or newspaper. If possible, choose one from the electronic media, one from the print. Don't spend too much time deciding on which interview would be the most interesting to analyze; you might learn as much from analyzing a poor interview as you would from analyzing a good one.

Now answer the following questions for each interview, referring to the material from the first part of this chapter.

1. Identify the opening, body, and closing.

2. What kind of strategy did the interviewer use (highly structured, nondirective, or combined)?

3. What was the question sequence?

4. Why might the interviewer have used the strategy and sequence he or she did?

5. How did the two interviews you chose differ with regard to the answers you gave for questions 1 through 4? Why might this be?

6. For each interview, describe the three aspects of the body that we discussed earlier in the chapter: turn-taking, the use of transitions, and coping with inadequate response. Why might the two interviewers have treated these aspects differently?

7. What can you apply from these interviews to the organizational interview?

● — ● — ● — ● — ● — ● — ● — ● — ● — ● — ● — ●

The Talk/Listen Ratio

In 1929, a researcher named Paul Rankin gathered information on the percentage of time spent by people carrying out the activities of speaking, reading, writing, and listening. He found that his subjects spent the greatest amount of time, forty-two percent, listening. This activity was followed by speaking (32%), reading (15%), and writing (11%).[3] By 1981, the ranking seemed not to have changed, although much of the time people now spend listening is carried out listening to the mass media. In 1981, a study indicated that college students spent fifty-three percent of their time listening (twenty-one percent spent in face-to-face interaction and thirty-two percent listening to mass media), seventeen percent speaking, sixteen percent reading and fourteen percent writing.[4] A pie chart of this information is shown in Figure 3.2.

As for specific interpersonal situations, we should adjust our talk/listen ratio (that is the amount of time we spend talking in relation to that spent listening) as appropriate. For example, during an interview, your ratio may be 25/75 or even 10/90. However, we suggest a rule of thumb for most conversations: that your talk/listen ratio be 40/60. To see what your ratio is, record a conversation or interview and then time the contributions to the interchange made by you and your partner. For most of us, such an exercise will indicate that the proportion of time we spend talking is higher than we expected.

Another exercise you can try to determine how much listening you are doing—and how well you are doing it—has been devised by psychologist Carl Rogers, who

Figure 3.2: Time Spent by College Students in Communicating

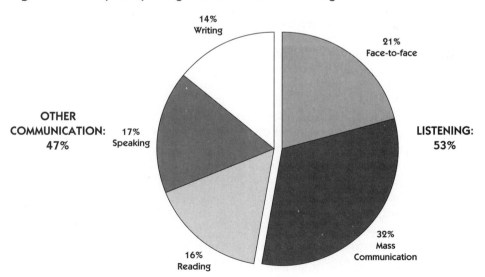

conceived the notion of active listening. Here is how it works. The next time you are talking with someone (your spouse, friend, or colleague at work), stop the conversation and establish a simple rule: Each participant must speak only after restating the ideas and feelings of the previous speaker accurately, and to that person's satisfaction. As with the talk/listen exercise, you may be surprised by what you find out. Most people find that it is easy enough to come up with a description of what the other person has said; it is much more difficult, however, to do it to the satisfaction of the other person. The implication of this is that many of us hear without listening. To carry out Rogers' exercise properly, you have to listen to the subtleties of meaning that others are trying to convey. In everyday communication we tend to assume that we understand the full meaning of what we hear. Paraphrasing to the satisfaction of the speaker tests this assumption. If you are like most people, you will fail the test (if only at first) or perform more poorly than you thought you would.

We will begin our discussion of active listening by suggesting three clusters of skills that can help you become, first, a reflective listener. After this, we will introduce the notion of dialogic listening. Both of these approaches are attempts to put into practice the notion of active listening.

Towards Reflective Listening: Three Clusters of Listening Skills

Many of us regard listening as a passive activity in which one person silently absorbs the messages being offered by another. No action is required of the listener. However, we suggest that listening requires the listener to be involved actively in the communication process. As devised by Robert Bolton, the three clusters of actions required for reflective listening are attending, following, and reflecting.[5] All three clusters of active listening skills appeal to most people's common sense; there is nothing surprising for most of us about the fact that we should maintain eye contact. On the other hand, actually incorporating these skills into our listening—and thereby becoming active listeners—is a difficult task indeed, requiring discipline and determination.

Attending skills. **Attending skills** are made up of those *nonverbal* behaviors (body movement and other actions) that help convey the message to the speaker that you are "there." The factors necessary for successful attending are a posture of involvement, appropriate body motion, and a nondistracting environment. A posture of involvement is a bodily expression of interest. It requires first that the listener choose an appropriate distance from the speaker. This will vary according to the social occasion and according to the culture. We will have more to say about this aspect of listening in Chapter 4, when we talk about *proxemics*, the study of physical closeness. Once the appropriate distance is established the listener must face the other squarely, maintaining eye contact and an open body position (legs and arms uncrossed). Appropriate body motion requires that the listener make some movement in response to what the speaker is saying. It is neither distracting nor forced or artificial. Rather, it is a natural way to convey the message that the listener is interested and attentive. A nondistracting environment is one in which aural and visual distractions are at a minimum. Thus, the noise from stereos, other conversations, and office equipment is low; similarly, large pieces of furniture (especially desks) and other items do not intrude between speaker and listener.

INTERPERSONAL SKILLS CLINIC

MAKING EYE CONTACT

Attending requires that you make appropriate eye contact with your partner. When you make eye contact, you convey a message of receptiveness to others, thus allowing them to express themselves more fully.

You can practise making eye contact with the use of a mirror and a newspaper. Choose two or three stories from the newspaper that you find interesting. Try to choose stories that deal with contrasting or varied topics: perhaps one from the lifestyle section and one international news story. Review each story until you can summarize them or discuss some of their implications. Now carry out the following steps:

1. Look at your face in the mirror, noting your expression when you are relaxed. Maintain eye contact with your reflection for a moment or two.

2. Begin to talk about the first story, noting how your expression changes. Which parts of your face change? Maintain eye contact as much as possible.

3. Stop talking about the story and note whether your expression has changed from the one you observed in step 1.

4. Begin talking about the second story. Note how your expression has changed from before. Try to decide why your expression differs, or does not differ, from the one you observed in steps 1 through 3.

5. Make a chart with the headings "Subject," "Facial Features," and "Movement." Record the title of the story under "Subject"; then record some of your observations about your facial expressions under the other two headings. You may wish to continue to record your observations as part of your listening journal.

Following skills. **Following skills** call for the formulation of questions or vocal articulations by the listener, so that he or she can assure the speaker that the message is getting through. If the first cluster of skills, attending, required the listener to indicate that he or she is paying attention, this cluster requires him or her to express that attention vocally.

The first skill that belongs to this cluster is the use of questions. For the purpose of following, open questions, as discussed earlier, are particularly valuable at the beginning of a conversation. Asking your partner a question such as "What's on your mind?" can initiate the conversation. Similarly, at points later in the conversation, you may wish to use questions that encourage the speaker to continue. Such questions may be related to the content of what the person is saying:

You felt, then, that your views were being ignored?

What happened after you left for the day?

Can we call for tenders in the next week or so?

Alternately, questions may not incorporate the content of the conversation. They may, instead, be forms of encouragement to the speaker, stated to indicate that the listener is following carefully:

Really?

I see. Please go on.

What happened then?

Was there anything else you wanted to talk about?

The second following skill is the use of nonverbal cues. These are used in the same way that questions are used and at similar junctures. However, they are vocalisms, rather than words. Here are some nonverbal cues that can be used as following devices:

Uh-huh.

Mmm.

Ah.

Ooo.

The third skill that we can use for following is, simply, silence. At certain points in an interchange, you may wish to avoid saying anything at all. If silence is used appropriately in combination with other aspects, such as eye contact and a posture of involvement, it can indicate to the speaker that you are following what he or she is saying. This can especially be the case for speakers who find the topic or issue painful or for those who are having difficulty expressing themselves.

VACATION

You will need a partner for this activity. Ask a friend to talk to you about the last vacation he or she took. Use the following procedure.

1. Ask your partner to begin talking about the vacation.
2. After about 20 seconds, use a following device. Use each of the three devices we discussed as the conversation continues.
3. Have your partner respond directly to your following devices. (You may wish to tell him or her in advance that silence is one of the three devices.)
4. After your partner has told you all about the vacation, ask him or her to comment on your use of following devices. Were they helpful? Did you miss any details of the vacation because you didn't use a following device?

- - - - - - - - - - - - -

Reflecting skills. Like following skills, **reflecting skills** also include certain types of questions, but they are intended to help the listener keep track of the message, not simply (as is the case with following skills) to encourage the speaker. Reflecting skills are used to hold a mirror up to the person with whom you are talking, with the intention of having the image improve the quality of the dialogue you are carrying on. Perhaps the most effective reflecting device for listeners to use is the *paraphrase*. A paraphrase has the dual purpose of providing information and asking for more information. It is a tentative interpretation of the other person's message, and it is a request for verification or revision of that interpretation. The following are examples of paraphrases:

So you had only two options left. Is that right?

Let me see if I understand. You were still trying to finish on time at that point?

You were running out of time. You had to act.

In the first two examples, the tentative aspect of the paraphrase is indicated by the interrogative nature of the sentence; that is, they are questions. In the third one, however, tentativeness would have to be indicated through the voice: perhaps through a rise in pitch towards the end of the sentence or through reducing the tempo of the words (slowing down).

You can use paraphrasing for three purposes. You can use it to clarify or consolidate the meaning the speaker is trying to convey. That is what the three examples above are intended to do. Or you can use it to reflect the feelings of the speaker. In this case, you would articulate what you take to be the emotional context of what the speaker is saying: "You were offended by the remark?" Or you may use paraphrasing to summarize what has come before, perhaps with the intention of encouraging the speaker to move on to something else. An example would be, "So you had done everything you could to explain the situation and decided there was nothing to do but go home." The common element in the three types of paraphrase is that all require the speaker to confirm or correct the paraphrase statement.

A caution. There is a dilemma to learning to paraphrase effectively in "real life." Paraphrasing must be done infrequently and with careful timing. If you try out your new paraphrasing skill with too much enthusiasm, you will find that others will catch on quickly; they may ask you to stop. The other side of the dilemma is that if you do not practise it enough you, and others, will not benefit from the check on meaning that paraphrases provide. A solution to this dilemma is to paraphrase silently at first. After you feel that you are paraphrasing effectively, try articulating a paraphrase or two in conversation. You will avoid feeling awkward, and you will begin to enjoy the benefits of enriched dialogue with others.

The following are examples of how you might respond with a paraphrase. A statement by someone is followed by a paraphrase.

Statement:	I've decided that the recognition I receive—or don't receive—at work is making my job intolerable. I need a change.
Sample response:	Are you saying you want to quit because your boss doesn't think you're doing a good job?
Statement:	The shipping department has always acted promptly to help us through the year-end rush. That's why I don't know whether I should ask them ahead of time to treat this order with special attention.
Sample response:	You don't want to threaten the good relationship you have with the shippers by appearing to nag. Is that it?
Statement:	This department is being run like a jail.
Sample response:	Are you feeling that morale is low because of the type of work we're being assigned or because management is being too heavy-handed in scheduling?
Statement:	I've met my daily and weekly sales targets for several months now. I don't think I've had a better year in my career.
Sample response:	You're feeling upbeat today, aren't you?
Statement:	That's three times this week I've missed the mail pick-up! This package has to go out today.
Sample response:	You seem frustrated with either the mail delivery system or with yourself. I'm not sure which.

WORKING PEOPLE

This activity can help you practise all the techniques we have introduced in this chapter. However, it is particularly useful for practising your paraphrasing skills. We provide several statements by different people in different occupations. Respond to the statements with a question or comment that carries out the two functions that we identified as being essential to a paraphrase: providing information and asking for confirmation or correction. If you can, have someone read the passages aloud to you, or record them yourself on tape.

Farmer "My job is not really a job at all. It's the way I think about everything. I can't get away from farming. It's tied up with who I am, the things I think are important. That's hard to explain to other people. I'm not sure I'm explaining it very well right now."

Hockey Coach "When I was a player I wondered what made professional athletes more intense than other people are when it comes to winning or losing. For a while I thought it was just youth. You know, the years will take the edge off. But now that I'm a coach I'm even more resolved to win than I was when I was on the ice. And the thing is, from behind the boards I feel helpless to actually do something to help the team win. So I do what I can, which is to help the guys plan strategy and use the tactics needed against a particular opponent."

Teacher "I taught high school before becoming an elementary teacher. People often ask me whether I consider it a bit of a demotion, especially since I'm a man. But I don't. I feel privileged, in a way, because no one is going to have the kind of formative influence that I have in the classroom every day. I guess it helps that I've got kids who are the same age as my students are, so I feel as if I'm learning things at work that I can apply at home."

Nurse "The thing that really gets to you is the shifts, because some days you feel as if you're just too tired to make another decision. Really critical situations don't happen that often in my ward, but when they do you have to act."

Lawyer "I've been doing this for more than two decades now, and I still find it hard to give people bad news. I do it, but it's hard. You do have to give people bad news, too. You have to tell them they are going to lose custody of their kids. You have to tell them they have no chance of winning a judgment. You have to say to them why don't you forget this whole thing and try to get on with your life. That's hard. When I started my practice I thought being a woman would be an advantage because maybe I could empathize with people. But I think it's just as hard for me as it is for any other lawyer to tell people what they don't want to hear."

These three clusters of skills—attending, following, and reflecting—provide a foundation for active listening. Active listening requires more than just hearing what another person has to say. It requires that you check the speaker's meaning and that you indicate to him or her that you are interested in the message. We have focused so far on specific skills for active listening. If used appropriately, these skills will help you become *reflective* in your interactions with others. In the following section we distinguish a slightly different approach to active listening than the reflective approach. We introduce the notion of dialogic listening.

Walk a Kilometer in My Shoes

Earlier in this chapter, we stated that an important part of a persuasive interview is to consider your audience. We suggested that you need to acknowledge your listener's point of view. For the purposes of learning to listen actively, you must go beyond acknowledging your partner's point of view to empathizing with his or her situation and feelings. Empathy is the capacity for participating in someone else's feelings or ideas. This capacity is difficult to develop for most people. We offer the following suggestions for trying to increase your empathy as a listener.

Let the other person talk. Only by keeping the conversation as a dialogue will you be able to put yourself in your partner's place.

Listen to the whole message. As we will discuss in Chapter 4, nonverbal language is entwined with verbal language. Body language must be considered with oral language. You must listen to the total message the speaker is trying to convey.

Treat your partner as a partner. If you adopt a stance of superiority or paternalism, you will find it difficult to consider matters from the other person's point of view. In an interpersonal situation, you are a person's equal, even if you are his or her boss.

But it is not enough simply to listen empathically. You must communicate your empathy to the people you talk to, so that they know you understand their feelings and situation and so that they will thereby be more likely to engage in meaningful communication with you. In Chapter 4 we will discuss various ways of communicating empathy; these include nonverbal techniques (facial expressions, an attentive body posture, touch and so on) and verbal techniques (such as paraphrases, perception checking, and mirror statements). Self-disclosure, a topic discussed in Chapter 5, can also be used to communicate empathy.

Empathy is the link between active listening and dialogic listening. Even if you are using all the techniques of active listening we have mentioned, you will not become a dialogic listener until you can actually see things from the other person's vantage point. Empathy is what will help you go beyond being an active listener (which is the position of the competent manager) to being a dialogic listener (which represents the attainment of authentic, meaningful, interhuman communication).

Beyond Reflective Listening: Dialogic Listening

"Dialogic listening"[6] is a term introduced by communication authors John Stewart and Milt Thomas to define their conception of active listening. In **dialogic listening**, paraphrases are less focused on reflecting what the speaker has just said, than on sculpting, or otherwise constructing, meanings of mutual interest to both parties. Another way of putting it is that dialogic listening is based on asking the question "What can I accomplish with my partner?"

Stewart and Thomas suggest that there are four ways of distinguishing dialogic listening from other kinds of listening. First, dialogic listening focuses on "ours," rather than on "yours" or "mine." A dialogic listener goes beyond a consideration of what one or the other is saying or seems to mean to what both people are saying or meaning. Second, dialogic listening is open-ended and playful. Because the two parties in a dialogic interaction do not know what the final outcome of their interaction will be, they must express conclusions tentatively and continually try out new conclusions. Third, dialogic listening occurs "in front of" the partners. That is, dialogic listeners focus on what the speaker is saying and feeling, not on what the listener believes the speaker means. Finally, dialogic listening focuses on the present, not on the past. As with the "in front of" distinction, focusing on the present requires the listener to take what the speaker says at face value.

In order to examine how dialogic listening can work, let's consider a conversation between two colleagues in a human resources office of a medium-sized company. Kathy, the manager, has asked Steve, a labor relations officer, to come up with some ideas for improving the atmosphere at the annual negotiations between the company's management and the unionized workers.

Kathy: Hi, Steve. Have you come up with anything specific for this year's negotiations?

Steve: Well, nothing specific, but I've been wondering whether something about the meetings themselves needs to be changed.

Kathy: How do you mean?

Steve: I was talking to the chair of the negotiating committee for the union. He said that he hoped management didn't try to, as he put it, "throw its weight around" this year.

Kathy: Was he specific about what he meant by that? I'm an observer every year, and I thought that both sides were courteous in their negotiations.

Steve: It seemed to be more than just the things that were said and the way they were said.

Kathy: What about our office providing figures a bit more promptly? Perhaps a couple of us could work evenings the week of negotiations.

Steve: I don't think that would help. From what I could understand, it had more to do with the way things were framed. I don't know exactly . . .

Kathy: Well, perhaps I'll let you think about it during your coffee break!

Steve: Coffee might help. Perhaps I'll walk around downtown after lunch. . . . You know, I wonder if a change of venue might be what we need.

Kathy: By all means. Have lunch somewhere else today.

Steve: No, I'm talking about the negotiations. Maybe we've settled into a bit of a rut by having the meetings in the boardroom. It's hardly common ground, after all. And the way management's delegation always seems to stake out the far end of the table . . .

Kathy: I think we ought to give it a try. Why don't you come up with some possibilities this afternoon, along with the costs?

In this interchange, we can consider the four distinguishing characteristics of dialogic listening. First, Kathy kept returning to "ours," rather than remaining concerned with "yours" or "mine," which she might well have done since she was checking on how an employee had carried out an assignment. A dialogic listener goes beyond what one or the other is saying or seems to mean to what both people are saying or meaning. Second, the interchange was open-ended and playful. The two almost broke off the conversation with a light-hearted agreement that Steve should think the matter over further at coffee or lunch. But then they resume the conversation when Steve made a connection between where to eat lunch and where to hold the negotiations. Recall that the two parties in a dialogic interaction do not know what the final outcome of their interaction will be; therefore they must express conclusions tentatively and continually try out new ones. Third, Kathy and Steve seemed to carry on their interaction "in front of" themselves. Steve and Kathy focused on what each was saying rather than dwelling on the fact that Steve had not come up with anything concrete as yet. And finally, they focused on the present, not on the past, both in regard to Steve's assignment and to failures of previous negotiations.

A Checklist for Active Listening

Having learned to practise the skills of active listening—and having become, in the process, a reflective and dialogic listener—you can use the following checklist to see how you're doing. Try using it before and after an interview or conversation.

Try to find the main idea. Active listeners can describe the details of what someone has said and how they have said it. More importantly, however, they can paraphrase the main ideas of a conversation. Most speakers cannot provide a perfectly structured argument that indicates the way all the minor ideas are subsumed in the one or two major ones. Instead, they express the whole thing organically, without apparent focus. Through paraphrasing and probing, determine what the really important ideas are and how they fit with the less important ones.

Keep an open mind. Try to determine the other person's feelings and the meaning he or she is trying to convey, rather than focusing on what is literally said. Certain words and phrases can have an inflammatory effect on people's emotions. Learn what these are for you personally, then try to ensure that you don't let your emotions get the best of you during a conversation. If you manage a budget, for example, don't assume that all requests for assistance are really requests for money. Sometimes, people want advice or encouragement, although they frame it in terms of money for a project. Don't say no right away; instead, try to listen for the underlying message.

Challenge your mind. The more you practise talking about difficult or challenging topics, and the more you listen to others doing the same thing, the better you will get at listening. Like any other skill, listening takes practice. So don't shy away from a good mental workout.

Find common ground. Before you get to the main topic of a conversation or interview, always find a topic of mutual interest. We suggested in the first part of this chapter that you talk about the weather or some other topic of broad interest. You should use your listening skills to try to find clues about what interests the other person and then focus on something that you can both talk about. This will make it easier for you to engage in dialogic listening.

Work at it. Pay close attention to the verbal and nonverbal signals that the speaker is conveying. Remember to attend, follow, and reflect. With each interpersonal interchange, try to ensure that you are not just feigning interest but that you are genuinely trying to improve your ability to take an interest in what other people are saying.

Avoid distractions. We have said that it is best to keep distractions to a minimum by preparing for the interview. However, when distractions do intrude, try not to let them affect your performance in listening. Use self-discipline and concentration to let the speaker know that his or her message is too important to be interrupted by a minor annoyance.

Use the speed of thought to your advantage. We can think much faster than we can speak. That fact was the basis for our suggestion that you silently paraphrase as a way to keep track of the speaker's meaning and to practise for spoken paraphrasing. But you can use the speed of thought, as well, to "tune out" occasionally from the speaker's words so that you can reflect on what he or she has already said or plan how you will respond to a message. An active listener will silently assess a message and try to respond in a way that will help both parties get more out of the conversation.

Bend a little. Don't hold the speaker to something he or she said a moment ago. Perhaps he or she has been persuaded by something you said or has simply had a change of heart. Summarize occasionally in your mind, or on paper, but don't use your summaries as a means of making the conversation overly rigid.

Judge the message, not the delivery. Most of us have some kind of fault in our oratory. We may blink, stammer, or say "uh" too much. Active listeners do not judge the speaker by such faults. Instead, they try to respond with empathy to the underlying message.

Wait a while. Sometimes the message takes longer to find expression than either of you would prefer. Allow the speaker the luxury of meandering a bit in order to find the right word or phrase and to let him or her know that you are more interested in discerning the message than in running an efficient meeting. Only when you feel that the speaker has had his or her say should you make a counterpoint.

And finally . . .

We have discussed several techniques for improving listening. However, keep in mind that, more than anything else, openness and authenticity are vital to the establishment of successful communication in the workplace. As we will see in the clinic in the next chapter, the skills we have discussed can become even more useful when combined with the effective use of verbal and nonverbal language.

CHAPTER REVIEW QUESTIONS

1. On what occasions might you use a persuasive interview?
2. Suppose you are the manager of a retail outlet that sells office supplies. You are going to meet with a supplier of office furniture whose deliveries have been unreliable. You are considering switching suppliers. How would you state your purpose at the beginning of the meeting?
3. Why is a combined approach recommended as an interviewing strategy?
4. Of the types of questions discussed in this chapter, which is most commonly used in the media interview?
5. Which type of question is almost never recommended for use in interviews?
6. When might a diamond question sequence be used?
7. Why is "climate control" important in an interview?
8. Why should an interviewer avoid spending too much time on the opening stage of an interview?

9. What are some of the words that might be used to allow for transitions in an interview?

10. What sequence of questions might be used to counter a reluctant respondent?
   a. pyramid
   b. stacked funnel
   c. tube or tunnel
   d. diamond

11. What are the five steps for structuring a persuasive interview?

12. What are the three clusters of skills required for *reflective listening*?
   a. attending, taking notes, reflecting
   b. reflective, dialogic, paraphrase
   c. attending, following, reflecting
   d. following, reflecting, taking notes

13. An effective reflecting device is:
   a. notetaking
   b. the mirror exercise
   c. proxemics
   d. paraphrasing

14. What are the two essential components of a paraphrase statement?

15. A paraphrase has the dual purpose of _____ information and asking for _____ information.
   a. reviewing; reinforced
   b. providing; more
   c. reviewing; detailed
   d. detailing; previous

16. Which is the best step for a listener to carry out after attaining empathy?
   a. empathy reinforcement
   b. communicating empathy
   c. repetition of empathy
   d. variation of empathy

17. What are the five characteristics of dialogic listening?

18. Discuss the relationships among reflective listening, dialogic listening, and active listening.

19. One of the suggestions on the checklist for active listening is to "use the speed of thought to your advantage." Discuss this recommendation.

20. The following are all recommendations offered for active listening *except*:
   a. Try to find the main idea.
   b. Keep a learning log.
   c. Keep an open mind.
   d. Avoid distractions.

21. One of the recommendations for active listening is to *Judge the message, not the* _____.

SUGGESTED ANSWERS

1. For proposals, presentations, or negotiations.

2. "We've had a long business relationship, but I don't want to encounter delays and missed shipments anymore. My customers count on me. I would like to solve this problem today."

3. In an interview with a combined approach, there is enough structure that both parties feel something has been accomplished but enough freedom to allow for both to express themselves freely and influence the direction of the interview.

4. prefaced probe

5. loaded question

6. For a situation in which the topic is sensitive, controversial, or difficult for one or both of the partners.

7. Climate control is important because people's needs are being met increasingly through the use of institutions and mass communication. The interview, on the other hand, brings human interaction and the meeting of needs to the level of one-on-one, a level at which needs are usually best met. By controlling the climate for such an interaction, you will be reinforcing the message that you hope your partner will be receiving: that you are hoping for a meaningful and free exchange of information and opinion, not an elicitation of responses. If the physical surroundings of the interview, along with the subsequent verbal and nonverbal cues of the interview itself, have been considered with regard for human needs, the chances increase that the interview will follow the course of meeting human needs.

8. Delaying the business at hand may cause the respondent to become anxious.

9. now
next
so
another
second
finally
also

10. a.

11. 1. State the issue.

2. State your point of view, with evidence.

3. Acknowledge your opponent's point of view and its merits.

4. State the shortcomings of your opponent's point of view.

5. Resolve the issue by restating your point of view, while incorporating any qualifications introduced by the opponent's arguments.

12. c.

13. d.

14. A paraphrase statement is a tentative interpretation of the other person's message, and it is a request for verification or revision of that interpretation.

15. b.

16. c.

17. Focus on "ours," rather than on "yours" or "mine."

Open-ended and playful.
"In front of" the listeners.
Focus on what the other is saying.
Focus on the present.

18. Active listening is the broader category in which reflective listening and dialogic listening are contained, since active listening requires all communication skills. Reflective listening skills allow a listener to check on the speaker's meaning and to indicate interest and empathy. Dialogic listening calls for not only empathy but mutual meaning-making.

19. We can think much faster than we can speak. You can use the speed of thought to "tune out" occasionally from the speaker's words so that you can reflect on what he or she has already said or plan how you will respond to a message. An active listener will silently assess a message and try to respond in a way that will help both parties get more out of the conversation.

20. b.

21. delivery

INTERPERSONAL COMMUNICATION SCENARIO

THORNLEA CITY COLLEGE

OVERVIEW AND ASSIGNMENT QUESTIONS

In the following scenario, which is based on a situation that could well occur in an organization, you will have the opportunity to apply the principles and skills you have learned in this chapter. The scenario can be used as the basis for a written or oral analysis or for role-play.

Ingrid Dawson, a supervisor, must deal with requests by a part-time employee, Christine Chartrand, for changes in the work schedule. The changes that have been made to date, on Christine's request, have caused annoyance among workers in the unit and are starting to disrupt work activities.

1. Assume you are Ingrid Dawson. Prepare an interview guide for dealing with Christine Chartrand face-to-face.
2. Determine exactly what you hope to accomplish and what compliance you are seeking.
3. Plan the opening, body, and closing of the interview.
4. Identify the kinds of questions you intend to ask and the sequence structure.

INTRODUCTION

It is Tuesday morning. Ingrid Dawson, head of Library Services at Thornlea City College, has just completed a terse, tension-filled telephone conversation with a member of her support staff, Christine Chartrand. Chartrand has called from home to say she will not be coming in to work the last two days of the week. Chartrand, who has worked part-time for both Library Services *and* the College's Department of Staff Development, says she will be working at home to finish typing a lengthy report for the director of Staff Development.

Dawson is becoming increasingly concerned with Chartrand's changes to her work schedule. The changes suit Chartrand's personal needs and the priorities of the Department of Staff Development. This is causing scheduling problems and dissatisfaction within Library Services, and Dawson is beginning to sense displeasure from her other support staff. She knows that she will have to discuss the problem with Chartrand face-to-face, not over the phone. She decides she must develop an interview guide and strategy for dealing effectively with the situation before it develops into a significant problem.

LIBRARY SERVICES

Thornlea City College is a relatively small college (4 000 students, 120 faculty, 200 staff), with only two full-time people (in addition to Dawson) in Library Services, plus two part-time support staff—Christine Chartrand and Michel Prost. Chartrand and Prost's support roles consist mainly of managing the library's collection of books, journals, films, and videotapes, as well as the audio-visual equipment used to run them. They are also responsible for coordinating bookings of equipment, materials, and viewing rooms for faculty and students. Bookings have to be made with care, since most resources are in short supply and often in high demand.

Both Chartrand and Prost work 20 hours per week—checking materials and equipment, arranging bookings, and sometimes assisting with AV presentations. In arranging the work schedule for the unit, Dawson has to ensure that at least one person is available to take bookings.

DEPARTMENT OF STAFF DEVELOPMENT

In addition to her part-time work in Library Services, Christine Chartrand also works 20 hours per week in the Department of Staff Development, but her reporting relationship is to Ingrid Dawson, who is responsible for supervising her.

Chartrand's role in Staff Development differs from the one she has in Library Services. In Staff Development she acts as part-time secretary to the director—typing reports, letters, and memoranda as required. Even when she is working in Staff Development, however, she can be called to assist with library matters, if that unit becomes unusually busy. Library Services has priority because client needs are usually more urgent. Staff Development services performed by Chartrand are primarily clerical and can be completed as time permits.

CHRISTINE CHARTRAND AND MICHEL PROST

Christine Chartrand has worked at Thornlea City College for some five years. Until the birth of her first child, two years earlier, she had been a full-time employee in the Department of Staff Development. After her son was born, she took a six-month leave of absence, and returned to work part-time in that department. In the past six months, she has increased her work load to include 20 hours per week in Library Services. Accustomed to flexible working hours in Staff Development, Chartrand has requested—and received approval from Dawson for—10 changes to her schedule since joining Library Services.

Initially, Chartrand's changes caused little concern for Michel Prost. Lately, however, Prost, who joined Thornlea's staff a year ago, has been reacting to the frequency of schedule changes with increasing signs of displeasure—although he has yet to complain directly to Dawson. This time, when Dawson informs Prost that Chartrand will not be coming in for the rest of the week, he does not respond with any statements of discontent, but Dawson senses disapproval in Prost's facial expression. Dawson decides not to pursue the matter with Prost at this time. However, it is obvious to Dawson that unless the situation improves, relations in the unit will deteriorate.

CLIMATE CONTROL

Ingrid Dawson feels it is time to plan an interview with Chartrand and the rest of her staff, including Prost, and to determine what approach to take to the growing difficulty. As she thinks it over, she wonders if she should meet with Chartrand and Prost separately, together, or both. She also considers the following questions:

Who should she speak with first?

What should she try and find out?

How structured should the interviews be?

Where should they be held and when?

What questions should she ask?

What propositions should she put forth?

What should the structure and sequence of her interview guides be?

POINTS TO CONSIDER

Assuming that Dawson and Chartrand have different orientations to their jobs—for Dawson, the job is the top priority in her life, while for Chartrand it is not—consider whether or not Dawson has the right to impose her own values on Chartrand, and whether or not this consideration should figure in Dawson's interview strategy.

● — ● — ● — ● — ● — ● — ● — ● — ● — ● — ● — ● — ●

ENDNOTES

1 From Paul McLaughlin, *How to Interview: The Art of the Media Interview* (Vancouver: International Self-Counsel Press Ltd., 1990), p. 126.

2   From Marco Adria,"Radio Days,"*Aurora* magazine 11, no. 2 (Winter 1987-88), p. 4.

3   Paul Rankin, "Listening Ability," in *Proceedings of the Ohio State Educational Conference's Ninth Annual Session*, 1929.

4   L. Barker, R. Edwards, C. Gaines, K. Gladney, and F. Holley, "An Investigation of Proportional Time Spent in Various Communication Activities by College Students," in *Journal of Applied Communication Research* 8 (1981). pp. 101-09.

5   Robert Bolton, *People Skills* (Simon & Schuster, Inc., 1979). Used by permission of Simon & Schuster.

6   John Stewart and Milt Thomas, "Dialogic Listening: Sculpting Mutual Meanings," in *Bridges Not Walls: A Book About Interpersonal Communication*, edited by John Stewart (New York: Random House, 1986).

CHAPTER 4

The Language of Employment Interviews

for Management ◆ Understanding Proxemics ◆ *Interpersonal Skills Clinic: Imagining an Office* ◆ Intercultural Communication ◆ Looking at Others ◆ *Interpersonal Skills Clinic: The Yearbook* ◆ And finally . . .

Chapter Review Questions

Interpersonal Communication Scenario: Ellis-McCraig Co. Ltd.

● ― ● ― ● ― ● ― ● ― ● ― ● ― ● ― ● ― ● ― ●

WORTH REPEATING

Competence, like truth, beauty and contact lenses, is in the eye of the beholder.

—Laurence J. Peter and Raymond Hull

Their little interview was like a picnic on a coral strand; they passed each other with melancholy smiles and looks sufficiently allusive, such cupfuls of water as they had saved.

—Henry James

One forgets words as one forgets names. One's vocabulary needs constant fertilization.

—Evelyn Waugh

Section 1 Employment Interviews

Before we get started . . .

We have suggested that one of the most important skills a manager can exercise is to listen and communicate effectively. This skill is particularly critical for performing the managerial responsibility of finding qualified and productive employees. This task is accomplished by conducting employment interviews. Degrees and previous positions held, along with other formal qualifications, are important factors in the hiring decision, but the recruitment process also calls for direct, interpersonal contact. Only the face-to-face interview can finalize the decision to offer a position to a candidate.

Along with the recruitment interview, we include three other interview types under the category of the employment interview. After an employee is hired, he or she must be oriented to a new working environment. This calls for an orientation interview, in which the employee will experience those important first impressions of working in the organization. The new employee will also need to gather information about his or her new job, about the organization, and about the tasks to be accomplished. This will require the use of information interviews. Our discussion of the information interview will be applicable to many workplace situations, from the press conference to the research proposal. The fourth type of employment interview, the disciplinary interview, requires the most forethought and sensitivity—we discuss it separately in Section 2.

As we claimed in Chapter 3, all interviews call for a plan. The employment interviews from which both the organization and the prospective employee benefit most are structured sessions in which thought has been given to the goals of the interview. We consider employment interviews—recruitment, orientation, information, or disciplinary—to be important elements of the process by which an organization reaches its goals.

Objectives

After you complete this section, you should be able to:

1. List and discuss the six steps of recruiting.
2. Describe a strategy for structuring a recruitment interview, using an opening, body, and closing.
3. List at least three interview formats that are alternatives to the traditional recruitment interview.
4. State why an interview should be evaluated after it has taken place and how this may be done.
5. Discuss some guidelines for being an interviewee for a recruitment interview.
6. Discuss the importance and use of the orientation interview.
7. State the four formats for an information interview.
8. Discuss the five points of a strategy for carrying out an information interview.
9. List 10 guidelines for an information interview.

The First Step of Recruiting: Write It Out

For a manager, the first step in the recruitment process is to create a job description for the position to be filled.

A job description should be more than simply a list of duties and responsibilities. The main points to be included are the title of the job, a description of the main function or role of the position, and a description of duties and responsibilities. The relative importance of each duty and responsibility should be stated. We suggest that the job description should be made available to all candidates who are invited to an interview. It should also be distributed to those who are part of the search process.

The second step for the manager is to determine the qualifications needed for the job. These should not be so unrealistically high that it becomes all but impossible to find a qualified candidate. Among the qualifications you should consider are education (including non-credit or informal education), work experience (including volunteer and community work), knowledge and abilities, and quality of contact with others, all of which will be indicated in the résumé, during the interview, and through reference checks. The information you look for when reviewing candidates' qualifications should correspond with the requirements of the organization and those of your department or unit. The requirement of a college degree, for example, should be directly related to some aspect of the nature of the position. Be prepared to show that the requirement is related to the job and that it will help you predict success on the job.

A caution. Some organizations now have formal hiring guidelines that are designed to increase the representation of certain segments of society in the workforce. For example, an organization may try to increase the female proportion of its professional workforce, or it may wish to encourage members of native or minority groups to apply for positions. Early in the recruiting process, you will have to determine whether your organization has such guidelines. If so, you must then decide how these guidelines might affect the position description and the qualifications required, and how the announcement of the job (including the wording of the advertising) will need to reflect the guidelines. Carried out with creativity, the process of adhering to your organization's employment guidelines can be exciting and rewarding. It will mean that you are contributing directly to the development of a society in which a wider spectrum of the population is encouraged to participate fully.

Even if you find that your organization has no guidelines for hiring representatives of certain groups, you may still wish to review the position description, the required qualifications, and the advertising to be sure that none of it discriminates. Ask yourself if these components are fair. Do they seem to favor one group over another, perhaps inadvertently? If they do, try to change them to make it clear that all qualified applicants will be considered equitably. (Of course, such a change would have to be cleared with your human resources department and with anyone else affected.) For example, if the required qualifications include a reference to "five years of full-time experience," you may be excluding a large number of women who have worked part-time in order to raise children. Are five years of full-time experience necessary? Why not ask, instead, for a combination of relevant part-time and full-time experience adding up to five years?

The Second Step: Get the Word Out

The announcement of a position through advertising is usually the first an applicant learns about the position. He or she may also be learning about your organization for the first time. The announcement should therefore be clear, concise, and accurate. It sets the tone for what comes after: the interview and, for at least one applicant, the beginning of a new job.

Recruitment is essentially a *matching process*, in which the job requirements are matched with the right man or woman to accomplish them. When looking for potential applicants, there are a number of sources you should consider, your choices of which will determine where you advertise. However, the obvious place to look first is within your own organization. Many staff development consultants recommend you "grow your own" candidates. In fact, some organizations have made it part of their human resources policy to promote from within their own ranks whenever possible. Such a policy lets employees know that they do indeed have opportunities for personal and career growth with the organization.

You may also be able to help your organization reach its goal of increasing the representation of certain groups by holding an internal competition first. As a manager, you know better than others what skills and abilities members of the organization have. The employment search process, along with the subsequent interviews, is an ideal opportunity to help these members achieve their personal and workplace goals. Even if the candidates in an internal competition turn out not to be suitable for the position you are seeking to fill, you can use the process to help you and the candidate determine future development opportunities. The benefit to the organization is obvious; a worker who knows that his or her needs are being considered, during employment searches and at other times, will be more likely to seek out opportunities to contribute to the organization's goals.

If you decide to search outside the organization for candidates, perhaps after exhausting the possibilities within the organization, you may wish to consider advertising in media such as newspapers, professional journals, or trade association newsletters. You should advertise in media that are likely to reach all qualified applicants.

Again, if you want to ensure that you are not discriminating against anyone, you may wish to consider altering the advertisement. Are references from previous employers essential to the selection process? If not, perhaps personal references would be satisfactory. If personal references are accepted, people who have not worked recently will have a chance to apply.

The ad should be clear about the position and about the qualifications required for an applicant. Use the following checklist to draft or revise the advertisement.

Have we stated whether this is an internal or external competition?

Are we asking for a résumé or curriculum vitae?

Are applicants to send us the names of referees, or are reference letters to be sent directly to the organization?

Are the mailing address and name of the contact person accurately stated?

Do we want to include a telephone number for inquiries about the position?

Have we included an application deadline date?

The Third Step: Take a Good Look—Résumés

The résumé is the first opportunity that you have to assess the applicants' written presentation of their skills and experience. You will offer an interview to one or more of these applicants based on this presentation, but you will have to wait until the interview to confirm the impressions you got from reading the résumés. Because the résumé is normally the first point of communication initiated by the prospective employee towards the organization, it's not surprising that readers of a résumé look for signals about how successfully the applicant would function in the organization. But résumés must be handled with care. You should read the résumé sensitively and avoid making hasty generalizations or assumptions. A résumé says a lot about a candidate, but it doesn't say everything and it cannot substitute for a personal encounter. It nonetheless remains the most widely used tool for screening prospective employees.

We suggest that the main thing to be sensitive to when you're screening résumés are signs, which may be hidden, that indicate the qualities or special abilities you are seeking. You need to learn to read between the lines to see what the résumé tells you about the candidate's past performance and about his or her stability and career direction. In this regard, be careful how you interpret the patterns. Some personnel specialists automatically eliminate all candidates who have changed jobs frequently over the past several years. Others, such as Robert Half, say that this approach might not be the best one. He says that if people have been hired so often:

> **66** there must be something attractive about them. I know one sales manager who deliberately seeks out such people. He figures that anybody who is good enough to repeatedly sell himself or herself at an interview has good sales potential.[1] **99**

Try to discern patterns among the statements the résumé makes with regard to increases in sales, profits, or productivity. Are they specific enough? You'll be able to explore such matters in more depth during the interview.

In summary, remember that although résumés are the most widely used tool for screening prospective employees, they do have limitations. In reading a résumé and, to a lesser extent, the covering letter or letter of application, do not expect to learn everything about a candidate, but try to look for answers to the following five basic questions.

1. Does the applicant have the basic qualifications and credentials to do the job? (Keep in mind that some candidates may have *equivalencies* to the qualifications you've listed, such as a combination of university or college courses and relevant job experience instead of a university degree).

2. Does the applicant have superior experience or training that makes the application stronger than others?

3. Does the applicant seem to possess personal qualities that may make him or her a reliable, long-term employee?

4. Is the applicant good at what he or she does? (How is this indicated?)

5. Does the applicant seem to know what he or she wants?

If you have read a lot of résumés in your career, you will know that most résumés transmit adequate information about the first two or three questions. Not many, on the other hand, answer the fourth and fifth questions.

A caution. The physical appearance of a résumé (the format) may be important, depending on the position. If, for example, the position calls for the production of a large number of documents—or simply for accurate typing—the appearance of the résumé may be a consideration in the screening process. For some competitions in the book publishing industry, for example, résumés or covering letters with even one typo are routinely and immediately rejected. However, there may be cases where you feel that there is something about the candidate that needs further investigation, even though the résumé is not refined in appearance or organization. Why not keep such a résumé in the "maybe" pile? That way, you will be providing a balance for the applications that are heavier on style than on substance. The screening interview, which comprises the next stage of the search, will help you decide whether your hunch was worth acting on.

The Fourth Step: Screen

This is the stage at which you separate those applicants who warrant closer inspection from those who are clearly unsuited for the job. Your organization may have a representative from the human resources department (if you have one) who will help you carry out this process. The goal of this stage is to end up with two piles of applications: the "interviews" and the "no interviews." However, while you are going through the process of deciding, you should have three groups of applicants: the "definites," the "possibles," and the "unqualifieds." At the end of this process you will move the possibles to one of the two final groups. Go through the possibles a second time and choose at least one or two to interview. This extra step will test your objectivity and help you determine the validity of your criteria. You may find that the possibles are turning out stronger than your definites; if that is the case, perhaps it's time to rethink your criteria.

In Chapter 3 we discussed two types of interview formats or styles that can be used in management interviews: directive and nondirective (structured and unstructured). Most human resources department interviewers use a directive interview for screening initial applicants. The interviewer follows a pattern based on a set list of questions. The interviewer may even use a checklist, which can be annotated with remarks about the candidate's responses. While this is a good method of comparing the qualifications of several applicants, it is, not surprisingly, too impersonal for the purpose of discovering the personality of individual candidates.

You or your human resources department may prefer to use a nondirective interview. This can be semi-structured to accomplish a fair comparison, but because nondirective questions are more general than directive ones, applicants are encouraged to talk more freely and openly about themselves and their qualifications. As a result, of course, the process takes more time, and it requires an interviewer with highly developed interviewing skills.

As we will discuss further in the section on information interviews, all interviews, including recruitment interviews, must be planned, even if they are nondirective. That is, even if you want to let the candidate determine much of the direction for an interview, you must consider the purpose of the interview ahead of time and draft questions and topics for reference during the interview.

The Fifth Step: Check Them Out

Reference checks are used to verify the accuracy of the information provided on the application or résumé and, in some cases, to get more information about the applicant. Usually, you will be asking for work-related references and contacting previous employers. However, in some cases personal references may be appropriate. These may help you to attract applications from some women, who, perhaps because of their situation, do not have formal work references (they may have worked extensively as volunteers) or from younger applicants who have little or no previous work experience.

As you check references, one slightly negative reference should not outweigh two or three positive ones. Consider all the information accumulated during your reference checks. When you decide whether or not to pursue an application further, the information you gathered during the reference checks can be helpful. Similarly, a strongly negative reference may be a signal that you should investigate the applicant more thoroughly.

Some organizations take a formal approach to references. Academic institutions, for example, often call for all applicants to have two or three referees submit letters directly to the institution. Other organizations treat references as an auxiliary process to be completed after most of the hiring process has already taken place. Most often, reference-checking is not done until the organization is relatively certain that a candidate is worth serious consideration for the job. You may even want to check references just before a formal offer of employment is offered.

The Sixth Step: Face-to-Face

We believe that the recruitment interview is the most vital component of the entire selection process. It provides the interviewee with an indication of what the culture of the organization is like. The recruitment interview allows both the employer and the applicant to obtain information, form impressions, and make observations that would not be possible through other means. The recruitment interview is meant to accomplish the following:

1. To allow the interviewer to gather enough information about the candidate to determine if the he or she is qualified and suitable for the position in question.
2. To inform the applicant about the organization and the particular job so that he or she can make a decision as to whether he or she would accept a job offer, if such an offer were made.
3. To create and maintain goodwill towards the organization from the applicant.

The recruitment interview is usually the first occasion employers have to discover the personal attributes of candidates. Communication skills are often cited by employers as being the main personal characteristics they look for during job competitions. Other important attributes include the following:

Sociability:	whether or not the candidate seems to be able to work well on a team and whether he or she appears to like people.
Maturity:	whether the candidate demonstrates that he or she can think clearly and exercise sound judgment.
Technical ability:	whether the candidate is familiar with recent developments in the field, with the language of those who work in the field, and with new or emerging approaches in the field.
Creativity:	whether the candidate shows flair and insight during the interview, especially with regard to issues directly connected with the job.
Appearance:	whether the candidate presents an image that is consistent with the organization's mission and image.
Poise and confidence:	whether the candidate seems to be comfortable and self-assured.

Before we move on to an examination of the structure the interview is likely to take, we should emphasize the importance we attach to the recruitment interview and its role in the culture and communication structure of the organization. We believe that the recruitment interview—as well as two other types of employment interview; orientation and information interviews—is an opportunity for helping the organization reach its goals through authentic communication among its members. The importance of the event is evident from the fact that many people can remember in great detail the experience of each recruitment interview of their careers. The process of matching that should occur during the recruitment interview sets the tone for each member's role in the culture of the organization. That culture, in turn, helps determine the organization's effectiveness and its potential for offering members the opportunity to achieve personal goals.

Structuring the Recruitment Interview: The Opening

As a representative of the employer, you should take the lead in managing the interview. Part of this responsibility is to see that potential distractions (such as telephone calls or unexpected visitors) have been eliminated. In Chapter 3 we discussed how the comfort and atmosphere surrounding the interview can have a great impact on the outcome of the process.

According to an informal poll of a few Toronto-area human resources executives, most interviewers' decisions do not change after the first four or five minutes of the interview. What are the implications of this fact for the interviewer and the candidate? For the interviewer, this means that the opening questions are the most crucial ones. After these, all other questions are likely to follow from the impression made while listening to the response to those first few questions. The implication of this is that the applicant will be considered a good candidate if he or she is characterized more by the absence of unfavorable characteristics (such as poor eye contact or sloppy appearance) than by the presence of favorable ones. Furthermore, the sooner the unfavorable information or impressions appear, the more potential for a negative outcome for the candidate.

The initial impressions that both participants gain is thus important in a recruitment interview. We suggest that you gain rapport quickly. Of course, you should be courteous, expressing sincere interest in the applicant. Your appearance, conduct, and attitude will influence the applicant just as much as his or her appearance and behavior will influence you. If candidates are made to feel comfortable, they will perform at their best in the interview. That, in turn, will make your task more pleasant and more productive.

After you have exchanged pleasantries, you should make a short statement about the position. The candidate will want to learn as much as possible about the organization and about the position for which he or she has applied. It is your responsibility to ensure that the applicant knows the specifics of the job and the relevant details about the organization and its environment. At this point, describe the job in general terms, perhaps providing a copy of the job description for the candidate's reference during the interview. When you feel that you have gained rapport and that both of you agree on the purpose and format of the interview, you can proceed to the next stage.

Structuring the Recruitment Interview: The Body

While you may have carried out the opening of the interview without reference to notes or a written plan (even though you will have prepared one), you will need to refer to your notes and lists of questions for carrying out the next stage, the body. We provide a sample of several lists of questions you might ask, in addition to a list of questions the applicant might ask you. We encourage you to revise and add to these lists to suit your purposes. First, however, we provide a brief description of a recommended sequence for your questions.

The *funnel sequence* (which we introduced in Chapter 3) is especially valuable for use in a recruitment interview, since it allows the candidate to respond with longer answers to open questions and provide more information in response to secondary or probe questions. Unless necessary, try to avoid asking closed questions, since they do not reveal much about the applicant's abilities in self-expression. Also, avoid leading questions (questions that suggest the "right"answer to the astute applicant) and questions that have already been answered in the résumé. Instead, use questions that focus attention on the applicant's experience and education, and open-ended questions that delve into bona fide occupational qualifications. Hypothetical questions such as the following are also useful:

> Suppose you are the manager of a development team in our organization. What would you do if . . .

When you respond to answers from the candidate, listen carefully to each answer and probe for details and explanations. Give the applicant time to answer each question, and rephrase questions if the applicant seems confused or unable to respond. Try to avoid evaluative responses (either verbal or nonverbal) to answers that reveal how you feel about what the candidate is saying. You may wish, however, to keep notes of your impressions of the candidate's responses to your questions. (As we discussed in the section on notetaking, be discreet. Most people are at least a little apprehensive about someone taking notes during an interview.)

Try to be patient when, having posed a question, you are waiting for a response. It is usually not in either party's interest to have the respondent mention the first answer that comes to mind. If you have asked the person for the accomplishment of which they are most proud, give him or her a moment to decide which to discuss. Patience will ensure better hiring choices.

The following are sample questions you might ask the applicant (including, at the end, a list of questions the applicant might ask you), presented under relevant headings.

The Candidate's Education, Training, and Upgrading

Which courses or subject areas provided the most challenge or enjoyment in university, college, or high school?

Which courses or subject areas did you like least?

Describe the most enjoyable experience you had in university, college, or high school.

Why did you choose the educational program you did?

Would you change your choice of educational program if you could?

Has your education or training helped you prepare for the job for which you applied to our organization? If so, how?

The Candidate's Career

What made you embark on the career you have chosen?

Of all the jobs you have held in your career, which one do you regard with the most pride or sense of satisfaction?

Which job do you regard with frustration or disappointment?

How would you describe your career to this point?

How has your career prepared you for the position for which you have applied?

Describe the supervisors you have had in your career and what kind of supervision they provided for you.

What would be the characteristics of your ideal supervisor?

If colleagues you have worked with in your career were here today, how might they comment on your strengths and weaknesses?

Which kind of colleagues do you enjoy working with best?

How would the job for which you have applied with us fit into the development of your career?

Describe your ideal organization.

The Candidate's Field

What are the trends and challenges in your field today?

In the next 10 years, which areas of your field do you think will expand?

What is the greatest challenge facing people working in your field today?

What might be the next important development in your field?

Describe briefly the history of your field.

What is the best way of keeping abreast of the developments in your field?

Is keeping abreast of developments in your field a difficult or time-consuming process?

What kind of professional or technical reading do you do?

The Candidate's Present and Previous Jobs

Most jobs have their positive points and their negative aspects, from the perspective of the incumbents. What are the positive and negative aspects of your job?

How would you describe the progress you have made with your present organization?

What do you find difficult to do in your present job?

What have you done about the problems you have encountered in your present job?

What have you spent most of your time doing in your present job?

What do you find most interesting about your present job?

What tasks have you completed most successfully?

Have you been recognized formally or informally for your job accomplishments?

Why would you want to leave your present job?

What else can you tell us about the job you hold now?

Will you comment on the general impression you have of the last organization for which you worked?

What have you learned in your present job and in your previous job?

Have you done anything creative in your present or previous job?

Why did you leave your previous job?

The Candidate's Interest in the Organization

Why did you apply for this position?

Why would you like to work for our organization?

Do you know much about our organization's history and its products or services?

Have you ever dealt with our organization as a client or customer?

If you have been a client or customer, how did you regard the organization's performance in providing you with our product or service?

If you were to be offered a position with our organization, how might you improve on the product or service we offer?

Would you accept travel or relocation as a part of a job with our organization?

The Candidate's Performance on the Job

What are your strengths and weaknesses with regard to performance?

In your field, what are the most important criteria for evaluating performance?

How does your employer appraise your performance?

How did you do in your last evaluation?

In what areas were you asked to improve your performance during your last appraisal?

How do you respond to the constructive criticism?

Do you offer such criticism to colleagues and subordinates?

The Candidate's Interpersonal Skills

With what kinds of people do you work well?

With what kinds of people do you not work well?

What were the greatest strengths and weaknesses of your previous supervisor?

Did you ever disagree significantly with him or her?

Were you able to resolve this disagreement? Why or why not? If so, how did you do it?

How do you usually deal with people with whom you disagree or with whom you find it difficult to work?

The Candidate's Plans and Goals

What position would you like to hold in five or 10 years?

Describe your long-term career goals, if you have any.

When do you want to retire?

Are you preparing yourself for advancement? If so, how?

When you consider your education and career, who influenced you most as you decided on your career plans?

In your field, what is the most important factor for ensuring career success or satisfaction?

Do you have plans to continue your education? If you do, how do you intend to carry them out?

Some Questions the Candidate May Ask

Have you had many applications for this position?
Can you tell me more about the position I would be entering?

Does the organization offer programs that consider the employee's personal and family needs? For example, does it offer flex-time, working at home, paternity leave, job-sharing?

With what kind of people would I be working if I took on this job?

Describe your ideal employee.

What have you liked most about working for this organization?

Does your organization encourage innovation? If so, how? If not, why not?

Would I have to undergo any training if I took on this job?

What is the procedure used by your organization to evaluate or appraise employee performance?

How often, on average, are employees promoted in this organization?

Where have people entering this position previously ended up in the organizational hierarchy?

Does your organization offer support to employees who want to go back to school, say for an undergraduate or graduate degree?

Is the support in the form of financial assistance? time off?

How might an advanced degree affect my position in your organization?

Could I expect a raise in pay or a promotion if I completed a mutually agreed-upon program of education or training?

What kind of supervision would I expect as an employee?

Which organization provides the stiffest competition for your organization?

When may I expect to hear from you concerning whether I will be offered the position?

Optional Exercises and Formats for the Recruitment Interview

We have described the most common form of recruitment interview, with someone asking questions and someone answering questions. You may wish to try something different. Stress interviews, for example, can be used to determine how a candidate will handle stress on the job. In such an interview, questions are asked in a context and manner that requires the candidate to show how he or she performs under pressure. The stress interview can be used instead of or in addition to the conventional recruitment interview. With the group interview, many applicants are interviewed at the same time. In the board interview, one applicant is interviewed by several interviewers.

As an example of how one of these alternatives can be set up, let's consider a form of the stress interview, called the in-basket exercise. This technique is used to test the candidate's ability to make quick decisions when encountering new and unfamiliar situations. You might present the following to the candidate: faxes, hand-written (perhaps illegible) notes, reports, proposals, memoranda, advertisements, telephone message slips, letters, and electronic mail. You would then describe to the candidate a scenario, such as the one that follows:

You are a salesperson for an office machine company and you have just been appointed the director of sales promotions. The manager you have succeeded was sent to prison on fraud charges, and a great many important details are unresolved. It is Monday morning, and you find the attached materials in your in-basket. What are you going to do for the first half hour?

As the candidate works through the material in the in-basket (you can present everything at once or pass items one at a time), he or she must justify a decision or action at each stage. Alternately, you may wish to wait until the candidate has completed the half hour of decisions before a discussion takes place in which he or she defends or explains the actions taken.

When you are deciding what kind of interview format will be the most suitable, keep in mind that the best interview format is the one that simulates the conditions of the job best. Such a situation will help you (and the prospective employee) decide whether a match exists between the candidate and the organization. For example, in a job that requires the employee to deal with many members of the public on a given day, perhaps the board format would be appropriate. On the other hand, for a job whose main requirement is initiative and independent action, you may want to try the in-basket exercise as part of a series of screening tests. Whatever the format, try to ensure that the applicant has an opportunity to observe how the organization operates and that he or she is able to offer comments and ask questions.

Structuring the Recruitment Interview: The Closing

During an employment interview most people want to know where they stand. If you will be making a decision soon, tell the candidate. Similarly, if you will not be able to make a decision in the next week or so, tell the candidate. People are grateful if you are direct and candid about such matters. Candor, in turn, contributes to authentic communication.

When it is time to bring the interview to a conclusion, your task will be to outline what steps will follow. If you have reached a decision during the interview as to whether you will extend an offer of employment, and if you have the power to do so, you may choose to inform the candidate of your decision. If you haven't, you should tell the applicant what will happen next. Tell him or her when a decision on the position will be made and when to expect to be contacted. By following through on this commitment you will help to fulfill the recruitment interview goal of maintaining a positive image for the organization. It will also confirm the sincerity of your interest in the candidate and your gratitude to him or her for applying. Finally, you will want to signal to the candidate that the interview is coming to a close and that now is the time to ask any outstanding questions he or she may have about the position or about the organization. At this point, pay particular attention to the applicant's behavior, since it may reveal how he or she feels the interview went.

After the Interview

Record your impressions of the interview after it is over. This will help you to make comparisons among the candidates later and, eventually, to make a decision. You may also find it helpful to record your impressions of the applicant. To aid you in this process, your organization may provide you with a standardized evaluation form that includes such categories as the following: the candidate's motivation, interpersonal skills, and self-confidence; his or her interest in the job and in the organization; the knowledge he or she demonstrated of the organization, the job, and the relevant field; and his or her experience, achievements, and goals.

An alternative method of evaluation that you may wish to try is to answer the following questions with a brief comment in point or paragraph form:

What are the candidate's strengths and weaknesses?

How does the candidate compare with other candidates for this position?

If the candidate took on the job, how well would he or she fit into the organization?

How would this candidate's strengths and weaknesses, goals, and abilities complement the organization's present situation?

How might this candidate grow and develop in the organization?

How mature and realistic is the applicant's self-image?

Did the résumé or interview reveal any issues that should be pursued further, through additional reference checks or a follow-up telephone call to the applicant?

Should an offer of employment be made to this candidate? Why or why not?

During an employment interview, you are deciding whether to hire a particular person for a particular position. You are also trying to improve your interviewing and communication skills. To help you learn from each interview, ask yourself the following questions:

Did I listen closely to what the candidate was saying and tailor the interview to what I was hearing?

Did I have enough questions?

Were all the questions relevant and phrased appropriately and effectively?

Did I stay in control of the interview, while allowing the candidate enough scope to answer questions freely?

Did I make special efforts, both before and after the interview, to put the candidate at ease?

Did I obtain the information I intended to get from the candidate?

Did I probe deeply enough into important areas of the candidate's experience, education, abilities, and aptitudes?

Did I end the interview on a pleasant note?

Will the notes I took be helpful in carrying out the next steps of the recruitment process?

Would more planning be in order next time?

What specific aspect of the interview do I plan to handle better next time?

Did some aspect of the organization's procedures or documents (the job description, the reference checks, the benefits package) show themselves to need improvement?

Did the choice of advertising media (whether internal or external) seem to provide an adequate pool of applicants?

If not, should I advertise through a different channel next time or use a different advertisment?

Some Cautions and Tips

In this section, we provide some cautions to be observed during the recruitment interview, as well as some tips for improving future interviews.

The first *caution* is that you will probably not be able to answer the question of whether to hire a particular candidate based on a single aspect of a candidate's behavior during an interview. Instead, you will probably have to draw on an impression based on everything you were able to learn about the applicant, from the reference checks to the appearance of the résumé to the farewell after the interview.

Second, when the candidate is responding to questions about any potential "weaknesses" they might possess, be wary of a non-defensive willingness to talk realistically about these weaknesses and what the candidate may be doing to overcome them. As well, when candidates respond to hypothetical questions about how they might go about solving a problem on the job, consider their approach to the problem rather than focusing only on their answer. Those with all the quick answers may be overly impulsive. Those who respond by first asking the relevant questions are more likely to make good decisions.

Third, many of us feel comfortable with others whose intellectual background is similar to our own. In fact, we quite naturally feel an affinity for those whose thinking and approach to the workplace are similar to ours. In making hiring decisions based on such affinities, however, we fall victim to the "cloning trap" whereby we hire people who are little more than images of ourselves. And, as a result, the organization will not benefit by varied experiences, personalities, approaches, and abilities. One way of thinking about a diverse organization is to consider a successful hockey team, whose management chooses players who can fill various functions on the team. Balance and variety are the criteria for such a selection procedure. Similarly, in an organization, you should try to hire people who will complement, rather than duplicate, the skills you already have. In short, hire someone who is strong where you are weak and weak where you are strong.

The first *tip* we offer is to spend a few moments before each interview to review the purpose of the interview and what you want to accomplish. Also, make sure you understand the job and its qualifications. This will help you focus your questions during the interview.

Second, take the interview seriously. If you regard, as we do, the employment interview as an important event in people's lives, as well as in the life of the organization, you should realize that interviews can result in costly mistakes if they are not handled properly. A bit of time and effort can save you and your organization problems in the future.

Third, picture the candidate in the job. How would this candidate perform on a typical day on the job? Or, how would he or she do on a tension-filled or difficult day? Try to visualize the candidate actually doing each element of the job requirements.

Fourth, show an interest in the personal qualities of the individual you are interviewing—his or her self-image, values, interests, and aspirations.

Fifth, look for specific examples in response to your questions about performance. Abstractions and generalities need to be backed up with evidence. For example, "I am conscientious and hard working" is vague, unless accompanied by "for instance, when I am given an assignment, I make certain I have asked enough questions to be sure of what I'm doing. When I was given the responsibility for that new program we spoke about, I spent an average of 50 hours a week with the design crew until I felt sure we were on the right track."

Sixth, try letting the candidate do the talking as much as possible. Keep your reactions to yourself. Don't do too much talking or talk for too long at any one time. You may wish, as we suggest, to start with broadly based questions and then move to more specific, but still open, questions to get the applicant talking more freely. Use your listening and other interpersonal skills. In short, pay attention!

Finally, be sure you are aware of the legal constraints of the interviewing process. In Canada, personal factors such as age, sex, race, religion, and ethnic origin cannot be considered when a decision is made to hire someone.

The Candidate's Guide to Employment

The main perspective in this chapter has been that of the manager. In other words, we have been assuming you will always be the interviewer. We now provide some advice on how to survive at the other side of the table, as interviewee.

The principal advice we offer is similar to that we provide for the interviewer: rehearse. Begin with an inventory of your strengths, interests, skills, values, and ambitions. Then link these to the job for which you will be interviewed. Find out as much as you can about the organization and the job. Talk to people in the same field or, if possible, in the same organization. If you can impress on your interviewer that you are familiar with the job and what it requires, you will immediately have common ground on which you can discuss your candidacy effectively. Next, even if you feel you have all the information you need at hand, practise aloud, either alone or with a tape-recorder. Even if you do not discuss all you know about the organization during the interview, you will still convey a sense of your knowledge through having prepared and rehearsed.

During the interview, consider the following advice:

1. Ask questions. Has the interviewer indicated all the liabilities—as well as the benefits—of the job? What about opportunities for promotion? Does the employer value the things that you value, such as further education or upgrading? Before an interview, review the questions that we offer the interviewer to ensure that you are ready to ask for the information that may be left out.
2. Try to bring the conversation around to a discussion of your skills. Remember to relate what you can do to what the prospective employer needs the new employee to do.
3. Avoid criticizing former employers or co-workers. Your interviewer won't be able to understand the context and may assume you are hard to get along with.
4. Don't apologize for your shortcomings or be overly aggressive. You should be trying to create a positive impression, and focusing on your shortcomings may create a negative one. Assume a physical attitude of respect and confidence. Don't fiddle with your hair, glasses, or a pen. Try not to slouch or mumble.

Take your leave at the end of the interview with an expression of good wishes. Good luck.

Orientation Interviews

After we have completed the recruitment process, it remains for managers to orient the new employee to the job and to see that the match, which we considered during the recruitment process, is completed. As a manager, the first impressions you make on the new employee will form part of his or her process of establishing a place in the organization. The orientation process is not as simple as handing someone an employee handbook and a set of procedures. Instead, it offers an opportunity to express expectations in another personal interview. It also allows us to emphasize to the new employee that we will be following up on his or her transition.

An employee who has been thoroughly oriented to an organization should feel that he or she has the resources and information necessary to meet performance expectations. The manager should also have established a positive impression—one that encourages interaction and recognizes the importance of each person in the organization. Treated creatively, the orientation interview offers an opportunity to take advantage of the fact that new employees are a wonderful resource for information about an organization. You may be able to determine what makes people comfortable or uncomfortable about their work situation. For example, ask a new employee for a comparison between his or her new experience and experiences in other organizations.

As with other forms of organizational interviews, the orientation interview requires a structure and a plan. The following points constitute a checklist that you can use for planning and conducting an orientation interview.

Put together a package of information for the employee to review later. Such a package should deal with organizational policy and structure, as well as procedures and guidelines. These can form the basis for future reference and discussion.

Make appropriate arrangements for the employee's office, telephone, parking, and supplies. Ask if he or she needs anything you may have overlooked.

Inform others beforehand of the new employee's arrival. Arrange for him or her to meet and perhaps share a meal with other employees.

If you have not already done so, give the employee his or her job description.

Introduce the new employee to people who can arrange for training on, for example, a computer or other office equipment.

Have a series of meaningful tasks and adventures set up to aid and enliven the staff development process. You might ask the employee to order a new computer for his or her office or to introduce him or herself by telephone to an external contact. Such an assignment will encourage the employee to feel that he or she is finding a place in the organization. The assignment might be one that can be accomplished over the next two weeks or so. It should be something informal, even fun, with no pressure attached. Whatever the assignment, ask for a report. Follow up on the report. This will provide a semi-structured opportunity to check on the employee's progress in the first few weeks of employment.

Information Interviews

Unlike recruitment and orientation interviews, which occur within clearly defined boundaries, information interviews can and do occur anywhere at any time. We carry out information interviews often, even if we don't realize it. For example, if you are in a department store to buy a pair of winter gloves and you want to know whether the store carries your size, you might ask a salesperson. Similarly, if you own a car, and it's not running well, you might ask a mechanic to tell you why. Although neither of these situations is a formal interview, they both involve seeking information and engaging in behavior that is characteristic of an interview; thus we consider them to be information interviews. In this way, interviews are part of our everyday routine of interpersonal communication. If you can master the use of the information interview, you will find more and more opportunities for its successful application. Your effectiveness as a manager can only improve. In the workplace we need to find out why customers or suppliers are complaining; who to go to for help and advice on planning and budget; who needs our help with a client; and who to reward for extra effort and a job well done. Information interviews are the way to get at this information.

In the following section, we discuss four interview formats. (These are distinct from the question sequences we discussed in Chapter 3; the interview format is the larger category in which the sequences must find a place.) You may have one or two formats in mind yourself. The characteristic that is common to all interview formats is that they are planned. Some may have more structure than others; some may allow for the interviewer to improvise to a greater degree than others do. Experienced and skilled interviewers often do not have to spend as much time preparing as do other interviewers. But we suggest that all interviewers should consider their own needs and aspirations, and those of the people they will interview, before sitting down for the interview session. We feel, in fact, that there is no such thing as an unplanned interview.

Four Formats for an Information Interview

Beginning with the format that has the narrowest scope, the **specific format** leaves little room for deviation from the survey or interview guide. This format is especially useful when you must interview a large number of respondents. In such a situation, it may be difficult to make comparisons among responses unless there are strict controls on both the questions that are asked and the choice of responses. But the rigid structure and limited choice of responses in the specific format means that the interviewer may miss any additional, creative, or spontaneous responses that the interviewee might otherwise have offered. An example of a situation in which you might decide to use the specific format would be a survey of employees' opinion on whether to institute a flex-time program. In such a situation, it would be important for everyone's response to be as specific as possible: yes or no. After this, another format might be used to decide what kind of flex-time program should be set up.

The **planned format**, by contrast, offers the respondent and the interviewer some flexibility. The use of this format encourages the respondent to offer any response he or she wishes. The questions are controlled, as in the specific format, but the respondent is free to include any relevant, or for that matter irrelevant, data in the response. You might, for example, use the planned format to conduct a focus-group interview for the purposes of marketing a product or service. Here, you want responses to specific questions, but you also want respondents to mention anything that comes to mind in their responses.

In the **free format**, the interviewer begins the conversation with only a few written questions in hand or with a topic or list of response categories. Since the respondent's answers may not follow the order expected by the interviewer, the interviewer must be ready to improvise on the structure as the interview proceeds. The way in which the interviewer improvises will be connected, of course, to his or her purpose. The free format might be used, for example, for the purpose of investigating a complaint arising out of an interpersonal dispute in an organization. The free format would allow you to begin by taking an objective or unbiased stance in the dispute.

Finally, the **flexible format** is a combination of the previously described formats. The interviewer prepares the questions in advance, anticipating the response categories that will be adapted during the interview. The interviewer modifies, revises, and edits the questions as the interview proceeds. It is a free-wheeling style that allows for the exploration of new topics, while preserving the purpose of the interview. For example, you might decide to use the flexible format for a type of information interview we will discuss in more detail in a later chapter: the performance appraisal. When you use the flexible format, be sure you have a clear purpose thought out in advance.

Setting a Strategy

The strategy you formulate for an information interview will be a result of your choice of an appropriate question sequence and interview format. Because every interview situation is different, we leave the details of that process to you, but suggest a possible general outline. In the case of most policy announcements, many organizations use a pyramid approach (which we described in Chapter 3) for the question sequence and a planned format. Such a strategy could be used if you are conducting a press conference, which is a form of information interview in which a person or organization provides information to others. Or it could be used in a much less formal situation, such as a session in which someone gives instructions to a colleague on how to run the photocopier. You may be surprised at how quickly the quality of your interactions improves with the use of a simple strategy like the one outlined below. Once you've used it successfully, you can improvise according to who you're talking to and what you're talking about.

1. Begin by providing an overview and summary of the information you are going to provide.

2. Describe any relevant background information or details.

3. State the information succinctly and directly.

4. List the effect, results, consequences, and benefits of the information you have presented.

5. Ask for and respond to questions from your partner or audience.

If you can master the use of a simple but effective structure such as the "press conference" interview, you will find that your effectiveness increases in situations where you are contributing to or leading meetings, presenting proposals, or, in the personal sphere, finding the best mortgage arrangements for your house.

And finally . . .

You may find the following guidelines useful as you plan and carry out employment interviews.

Try to gain as much information as possible from the respondent. Once the interview is over, the unique circumstances—good or bad—will be gone. Use your plan and your notes to ensure that you get the information you need.

Listen to your respondent carefully. Sometimes, the message we receive in an interview is ambiguous. Try to interpret both the respondent's words and non-verbal behavior to obtain the intended (or unintended) message. As well—and this is especially the case with famous interview respondents—you may find that the subject responds with answers that he or she has rehearsed in previous interviews. If you have done your research thoroughly, you may even recognize some of the responses.

Research as much as possible. Most interview subjects are flattered that you have taken the time to look into their work. This can only improve the atmosphere of the interview. Keep in mind that what a person says must be balanced with who that person is and what he or she has done.

Preview your questions for the respondent. The use of prefaced probes and other devices allows your respondent to prepare for your questions, thereby improving the quality of the responses he or she gives.

Use transitional language, and polish your transitions before the interview. The interview will proceed more smoothly if you use phrases like the following:

"As you may recall, I'm here to discuss . . ."

"Let's review what we talked about at our last meeting. . . ."

Clarify what your respondent is saying. Practise the use of the devices we discussed in Chapter 3—mirror questions, paraphrases, and other probes or feedback devices to help you pursue a particular line of questioning.

Use appropriate language. The way you phrase a question will determine, in part, how your partner responds. The more technical or sosphisticated the language, the more specific the answer can be. Your language can indicate that you have researched the area you are discussing and that you know something about the respondent.

Use nonverbal and body language. To enhance your ability to maintain the attention of your respondent, use the techniques we introduced in the clinic in Chapter 3: paraphrasing, vocal pauses, gestures, and so on. Indicate to your respondent that what is coming next is of particular importance.

Recapitulate and summarize often. You can do this by reiterating your own or your respondent's statements. It is an effective technique whether you are giving or receiving the information in an interview. Through summaries, you can ensure that both of you understand what the other has said. Also, summaries can reveal inconsistencies in the information being conveyed.

Plan your questions thoroughly. The most important thing to keep in mind as you plan your questions is the purpose of the interview. Write out at least a few questions in full.

Section 2 ▸ Constructive Disciplinary Interviews

Before we get started . . .

Constructive discipline usually refers to both a formal management system that gives rise to disciplinary action, as well as an informal method of problem solving and providing performance-related communication. The goal can be to gain compliance with performance standards, to bring about some positive change in individual behavior, or to build a commitment to higher quality performance in the organization. When constructive discipline is used, clear expectations must be established; the employee must understand what needs to be changed, why, and how the change can happen.

Along with performance appraisals, disciplinary interviews are among the manager's best tools for helping to bring about change in work performance—provided they are used for their constructive potential. Blaming or fault-finding seldom, if ever, work.

Objectives

After you complete this section, you should be able to:

1. Discuss the objectives of constructive discipline.

2. Explain *progressive discipline* in organizations, and discuss when a disciplinary interview is in order.

3. List and discuss four purposes of a disciplinary interview.

4. Describe the steps that a manager must take or consider in order to prepare for and conduct an effective disciplinary interview.

5. Describe the special steps one must take when dealing with the uncommitted, or when giving more positive direction to an employee with a problem.

6. Discuss the importance and use of the exit interview.

What Is Constructive Discipline?

Constructive discipline is a process of reviewing the performance of an employee in which the employee is not judged, intimidated, or punished. It focuses on empowering employees to correct their own problems through self-discipline, rather than through external pressure. There are plenty of things wrong with disciplinary punishment, the most important of which is that it usually doesn't work. Even if you gain short-term compliance, the longer-term consequences of anger and resentment defeat any further progress. The objective of constructive discipline, in the short-term, is to correct any dysfunctions standing in the way of positive self-discipline. In the longer-term, what we are after is a commitment to change, to getting the job done better, to improving our performance, and so on. If you can get employees to solve their own problems, then you have discipline in the best sense of the word.

It should not be the manager's responsibility to regulate the discipline of employees. It is really the responsibility of the employee to regulate his or her own constructive behavior. Discipline works best when, instead of making demands, the manager asks the employee to offer ideas or solutions to a problem. If someone is always griping or complaining about everything and everybody, try asking questions such as the following:

How would you improve morale in this department?

Do you see a way your job could be restructured that would make the atmosphere more productive around here?

Complainers will often abandon their complaints when they are given the chance to act positively. It's certainly worth a try—maybe more than one.

The focus in constructive discipline is not on what is wrong with the person, but rather on what is not working, and how much management intervention may be required to rectify the situation. Although it is common to explain people's actions in terms of their personality, this is not a helpful approach. People rarely change their personality, but people can and do change their behavior. If you have an employee who misses work frequently, what you want is for the employee to come to work—not to become a different person. The responsibility for coming to work and doing a good job ultimately rests with the employee, and so does discipline. According to constructive disciplinary practices, if an employee agrees to, and successfully carries out the plan for correction, then no further disciplinary action is necessary. If the person fails to come to work or otherwise improve performance as planned, management must take progressive steps to further evaluate the employee's position.

How to Begin Discussing a Problem Without Creating a New One

The best and easiest way to introduce and describe a discipline problem to an employee is to be as specific as possible. For example, when an employee arrives late for work, you don't need to mention that he or she is late—just say "You arrived for work at 9:35 a.m. for the third day in a row." If how fast or slow something is done is the concern, give the exact speed, instead of stating that the person is too fast or too slow. Tell people exactly what they are doing, and exactly what is to be done. But don't fall into the trap of judging them or condemning their behavior with sarcasm.

Unfortunately, it is often possible to be specific about behavior, avoid using punishment or evaluations of character and personality, and then destroy the entire process by being punishing in tone. When you treat someone badly, problems are created, not solved. Punishment focuses the person's attention on their treatment, and away from the problem you are seeking to correct. What we are aiming at is to be both specific and non-punishing. But this is still only one half of the constructive discipline equation.

What about situations where there are positive things going on—where someone is doing a good job, tasks are being performed effectively, discipline is being maintained, and people are making a real effort? Situations such as these call for *equally specific* positive reinforcement. For example, if an employee did in two hours what normally takes four—let him or her know why that is important to you or the organization. Try using the following steps.

1. Communicate how this performance differs from normal expectations.

2. Tell your employee why you value what's been done.

3. Explain the difference this will make to you, the group, or the organization as a whole.

The Notion of Progressive Intervention

While there are many reasons for disciplinary problems within organizations, poor interpersonal communication is a common one. In some cases, employees simply do not understand the essence or spirit of a rule or policy, or for some reason do not think it applies to them. Such situations may indicate a failure of management to communicate its policies and procedures effectively. These considerations are related to the duties and responsibilities of management to align work performance to the goals of the organization.

The disciplinary interview is an important tool managers have for monitoring work performance and for communicating the organization's goals. It is not an opportunity to threaten, blame, or control. A constructive feature of this kind of progressive intervention—and its real advantage—is that it provides individuals with another chance to improve. A well-planned program, thoroughly prepared and consistently adhered to, can be a most effective instrument of management communication.

Progressive Purposes, Preparations, and Procedures

As we have stated, the goal of constructive discipline is to get people to solve their own problems. In order to improve performance, the emphasis must always be on the future. Although there is a tendency to rehash previous arguments or to focus on minor infractions, the ultimate purpose of constructive discipline is to get past old obstacles and to look ahead to brighter futures—as naïve as that may sound. The manager and employee should spend relatively little time discussing the existing rules or past infractions. Instead, they should spend their time developing a long-range action plan, whereby the employee can enhance his or her positive contributions to the organization. The following is a framework within which disciplinary interviews should take place.

Purposes

◆ *Disciplinary interviews aim to change or "correct" behaviors that violate the rules of the organization.* Thus, discipline serves to guide the employee towards a more appropriate course of action.

◆ *Disciplinary interviews serve as notice to other employees that the rules of the organization are being enforced.* By setting an example, it becomes clear to all employees that if rules are broken, violators will be confronted with the consequences.

◆ *Disciplinary interviews are also concerned with the protection of employees. Rules against theft, sabotage, and negligence are all designed to protect employees and ensure their safety at work.*

◆ *Disciplinary interviews should preserve justice and fairness.* This is perhaps the most important purpose of all. The manager needs to ensure that everyone is heard and treated fairly and equally.

Preparation

Like performance appraisals, disciplinary interviews depend heavily upon thorough preparation for their success. There are at least five things you should do before you call an employee in to your office and close the door:

1. *Identify the problem.* Make sure that a problem exists that truly calls for disciplinary action before you confront the employee.

2. *Check the employee's work record.* Determine whether he or she has been disciplined before and, if so, for what reasons. Has this person asked for help, and, if so, from whom? Managers need to form an overall view of the employee's performance to determine whether the present situation represents a set pattern or a change of behavior.

3. *Review the organization's disciplinary rules.* Most collective agreements or employment contracts specify disciplinary procedures and punishable offences. Above all, managers need to be seen as being consistent in enforcing the rules. So ask around.

4. *Don't let frozen judgments get in the way.* Sometimes ability and potential become tied to past performance. In organizations, there is a tendency to label people—thus reducing the chances of positive change.

5. *Examine your own attitudes and motives.* The relationship between managers and employees also shapes the impact of the disciplinary interview. In what way do you expect this person to change his or her behavior? Both sides need to be aware of their feelings about each other. Also, they must remain calm and objective.

Procedures

Disciplinary procedures are really the same as any other mutual problem-solving procedures. As such, confronting poor performance should never come as a threat, but rather as an opportunity to solve a problem. Once the problem has been identified, and you have arranged a private face-to-face meeting with the employee, there are four more steps that need to be taken to ensure corrective and responsible action on the part of the employee.

1. *When the employee arrives (and the door is closed) come straight to the point of the meeting.* This is not the time for building rapport. Get to the point immediately, but do not begin by accusing the employee. Be certain of your facts as you present them. And don't jump ahead of yourself without evidence to support your claims. Ideally, as with good performance appraisals, disciplinary interviews should be treated as problem-solving sessions. Both the manager and the employee have a mutual problem, and together they must arrive at some solution. The best way to begin the interview is to define the problem by stating first, the appropriate rule or job requirement; and second, the information you have about the employee's behavior.

2. *Your next task is to listen.* By letting the employee talk—and by attending, following, and reflecting—you should determine what, especially from his or her point of view, actually took place. You must hear the employee's side of the story. Be empathetic. Then ask the employee to explain his or her understanding of the rules to you. Having heard this, ask the employee what he or she is planning to do to take action. You must be willing to work together to determine how the employee will improve in the future. Set up follow-up dates on which you can agree to assess the progress.

3. *Ask one or two open questions, and probe for ideas with an encouraging and positive tone.* Examples of such questions are, "What do you think is at the root of the problem?" and, "How do you think the problem could be solved?" It is largely the verbal or nonverbal "music" that conveys the message here, not simply the words or "lyrics."
   The following are some probe questions that can be used at this stage: "Who or what has contributed to the problem?"
   "What needs to happen next?" "What assistance do you need?" "What can I do to help?" "Is there anyone else, or some professional perhaps, who should be told or involved in this?"

4. *Finally, record the actions taken, reasons for the discipline, and plans for future improvement.* State what you expect, as well as what will happen if you don't get what is expected. It is important that all of this be clearly understood by both parties and recorded by you. This record will guide further action and, if needed, will remain a part of the organization's documentation. During the course of the meeting you should ensure that future expectations are clearly understood. We will discuss an important means of doing this—perception checking—in detail later in this chapter. Then follow up!
   Formal documentation should include: a *salutation*—stating who the document is to and from, and what it is about; the *date*; a *specific problem*—spelling out exactly what happened; its *implications*—why this is a problem; the *prior record* of the employee; any *disciplinary action* to be taken; *expected solutions* according to the specific steps to be taken; the *consequences* if these steps are not taken; and a *follow-up schedule* to determine if further discipline needs to be considered.

Dealing with the Uncommitted

The disciplinary approaches we have discussed so far work best with employees who truly want to improve their performance. This isn't always the case. When people are uncommitted to a project, or unconcerned how their negligence of duty may be affecting others, there are some special steps that can be undertaken in conjunction with those already mentioned.

◆ *Help them link the task at hand to personal goals they have set for themselves.* For example, you might say, "Last month you agreed to improve and expand your job skills so you could apply for a promotion. Is there some way we can get you back on track?"

◆ *Explain how their job contributes to the total effort of the team or organization.* Try a statement like the following: "Training and development are central aspects of our strategic plan; therefore we need one hundred percent input from everyone in your department."

◆ *Reassure them of your confidence in their ability to accomplish what they set out to do.* For example, you might offer words of encouragement such as the following: "I know you are capable of creating many innovative programs for our organization—that's why we hired you."

◆ *Design a system for enhancing performance standards and improvement patterns.* You might start by asking: "Is there some other way that you feel you can contribute more to the organization?"

◆ *Celebrate positive results!* Compliments like the following are always welcome: "You did a wonderful job on that last project; I want you to know how much we appreciated having that come in on time. It's made a difference. It's a real contribution."

More Positive Directions

If you have tried all of the things we have suggested up to this point, and problems still remain, here is one more problem-solving template you can use. Some of the items repeat or reinforce some of the advice we have offered previously. However, repetition of some of these key items may be just what is needed in some situations.

◆ *Recommend that the individual take a day or two, or more, to think about whether he or she wants to go on working for this organization.* Remember to say something positive such as, "We hope you will decide to stay and work, but if it turns out later that your performance falls off, and we have another problem like this one, then we may have to consider other alternatives."

◆ *Show your acceptance of people.* While you may disagree with something they have done or suggested, you should respect them as members of your team and as individuals who will make useful and significant contributions to your organization. They are more likely to improve performance if they feel accepted than if they feel rejected.

◆ *Provide meaning and context for the action you are taking.* You should ensure that people understand the issues you are dealing with and that they know that you understand their concerns. You should provide a rationale for your decisions. This rationale should be linked to the objectives of both the organization and the individuals. Failure to do this will mean that individuals may leave your office feeling uncertain about why something is happening. This may lead them later to question whether your concern is genuine.

◆ *Provide a clear statement of direction.* The other person should not be in doubt as to what is expected as a result of your giving direction. Ensure that he or she understands what is being said and what is expected.

◆ *Indicate the rewards and benefits of following your direction.* Just as individuals should know what and why something is being asked of them, so should they be clear about what the consequences of following your direction will be. A manager may sometimes expect the outcome and benefits of a particular course of action to be obvious, when they are not. Explain in simple and clear terms what it is you expect will result from following your direction.

◆ *Explain the follow-up process.* The individual should know the way in which you intend to follow-up the discussion you are having. Will you check back with him or her about progress? When will you do this? How will you do this? What is it that you will be looking for? Will others be involved in this follow-up?

More Serious Measures

We need to mention discharge, of course, but it is really not a part of progressive discipline. Discharge follows the failure of discipline. As we mentioned previously, the goal of discipline is not to punish or give up, but to seek ways of improving performance. The goal is to get the job done, not to build a case for suspending someone. Nevertheless, there are times when letting someone go is the only option left. If you must do this, you will need to consult with the human resources office first, since there are legal implications to discharge. Assuming you have taken the necessary steps in that regard, invite the person into your office, close the door, and tell him or her immediately why it is time for the organization and the person in question to part company. If possible, allow the other person to decide whether he or she needs to use the office for a couple of days or longer, or would rather receive pay in lieu of notice. Find out if he or she would like others in the group to be told or not. In sum, treat your employees with respect at this stage, and don't be afraid to ask them for ideas on how the organization might be improved. Even though they are leaving, exit interviews can give you some good information about how things can be improved in the workplace.

Exit Interviews

If you do let an employee go, or if he or she decides to go, you should carry out an exit interview. An exit interview, used with discretion and tact, can help you find some of the hidden strengths and weaknesses of your organization. You might assume that an employee will use the exit interview as an opportunity to "get back" at others. Such is not usually the case. Often, employees are helpful and objective as they leave the organization, because they do not have anything to lose by being frank. Here are some tips for carrying out an exit interview:

Have someone other than the person's supervisor carry out the interview. This usually makes the person feel freer to say what's on his or her mind.

Be informal. The employee must be encouraged to participate in the interview. After all, he or she has the option of refusing to meet with you.

Listen to the bad news. Take notes, assess later. Let the employee talk, even if what he or she is saying sounds unlikely, especially concerning things you did not know about.

Don't get into personal matters. The interview should be about the workplace and how people could function better in it. Avoid listening to vendettas.

And finally . . .

Be positive about discipline. Discipline can be an effective way to guide employees toward the constructive goals of the organization. Encouragement should be used as part of the disciplinary process—to instill self-reliance, self-direction and responsibility in the other person. To be of benefit to both the employee and the organization, discipline must be viewed as a constructive learning experience.

Confrontation means that change is imperative. Progressive, constructive discipline can involve any level of change from making a decision and setting a deadline, to reassigning or restructuring the current job, to the curtailment of job responsibilities, or dismissal. At each stage, the manager and employee must examine the alternatives, and the consequences of each action contemplated or implemented.

Section 3 ▶ Understanding Verbal and Nonverbal Language

Before we get started . . .

Imagine a meeting room in a rapidly growing software development firm. Before the meeting is called to order, several senior staff members are chatting about past experiences, some unsuccessful, some successful. The subject of conversation turns to the development of new products. The mood in the room and the body language of the young middle managers shows that they are jovial, even irreverent. The handshakes, smiles, and gestures are symbols of their collegiality and success. In fact, the atmosphere in the room may be more revealing than what they are saying. The atmosphere suggests that the way to become a contributing member of this organization is to participate in developing a new product.

In Chapter 3 we studied the concept of active listening by considering three clusters of skills: attending, following, and reflecting. We also discussed the notions of dialogic listening and reflective listening. In this section, we consider a fourth cluster of skills: the skills that are associated with the use of verbal and nonverbal symbols. We recommend that as you consider nonverbal language you imagine clusters of gestures, much as we suggested in Chapter 3 that you consider clusters of listening skills. Suppose someone becomes angry. Many gestures occur simultaneously. The arms tighten across the chest, the body becomes rigid, the jaw sets, the eyes narrow. Taken separately, each of these gestures may not mean much. Taken as a cluster, they have significance. You should look for congruency as you make inferences about mood from others' behavior.

We will discuss aspects of verbal and nonverbal language which we will then encourage you to explore on your own by trying related activities. The benefit of practising is that it offers you a situation in which the risks of failing are low. Anyone who has tried paraphrasing in everyday conversations has found that people can take offence quickly if they feel they are being manipulated or mocked. ("Why do you keep repeating what I've said?") The activities in this section offer you a chance to practise taking the sting out of such reactions. Don't be discouraged if you get a negative reaction; try again, perhaps with more care the next time.

Verbal and nonverbal language occur together. The two should be seen as a complete and inseparable unit. The nonverbal aspect is used primarily to express emotion, present personality, and convey attitudes (like/dislike, dominance/submission). It also plays a part in accompanying speech for the purposes of managing feedback. In fact, verbal and nonverbal language are so interwoven that it is difficult to consider one without considering the other. For the purposes of analysis we will try to consider them separately, but in reality, they always occur together.

In this section we will examine those expressions of communication that cannot be found in the transcript of an interview or conversation. In fact, they may not even be evident on an audiotape or videotape. Both the sender and receiver may be transmitting or processing these signs unconsciously. These are the words, phrases, gestures, gradations of volume and tone, cues, and signals that we rely on to provide shades of meaning.

Objectives

After you complete this section, you should be able to:

1. Discuss examples of words having different meanings in different contexts.
2. List and discuss four verbal barriers to meaning.
3. Describe techniques for overcoming verbal barriers to meaning.
4. Discuss the importance of nonverbal language.
5. Discuss briefly the messages that dress in an organization may send.
6. Name four categories of kinesics and discuss their uses.

7. Describe how perception checking may be used to improve communication.

8. Discuss the importance of proxemics in the workplace.

9. Discuss the importance of facial expressions and features in communication.

INTERPERSONAL SKILLS CLINIC

AN INTERVIEW

Throughout this section, we suggest activities that you may wish to try, either by yourself or with a coach or partner. The activities are intended to help you move the ideas we discuss from the realm of theory to the realm of practice. In addition to these activities, we suggest a project that will help you to draw several strands of the section together in one activity. To complete it, you will need access to an audiocassette tape recorder.

For this activity, you will role-play an organizational interview. You will need to complete four documents; a covering letter, two interview guides (one for you, the interviewer, and one for your partner), and an annotated transcript of a portion of the interview.

We suggest that the type of interview be one of the employment interviews we discussed in the first two sections of this chapter (that is, a recruitment, orientation, information, or disciplinary interview). However, you may wish to carry out some other kind of interview, such as a media interview or a performance appraisal. If the type of interview you choose is covered later in this book (such as the performance appraisal), you may want to complete the activity after you have skipped ahead to preview the relevant portion of the book.

Here are the steps to follow.

1. Choose a partner. It may be helpful to choose a partner who has actually been interviewed, perhaps recently, in an interview of the type you have chosen.

2. Write interview guides for both you and your partner. An example appears below.

GUIDE FOR INTERVIEWER

Type of interview: Recruitment

Position: Supervisor of clerical staff for a small manufacturer

Objective of the interview: To discover the candidate's fit with the organization. (Note: the advertisement called for five years of relevant experience, but the candidate only has three and a half years of full-time employment.)

Opening strategy: Nondirective at first, combined with probing where appropriate.

Body: Funnel sequence—open at the beginning, narrowing as we go along.

Close: Leave lots of time for processing questions.

Questions:
1. Describe your career and education.
2. What are your long-term career goals?
3. What kind of people do you like working with?
4. How would you describe the manager for whom you now work?
5. How would you describe your qualities as a supervisor?
6. With what office automation systems are you familiar?
7. Why would you like to work for us?

Checklist:
credentials?
special talents?
references?
general impressions?
poise and confidence?
creativity?
appearance?

GUIDE FOR CANDIDATE

You are a female with three and a half years of relevant experience in word-processing and administration. You have supervised the work of freelance data-entry clerks in your present job as secretary at a publishing firm.

You also have the following experience:

—two-year community college diploma in business administration
—treasurer of the local cub scout pack for the last four years
—attended several workshops and courses on electronic publishing

You have an infant son (10 months old), and in your present job, you work at home for three afternoons a week so that you can be with him. You would like to continue this arrangement.

3. Meet with your partner to rehearse and tape the interview. As you conduct the interview, try to answer the following questions for yourself:

How well are you accomplishing your stated purpose?
What image are you trying to convey of yourself and your organization?
Have you covered relevant areas of information?

4. Transcribe a selection of 10 minutes' worth of continuous dialogue for analysis and annotation. The annotations (occasional, brief comments interpersed with the actual interview) should answer the following questions: What communication skills have been intentionally applied? What specific interviewing strategies were used? Did the skills and strategies used help accomplish the stated purpose of the interview?

The following is a portion of an annotated transcript that might follow from an information interview.

INTERVIEWER: You seem to be working pretty intensively lately. Is that right?

[Open question suited to uncovering the respondent's attitudes, values, and so on. Part of the funnel strategy.]

RESPONDENT: Yes, I've had several projects going at the same time. But I must admit I enjoy a bit of challenge, even a bit of pressure. For a while anyway! And I have flexible work hours. That's the best part. But I'm not too crazy about the pay scheme there. Some people need the security of a regular salary. I prefer to work alone for commission. I bring in a lot of business on my own. That's what inspires me to work as hard as I do.

INTERVIEWER: So what you're saying is that you like to work on your own and that if you're given the chance to do so, you don't mind working extra hard? If that's true, given the project I have in mind, you may be able to work largely on your own.

[Mirror statement is used to paraphrase and check perceptions. Also, prefaced probe used to continue flexible format and strategy.]

RESPONDENT: I am happy now. But I'm not sure that I want to take on anything new just now.

INTERVIEWER: Mmm . . .

[Strategy: minimal encouragement used to help stay in control without doing too much of the talking.]

5. Summarize what your strategies were in the interview, including any specific skills used, in a one-page covering letter. The following is an example of such a letter:

November 1, 199X

Dear Professor,

I have finished the interview project, as we agreed. Please find enclosed an audiocassette of the entire interview, two interview guides, and an annotated transcript.

In the interview, I used a nondirective strategy because I was more concerned with the candidate's attitude and fit than with specific credentials. References confirmed the basic credentials. I was concerned by the fact that the candidate did not have all the formal qualifications the advertisement had called for. However, I was impressed by the candidate's determination to improve her skills through taking non-credit courses in her area.

I began with open questions aimed at getting the applicant to relax. Eventually, she did relax and was able to describe the way that her volunteer and part-time experience would find direct application in this job. I used prefaced probes to get her to begin to do this.

The candidate had asked about whether working at home some of the week would be possible. I said I would check this the next day with the human resources office and let her know. In order to do this, I had to get some information from her on exactly what kind of arrangements she had in mind. I used closed questions for this, taking note of her answers in writing.

At one point in the interview, we did get off topic. After she inquired about working at home, we began to talk about our kids. It turned out that this was a good springboard for moving on to how she became interested in publishing and why the area is especially attractive for women. Thus, the nondirective technique turned out to be effective.

Sincerely,

Student

6. If required, submit the project to your instructor.

● — ● — ● — ● — ● — ● — ● — ● — ● — ● — ● — ● — ●

Making Meaning with Words

When we use words and other symbols, we are engaging in a process of making meaning with others (communication). This process is often accomplished without our having to expend much effort. This is especially true if we, as listeners, are in harmony with the speaker's intentions. But even if we don't know the person's intentions, we are still able to attend to the total message, which includes nonverbal as well as verbal signals. We do not interpret each word, phrase, or signal separately, but as part of an integral message.

We make meaning from the many learned experiences that we associate with the use of particular words and signals. If you were to consider the word *student*, for example, the meaning you would associate with the term would be different from that of someone else. It is true that you might agree with someone else on how the word can be used (that is, in the context of schools, colleges, universities, and so on), but your feelings about the word would be different because your experience (or lack of experience, as the case may be) as a student would be different. **Affective meaning** is the term we use to describe the different associations people make with the same phenomena. Affective meaning is anchored in the feelings and attitudes of each person. When we communicate with others, the affective components of the interaction are as important as the literal meaning of what we say.

Semantics is the study of meaning. Like words such as *myth* or *rhetoric*, *semantics* has taken on a popular meaning that is removed from its formal meaning. In popular parlance, 'semantics' is used to refer to a level of discussion that restricts itself to insignificant detail and nuance. This definition relates to the use of semantics for the purposes of exploitation. For our part, we will rely on the formal definitions of **semantics**, which include the *relationship of words and symbols to the ideas or objects that they represent* and the *history of meaning*.

For an example of the first type of semantics—the connection of words to things—suppose we were to ask two individuals to think about the same word or object. Let's take the word *sun*. One person might report that the first thoughts to come to mind had to do with the natural power of the sun, its almost unimaginable capacity to influence weather and, consequently, the very shape of the earth's land forms. The other person might have thought only of pleasant memories of sunny days, the beach, languor. A simple example of the second type of semantics—the history of meaning—is the way the term *individual* (in reference to a person) has, since the seventeenth century, lost its pejorative, or negative, connotation. Formerly suggesting eccentricity, the term has come simply to mean, in our day, "a person."[2]

So we would be wrong to assume that words mean the same thing at all times and in all places. Words are not repositories for meaning; they are focal points for the associations that people use to make meaning. In this sense, words have a degree of "portability" that makes them applicable to different contexts. Words mean different things to different people at different times.

Four Verbal Barriers to Making Meaning

While verbal language is the frame within which people make meaning, it is also a potential barrier to the creation of meaning. We can point to four common means by which language can stand in the way of communication: labelling, polarization, emotive words, and stereotyping.

In a complex organization people often tend to want to reduce the world and the people who live in it to phenomena that can easily be manipulated. This is done by **labelling** people according to various limited categories; what begins as a symbolic process of naming can become an act of reduction. Semanticists (those who study the meaning of words) and psychologists have agreed that labelling persons as we do objects can cause us to lose sight of the true purpose of interpersonal communication, which is contact with others. By using statements such as the following, which are barriers to communication, contact with others is limited, not improved:

He's going to try to push me to make a hasty decision again.

There's no point in asking. She's made up her mind.

I've seen her type before.

They have all the answers.

All of these statements are evidence of a tendency to categorize, a process that is fundamental, ironically, to our notion of objectivity. Abraham Maslow has warned of the social danger of applying the "objective" stance of classical science to the study of human beings. He states that for the study of human relations we need a humanistic, rather than mechanistic, science:

> 66 While it was necessary and helpful to dehumanize planets, rocks, and animals, we are realizing more and more strongly that it is *not* necessary to dehumanize the human being and to deny him human purposes.[3] 99

Authentic communication cannot occur in a situation in which one person treats another person as an entity to be studied at a distance, without empathy or understanding.

Polarization is another barrier to making meaning; this is the act of refusing to acknowledge the existence of anything other than two alternatives. Polarization occurs when someone insists on a clear distinction between right and wrong, my way and your way, the best and the worst, for and against. As with labelling, polarization is connected to the notion of objective consciousness: When someone or something is labelled, it can more easily be placed in one of two polarized categories.

When a word is used in a way that announces the speaker's attitude towards it, we call it an **emotive word**. Examples of words that can easily be used emotively are *reactionary* and *emotional*. By using these words dismissively, we reduce the opportunity to make meaning with others, because we announce our attitude without having to engage in dialogue, or to explain or justify our opinions.

Similarly, **stereotyping** stifles genuine dialogue by providing the stereotyper with a cloak behind which he or she can avoid debating the issue in question. Stereotyping is often used to blame a group. The difference between stereotyping and labelling is that labelling represents an attempt to categorize based on valid information, while stereotyping is based on misinformation and distortion. Both labelling and stereotyping can be very damaging in interpersonal communication; stereotyping is perhaps easier to identify. The following are examples of expressions of stereotypical views:

"Canadians are polite."

"Americans are pushy."

"Women are touchy."

"Men are aggressive."

"Business schools are practical."

Overcoming the Verbal Barriers

In order to avoid creating barriers to meaning, we should use language for its real purpose—to improve communication. The techniques that we will discuss are the following: the mental use of *et cetera*, indexing, using a calendar, summarizing, and refining verbal habits.

If you find that you are labelling, silently use the term *et cetera* to initiate a mental process whereby you imagine all the other associations that the label did not convey. For example, using et cetera after labelling someone as "aggressive" may cause you to think about more positive attributes such as energetic, industrious, and courageous.

Indexing can also help to overcome the problem of labelling. When you meet someone, associate his or her name, mentally or graphically, with some aspect of your experience. You might keep a running list for each person, in which you enumerate the person's characteristics. Or you might sketch spokes and wheels, in which you are at the hub and in which each spoke leads to a person you know and whose name is written on the rim; each person's characteristics can be listed along his or her spoke.

You can also jot people's names on a *calendar* or some other representation of the passage of time, such as a time-line or a diary. As you plan a meeting or recall your interactions in the past with someone, you can assess and reassess your impressions and conclusions of him or her. This can help remind you that relationships change and that labelling tends to stifle opportunities for change.

If we are to understand what others are trying to convey to us, we must engage in a process of comprehending and consolidating information. The ability to *summarize* accurately and concisely is an important skill in this process, and it is more difficult to do than you may think. Summarizing is not the same as paraphrasing, a skill that we dealt with in Chapter 3. Paraphrasing is the act of holding a mirror up to the speaker; summarizing is the act of condensing and synthesizing. Both call for the use of words and phrases that are different from the speakers. But summarizing calls for a deeper consideration of the speaker's message than does paraphrasing. That's why it is perhaps more suitably carried out with regard to a written, rather than a spoken, passage. The skill can be applied, however, to both written and spoken communication.

INTERPERSONAL SKILLS CLINIC

SUMMARY SENTENCES

Read a short article from a newspaper or magazine, an excerpt from a non-fiction book, or a document from the workplace. Try to choose a piece that deals with a topic with which you already have some familiarity. Your passage should be no longer than 2,000 words.

Write a summary sentence that begins as follows, filling in the brackets as appropriate:

In this [article, book excerpt, memo], the [author, reviewer, manager, professor] tries to [argue, illustrate, demonstrate] that . . .

You must not use the same words that the writer has used, and you must restrict yourself to one sentence. After you've come up with a version that you feel summarizes the passage, ask a friend or colleague to do the same thing. Compare. After discussing your summaries, you will almost certainly have learned more about the topic of the excerpt. And you will both probably want to revise your summary sentences.

━ ━ ━ ━ ━ ━ ━ ━ ━ ━ ━ ━ ━ ━

Finally, we should try to refine our verbal habits. Impersonal designations for someone ("Hey, buddy") must be used with care. Although you may think you are using such a designation in a friendly manner, your listener might take offence. Also, if you use certain greetings or farewells repeatedly or without sensitivity, your listener may feel that you are not treating him or her with respect. Therefore, be careful when you say such things as "Have a nice day" or "Take care." Nothing beats the following phrases for routine dullness: "You know?" "Yeah?" "No kidding?" Finally, improper grammar or vulgarity can hurt your image and credibility in any setting. Watch your language. The person who can maintain coolness under fire and professionalism when dealing with others is the person who will earn other people's respect and confidence.

Making Meaning Without Words

Have you ever walked away from a conversation convinced that you have made a very good impression and that you will receive positive results from the encounter? Or have you ever sensed that you somehow left a negative impression with your partner? In either case, you may not be able to identify exactly what words you or your partner used that left you thinking the conversation went particularly well or particularly badly. When you have such feelings, you are probably in a situation of trying to identify nonverbal or body language.

In the first few minutes after meeting someone for the first time, we often try to come to some conclusions about the person. Our verbal language may be mundane; we may talk about current affairs or the weather. But at another, nonverbal level, we are trying to convey and receive messages about such matters as whether we are compatible with this new person.

A popular story about a horse named "Clever Hans" is recounted by Mark Knapp.[4] In 1900, Herr von Osten of Berlin bought a horse that could tell time, count, add and subtract. In fact, he could do almost anything that required him to tap his hooves a number of times in response. The horse became famous, as did his owner. Eventually, though, it was discovered that what Clever Hans had been doing was responding to nonverbal language, not verbal language. He always performed, it turned out, with a confederate in the audience. The accomplice would adopt a posture of expectancy while Hans was tapping. When the horse reached the correct number, the accomplice would indicate relaxation by tipping the head slightly. Hans would stop. The power of nonverbal language was evidently something Clever Hans had learned well!

The book that popularized the analysis of nonverbal signals was *Body Language* by Julius Fast. Fast suggested interpretations for various body language phenomena. He suggested that if you look away while you speak, it signals that you are explaining yourself and that you shouldn't be interrupted. If you then look your partner in the eye and pause, you are seeking interruption or feedback. If you pause without looking your partner in the eye, you want to go on. A listener who looks away from a speaker is perhaps expressing dissatisfaction with what is being said; perhaps he or she is concealing a reaction to the speaker's ideas. If a listener looks the speaker in the eye, he or she is signalling agreement with the speaker.

This summary of some of Fast's interpretations is only an introduction to the topic of nonverbal, or body, language. In order to understand body language, you must observe and perceive acutely and accurately. One way of practising your powers of observation and perception is to guess the occupations of people you see at an airport or bus terminal. Then try to determine how you came to your conclusions. Was it by style of dress and appearance? Was it by their gestures and gait? Was it by their companions? Or, more likely, was it a composite of all of these factors and more? Often, behavioral patterns reveal a lot about a person; a simple action such as a kiss of greeting is charged with cultural convention. Even within Canada, some people, especially of European extraction or those living in Quebec, think nothing of greeting one another, male or female, with a kiss on both cheeks. English-speaking people in Quebec, as well as those in the rest of the country, might not feel comfortable doing so. For the exercise, of course, you won't be able to confirm the accuracy of your guesses unless you ask, but after some practice you might try it in interpersonal situations in your work and personal life.

The Message of Dress

Just as gestures, office layout, and personal space (which we'll discuss later) are part of nonverbal language, so too is dress. Of course, style of dress is a relative thing. In some organizations, informal dress is part of the culture of energy and creativity. In others, the same style would convey a lack of care and respect. Today, there seems to be more diversity in what is considered appropriate dress. In the computer industry, for example, IBM has traditionally encouraged its male employees to wear dark blue suits, white shirts, and conservative ties. At IBM's competitor, the upstart Apple, there are fewer rules on proper attire. In fact, diversity seems the only rule, and many employees choose to dress informally. But in all organizations, clothing serves as more than protection from the elements. It is an indicator of status, high or low, and of success. We do not recommend "dressing for success" or any particular style of dress. We do, however, point out that whatever you wear will send a message. The question you must answer is whether the message you are sending is the one you want to send.

Listening to Nonverbal Language

In the same way that we learn to use verbal language—by observing, then imitating, how others do it—we learn to use nonverbal language. The nonverbal language that we learn will be determined by such things as our social class, lifestyle, and ethnic background. To become active listeners, we must understand the whole repertoire of nonverbal language. In an organization, the ability to understand and respond to body language can affect decisions regarding hiring, performing well on the job, and influencing others. Through "reading" body language, we may improve the quality of our contact with others and refine the accuracy of our listening.

The nonverbal aspect of interpersonal communication has not been given much attention in studies of communication. We believe that, in interpersonal situations, nonverbal language says as much about us as the words and verbal symbols we use, perhaps more. Many experts believe that when verbal and nonverbal behavior are in contradiction, it is the nonverbal cues, not the words we say, that reflect our true feelings and intentions. While the verbal message is what we worry about most in forming meaningful impressions, nonverbal action is what listeners rely on to help them interpret motives and behavior.

Before we discuss particular nonverbal cues, we should introduce a distinction between two categories of nonverbal communication: kinesics and proxemics. The term *kinesics* is from a Greek word referring to motion; the term *proxemics* is formed from a Latin word meaning near. By the end of this section, you should be able to recognize various nonverbal cues and be able to classify them as being part of the realm of kinesics or of proxemics.

Understanding Kinesics

Kinesiology is the study of movement and **kinesics** are the meanings ascribed to or conveyed by the motions and tensions of certain parts of the body. The waving, tapping, shrugging, and slouching that we do are examples of kinesic behavior. The facial expressions, postures, and gestures people use as they communicate are all part of their kinesic repertoires. There are five principal categories of kinesic behavior.[5] Note that all of them are associated, directly or indirectly, with verbal expression.

Regulators are the cues that accompany speech for the purpose of providing order in a conversation. They may aid in turn-taking. If you raise your hand in class, you are using a regulator.

Adaptors are kinesic devices used to release physical or emotional tension. Tapping your foot or a pen are examples of adaptors. Adaptors are used to reduce the arousal or impatience as our emotions become stimulated in an interpersonal situation. A particular type of adaptor is known as "nonverbal leakage"; in which something being indicated through one nonverbal behavior is contradicted through another. For example, if you have glanced at the clock several times while trying to express interest through other means in what someone is saying, you have engaged in nonverbal leakage.

Emblems are those nonverbal cues that can stand alone. They are symbolic of a verbal expression. The "V for victory" (or for peace) is an emblem.

Illustrators are nonverbal behaviors that emphasize or clarify what we are saying verbally. Pointing which way to walk to a stranger on the street would be an example of an illustrator.

Regulator

Adaptor/ Nonverbal Leakage

Emblem

Chapter 4: The Language of Employment Interviews

Illustrator

Affect displays are cues that usually convey emotion. (The term "affect" here is in the psychological sense, as in the concept of affective meaning discussed at the beginning of this section.) A pout or grin, snapping one's fingers in regret: These are examples of affect displays.

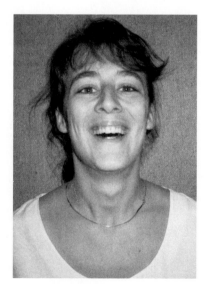

Affect Display

CATEGORIZING KINESIC BEHAVIOR

If you can classify certain physical behaviors, you have taken the first step towards understanding, responding to, and conveying unspoken messages.

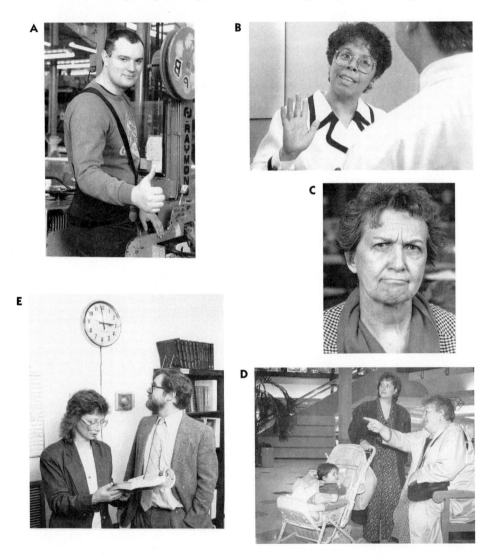

Answer: **A**, emblem; **B**, regulator; **C**, affect display; **D**, illustrator; **E**, adaptor

For each of the preceding photographs, determine under which kinesic category the behavior depicted belongs.

● ● ● ● ● ● ● ● ● ● ● ● ● ● ●

Perception Checking

The words we use to represent our experience influence what we perceive. They can also be used as an effective means of checking the accuracy of our perceptions. *Perception checking* is paraphrasing by another name. In both cases, the receiver puts a mirror up to the sender to confirm understanding, so that both can move on to the next message. The difference between the two is that, with a perception check, we are trying to interpret nonverbal, not verbal, language; we are not putting communication "in other words" but "in words."

A device related to the perception check is *descriptive feedback*. This device is a less direct form of the perception check. Descriptive feedback takes the form of a comment that incorporates what the speaker has just said. It is offered by the listener for the purpose of clarifying the speaker's ideas for the benefit of both parties. We will regard perception checks and descriptive feedback as the same thing, because they are both methods of interpreting what is going on around us by holding a mirror up to the person to whom we are speaking. And both devices call for a verbal response.

We do not suggest that you use perception checks to express approval or disapproval of what your partner is saying. Rather, we suggest you use them to improve the accuracy of your perception. Here is an example of how a perception check can work, followed by a clinic which gives you practice in perception checking.

At work, Leslie offers some advice to June about a brochure she has just finished writing. June has spent several weeks working on the brochure. As Leslie speaks, she begins to sense that June is exasperated. She puts her chin in her hand several times, and she sighs just loud enough so that Leslie can hear it.

Leslie says, "June, how do you feel about the suggestions I've made so far? I sense you have a concern."

INTERPERSONAL SKILLS CLINIC

PERCEPTION CHECKING

For practice, write a statement to respond to each of the following situations.

During a performance appraisal that you, the manager, are carrying out with an employee, the employee stares at the table, rather than looking at you. Usually the employee is amiable. You ask what she thinks of the new appraisal process. She states that "the appraisal process seems to be working well, in the opinion of some members of the organization." You would like to have the employee clarify the point.

How might you do it?

A clerk in the office has a child whom he picks up every day before lunch. You are talking to the clerk at about 10 minutes before noon when he begins to look at his watch every half minute or so. You suspect he wants to leave.

How would you check your perception?

Your colleague, Bill, comes into the office late in the morning. He has been at the dentist. He seems tired. When you ask him how the appointment went, he says, quietly, "Pretty well," and absorbs himself in the day's work.

What might you say?

Next, choose a partner. Say that you would like to try out an exercise in communication, but don't, for the time being, mention nonverbal language. (This is so your partner does not become self-conscious and perhaps reluctant to use nonverbal language.)

1. Discuss a topic of mutual interest, preferably one about which you both have distinct and developed ideas.

2. Observe the nonverbal cues coming from the person with whom you are interacting, making a mental or written note about each one.

3. Ask yourself what the behavior means to you.

4. Put your impressions into words, and then ask your partner if your perception was accurate.

Implications for Management

As a manager, you may be able to use your understanding of nonverbal language to help employees clarify the power relationships among them. You may observe, for example, how someone uses turn-taking cues to maintain his or her status as an opinion leader. Such knowledge may help you to suggest ways of improving the communication channels in the organization.

A caution. When observing gestures, avoid the temptation to generalize or jump to conclusions. Observing is hard work. You will need to educate your eye and exercise your awareness to the point that you can recognize fine detail. And no matter how proficient you become at observing and responding to body language, your conclusions must remain provisional. Body language, like verbal language, is subject to various interpretations. Nonverbal signs are not evidence, but clues. Try to use the clues of body language as a method of improving your empathy and understanding, not as a means of acquiring information that others may consider private. Respect people's desire to keep true feelings hidden, even though inconsistencies between verbal and nonverbal language may mean that these feelings are not hidden at all.

Understanding Proxemics

Edward T. Hall, an anthropologist, is perhaps best known for his insights into the importance of cultural differences, made popular through such books as *Beyond Culture* and *The Silent Language*. He suggests that cultures structure themselves according to varying conceptions of time and space. If we want to know why we find another culture strange, exotic, or bewildering, Hall claims, we should examine how that culture's use of time and space differs from our own.

In the late 1950s, Hall began publishing his ideas about what he called proxemics. **Proxemics** is the study of the way we think about and use our personal and social space. Simply stated, it is the study of proximity, or physical closeness. For example, we can consider the seating arrangement at a business meeting or the width of a hallway as proxemic factors.

Hall claims that in North America, the four categories of personal space are as follows: intimate distance (up to 18 inches), personal distance (to four feet), social distance (between four and 12 feet), and public distance (anywhere from 12 to 25 feet). Hall's assumption is that human beings are territorial. That is, they treat space as a possession to be held or ceded, as necessary or desirable. Thus closer distances are reserved for friends and family, while larger distances are for those whom we view with some hesitation. You may want to consider whether Canadian culture (which you may know well) varies from American culture (which has been the subject of Hall's scrutiny) in its expression of time and space. Furthermore, should we consider the subcultures that go into creating the Canadian culture (native, European, East European, Oriental, and so on) for clues as to how Canadians structure their culture? Are there aspects of your heritage or ancestry, if you are aware of them, that you might consider in your communications with others? To analyze such matters, you may have to begin with a consideration of some of the family and community customs and beliefs that provided a background to your upbringing.

Studies of the proxemics of organized meetings have indicated that seating preferences are based on allowing for interaction, for leading, or for the expression of attraction. Not surprisingly, leaders (or those who want to be leaders) choose seats at the head of a table or in some other prominent position. Proxemics can also indicate more complex messages about status. In large, complex organizations in particular, proxemics are used by members to vie for status or power. While we might want to believe that we are not territorial in the same way that wild animals are, the evidence indicates that the control of space and location is typically seen in an organization as an extension of one's personal power range. It is thus an indication of rank. More is better than less, higher is better than lower, private is better than public, and windows are better than walls. As a result, the corner offices (affording more windows) on the highest floors are commonly reserved for senior executives.

A caution. We are not advocating that you use your knowledge of proxemics to gain or express power. You may not agree with the values underlying the indications of status and power suggested by proxemics, but you should be aware that they exist as part of the spectrum of nonverbal language. In fact, we hope that such knowledge will help you to debunk the use of such devices in the workplace.

Since physical setting is part of the nonverbal language we use, it follows that we should make that setting as amenable to participation as possible. The traditional, formal office usually has a desk placed between two parties. The desk in that position acts as a physical and psychological barrier. It guarantees, for example, that conversations will take place at a safe distance. Participative arrangements (chairs facing one another or adjacent to one another, or perhaps a round table) convey a very different message and are used by counsellors and other professionals who try to encourage their clients to feel that their relationship is not adversarial.

INTERPERSONAL SKILLS CLINIC

IMAGINING AN OFFICE

1. Think of the living room of a friend. Ask yourself the following questions.

   How closely are the pieces of furniture arranged?

   Is the furniture arranged in a way that will encourage conversation or discourage it?

   Is there provision for more than one conversation at once in the room?

   How does the arrangement of things such as lamps, bookshelves, and tables enhance or interfere with conversation?

   What kind of lighting is used in the room, and what does the lighting do for conversations?

   How do the colors and textures of the walls affect human interaction?

2. Now think about a place where you have worked, perhaps your office (if you had one) and your boss's office. Try drawing one or both of these. Figure 4.1 is an example of such a drawing. Then answer these questions.

What do these rooms convey about the following: productivity? creativity? individuality? competence? power? participation? What do they convey about the personalities and positions of their occupants?

3. If you were given the resources to rearrange, redecorate, or even renovate the place where you work, what would you do? How would you deal with furniture, windows, plants, and doors? Why would you do these things?

Figure 4.1: Office Layout

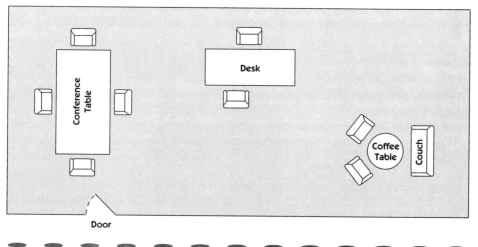

Intercultural Communication

For many organizations, the international aspect of their operations is taking on more importance. The degree to which members of the organization can communicate with people of other cultures is also becoming more important. In Canada, where immigration and official multiculturalism are part of the social fabric, interactions within the organization often call for a recognition of cultural differences in the ways people communicate. The temptation is always to ignore the differences in meaning that members of different cultures bring to an interaction. However, ignoring the differences usually only compounds the problem. Another temptation is to treat differences in others negatively. That is, rather than trying to understand others' views, we simply dismiss them as "foreign" or "eccentric." Again, while this may be a coping mechanism that saves time in the short run, in the long run it can only create further difficulties.

As an example of how to begin considering cultural differences in business, we can turn to the case of the Japanese. We can summarize the cultural differences between Americans (and, to some extent Canadians) and Japanese in the following way. While North American business culture is based on fact, on risk-taking, and on appeals to reason, Japanese business is based on information and on consensus in the group.[6] If you realize this basic difference in approach to decision-making, you can begin to tailor your communication with people in a Japanese organization accordingly.

Initial interactions are particularly important in intercultural communication situations. At the first meeting between two people of different cultures, they should try to determine what differences are likely to impede their communication. The first meeting should therefore be tentative, especially if the stakes for the interaction are high.

The term *intercultural differences* may imply that we are dealing with differences simply of ethnicity or race. In fact, intercultural differences can exist in communication among people who differ in one or more of the following categories:

1. Nationality (Germans communicating with the French, for example).
2. Ethnicity (such as a Canadian of Ukrainian ancestry communicating with a Canadian of Chinese ancestry).
3. Religion (say, Moslems communicating with Christians).
4. Subculture (federal civil servants communicating with their provincial counterparts, for example, or gay men and lesbians communicating with the dominant culture).
5. Sex (men and women communicating).

We identify four aspects of communication to be examined when you are considering intercultural differences: language, perception, rules, and the direction of communication.

Language is the most complex reflection of intercultural difference. It may involve something as difficult to learn about as taboos (the words or ideas that a culture designates as forbidden or inappropriate for discussion—in North America these might be incest or the revelation of one's income bracket); or it may involve the jargon of a particular professional group (such as the terms and expressions particular to the government bureaucracy; "policy evaluation research design" or "program budget"). The only way to improve your understanding of intercultural differences in language is to learn what you can about other cultures.[7] Particularly sensitive things to consider in language differences are racist and sexist expressions—what one culture considers acceptable may not be acceptable to another.

Perception is, like language, a subtle aspect of intercultural differences. Areas in which perceptual differences may occur are given in the section of this chapter entitled "Understanding Kinesics" and "Understanding Proxemics." For example, a large office is not the symbol of influence and status in Japan that it is in North America; therefore, if you were touring a Japanese office building you might have to change your assumptions about the organizational structure to avoid basing your perceptions on the layout and size of the offices. The only way to improve your practice in this area is to learn as much as you can about the culture of the person with whom you are communicating and then try to adjust your communication patterns accordingly.

Rules are the stated and unstated prescriptions and proscriptions for social behavior. Not surprisingly, they are important in any consideration of intercultural differences in communication. In some cultures, for example, an organization is characterized by hierarchy in which only members of the same level communicate about significant matters; communication between levels is discouraged. In others, a recognizable hierarchy may be difficult to detect. Furthermore, rules in some cultures may relegate discussion of personal matters to outside working hours, while in others the whole person may be considered in organizational deliberations.

Direction of communication is the easiest to discern and accommodate in intercultural situations. Put simply, some cultures encourage upward communication while others encourage downward communication. In Canada, while the tendency in the past 20 years has been to begin to encourage upward communication in the organization, much of the communication that actually goes on is downward. In most of Western Europe, including France and Germany, downward communication is the norm. In Japan, on the other hand, upward communication has been a part of the organizational communication culture for a long time. Discovering the direction of communication in another culture should be a matter of asking—or finding out by less direct means, such as through research in the management literature—and then adjusting your communication patterns accordingly.

The emerging technology of communication creates the impression that cultures are "coming together" and that cultural differences will in future be less important than they were in the past. Won't the fact that different cultures are all using the microcomputer, for example, reduce the cultural differences? Probably not. Cultural patterns of behavior and understanding are fundamental. The fact that the Japanese, for example, have embraced and developed the technology for fax machines does not mean that they feel any less committed to their particular conception of the individual in society, which calls for more deference to authority than is practised in North America.

Managers who are responsible for workers who must adjust to different cultures, either in Canada or abroad, should remember that the adjustment required can be stressful. By providing training and support in the area of intercultural issues, managers can ensure that the transition will be as rewarding for the employee as possible.

Looking at Others

Be aware of the signals people make with their eyes. As we discussed with regard to Fast's principles of what eye contact means during a conversation, we seek eye contact with others when we want to communicate with them or when we desire feedback from them. Conversely, we avoid contact with others when we wish to avoid communication. Eye contact is generally perceived as a sign of honesty, interest, openness, and confidence. And, accordingly, people will avoid eye contact when embarrassed or nervous. Distance being held constant, it has been observed that employees make less eye contact with supervisors and more eye contact with subordinates.

We are constantly receiving and processing information conveyed by other people's facial expressions; by the signals they send by smiling, furrowing their brows, or just staring. As a manager, you may not be interested in determining what many of these expressions mean or might mean. But you should recognize that facial expressions, like other nonverbal behavior, contribute to the fact that all authentic communication is unique. As with the other nonverbal signals we have discussed, facial expressions must be dealt with carefully. Respond to such signals, but don't be surprised if your partner doesn't readily accept your response. Perhaps you got it wrong; try again, with care.

INTERPERSONAL SKILLS CLINIC

THE YEARBOOK

In our lifetime, we observe thousands of human faces. Interestingly, we can recognize what seems a limitless number of them. We can match names to many of them.

Take out your high school yearbook, if you have one, and find the photos of people you knew, including those depicted in teams and activities of which you were a part.

Now try to match the faces with the correct names.

Many people are able to match ninety percent of the faces they recognize with the correct names, even 15 years after graduation. Fifty years after graduation, people are still able to match faces with names with an accuracy of seventy percent.

- - - - - - - - - - - - - -

And finally . . .

In this chapter, we have learned about what makes interviews work and how an examination of our language (both verbal and nonverbal) can help us improve our interpersonal communication. We considered the approaches we can take to employment interviews, and provided several lists of possible questions for the interviewer. We stated that the employment interview is an auspicious occasion for the organization and that, consequently, care must be taken in its planning and execution. We practised several methods of improving our knowledge and use of verbal language. Then we went beyond the use of only words into the realm of nonverbal symbols. The most common method of enhancing interpersonal communication, we suggested, is through the use of feedback. Feedback may be in response to either verbal language, as is the case with paraphrases, or nonverbal language, as is done with perception checks.

CHAPTER REVIEW QUESTIONS

1. What are the four types of employment interview?
2. What is the main activity of the first step of recruiting?
3. Where is the first place to look when you are recruiting?
4. What are some of the questions to be addressed as you draft the advertisement for a job competition?
5. What do many résumés not address?
6. What are the three things that the recruitment interview is meant to accomplish?
7. Why is the funnel sequence of questions especially valuable for recruitment interviews?
8. What are some alternative interview formats for the recruitment interview?
9. After the interview has taken place, what are two means of evaluating it?

10. The main piece of advice for interviewees is the following:
    a. study
    b. rehearse
    c. smile
    d. think

11. What are some of the things you can do to accompany an orientation interview?

12. List the four formats for an information interview.

13. What are the steps for a "policy announcement" interview?

14. Notetaking can aid in _____.

15. Constructive discipline focuses on empowering employees to correct their own problems through _____ rather than through external pressure. Choose the best word to fill in the blank:
    a. suggestive action
    b. contemplation
    c. self-discipline
    d. progressive warnings

16. Which of the following is *not* a purpose of the disciplinary interview?
    a. to change behaviors.
    b. to serve as an example to other employees.
    c. to protect employees.
    d. to create an appropriate organizational climate.

17. What is the first step in the process of preparing for a disciplinary interview?
    a. identify the problem.
    b. make an appointment with the employee.
    c. check the employee's work record.
    d. decide on the disciplinary action to be taken following the interview.

18. What should be discussed at the outset of a disciplinary interview?
    a. matters of mutual concern for the purposes of rapport-building.
    b. the appropriate rule or job requirement and the information you have about the employee's behavior.
    c. the steps leading up to the interview.
    d. the disappointment you feel at having to discipline the employee.

19. Often, employees are helpful and objective as they leave the organization, because they do not have anything to lose by being _____.

20. Verbal and nonverbal language occur:
    a. in equal measure in most conversations.
    b. together.
    c. most often as emotional "foils" to one another.
    d. as separate expressions of a single idea.

21. *Affective meaning* and *semantics* can best be described as follows:
    a. affective meaning results from a particularly emotional form of associative thinking; semantics is the study of the history of debate.
    b. *affective meaning* refers to the different associations people have for the same phenomena; *semantics* is the study of meaning.
    c. for our purposes, the terms mean essentially the same thing: the study of words.
    d. affective meaning is the modern form of semantics, which is the ancient study of lexicography (the study of words).
22. Name four verbal barriers to making meaning.
23. List the five means of overcoming verbal barriers to making meaning.
24. Discuss the following categories of kinesics:
    regulators
    adaptors
    emblems
    illustrators
    affect displays
25. Distinguish between perception checking, paraphrasing, and offering descriptive feedback.
26. On what assumption about human beings did Edward T. Hall base his work?
27. If an employee believes that the language of the collective agreement which she has signed does not use language that includes reference to women, she is referring to an intercultural difference. True or false?
28. What are the four areas in which intercultural differences can arise in communication?
    a. language, perception, rules, and the direction of communication.
    b. perception, taboos, kinesics, and language
    c. language, communication patterns, perception, and taboos
    d. prescriptions, proscriptions, persuasion patterns and taboos

SUGGESTED ANSWERS

1. recruitment, orientation, information, and disciplinary
2. Writing or revising the job description.
3. Within the organization.
4. Are we asking for a résumé or curriculum vitae?
   Are applicants to send us the names of referees, or are reference letters to be sent directly to the organization?
   Is the mailing address and the name of the contact person accurately stated?
   Do we want to include a telephone number for inquiries about the position?
   Have we included an application deadline date?

5. Whether the applicant is good at what he or she does and whether the applicant seems to know what he or she wants.

6. To allow the interviewer to gather enough information about the candidate to determine if the he or she is qualified and suitable for the position in question.

   To inform the applicant about the organization and the particular job so that he or she can make a decision as to whether to accept a job offer, if such an offer were forthcoming.

   To create and maintain goodwill towards the organization from the applicant.

7. It allows the candidate to respond with longer answers to open questions and provide more information in response to secondary or probe questions.

8. Stress (which may include the in-basket exercise), group, and board interviews.

9. Using a standardized evaluation form and answering a list of your own questions in point or paragraph form.

10. b.

11. Put together a package of information; make arrangements for the new employee; inform others of his or her arrival; give him or her the job description; introduce the employee to others; and arrange for a series of meaningful tasks.

12. Specific, planned, free, and flexible.

13. 1. Begin by providing an overview and summary of the information you are going to provide.
    2. Describe any relevant background information or details.
    3. State the body of the information succinctly and directly.
    4. List the the effect, results, consequences, and benefits of the information you have presented.
    5. Ask for and respond to questions from your partner or audience.

14. paraphrasing

15. c.

16. d.

17. a.

18. b.

19. frank

20. b.

21. b.

22. labels, polarization, emotive words, and stereotyping.

23. Mental use of *et cetera*, indexing, summarizing, using a calendar, and refining verbal habits.

24. *Regulators* are the cues that accompany speech for the purpose of providing order in a conversation. *Adaptors* are kinesic devices that are used to release

physical or emotional tension. *Emblems* are those nonverbal cues that can stand alone, symbolizing a verbal expression. *Illustrators* are nonverbal behaviors that emphasize or clarify what we are saying verbally. *Affect displays* are cues that usually convey emotion.

25. With a perception check, we are interpreting nonverbal language; with paraphrasing we are interpreting verbal language. Descriptive feedback and perception checks are similar, but descriptive feedback is less direct than a perception check.

26. That human beings are essentially territorial.

27. True. This is a matter of sex differences, which is an area of intercultural communication differences.

28. a.

INTERPERSONAL COMMUNICATION SCENARIO

ELLIS-MCCRAIG CO. LTD.

OVERVIEW AND ASSIGNMENT QUESTIONS

In the following scenario, which is based on a situation that could well occur in an organization, you will have the opportunity to apply the principles and skills you have learned in this chapter. The scenario can be used as the basis for a written or oral analysis or for role-play.

Brian Forbes, Chief Accountant and Director of Human Resources of Ellis-McCraig, an accounting firm, is faced with the task of interviewing applicants for the position of Woodlands Accountant. The person selected for the position will work closely with one of Ellis-McCraig's new clients. Forbes is examining the application forms of his best candidates for the job—with a view to selecting someone who is likely to remain with the firm and grow in the job.

1. Assume you are in the position of Brian Forbes. Decide on a basic interview format and the sequence of events that should lead to the recruitment interview stage.

2. State the objectives of the recruitment interview and make a list of the personal attributes you are looking for.

3. Consider which key questions you intend to ask applicants about their interest in the position, education and training, career plans, and so forth.

4. Be prepared to evaluate both the applicant as well as your own performance in conducting the interview.

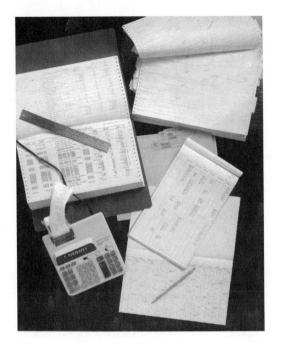

5. Assuming that Andrew Collins, whose résumé appears at the end of the scenario, is a suitable candidate, plan an interview with him.

INTRODUCTION

Brian Forbes, Chief Accountant and Director of Human Resources at Ellis-McCraig Co., Ltd., sits staring at the pile of résumés on his desk. Ellis-McCraig is the newest chartered accounting firm in Peace River, Alberta, with a staff of four accountants and an equal number of support staff. The company has recently acquired a contract to provide accounting services to Lakeforest Corporation, a pulp and paper products firm operating in the town of Peace River, 490 km northwest of Edmonton.

Forbes has to fill the position of Woodlands Accountant with one of the seven remaining applicants whose résumés he has in front of him. He has narrowed the list down from over 20 original applicants and has short-listed seven for interviews.

Since Ellis-McCraig is a small firm just starting out, Forbes intends to oversee the Lakeforest account himself, and has been looking for someone he can train to take over from him as the firm grows. Forbes had a limited budget for recruiting and decides to interview one candidate at a time—taking the best candidates first and hoping he won't have to interview all of the others if one of his first choices proves satisfactory. Unfortunately, there are no local candidates on his short list so he decides he will interview people from as far away as Ontario, Quebec, Nova Scotia, and Newfoundland.

THE PRE-SCREENING PROCESS

Ellis-McCraig uses a standard application form to pre-screen candidates. Forbes feels that having a standard application form makes pre-screening easier and quicker to check. The job description for the position in question reads as follows:

WOODLANDS ACCOUNTANT

A challenging position exists for a highly motivated individual capable of managing and maintaining the M.I.S. reporting system for our Woodlands Department.

Reporting to the Chief Accountant, the successful candidate will be involved with working in a computerized environment with specific responsibilities including maintaining controls and procedures for tracking log and chip inventories, and budgeting. Responsibilities will also include all the accounting functions of an integrated wood supply system which includes harvesting and delivery. The opportunity will be of interest to individuals who are currently enrolled in a CMA or CGA program. In addition, experience with and competence in Lotus and dBase are considered an asset.

The town of Peace River (population 6500) and surrounding communities provide good cultural, educational, medical, and other urban amenities. Sport facilities include a golf course, racquet courts, curling and hockey rinks, and an indoor swimming pool. The surrounding area affords excellent outdoor recreation activities.

Interested candidates should forward their résumés, including the names of references, to the Director of Human Resources.

THE SELECTION PROCESS

While previous employment experience is important, Forbes expects that the successful candidate will take on increasing levels of responsibility if he or she remains in the job for more than three years. Therefore, it is essential for the successful applicant to indicate his or her long-term plans in the interview.

POINTS TO CONSIDER

There is increasing competition in the accounting field from non-accounting firms such as data processing consulting companies, computer software and network services, and systems design bureaus. Consider how your hiring, orientation, and staff development practices and programs can ensure Ellis-McCraig's ability to combat the intensified competition, and how you plan to retain skilled personnel who may find other opportunities once you have trained them for advancement and promotion.

APPLICATION FOR EMPLOYMENT
Name: Andrew Collins
Address: 41 Marchbrook Lane, Milton, Ontario, M1X 8P3
Telephone: (416) 876-2232   Age: 27
Languages: English and French

EDUCATION

Institution	Faculty or Dept.	Discipline	Degree	Dates
Brock University	Admin. Studies	Accounting	B.B.A.	1989-92
U. of Ottawa	Computer Science	Computer Sc.	B.Sc.	1985-88

WORK EXPERIENCE

Job Title	Organization	Duties	Dates
Staff Assistant	Dayton-Hawkins	Computer Programming	June-Sept 91
Warehouse Operator	Ultra Wood Supplies	Shipping & Receiving	June-Aug 90
Plumber's Helper	Collins Mechanical	Repairs & Delivery	1988-89

EXTRA-CURRICULAR ACTIVITIES

While not attending classes much of my time is spent playing ball games with my friends. Living adjacent to a park and having several long-time friends in the area, I try to get outside as much as possible. I also have a membership at a local racquet club and try to get in there as much as possible on weekends. My evenings are often occupied with having to answer my father's business phone (he is a plumber) as my mother works three evenings a week. This responsibility, of course, has limited my membership in student organizations such as the computer and commerce clubs.

ADDITIONAL INFORMATION

When I went to the University of Ottawa I did not have any real career goals in mind. My main reasons for going to university—at the time—were to please my parents and because I had an aptitude for mathematics. I worked part-time, but none of the jobs I've held to date have been too exciting for me. I'm looking for a real challenge—and a chance to move away from home.

It wasn't until I started to study business administration that I got excited about a career. I found the accounting courses the most interesting and became committed to becoming a CMA. To help achieve this goal, I decided to use my strengths in math and computers, and to search for the kind of position that would give me the opportunity to carve out a special area for myself. My greatest asset is my willingness to work hard and to continue learning. What I am seeking now is more responsibility, a chance to prove myself a hard worker, and the opportunity to learn more about business and accounting.

● ● ● ● ● ● ● ● ● ● ● ● ● ●

ENDNOTES

1   Robert Half, *Robert Half on Hiring* (New York: Crown Publishers, Inc., 1985), p. 61.

2   Though words have different meanings in different contexts, it appears that limits on the number of these meanings might be lower than we have thought. The notion that Eskimos have "23 words for snow" has recently been questioned. In Geoffrey K. Pullum's article *The Great Eskimo Vocabulary Hoax* (University of Chicago Press, 1991), the number is shown to be less, about 10. This is in spite of the fact that in popular mythology, the number is sometimes pegged at 100 or more.

3   Abraham H. Maslow, *The Psychology of Science* (South Bend, Indiana: Gateway Editions, Ltd., 1966), p. 2.

4   "Nonverbal Communication: Basic Perspectives," in *Bridges Not Walls*, edited by John Stewart (New York: McGraw-Hill, 1990, p. 79.

5   As discussed in P. Ekman and W.V. Friesen, *Unmasking the Face: A Guide to Recognizing Emotions from Facial Expressions* (Englewood Cliffs, N.J.: Prentice-Hall, 1975).

6   Farid Elashmawi, *Tokyo Business Today*, November 1991, p. 66.

7   Here are three books that can help you understand intercultural differences: Edward T. Hall, *Beyond Culture* (Garden City, N.Y.: Anchor Press, 1976); David A. Ricks, *Big Business Blunders: Mistakes in Multinational Marketing* (Homewood, Ill.: Dow Jones-Irwin, 1983); and Richard Tanner Pascale and Anthony G. Athos, *The Art of Japanese Management* (New York: Warner Books, 1981).

CHAPTER 5

Conflict Resolution and Trust Through Self-Disclosure

Chapter Review Questions

Interpersonal Communication Scenario: Valtec Controls

- - - - - - - - - - - - - - - -

WORTH REPEATING

Conflict is a dangerous opportunity. Many of us are more aware of its perils than its possibilities.

—Robert Bolton

Trusting relationships are a necessary condition for the long-term effectiveness of any organization.

—Samuel Culbert & John McDonough, *Radical Management.*

I was angry with my friend:
I told my wrath, my wrath did end.
I was angry with my foe:
I told it not, my wrath did grow.

—William Blake

Section 1 Constructive Versus Destructive Conflict

Before we get started . . .

In this chapter we will examine how communication can play a part in shaping and resolving conflict, and how trust can help prevent certain conflicts from occurring in the first place. We will also suggest—and you may find this surprising—that conflict, when it is managed constructively, can lead to positive results for both the individuals involved and the organization as a whole.

We all have plenty of opportunities to take away with us something positive from every conflict we encounter. Managed constructively, conflicts can improve the quality of the work we do. They can also be used to establish a climate of openness and trust, in which destructive conflicts can be prevented from escalating out of control.

In this section we begin by distinguishing between constructive and destructive conflict. Although conflict is inevitable, it need not be negative or destructive. Conflict is a common feature of everything we do in life and at work, and can often result in some positive change or improvement in the way we do things. In addition to examining some of the conditions that give rise to conflict, we will introduce several basic problem-solving templates, as well as five strategies for resolving conflict and an exercise you can use to investigate your own conflict situations. The purpose of this last exercise is to help you learn to recognize greater options and opportunities for getting something positive from the conflicts you experience daily.

Objectives

After you complete this section, you should be able to:

1. Contrast destructive conflict with constructive conflict.
2. List five sources of conflict, and explain the conditions that give rise to them.
3. Demonstrate a strategy for reducing the negative aspects of unnecessary conflicts.
4. Demonstrate the use of a problem-solving template for dealing with verbal assault; arrogant, self-centred people; and procrastinators and perfectionists; and for making third-party interventions in a conflict.
5. Discuss five strategies for resolving conflict, and state the degrees to which you use them in your own experience.
6. Discuss how, in political terms, conflict simultaneously divides and unites.
7.. List some opportunities for using conflict creatively at work and elsewhere.

Beyond Good and Evil

Many organizational leaders look upon conflict as something to be avoided at all costs. It needn't be. In many cases, conflict can be a positive and constructive experience if we take pains to put things in the right perspective, one that highlights the value of the conflict as a learning experience. The learning experience will be of benefit to the individuals involved and, in a larger sense, to the organization.

Gordon Lippitt has distinguished between destructive and constructive conflict this way:

Destructive Conflict

◆ Diverts energy from the real task;
◆ Destroys morale;
◆ Polarizes individuals and groups;
◆ Deepens differences;

- Obstructs cooperative action;
- Produces irresponsible behavior;
- Creates suspicion and distrust.

Constructive Conflict

- Opens up an issue in a confronting manner;
- Develops clarification of an issue;
- Improves problem-solving quality;
- Increases involvement;
- Provides more spontaneity in communication;
- Initiates growth;
- Strengthens a relationship when creatively resolved;
- Helps increase productivity.[1]

Conflict can be mobilized for good or evil. It can stimulate improvement and foster creativity, or it can escalate into a kind of fire fight that consumes the energies of all those it touches. Sometimes it can do a bit of both. Conflict may be unavoidable, but it needn't be all negative or destructive. By viewing conflict as a "healthy challenge," we can reframe many conflict situations and find in them opportunities for positive action.

Conflict Over What?

Although to this point we have distinguished simply between constructive and destructive conflict, we can identify several types of conflict that commonly occur in almost every organization. We classify conflict by reference to the sources of conflict and the conditions that give rise to conflict:

Conflicts over facts or feelings occur when two or more individuals recognize that they disagree about facts, or that their feelings about certain issues are incompatible. One result of such a conflict might be that whenever the people involved meet, they become tense, defensive, or argumentative. Sometimes these conflicts are the result of temporary frustrations; but they can also stem from more enduring clashes in personality.

Conflicts of needs and interests occur when individuals fail to disclose their vested interests in seeing certain outcomes come about, or when they do not state their need to influence some decision in which they have a stake. For example, there may be direct competition for budget resources between various individuals or departments in a larger organization. Who gets what may lead to some dispute, especially if the needs and interests of those involved are not stated in discussions about the budget.

Conflicts of values occur when individuals have fundamental differences in ideology or attitude. For example, one supervisor may disagree with another about the need to practise "equal pay for equal work"—or to correct a hiring imbalance that strongly favors men over women.

Conflicts of methods of understanding occur when people draw different conclusions from the same data, or when ineffective communication contributes to some misunderstanding. For example, one person might feel confident relying on previous experience in making a decision; another person might resist any decision that cannot be verified by experts or by some other source of authority.

Goal conflicts occur when people disagree fundamentally about the goals they are pursuing within the organization or about the best way of achieving them. For example, in early 1985 a dispute arose between Steven Jobs and John Scully at Apple Computer over which new product to launch (and, consequently, which new direction the company would take). Jobs favored a multi-product launch while Scully favoured a single product-line focus. The goals of each campaign were quite different. As a result of the conflict, Jobs left the company. This conflict of goals for the company was so serious that the future of the company itself was threatened.

Substantive conflicts occur when individuals find themselves unable to agree on issues of substance. In business, an example of a substantive conflict may be a dispute involving the establishment of a collective agreement; management might state that job security should not form part of the agreement while labor might argue that it should.

False conflicts occur when individuals are at odds with one another because of a misunderstanding or mistake that can be rectified through clarification. This kind of conflict is the easiest to deal with, since it requires only that the two parties discuss the issue until the misunderstanding or mistake is acknowledged.

Mixed conflicts, which involve more than one of the categories we have discussed, are probably the most common type of conflict in an organization. For example, what began as a conflict of understanding between Jobs and Scully at Apple quickly became a conflict of values with emotional and substantive conflicts added to the mix. Over a five-month period, this conflict escalated from a series of smaller skirmishes, into a goal conflict which resulted in one of the founders of the company quitting.

Dr. Pierre Blais and the Bureau of Medical Devices

In January 1989, Pierre Blais, a scientist at the Bureau of Medical Devices at Health and Welfare Canada, recommended that the manufacturer of a commonly used breast implant remove its product from the market.[2] Blais felt he was doing his job. His role was to track developments in the area of medical devices and to advise the government of his findings. He believed that there could be serious health dangers for women who had the implants, and he wanted to have the manufacturer halt distribution until the matter was studied further.

Health and Welfare Canada, on the other hand, had been changing its approach to such issues. It no longer wanted to be a "thorn in the side" of industry. Instead, Health and Welfare would encourage industry to monitor itself. According to the deputy minister, the days were over when bureaucrats prided themselves on embarrassing industry. It was better, she said, to cooperate with industry, since government regulators and company officials were, after all, working for the common goal of public health and safety. The approach of Dr. Blais, she implied, was outdated. The two approaches—and their proponents—were in conflict in this situation.

A couple of weeks later the recommendation by Blais was overturned by his superiors. Further, Blais's immediate superior ordered him to destroy documentation connected with the issue. After these events were reported in the Montreal *Gazette*, Blais became a national figure of controversy. Believing that he had a duty to continue to pursue the matter, Blais did not remain silent. In July he was fired from his civil service position. Eventually, the implant was removed from the market by the manufacturer. Blais, after being reinstated by the government, negotiated a severance agreement. In early 1992, the deputy minister resigned to take a position at the United Nations; in January 1993, the Minister of Health banned the use of the breast implants.

The Body's Fight or Flight Plan

Throughout his ordeal, the psychological stress on Dr. Blais became intense. The aims of the organization and what he understood to be his professional mandate were in conflict. He felt he had a duty to speak out; the management of Health and Welfare, on the other hand, believed his approach was not the most effective one. Of course, interpersonal and organizational conflicts of this magnitude are not common occurrences for most of us. What is common, however, is the way our bodies respond to the stress of conflict. As with all threats to our bodily and psychological integrity, conflicts tend to trigger a "fight or flight" mechanism.

The "fight or flight" urge happens whenever you are faced with a stressful conflict situation: Right away you tense up. Your heart starts beating faster. Your breathing speeds up as well. Adrenaline and hormones stimulate the central nervous system; as a result, your liver starts pumping more sugar through the bloodstream. Overall muscular strength increases twenty percent on average, as more blood volume is diverted to the trunk and limbs. All the nutrients in the body are used to support the work of the muscles in your arms and legs. The cortical center of the brain (where thinking and problem solving take place) is therefore drained of blood. You are ready to scrap with someone or to run away, but you are not in a good position to solve problems or to resolve conflict rationally.

How to Deal with People's Strong Emotions

There is basically one rule to follow here: *encourage expression*. Since emotions produce tension and press their way to the forefront for release, they tend to interfere with incoming messages from the environment. If you want to get a problem-solving idea through to someone, you may have to wait until he or she has finished expunging any interfering thoughts and feelings.

Get the other person to talk. Otherwise, he or she will be too distracted to think about anything you have to say that might help resolve the problem. For example, if an associate at work were to complain bitterly about overtime assignments, you, as the manager, might try to draw her out, or get her to clarify her position:

Alice: Hell, I don't mind it once in a while, but this is the fourth weekend in a row! I'm sick of it. Adam is off—doing who knows what? I'm always the one stuck in this office on Saturdays and I'm sick and tired of it!

Manager: You feel that I haven't assigned any of the extra work to others on the team?

Alice: Oh sure, they get a lot of take-home work. I know they have a lot to do—and they work hard. I know that. But they get to be at home—near their barbecues, near their kids, and with a view of their own backyards. I'm stuck in here staring out at this alley full of loading vans and garbage cans.

Manager: I didn't know you felt that way. I'm glad you told me.

Alice: *[Continues to vent and elaborate—until her anger subsides.]*

Manager: Let's see if we can come up with a more flexible schedule that allows you to do some of your work from home, okay?

Having had the chance to release an initial wave of anger and frustration, Alice may be ready to begin viewing the situation more rationally. Talking about feelings not only lessens the tension, it enables a more realistic appraisal of the problem as well. Before you can present a solution, you must focus on being able to talk about the problem. Similarly, if a person expresses joy or excitement about something that happened—ask him or her to tell you more about it before you attempt to cut in or return to the problem. And you must be careful not to take the conversation away by associating it with too many of your personal views. Instead, concentrate on making the other person aware of his or her own feelings.

Strong feelings—whether positive or negative—tend to get in the way of problem solving. Too many digressions destroy momentum. Feelings of anger may be expressed as gossip, destructive criticism, or unhelpful teasing. Excessive talking, intense secretiveness, joke-telling, avoidance—these are other ways people have of expressing anxiety or intense emotion. One way of dealing with these digressive behaviors in others is to acknowledge that you understand that they feel angry or anxious. This does not mean that you agree with their arguments or sentiments—but simply that you accept their right to express their feelings without judgment or condemnation. After all, one can control only what one *does* about emotions. The experience of the emotion itself is entirely uncontrollable.

Basic Problem-Solving Templates

When conflicts do occur, it is usually best to deal with the emotional aspects first. The issues themselves can be handled more readily once strong emotions have subsided.

To prepare yourself for some of the more common skirmishes that may occur in an organization, consider the following problem-solving templates, and try to decide how you might adapt them for your own use.

I. HOW TO CONSTRUCT AN ALL-PURPOSE PROBLEM-SOLVING TEMPLATE

1. Communicate the problem in a specific, non-threatening, non-punishing way. Start with:
   (a) ACTION   "We need to talk about . . . ."
   (b) FEELING   "I'm worried that . . . ."
   (c) CONSEQUENCE   "We may be in danger of having the project cancelled."

2. The response to this will allow you to assess whether the problem is one of ability or of motivation. If it is an ABILITY PROBLEM:
   (a) ASK FOR IDEAS. When someone comes up with a solution that meets your needs, acknowledge the contribution.
   (b) PARAPHRASE. Repeat the solution in your own words, to reinforce the solution.
   (c) FOLLOW UP. Determine who does what and when. Set a follow-up schedule and stick to it. Agree to a specific time for checking to see that the solution is still working.

3. If it is a MOTIVATION PROBLEM:
   (a) Begin by communicating the NATURAL CONSEQUENCES or "pressures of reality" *on others*.
   (b) Progress to LOGICAL CONSEQUENCES *for your listener personally. IF, ..., THEN.......*

Finally, ask if there is anything keeping the other person from future compliance on these issues.

II. DEALING WITH ARROGANT, SELF-CENTRED PEOPLE

1. *Recognize their need* to exaggerate their own importance or to otherwise attempt to win your admiration.

2. *Acknowledge their expertise.* The more they are made to feel their own self-worth, the less they will feel they have to attack you.

3. *Listen carefully* in order to formulate good questions that you can use to challenge their assertions. Don't challenge their expertise, but suggest other ways of viewing the situation.

4. *Give them a way out.* If they are arrogant, they will have some pride to protect. Invite them to join the team, but make it conditional on following certain rules and procedures.

III. DEALING WITH PROCRASTINATORS AND PERFECTIONISTS

1. *Calmly get them to agree that their procrastination is a problem.* Make sure they are aware of the trouble this behavior is causing them, you, and others.

2. *Decide together how the problem will be solved.* Determine if there is some mismatch or overload. Renegotiate goals, responsibilities, and deadlines.

3. *Reassure them that not everything has to be perfect.* Explain how they will have more time for important projects if they spend less time on minor tasks.

4. *Follow up at specific check points for giving feedback and for recognition of progress.* Positively reinforce or reward the completion of each important stage or phase of the process. Even if the work isn't done properly or on time, be sure to let them know you realize they are trying to improve their performance. Encourage them to do better next time.

IV. THIRD-PARTY INTERVENTIONS

1. Begin by establishing some agreed-upon *procedures for handling disputes,* rather than dealing immediately with the disputes themselves.

2. *Break larger issues down to smaller ones* and deal with them one at a time. Start with those you think can be most easily resolved, and progress to more difficult ones.

3. *Generate as many solutions as you can.*

4. *Evaluate which solutions both sides can live with.*

V. WHAT TO DO WHEN YOU ARE VERBALLY ATTACKED

It's nothing to look forward to, but it does happen to everyone at one time or another: You are verbally assaulted with angry words. Maybe you inadvertently took a private parking spot or cut in on someone in lineup at the cafeteria or at a movie.

If you become defensive or aggressive in retaliation, this will trigger more defensive or aggressive behavior from the assailant. As the argument proceeds, the conflict may escalate out of control. Also, when we act defensively with one another, there is usually a greater distortion of messages sent and received. Unless checked, a vicious cycle of personal attacks and recriminations is likely to develop.

Here are five steps to help redirect angry emotions in positive directions when you are verbally attacked.

1. *Let them vent their feelings.* Invite the angered parties to continue in a concrete fashion. It is critical that you make people feel heard. Instead of trying to impede the outpouring, focus on listening and try to understand things from *their* point of view.

2. *Use the "sounds of silence."* Don't respond immediately to the first outpouring of anger. The second round is often less emotionally charged than the first—if you wait it out.

3. *Employ reflective listening skills (paraphrasing)* to confirm your understanding of the underlying causes of anger in the other party. Example: "You're angry because I inadvertently took your parking space. Is that it?" Or, in a work situation, "Are you yelling at me because I haven't kept you informed of my progress on this report?"

4. *Agree on at least one part of the argument.* This does not necessarily mean that you are capitulating or changing your position—you are just establishing some common ground. For example, you could start by saying "There is no doubt that we need to change a few things . . .", then confront the rest of the issue.

5. *Explore how the other person thinks the situation could be improved.* When someone attacks you personally, try to recast the attack in the direction of the problem, not yourself. For example, if someone accuses you of "not having enough sense" to do things his or her way, you might respond: "I agree that the way we have been doing things has not worked. Let's talk about what we can do to work it out, okay?"

Five Strategies for Resolving Conflict[3]

One of the first management theorists to discuss how administrators could go about resolving conflict was Mary Parker Follet, circa 1918. Follet suggested three ways of solving a conflict:

- ◆ Domination—whereby one side wins all and the other loses,
- ◆ Compromise—whereby each side gives up something, and
- ◆ Integration—whereby both sides gain without losing a thing.[4]

More recently, other prominent writers in the field—including Robert Blake and Jane Mouton (1970), Kenneth Thomas and Ralph Kilmann (1976, 1988), and Will Schutz (1982)—have expanded Follet's model to explain how each party in a conflict will exhibit one of five different orientations to resolving the conflict:

Figure 5.1: The Five Orientations of Conflict

(Source: Adapted from Thomas, 1976.)

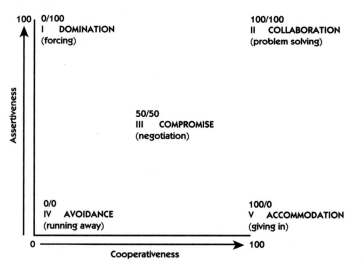

- ◆ I. Domination—one side wins all at the other's expense;
- ◆ II. Collaboration—both sides work to satisfy the concerns of both parties;
- ◆ III. Compromise—both sides gain something as well as lose something;
- ◆ IV. Avoidance—one or both sides refuse to deal with the conflict or concerns of the other side all together.
- ◆ V. Accommodation—one side puts the concerns of the other side ahead of their own;

In each case, the strategy chosen depends upon two major concerns:

1. Concern for oneself and one's own goals (assertiveness).
2. Concern for others and one's relationship to them (cooperativeness).

Of the five basic styles or strategies outlined here for dealing with the resolution of conflict, there are only three types of outcome: win-win, win-lose, and lose-lose. In Western culture, win-lose outcomes are the most common because they are deeply rooted (some say) in our competitive or combative society. In this "all-or-nothing" mode, each side strives to force its will on the other. Although a win-win outcome is by far the most effective for conflict resolution, it occurs far less often than win-lose outcomes. Lose-lose outcomes are obviously the most defeating; no one accomplishes exactly what he or she wants. But they do have their place. In fact, all five modes can be effective strategies in certain circumstances. Let's look at each one in more detail.

I. Domination or Forcing (win-lose)

The domination style can be appropriate when a quick, decisive solution is required, as in emergency situations or those involving someone's safety. When important issues need to be addressed immediately, forcing may be the only appropriate action. But as a general mode of managing conflict, it tends to do more harm than good. It can create many resentments if one side is always trying to win everything possible at the other's expense.

II. Collaboration or Problem Solving (win-win)

Ideally, the most desirable mode of conflict management is one that allows all parties to gain something without losing anything vital. Collaborating involves working to find a suitable alternative that combines a high concern for the interests of others with a high degree of concern for oneself. It often means that conflicts will need to be explored a bit before they can be finally resolved. There are, however, times when both sides' sets of concerns are too important to be reconsidered. Obviously, collaboration works best when both parties respect and trust each other. One drawback is that it takes a great deal of time and energy to establish such trust—resources not every conflict strategist enjoys.

III. Compromise or Negotiating (win-lose)

Between forcing and cooperating is compromise. The objective here is to find some expedient, mutually acceptable solution that can at least partially satisfy both parties.

Compromising may mean bargaining or splitting the difference, or it may mean establishing a quick middle-ground solution. This may be the best approach for two opponents with equal power who are strongly committed to mutually exclusive goals. Although this mode may be appropriate when two sides are fighting for limited resources, or when one side cannot possibly win it all, each side must give up something. And not everyone is happy taking the risks that result from giving something up.

IV. Avoidance or Running Away (lose-lose)

One conflict resolution strategy is to do nothing. This is the opposite of problem solving or collaborating. One side might choose to ignore the situation until it goes away or "blows over." If the problem does blow over, the parties may have done the right thing. Often, however, the inevitable decision-making process will only have been postponed.

A second sort of conflict-avoidance strategy involves a process of "playing down the differences." This *smoothing* process might work well when the potential for damaging a critical working relationship outweighs the issue in dispute. It can also work when an issue is trivial or of passing importance, or when there are other more important issues pressing their way to the forefront. The trouble with most avoidance strategies is that they simply do not address the conflict. Rather than confront the problem, avoiders side-step issues, postpone decisions, or simply withdraw from taking any position at all; all of which leave the conflict unresolved.

V. Accommodation or Giving In (win-lose)

Occasionally, some conflict resolutions will depend on one side giving in to the concerns of the other side.

This mode can work to your advantage if the issue is not of any particular importance to you, but means a lot to the other party. Accommodation is cooperative but unassertive. A manager who "gives in" on a regular basis might be seen by others as "soft" or ineffectual, rather than supportive or cooperative. The accommodating or obliging mode can be appropriate on occasion, but as a general style, it will only make the person you give in to feel satisfied for a while. It usually does little to resolve any real substantive conflict in the long term.

INTERPERSONAL SKILLS CLINIC

THE MANAGEMENT OF DIFFICULTIES EXERCISE (M.O.D.E.)[5]

The Management of Difficulties Exercise (M.O.D.E.) is an instrument for making an assessment of our personal use of conflict resolution styles and strategies. It can be a useful tool for enhancing awareness if used as a starting point for deeper reflection into either the general or specific ways we resolve conflicts. An example of this exercise follows the set of 10 instructions.

1. First, consider how you usually respond to conflict situations at home or where you work. Think of a recent day that you would characterize as an average "day in the life" for you. Ask yourself how you tend to react to daily conflicts and ordinary differences of opinion.

2. Read the M.O.D.E. questionnaire and complete the 25-item list by choosing what you "tend to do" when faced with either option. This is a forced choice questionnaire. Choose either the "A" or "B" statement—whichever is most characteristic of your general behavior—and check the appropriate box on the *lefthand* side of the page. Try not to think too much about the choices. Read them over quickly, and respond impulsively.

3. Do not read on until you have first completed your answers for situation #1. Then fold the lefthand side of the page under so you *cannot* see the checks you have just made beside each item on the questionnaire.

4. Think back to another time when—in contrast to this "normal" day—you have been faced with some significant conflict or crisis on the job or elsewhere. Perhaps you got into an argument at work, or argued with a representative of the airline that lost your luggage. Think of a time fraught with stress and difficulty. Try to recall the last major difficulty you faced at work. Who was it with? What was it over? How did you feel about it before, during, and after it was over?

5. With this conflict situation in mind, complete the questionnaire again. This time check your choices on the *righthand* side of the page.

6. Once you have completed the questionnaire a second time, assign the numerical scores provided for each item on the scoring sheet. You should enter this score in the square brackets beside each of your check marks. (For example, if you checked A for question #1, give it a 4; if you checked B, give it a 2.)

7. Add up the number of times you scored a 1, 2, 3, 4, or 5 and enter those totals in the appropriate box. These numbers correspond to the roman numerals I-V used in Figure 5.1.

8. Using a *mean score of five*, fill in the brackets with the value (plus or minus) of your score against the mean. For example, if you have a total of ten responses under any item, count that as +5 (10 – the mean of 5 = +5). If, instead, you had three responses, this would count as -2 (3 – the mean of 5 = -2), and so forth.

9. The way to interpret these scores is to look for variances between situation #1 and #2. The variance is worked out by subtracting the value in situation #2 from that in #1. A spread of three or more positions around the mean of five is a significant variance. Thus a variance value of 4 is "high," and a variance of −3 is "low." Plus or minus one or two is "normal."

10. Write a description or summary interpretation such as the one given with the example that follows the questionnaire.

Name:_____ Date:_____

"Normal" Conflict		*"Stressful" Conflict*
Situation #1		*Situation #2*

How Do You Tend to Resolve Conflicts?

( )   1. A. Stay away from trouble.   ( )

     [2]   [ ]

(✓)   B. See that everyone's concerns are dealt with. (✓)

(✓)   2. A. Give in to the wishes of others you trust.   ( )
        [5]   [4]
( )   B. Go for what you want—all or nothing.   (✓)
(✓)   3. A. Seek others' help in finding an optimal solution. ( )
        [2]   [3]
( )   B. Negotiate an expedient compromise solution.   (✓)
(✓)   4. A. Quickly move away from the problem.   (✓)
        [4]   [4]
( )   B. Accommodate the concerns of others before yourself. ( )
( )   5. A. Let nothing stand in your way.   ( )
        [2]   [2]
(✓)   B. Express confidence that, together, you and
                     the other side can work things out.   (✓)
        [ ]   [ ]
(✓)   6. A. Get everything quickly out in the open.   (✓)
        [4]   [2]
( )   B. Work towards establishing a middle ground
                     between you and the other side.   ( )
(✓)   7. A. Stick it out until everyone's wishes are met.   (✓)
        [2]   [3]
( )   B. Leave the scene before more trouble starts.   ( )
(✓)   8. A. Give something up in order to get something else. (✓)
        [3]   [2]
( )   B. Cooperate with others to the fullest extent.   ( )
( )   9. A. Satisfy the needs of others first.   ( )
        [3]   [3]
(✓)   B. Bargain for an even split.   (✓)
(✓)   10. A. Fairly exchange one thing for another.   (✓)
        [4]   [4]
( )   B. Postpone the issue to think things over.   ( )
( )   11. A. Try to win at all costs.   ( )
        [3]   [5]
(✓)   B. Try to find something both sides can agree on.   (✓)
(✓)   12. A. Avoid further difficulties as much as possible.   (✓)
        [4]   [4]
( )   B. Let others have their own way as much as
                     possible.   ( )
(✓)   13. A. Listen to the other side, but have your own say.   (✓)
        [4]   [4]
( )   B. Let others have things their own way.   ( )

(✓) [4] 14. A. Avoid useful tensions. ( ) [3]

( ) B. Press for an even split. (✓)

(✓) [5] 15. A. Be as obliging or accommodating as possible. (✓) [5]

( ) B. Accept nothing but complete victory. ( )

( ) [4] 16. A. Win at all costs. (✓) [1]

(✓) B. Ignore issues that don't concern you. ( )

( ) [1] 17. A. Give and take—in an open forum of debate. ( ) [4]

(✓) B. Get all of what you set out for. (✓)

(✓) [5] 18. A. Maintain a cooperative relationship first and foremost. (✓) [5]

( ) B. Avoid controversy. ( )

(✓) [3] 19. A. Settle for a compromise. ( ) [1]

( ) B. Accomplish your own goals. (✓)

( ) [4] 20. A. Press your own points. ( ) [4]

(✓) B. Collaborate to find a solution. (✓)

( ) [1] 21. A. Steer clear of trouble and controversy. ( ) [1]

(✓) B. Charge ahead with new challenges. (✓)

(✓) [1] 22. A. Assert your own ideas. (✓) [1]

( ) B. Satisfy the needs of others. ( )

(✓) [3] 23. A. Propose a middle-ground solution. (✓) [5]

( ) B. Avoid useful tensions. ( )

(✓) [5] 24. A. Negotiate a compromise solution. (✓) [3]

( ) B. Seek to have everyone's concerns heard. ( )

(✓) [5] 25. A. Allow others the freedom to learn from their own mistakes. ( ) [2]

( ) B. Participate as much as possible in mutually solving the problem. (✓)

SCORING

1. A	4	11. A	1	21. A	4
B	2	B	3	B	1
2. A	5	12. A	4	22. A	1
B	1	B	5	B	5
3. A	2	13. A	2	23. A	3
B	3	B	5	B	4
4. A	4	14. A	4	24. A	3
B	5	B	3	B	2
5. A	1	15. A	5	25. A	5
B	2	B	1	B	2
6. A	2	16. A	1		
B	3	B	4		
7. A	2	17. A	2		
B	4	B	1		
8. A	3	18. A	5		
B	5	B	4		
9. A	5	19. A	3		
B	3	B	1		
10. A	3	20. A	1		
B	4	B	2		

SUMMARY INTERPRETATION: *Eddie Sedgewick*

mean score = 5

	I	II	III	IV	V
Normal Situation #1:	8	7	4	3	3
	[+3]	[+2]	[-1]	[-2]	[-2]
Conflict Situation #2:	4	7	3	6	5
	[-1]	[+2]	[-2]	[+1]	[0]
Variances:	<4	-	<1	>3	>2

By calculating the difference of score between situation #1 and situation #2, we can recognize variances in particular attributes. The following interpretation is based on these variances:

SAMPLE CONFLICT RESOLUTION PROFILE: EDDIE SEDGEWICK

[<4 Forcing, >3 Running Away, >2 Giving In]

I [<4] on the Domination (forcing) scale suggests there is significant variance in the degree to which Eddie forces his opinions ("high" in normal situations, "normal" in conflict situations). Under ordinary circumstances, Eddie is a problem solver, even if he likes to get his own way most of the time. He generally likes to do a lot of talking relating to others to get the job done. He may tend to dominate conversations, but his intent is usually to find a solution to the problem.

IV [>3] on the Avoidance (running away) scale is also a significant variance. But in this attribute Eddie is less avoiding in "normal" situations than in "conflict" situations. Under conditions of stress or difficulty, Eddie backs off. He may not press his points so hard. He quiets down and has a good look around. His focus is still on solving the problem, but now he asks more questions.

Under difficult circumstances, Eddie will tend to manage conflict by putting more of his energy into preserving relationships, rather than by forcing the issue. He is also more inclined to make concessions to others' points of view than he would be normally.

V [>2] on the Accommodation (giving in) scale is not a significant variance— Eddie's accommodating behavior doesn't vary too much from situation to situation.

- - - - - - - - - - - - - - -

M.O.D.E. Aftermath

No one uses a single, rigid resolution style suitable for dealing with all conflicts. Each of us is capable of using all five conflict resolution modes, when appropriate, despite any particular patterns of reliance we may generally exhibit. All five of these modes are helpful in some situations and each represents a set of useful social skills.

Awareness of our own personal predispositions may also lead us to examine alternative conflict resolution strategies that may not have been previously recognized or practised. Increased awareness may lead us to use strategies with greater finesse and flexibility, according to the particular requirements we face with each new conflict.

After you have taken the M.O.D.E. questionnaire. As a means of exploring the implications of your conflict resolution modes further, we have summarized some of the potential uses and obvious risks to each strategy and have suggested questions for you to reflect upon further.

I. Domination

Potential uses/obvious risks:

Dominating or forcing your concerns can be a most useful strategy when important issues need to be addressed immediately, such as in cases of extreme time pressure, or emergencies. This strategy is generally useful whenever quick, decisive action is called for. If misused, it can create resentments from those who may have been opposed or overruled.

If you scored high, ask yourself:

◆ How much influence do you allow others to have on you?

◆ Do you talk too much in group situations? How much free or open interaction with others are you comfortable with?

◆ Do you try to take over a lot? What are the limits or costs of this pattern to you? To others?

If you scored low, ask yourself:

◆ How often do you feel frustrated or let down by your own inaction?

◆ How often do you wish you had the self-assurance to say what is on your mind, and to act on it with confidence?

II. Collaboration

Potential uses/obvious risks:

This is an appropriate strategy to use when each side's sets of concerns are too important to be compromised, or when your own primary objective is to learn more by understanding the views of others. Although this is the best ("win-win") alternative for resolving conflicts, the process can be time-consuming and requires a considerable investment of energy and resources.

If you scored high, ask yourself:

◆ Do you often spend time on issues or problems that don't deserve it?

◆ How successful are you at setting priorities and at getting others to go along with your plans?

If you scored low, ask yourself:

◆ Are you missing any opportunities for developing successful joint-ventures with others?

◆ Are you experiencing any difficulty gaining the cooperation and support of others? How do you explain this?

III. Compromise

Potential uses/obvious risks:

Compromise or negotiation can be a useful strategy when each side is strongly committed to mutually exclusive goals, or when there are complex issues to be resolved and limited resources with which to accomplish them. Although bargaining is often a useful tactic for arriving at expedient solutions under conditions of time pressure, the downside is that neither side is entirely satisfied with the outcome when they've had to give up something of value.

If you scored high, ask yourself:

◆ Are you so much of a tactician that you sometimes lose sight of the larger picture?

◆ Are you so fond of wheeling and dealing that it undermines relationships or deflects attention away from important issues?

If you scored low, ask yourself:

◆ Are you ever timid or reluctant when negotiating for something you want?

◆ How can you satisfy yourself that enough of your own needs are met?

IV. Avoidance

Potential uses/obvious risks:

Obviously, the "do nothing" option works best in situations where the problem is likely to blow over. But what if the problem doesn't blow over? It's either a brilliant choice or a complete blunder. When an issue is trivial or of only passing importance, or when other more important issues are pressing their way to the forefront—it may be best not to act. Avoidance is an appropriate strategy to use when the potential damage of confronting a conflict outweighs the benefits of its resolution. It can also serve as a "cooling off" period in the midst of a dispute. But if you choose to ignore a problem which then gets worse, it will likely be much harder to resolve than if you had "nipped it in the bud."

If you scored high, ask yourself:

◆ Are your contributions or potential contributions to projects being realized?

◆ Are important decisions being made without your input on issues?

If you scored low, ask yourself:

◆ Are you stirring things up unnecessarily, or creating hostilities towards you or your cause?

◆ Do you often feel overwhelmed with obligations? Do you feel compelled to act on issues beyond your control?

V. Accommodation

Potential uses/obvious risks:

This mode can work to your advantage if the issue is not of particular importance to you, but means a lot to the other side. If you find it reasonable to admit when you are wrong, you can step aside gracefully and accept a better position put forward by others. But, if there is something more substantial at stake in it for you, it won't do you any good to resolve the conflict by giving in entirely.

If you scored high, ask yourself:

◆ Do you feel that your own ideas and concerns are not getting the recognition and respect they deserve?

◆ Do you feel that you may be giving away too much in disputes that affect you or the organization?

If you scored low, ask yourself:

◆ Do you have difficulty building strong relationships with others at work?

◆ Do you have trouble admitting when you may be wrong, with letting go, or with recognizing legitimate exceptions to the rules?

The Contagion of Conflict

In *The Semisovereign People: A Realist's View of Democracy in America*[6] (1960), political scientist E.E. Schattschneider argued that organizations and politics are mainly informal systems rather than (formal) legal institutions. He further observed that nothing draws a crowd like a good fight. Conflict is almost irresistibly fascinating to people. And every conflict has, at its core, a few individuals in opposition to one another, plus an audience that is attracted to the scene.

The spectators are an integral part of the scene in as much as, by joining or not joining the fray, they can influence or determine the outcome. Furthermore, the relations between the audience and the combatants are highly unstable—allowing for changes or shifts in alliance. By changing the number of participants you can affect the results. It follows that the outcome of a conflict is determined by the ability of the contestants to involve more or less of the audience in the fight.

In modern business the way to preserve power relations is to keep conflicts out of the public arena, that is, to minimize the number of participants. The bias of the system favors *privatization* of conflict to protect private interests and maintain control. For the most part, the special interests in positions of power want private settlements in which they can dictate the results. Whenever possible, they want to keep government or the public out of it. On the other hand, those with a public interest in mind seek to *socialize* conflict by expanding the scope or number of people involved.

According to Schattschneider, the dynamics of conflict occur on four dimensions: intensity, visibility, direction, and scope. Assuming that the potential for conflict lies dormant until activated, the intensity and visibility of conflict can be raised through increased controversy on an issue. Assuming that some conflicts displace others as they become more visible and intense, the direction and scope can be altered by the priorities people set when taking sides on issues they know and care most about. Those on each side of a conflict tend to consolidate around the most important issues, even though they may continue to differ on lesser ones. Whichever way the lines are drawn, the mobilization of opposing forces involves a consolidation on both sides. Conflict divides and unites at the same time.

The failure, wrote Schattschneider, to understand that consolidation and division are part of the same process has produced several misconceptions about politics and political strategy. Conflicts, he said, compete with each other. A shift in cleavages produces a substitution of conflicts, new coalitions, and shifts in the allocation of power. New alliances are formed and reformed; old alignments and combinations are destroyed or abandoned. To exploit these cleavages, the strategy of opposition seeks to substitute certain conflicts with other issues. Splitting the dominant alliance is at the heart of all political strategy.

Investigating Conflicts

There are a number of questions that may be useful to ask in situations where conflict, or the potential for conflict, exists. Asking these questions can reveal more about a conflict and its context than appears noticeable at first glance. Here are some more questions for you to consider:

1. *Can we agree to disagree?* A good way of initiating a resolution of conflict is to do it when things are calm or peaceful between you and the other party. For example, you might begin by saying: "I haven't been entirely satisfied with the way we have handled our differences in the past. I don't think you have been very happy either. Why don't we try one or two new ideas and see if it helps to clear things up?"

2. *Has anything like this ever happened here before?* Few conflicts arise without a prior history. How does what is happening now relate to what has happened previously? Can you detect patterns or elements of repetition in the behavior of key players?

   For instance, one member of the team may be consistently absent whenever key decisions are being made. Once the decisions are subsequently announced, she challenges them on grounds of process: "Not everyone involved was in on the decision." She may repeat this process several times before others recognize a pattern. This can lead to a confrontation between her and others on the team. The conflict may escalate before any longer term solutions emerge.

3. *What does the conflict have to do with the roles people play in the organization?* Some conflicts are due to the way one person is expected to relate to others' official authority within the organization. A second-tier supervisor may, for example, have been told by a senior manager to change the work schedule of her staff. In doing so the supervisor is only carrying out mandates from above in the hierarchy, but the staff concerned about the changes have no one else to blame. Those involved need to recognize this potential problem, and make the chain of command and responsibility more explicit.

4. *To what extent is the conflict a reflection of the personal style (as opposed to the designated role) of those involved?* While some conflicts can be associated with the roles individuals occupy within the organization, others reflect the personalities of the people involved. The thing to remember is that different peo-

ple with different personality types have different needs. These needs are often reflected in the kinds of issues that lead to conflict.

5. *To what extent is the conflict premeditated?* Some conflicts are deliberately engineered. For example, certain types of questions can be asked with the intention of creating conflict. We know of one case where, at a regular board of directors meeting, a significant company shareholder asked a deliberate schedule of questions of the incumbent CEO, heard his responses, then produced documents to refute each of the CEO's replies. This led to a vote of non-confidence—and a new CEO! All according to the shareholder's conflict plan. Invariably, the best way to deal with people who manipulate conflicts is to "blow their cover" by using a relevant hypothetical question. In this case, the CEO might ask the shareholder: "What response would you give to someone who was deliberately setting you up for a fight?"

6. *To what extent is the conflict a symptom of a problem elsewhere in the organization?* Conflicts have been known to move around in organizations and become expressed at locations quite removed from their places of origin. Professor Kenwyn Smith reported that a White House staff member of the Kennedy administration once commented that it was always clear when the president and the First Lady were fighting, and when they were relating amicably:

> **❝** we knew when they were fighting simply by watching the interactions of their personal staffs. When the hairdressers or the limousine drivers were arguing, this was because JFK and Jackie were in conflict. When these groups had their act together we knew the first couple was getting on okay.[7] **❞**

It is also quite common for organizational consultants to intervene in an organizational setting to resolve a conflict at one point, only to see the same, or similar, problems emerge somewhere else within that same organization. When this occurs, the organization may have a problem that goes beyond a specific group, and concerns the way the organization is structured and managed.

Constructive Conflict Consciousness-Raising

Conflict is indeed a common feature of our lives, as we have discussed. And we have no doubt that each conflict can be a valuable learning experience for individuals and organizations alike. For individuals, conflict can provide the opportunity to demonstrate and expand their skills and confidence. For organizations, conflict can stimulate change and innovation.

The challenge for individuals in organizations is not so much to avoid conflict, but to create opportunities for conflict to be experienced positively. To accomplish this, the essential task is to build an organizational climate in which there is a strong sense of trust. Such climates of trust usually require:

◆ openness and clear communication as to shared objectives and agreed upon goals

◆ real encouragement to express views openly and to confront issues in a way that does not personalize them

◆ honest relations based on mutual trust and support for all team members

◆ substantial resources for personal development as well as organizational development

Well-managed conflicts may present us with special opportunities—dangerous as some may be—that increase the overall innovativeness of the organization. Here are just some of the kinds of things that constructive conflict consciousness-raising may do:

◆ *Heighten awareness of conflict patterns and personal biases.* (Ask yourself: how do others see themselves and their jobs? In what contexts? Is there another perspective to this conflict? Can events be understood in a more positive way?)

◆ *Increase awareness of the subjective frameworks underlying people's actions, and become more sensitive and respectful towards them.* (Think about the other people involved for a moment. What are they trying to do? What do they see as the conflict or dilemma? How would *they* like to see things handled?)

◆ *Raise awareness of some aspect of the organizational system, and adaptations that must be made for change to occur.* (What organizational dynamics and motives do others think are important? What resolutions would satisfy both sides of the dispute?)

◆ *Encourage a new perspective that highlights the value of an individual or department's efforts and contributions.* (How can the situation be framed or structured to appreciate the unique skills, interests, and abilities of those who work there? What can we do to strengthen our mutual resolve as an organization?)

And finally . . .

As we have seen, just as there are many types of conflict, and many variants of each type, there are many ways to approach their resolution, and even to prevent certain conflicts from occurring in the first place. By adopting a constructive stance with regard to conflict, what we hope to create is a climate of trust and support. In the Interpersonal Skills Clinic that follows in the next section, we will explore ways of using conflict creatively and attempt to define some of the interpersonal and organizational conditions necessary for establishing a climate of trust through self-disclosure.

Keep in mind the following tips when dealing with conflict:

Treat the other person with respect. Respect for another person is an attitude best conveyed through specific actions—such as the way we listen and the things we disclose.

Take the other point of view for a moment. Experience the other side of the argument if you can. Try to see what others see, rather than just listening to the way they try to say what they see.

Recap or reflect the other person's main themes—as you understand them. A quick review can help us to gain a more complete or integrated picture of what the other person is really saying, i.e. "One theme you keep coming back to..."

"I've been thinking about what you said..."

"I recognize a pattern in what you are saying..."

State your own views, needs, and feelings on the matter. After demonstrating respect for the other person it is your turn to:

◆ State your own point of view briefly and succinctly, i.e. *be short and to the point.*

◆ Say what you mean and mean what you say. While there may be occasion when it is best to remain guarded, this is not one of them.

◆ Disclose your feelings as well as your ideas. If you have been accused unjustly, and feel injured, say so. This needs to be done if the conflict is ever going to be fully resolved.

Section 2 Establishing Trust Through Self-Disclosure

Before we get started . . .

Trust, in any relationship, must be established through an open willingness to be honest with one another. This process of establishing trust by revealing honest and personal feelings and sharing experiences with another person is called self-disclosure.

To be effective, self-disclosure must be appropriate to both the situation and the existing levels of trust between the parties involved. In order to build trust and deepen relationships, people need to take account of the effect their disclosures will have on other people.

What's the advantage in possessing the skills associated with self-disclosure? Self-disclosure is the best preventive medicine against destructive conflict. This is because appropriate self-disclosure engenders trust, and people with a high degree of mutual trust are less likely to find themselves in conflict. Trusting relationships or friendships are established when two or more people exchange information about their values, interests, goals, and activities. If I trust you, one of the ways I can demonstrate my trust in you is by disclosing myself to you. To trust me, you must know who I am, and vice-versa.

Too much self-disclosure, on the other hand, or disclosure that is poorly timed, can lead to many unfortunate consequences—as we will see. While it may be true that, in many organizations, most people tell too little about themselves, rather than too much, sometimes self-disclosure can be risky. Therefore, self-disclosure requires our best judgment and understanding.

In this section we will discuss some techniques for bringing about effective, but measured, self-disclosure in the workplace. We will also reflect upon the extent to which we are, or should be, open about ourselves with those we work and live with. There are risks involved in establishing such a climate of openness. Inappropriate self-disclosure or disclosure that is ill-timed can damage one's credibility. We will, therefore, examine some appropriate settings and stages for self-disclosure, as well as some of the dangers involved in using self-disclosure as a means of establishing trust in relationships in general, and at work in particular. Self-disclosure is another of the double-edged swords we have discussed—it is both necessary for establishing trust in relationships, and potentially ruinous if not executed with skill, caution, and care.

Objectives

After you complete this section you should be able to:

1. Define managerial godfathers and disclosure climate.

2. List seven reasons for self-disclosing and give an example of each from your personal experience.

3. Describe four stages of self-disclosure through which most relationships progress, and discuss how to encourage others to be more open or disclosing to you.

4. Explain the meaning of the Johari Window in terms of its "ideal approach" to self-disclosure.

5. Recognize the potential risks and benefits of disclosing in many organizational situations.

Managerial Godfathers

In some Japanese management systems, young managers are formally or informally assigned a *godfather* to look out for them as they establish their careers within the organization. The godfather is always a male—as are most of the young managers—and is almost never a young man's direct superior. The godfather is usually a highly respected member of the upper-middle management group, assigned to act as a mentor or counsellor to a younger managerial trainee.

No one quite seems to know exactly how a godfather is chosen for a young man. One qualification that management professor Peter Drucker has mentioned is that the godfather should be a graduate of the same school or university from which the young man graduated. The "old school tie" binds even more tightly in Japan than it did in Great Britain at one time. Everybody inside the organization knows the identity of a given young man's godfather and respects their relationship.

This is how it works: Managerial godfathers are expected to know their charges, see them fairly regularly, and be available for advice and counsel. If, for example, a young man gets stuck under an incompetent manager and wants to be transferred, the godfather knows where to go and who to talk to. If the young man needs to be disciplined, very often the godfather will deal with him in private. When a young man is ready for a challenging assignment, it is the godfather who sits down with top management first, and discusses what project to give him.

This Japanese godfather concept is similar, but not identical, to long-standing mentoring and coaching relationships that exist in many western organizations. Mentoring relationships in the West tend to be less formal and are not necessarily patriarchal. All managers need guidance and protection during their learning period from advisors to whom they can disclose their goals and aspirations, and from whom they can learn by example.

Godfather relationships represent an institutionalized means of self-disclosing. Most occurrences of self-disclosure are considerably more informal, and often have risks of their own associated with them. We should consider those risks carefully.

Sayonara, Marlon Brando

When Warner Brothers Studio director Joshua Logan was shooting a big-budget picture called *Sayonara* on location in Kyoto, Japan, he warned his star, Marlon Brando not to be left alone with author Truman Capote, who wanted to interview him. "He's after you" Logan told Brando. But Brando—who had a reputation among interviewers as being "a hard nut to crack"—met with him anyway.

Interestingly, Brando revealed himself candidly and without any apparent restraint during the interview. No subject was spared. How was Capote able to get Brando to open up so far? In large part, through a *reciprocity of self-disclosure*—where an act of self-disclosure by one person leads the other person to reciprocate. Capote was a master of this technique—as he had proven in numerous other interviews. By trading confidence for confidence, Capote was able to get Brando to reveal many privacies that Capote's readers were to find shocking.

Here is one comparatively modest example. Knowing that Brando's mother had been an alcoholic, Capote described his own problems growing up with his mother Nina, also an alcoholic. These confessions induced Brando to describe, in terrible detail, the torture of watching his own mother fall apart emotionally in front of his eyes. "One day I could just step right over her, her lying on the floor, and not feel a thing, not give a damn," Brando told him.

Capote's own revelations, of course, did not appear in the final text of his profile of Brando. "The Duke in His Domain" was published in *The New Yorker* in November 1957. Gerald Clarke, Capote's biographer, describes Brando's discomfort once he realized that he had been tricked by the interviewer. In a letter to Capote, Brando later wrote:

Here, of course, is the inevitable communication. . . . It is, indeed, discomforting to have the network of one's innards guywired and festooned with harlequin streamers for public musing, but, perhaps, it will entertain. . . . In closing let me just say . . . [t]here are few who are as well equipped as yourself to write, indeed, the comedy of manners.[8]

This story illustrates the potent danger, as well as the pleasure, of self-disclosure. After Capote's profile appeared, Brando vowed to Joshua Logan that he would kill the writer. To which Logan replied, "You should have killed him before you invited him to dinner." In spite of how Brando may have felt when he read about himself in *The New Yorker*, on the day after the interview was actually conducted in February 1957, Brando told his makeup man in Japan just how much he had *enjoyed* his joint confessional the evening before. Catharsis, along with reciprocity, are just two of the potent motivations for self-disclosure.

Why Do We Disclose?

People have many reasons for disclosing. Ronald Adler and his colleagues have divided them into the following categories: catharsis, self-clarification, self-validation, reciprocity, impression formation, social control, and relationship maintenance/enhancement.[9] As you read, try writing an example from your own experience beside each of the categories. Ask yourself if there are any obvious reasons why you use some more often than others. Keep these categories in mind when you come to think about how to encourage self-disclosure in others.

Catharsis

Catharsis is emotional release. Following an act of catharsis, we feel as though a psychological burden has been lifted. This is part of the reason why Marlon Brando seemed to enjoy revealing so much of himself to Truman Capote.

Self-Clarification

Sometimes just thinking out loud can help you to clarify your own feelings or ideas. "Talking the problem out" is used in many kinds of psychotherapy, but it can also occur in more mundane settings, such as the hairdresser's shop or the local park or tavern.

Self-Validation

If you disclose information with the hope of getting the listener to agree with you, you are seeking validation—confirmation of a belief you hold about yourself. For example, if you explain to someone that you reprimanded a subordinate in front of others to make a point to them all, you may be seeking validation for your behavior.

Reciprocity

One act of self-disclosure leads to another. In some situations, you may choose to disclose information about yourself to encourage another person to begin sharing personal information. Likewise, you may find yourself wanting to disclose after someone else has just done so.

Impression Formation

In some situations, you may choose to self-disclose in order to convey a particular impression of yourself to others. To look good, we might share selected bits of information about ourselves, such as those pointing to our accomplishments or grand ambitions.

Social Control

Sometimes you may use self-disclosure to increase your control over a situation by deliberately communicating certain options which favor your own interests. For example, you may encourage your boss to give you a raise, simply by letting her know about other organizations interested in your services. Or, you may let a car dealer with whom you are negotiating know about other deals you have pending with the competition.

Relationship Maintenance and Enhancement

Relationships all need mutual trust and disclosure in order to develop over time. If you never reveal how you feel about your partner, your relationship will become shallow. People in any kind of relationship or friendship have to be open with one another if they ever expect their relationship to deepen and grow.

Finally, people may misuse self-disclosure to manipulate others. The example of Brando and Capote is an example of self-disclosing for manipulative purposes.

Four Guidelines for Self-Disclosure

For the purposes of establishing trust in any relationship, the basic guidelines emphasize the importance of engaging in disclosure:

♦ to the right person (someone capable of understanding);

♦ at the right time and place (when and where others' needs are not more pressing than our own);

♦ for the right reasons (wanting to get to know someone better); and

♦ to the right extent (in gradual stages).

Stages of Self-Disclosure

Most trusting relationships are established in stages. That is, we reveal ourselves to the other person over time. If all goes well in the early stages of limited disclosure and we are able to sense the interest and acceptance of our partner in return, we open ourselves up some more. The amount of disclosing that is deemed appropriate will, of course, vary with each relationship, but the general stages of self-disclosure roughly follow this progression:

♦ cliché communication

♦ basic facts and histories

♦ personal interests, feelings, and opinions

♦ friendship, bonding, or intimacy

In order to have satisfying and meaningful relationships you must first meet people and get to know them better. From the earliest stages of initiating contact, partners exchange *cliché communication* through a variety of standard queries such as: "How's it going?" "How are you today?" "Don't I know you from someplace?" "Do you come here often?" and so forth. Such openers are rarely original—but that is not their purpose. They are used as a means of getting acquainted with people. We begin this process by getting people to open up and looking for signals from them (which should be almost instantaneous) that this is something they want to do.

If those signals (smiling, light touching, wide-open eye contact) appear, the conversation moves forward to an open exchange of *basic facts and histories* about each other. Questions about names and occupations are asked and answered, e.g. "What's your name?" "What do you do?" "Where do you live?" "Who is your friend?" "What kind of car do you drive?" Once it becomes obvious that people have interests in common, the conversation is likely to move on to more significant topics.

The need to know others' personal interests, feelings, and opinions causes us to open up to a greater degree as time goes on. Before long, the conversation moves away from clichés and mundane facts to swapping more important personal information. As the desire to move to a new level of trust intensifies, routine exchanges of information become less and less satisfying. But it is especially important at this stage to remember that it is not usually a good idea to disclose too much personal information too soon. Rather than enhance the relationship, rapid disclosure can inhibit further development—and sometimes even terminate the friendship.

If a relationship continues to develop, and more time is spent together, partners will tend to disclose more and more of themselves at various (appropriate) times and places. When a relationship reaches a peak of *friendship or bonding,* the level of self-disclosure plateaus as well. In most friendships there is a natural limit to how much we can know about or reveal to one another.

Beyond that, true *intimacy* is a rare condition, and normally takes a great deal of time and trust to develop. Most working relationships never progress to this stage of disclosure. And even the most intimate relationships are not always focused on the deepest revelations. Most mature relationships are a mixture of mundane, routine, everyday conversation, with occasional deeper revelations thrown in every now and then. Besides, there are many things about ourselves to which even we are blind, and which cannot therefore be disclosed.

The Johari Window

No discussion of self-disclosure is complete without reference to the "Johari Window", named after its originators, Joseph Luft and Harrington Ingham.[10] The Johari Window, as shown in Figure 5.2, suggests that people possess four types of information about themselves:

♦ things known both to themselves and others.
♦ things known to others, but to which they themselves are blind.
♦ things known to themselves, but hidden from others.
♦ things unknown to both themselves and others.

Building a relationship usually involves working to enlarge the free area known to both yourself and others, while decreasing the blind and hidden areas. As you disclose, you free the area known to yourself and others, and reduce the hidden area. As you become more open to feedback and disclosure from others, the blind area is reduced, and more of yourself is revealed, as shown in Figure 5.3.

Before you start opening up to others at work and elsewhere, we caution you to do some more thinking about how much disclosing you do now, and the implications of any change. We all have opportunities to develop deeper personal relationships at work. But we may prefer not to establish too many close relationships on the job. In any case, we will quite naturally develop closer relationships with some of our fellow workers than with others. It is from them, and the *feedback and disclosure* they offer us, that we begin to learn the inside

Figure 5.2: The Johari Window

Source: Joseph Luft, *Of Human Interaction*, Palo Alto, Calif.: Mayfield Publishing, 1969.

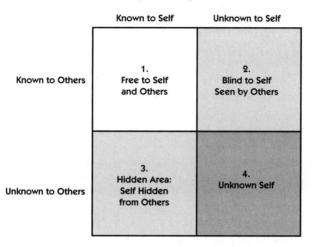

story of what is really going on in the workplace. Handled with care, such information is vital to individual and organizational development and survival.

For example, a newcomer is slowly brought into the social reality of the organization by progressing through two or three stages of self disclosure with some other employees. The inner workings and informal mechanisms of the organization are learned largely through such increments of disclosure provided by the organization's more senior members.

The degree and type of self-disclosure that occurs among organizational members can result in a "disclosure climate," where appropriate behavior is "sensed" much the same as some sense rainy weather. Some disclosure climates may be de-

Figure 5.3: Areas Known According to Johari

Source: Luft, 1969

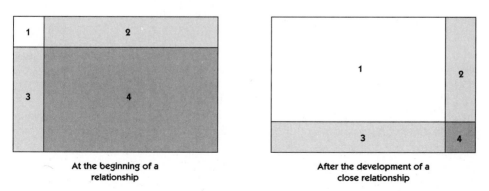

scribed as chilly or cold, others as warm and friendly. Like the weather, most organizations have variable conditions.

In a moderate climate, the ideal approach (in Johari Window terms), would be for individuals to increase the size of their open self (window #1) by making their hidden selves more known. People who are open to feedback, and who are willing to disclose information about themselves to others, have adopted the optimal profile. *If only it were that simple.* In reality, how much of ourselves we leave open for others to see will depend on many factors—including how well we know ourselves to begin with.

INTERPERSONAL SKILLS CLINIC

SELF-DISCLOSURE QUESTIONNAIRE

This questionnaire may help you discover more about how you communicate with other people. Like all the other questionnaires in this book, this one has no right or wrong answers. And it makes no claims to scientific validity. It is simply an instrument for stimulating awareness of how willing we are to disclose ourselves, and how open we are to feedback or disclosure from others.

You can take the test yourself, or compare your scores with those of someone you have a personal and/or professional relationship with. It might even be interesting to compare your scores with those of members of groups or teams with which you are affiliated.

To complete the questionnaire, indicate the extent to which you have disclosed or talked about each of the following topics (or a related topic from your experience):

   0 = I haven't disclosed or spoken about this at all;
   1 = I have seldom disclosed about this, and only in general terms;
   2 = I have sometimes disclosed or spoken about this;
   3 = I have frequently disclosed quite a bit about this;
   4 = I have disclosed fully and completely about this.

1. Your hobbies. How you like to spend your spare time, or how you are able to avoid working.

2. Times when you have asked your colleagues for more feedback regarding the quality of your work.

3. Occasions in your working life in which you were the happiest or most successful.

4. A time when you asked a friend to respond to your admission that you betrayed his or her confidence by giving away a secret you were asked to keep.

5. Those aspects of your daily work that satisfy you least.

6. Times when you have waited an hour for a scheduled appointment, and expressed your impatience over this to the person who kept you waiting.

7. The unhappiest moments in your work life, why they were unhappy, and who you view as responsible.

8. Your response to a colleague who has just confronted you about not standing up for yourself at a critical moment.

9. Your views on the way your boss should do his or her job.

10. Your pledges of improvement on assignments or maladjustments at work or in relationships.

11. Your personal views on organizational politics or business policy where you work.

12. Times when you deliberately ignored someone who had spoken critically to you.

13. Personal characteristics that give you cause for pride and satisfaction.

14. Your retelling of the "chewing out" you got from your boss for being late or over-budget with some assignment.

15. The person in your organization you most resent, and the reason for your resentment.

16. When you shocked a friend by revealing a guilty secret related to work or relationships.

17. The circumstances under which you become depressed and your feelings get hurt.

18. When you told your employer about circumstances at work that make you uncomfortable.

19. Your personal goals or ambitions for the next five years or so.

20. When you invited a loved one to give you some advice after you confessed a long-standing and deep-seated regret.

SELF DISCLOSURE ANSWER KEY

Willingness to Self Disclose	Openness to Feedback & Disclosure
1. _____	2. _____
3. _____	4. _____
5. _____	6. _____
7. _____	8. _____
9. _____	10. _____
11. _____	12. _____
13. _____	14. _____
15. _____	16. _____

17. _____	18. _____
19. _____	20. _____
Total _____	Total _____

AREA OF SELF-DISCLOSURE AND OPENNESS TO FEEDBACK

To arrive at an index of the amount and type of openness and interpersonal risk taking you have with regard to self disclosure, draw a square and plot your totals along the top and left side of the square as shown in Figure 5.4. Now draw vertical and horizontal lines through your scores to create a Johari window of your own disclosure profile.

Consider the example shown in Figure 5.5.

Figure 5.4: Self-Disclosure Questionnaire Answer Key

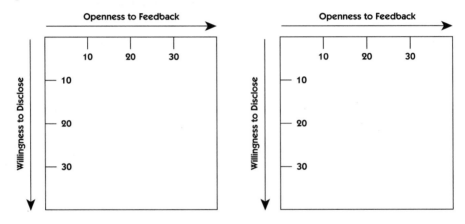

Figure 5.5: An Example of Self-Disclosure Questionnaire Results

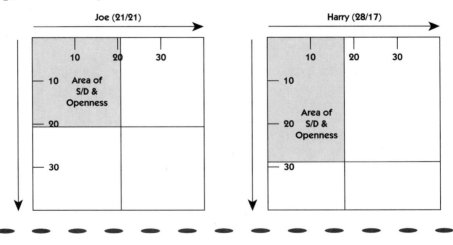

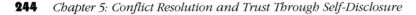

Disclosure Climates in Organizations

Each and every one of us has to make very tough decisions about whether or not to trust and be open with information about ourselves or others we know about. Therefore it is important that we develop the capacity to size up situations in a hurry and to make enlightened judgments about who, what, and how much to allow others to know about us.

The degree to which self-disclosure establishes trust will differ from place to place, and culture to culture. While some organizational cultures can accommodate a lot of openness, others are not so fortunate. All people must determine what is appropriate for the circumstances in which they work, and adjust their behavior to suit each situation.

In some organizational cultures, openness and self-revelation may be an accepted practice; in others such acts are so far outside the norm they are explicitly or implicitly discouraged. Consider the extent to which your primary organizational culture encourages or discourages self disclosure, and how this is related to the levels of trust you experience. As much as it is necessary for the development of trusting, productive relationships, there is a negative side to openness and self- disclosure in many organizations. Disclosure makes us as vulnerable to deception, rejection, and attack as to the pleasures of trust, friendship and openness.

It Cuts Both Ways

Self-disclosure is indeed a double-edged sword. On one side it is a necessary part of our social existence. It is an organizational requirement. On the other, it has a price and risks attached to its many benefits. It can help you to develop trust in a relationship, or it can tear your trust apart.

There are many ways in which inappropriate communication can compromise your best interests. At the level of face-to-face exchanges, disclosing too much or inappropriately can put a damper on a conversation or trigger barriers that eventually harm the relationship. For example, you may have a mean-spirited co-worker with whom you have been open in the past. If he or she consistently betrays your trust, you would be a fool to continue this trust in the future.

To gain trust, you must give it. We need it to learn and grow. Trust makes us secure enough to ask for constructive feedback about ourselves. Feedback from people you trust can be extremely helpful in revealing your "blind spots" to you, or showing you aspects of yourself you never knew existed.

Some Friendly Advice

Although it may be hard at first, requesting feedback from others is an especially important skill for managers to practise. The following six points are important for managers to keep in mind when practising self-disclosure in interpersonal or organizational settings:

1. *Move gradually through deeper stages of self-disclosure.* Disclosures about deep feelings or beliefs are appropriate (most often) in established, trusting relationships. If self-disclosure is made before a certain stage or before a bond of trust is established, it can lead to problems, such as prejudicial preformance ratings where your confessions of discontent may be used against you.

2. *When it is asked for, focus your feedback on the other person's behavior, not on his or her personality.* Refer to what the person does, not what you imagine his or her personality traits to be. For example, you might say the person "spoke frequently during a meeting" rather than saying he or she "is a loud-mouth". One statement is an observation; the other is a judgment of character.

3. *Reciprocate self-disclosure.* Unequal self-disclosure creates an unbalanced relationship and one that is doomed to fall apart.

4. *Focus your feedback on the "here and now", not on the "there and then".* The more immediate the feedback, the more helpful it is.

5. *Use self-disclosure to improve a relationship.* Focus your feedback on actions that the other person can change, not ideal behavior that is probably impossible to achieve.

6. *Do not give people more feedback than they can handle at the time.* If you overload people with feedback, it reduces the chances that they will use it to good advantage.

Giving constructive feedback is a serious business. We do not recommend you give it lightly. Be sure you are willing to accept responsibility for what is heard as well as said, and clarify as much as the receiver wants clarified. Keep in mind that the purpose of feedback is to increase others' self-awareness and to assist them in the process of self-improvement.

And finally . . .

Self-disclosure is necessary in order for us to have better, more trusting, and more satisfying relationships. It is also a way to grow closer and more supportive of others. But it is also a daring proposition. We pay a price. It is a risky business to reveal important information about ourselves—especially in most contemporary working situations. If you admit to a co-worker what you *really* think of your new supervisor, you may find that those comments will come back to haunt you. Then again, as much risk as there is, trust through self-disclosure is often what transforms our relationships from superficial, masked role-play arrangements into unique and important interpersonal adventures. We are, after all, attracted to people who disclose themselves to us in an appropriate manner. They are the ones we trust and go to for support.

CHAPTER REVIEW QUESTIONS

1. Identify three or four outcomes of constructive conflict.

2. Describe briefly when the body's "fight or flight" response occurs.

3. Why are conflicts that trigger a fight or flight mechanism not conducive to problem solving?

4. _____ and _____ conflicts are the types of conflicts found in organizations that are usually the most difficult to solve.

5. What is the first step in dealing with procrastinators or perfectionists?

6. What is the first step in third-party conflict intervention?

7. What are the first steps in handling matters when you are verbally attacked?
   a. Consider your options. Ask for clarification. Attack.
   b. Invite the angered parties to vent their feelings. Then use silence. Wait it out.
   c. Wait. Use silence. Invite negotiation.
   d. Use silence. Wait for the angered parties to vent their feelings. Talk.

8. What are five strategies for resolving conflict and which ones usually have the best outcomes for both parties?

9. In Japan, what is a *managerial godfather* and what is a managerial godfather's role in the organizations that have them?

10. How might you use *catharsis* and *reciprocity* as means for getting others to disclose more of themselves to you?

11. For the purposes of establishing trust in a relationship, when is self-disclosure most appropriate?

12. What is the final stage of self-disclosure and how soon should a friendship or intimate relationship take to get there?
    a. love; two to three years
    b. intimate friendship; after the bonding stage
    c. marriage; after a trial period of bonding
    d. bonding, friendship, or intimacy; after a great deal of time

13. Why is it impossible to disclose everything about yourself to someone you are intimate with?

14. Respond to each of the following by placing a (T) or (F) before the question.[11] Answer according to what you think is the case. Your answers will reveal your attitudes about self-disclosure, and can be compared against Gibson and Hodgetts' findings.
    ____ 1. It is usually better not to tell your employees more than they need to know to do their specific job. This minimizes office politics and gossip.
    ____ 2. A manager who is open and friendly with his or her employees is often seen as a soft touch.

_____ 3. Open sharing of goals and attitudes by the manager will help the employee to be more productive.

_____ 4. A manager should be careful how much personal information he or she discloses to employees. Workers who know you too well tend to lose respect for you as a supervisor.

_____ 5. In personal relations, the more open and candid you can be, the healthier the relationship will be.

_____ 6. Openness in personal relationships is fine, but sometimes it's better to maintain your privacy on certain issues. You can avoid a lot of disagreements this way.

_____ 7. If telling others what you really think, especially when you know they do not agree, is very uncomfortable for you unless the topic is of extreme importance, you should not mention it.

_____ 8. Consistently disclosing information to employees at work is extremely time consuming. The motivational value that might be gained is lost due to the amount of time and effort consumed in the process.

_____ 9. Being open with others and sharing things with them, like everything else, has its time and place. For example, it is appropriate at home with family and friends. However, it has no place in the office.

_____10. Being open and sharing with superiors at work can cause many problems. They may see you as pushy or egotistical, if not a little eccentric in your behavior.

15. What are the six points managers should keep in mind when practising self-disclosure?

16. State how conflict simultaneously divides and unites people.

SUGGESTED ANSWERS

1. Constructive conflict:
   ◆ Opens up an issue in a confronting manner;
   ◆ Develops clarification of an issue;
   ◆ Improves problem-solving quality;
   ◆ Increases involvement;
   ◆ Provides more spontaneity in communication;
   ◆ Initiates growth;
   ◆ Strengthens a relationship when creatively resolved;
   ◆ Helps increase productivity.

2. The "fight or flight" response happens whenever you are faced with a stressful conflict situation.

3. Because all of the energy and nutrients in the body are drained away from the brain into the muscles of your arms and legs.

4. substantive; mixed

5. Getting them to agree that procrastination or perfectionism is a problem.

6. Establishing some agreed-upon procedures for handling disputes, rather than dealing immediately with the disputes themselves.

7. b.

8. Collaboration is the only strategy in which both sides win. Compromise means that each side must give something up in order to get something in return. Domination and accommodation result in one side of the dispute coming away with the lion's share of the benefits. Avoidance usually results in a no-win situation for either side.

9. The godfather is usually a highly respected (senior) member of the organization who is assigned to act as a teacher or mentor to younger managerial trainees.

10. People enjoy getting things "off their chest" through catharsis. Let them vent when they need to. They can also be encouraged to disclose by responding to information you disclose about yourself to them (reciprocity).

11. Disclosure is appropriate when it is to the right person, at the right time and place, for the right reasons, and to the right extent.

12. d.

13. It is impossible to disclose everything because there are some things about ourselves that are unknown or to which we remain blind.

14. Answers seen as indicating comfortableness with self-disclosure behavior are as follows:
    1. _False._ Office politics and gossip will flourish when information is restricted and guarded.
    2. _False._ While initially some employees may perceive this to be the case, long-term authentic, open relationships can be fostered only by the manager's setting an example.
    3. _True._ Employees like to know where they stand and where they are headed. Trying to "figure out" the boss is both nonproductive and time-consuming.
    4. _False._ Though a commonly held belief, "familiarity breeds contempt" has not been proven. Open, comfortable, interpersonal relationships foster a good working climate.
    5. _True._ Why spend time trying to guess what the other folks you relate to are thinking? The best way to gain accurate knowledge is directly from them!
    6. _False._ Privacy is read as secrecy by others and they will try to figure out your motives—usually incorrectly!
    7. _False._ Failure to confront issues may lead to fewer arguments now, but substantially bigger problems will occur later on. When you finally ex-

plode, people will not understand because it will appear as though you have gone along with everything previously.

    8. <u>False.</u> Disclosure may be time-consuming, but in the long run it is far less so than operating on erroneous assumptions and partial knowledge.

    9. <u>False.</u> Just as disclosure works at home, it will work to promote healthier professional relationships as well.

    10. <u>False.</u> This is a tough one and particularly problematic with supervisors who are secretive themselves. They may indeed see you as a little eccentric. Nevertheless, they will have more knowledge of who you really are and how to motivate and reward you.

15. 1. Move gradually through deeper stages of self-disclosure.

     2. When it is asked for, focus your feedback on the other person's behavior, not on his or her personality.

     3. Reciprocate self-disclosure.

     4. Focus your feedback on the "here and now," not on the "there and then."

     5. Use self-disclosure to improve a relationship.

     6. Do not give people more feedback than they can handle at the time.

16. The mobilization of opposing forces involves a consolidation on both sides. While conflict divides people on lesser issues it often unites them on larger ones.

INTERPERSONAL COMMUNICATION SCENARIO

VALTEC CONTROLS

OVERVIEW AND ASSIGNMENT QUESTIONS

In the following scenario, which is based on a situation that could well occur in an organization, you will have the opportunity to apply the principles and skills you have learned in this chapter. The scenario can be used as the basis for a written or oral analysis or for role-play.

Jim Hnatyshyn, a vice-president of manufacturing, is faced with a series of disputes between his direct subordinate, Dipak Sari, a maintenance manager, and Dwayne Sather, one of his maintenance supervisors. These conflicts have resulted in a formal complaint by Sather against Sari. The situation is threatening to disrupt maintenance operations. As a VP, Hnatyshyn believes he should intervene.

1. Assume you are Jim Hnatyshyn. What is your perception of how Sather and Sari view one another? Why do you have these perceptions?

2. How would you explain the behavior of the two men?

3. Does Sather's complaint against Sari have any basis in fact?

4. Does Sari's authority entitle him to reprimand Sather?

5. Do intercultural factors have a role to play in this scenario? If so, how should they be identified and treated?

6. How would you deal with this situation?

INTRODUCTION

"This is the worst part of the job for me," thought Jim Hnatyshyn, vice-president of manufacturing at Valtec Controls in Ottawa.

"I can handle the technical side, but the greatest problem in this company is with the people side of things. Yesterday morning one of my supervisors, Dwayne Sather, stormed into my office to complain about the tongue-lashing he got from his manager, Dipak Sari, over some scheduling problems in the department. I don't see why two good men can't learn to get along. In any case, it's time for me to do something before they come to blows.

"If I don't intervene, the whole department is going to get caught up in the conflict and we will fall behind schedule. I can't afford to let that happen. But what can I do? When a machine breaks down I fix it. But when the relationship between one of my managers and his supervisor breaks down, it's a more difficult problem."

PROFILES OF SARI AND SATHER

Dipak Sari is one of six managers reporting to Jim Hnatyshyn. Sari manages the maintenance department which includes workers, machines, building, and electrical maintenance. He is 47 and has 12 years of experience at Valtec. Sari is married with two children in high school. He is a graduate civil engineer, and is currently working towards his master's degree in civil engineering.

Dwayne Sather is one of three supervisors reporting to Sari and is responsible for building and electrical maintenance. He is 51 and has 17 years of experience with the company. Prior to becoming a maintenance supervisor, he had been an assistant supervisor in the tool room for six years. He is married with two sons and a daughter, all of whom are in elementary school. For the past 10 years, Sather has been an elected councillor on the local public utilities commission. He has held the post of chair for the commission for the past four years.

SARI TALKS ABOUT HIMSELF AND THE JOB

I'm a graduate student at university, working my way towards a master's degree in civil engineering. When I started at Valtec, there was only one other person in the engineering department. My first assignment was to plan a revised layout for the plant. I think I did a good job.

In my current position, my main duty is to keep the place on schedule, with a minimum of downtime. I like to keep in close contact with all aspects of the department. I go over whatever problems arise, check with the supervisors to see that everything is satisfactory. Sometimes I even discuss sales and marketing issues with senior management and my boss, Jim Hnatyshyn. Or I might have the odd discussion with the cost people as to how we are going to determine charges on certain jobs.

The supervisors I have working for me are pretty decent workers, for the most part. Sometimes one or two of them seem a bit reluctant to do their job or assume responsibility. I am having a lot of trouble with one man, Dwayne Sather, right now. I can't get him to accept responsibility for simple maintenance scheduling. I give him the policy and he still can't keep up to the task. Most of the time I can handle this sort of thing myself. Other times I have to take the problem to Jim and seek his advice. Dwayne is on the public utilities commission, and that's part of the problem. I think his first priority should be the company. I've tried to talk to him about which side his bread is buttered on, but he just clams up and makes me feel uncomfortable. I don't know how to get through to him.

DWAYNE SATHER TALKS ABOUT HIMSELF AND THE JOB

I'm a happily married man with three terrific kids and a modest home with three and a half acres of land in the Ottawa Valley. I have served on the local public utilities commission as chair for the past four years, and this puts extra demands on my time. It has meant that I have had a lot less leisure time to spend with my family. Still, I am proud of my work with the commission and think the experience has helped me in my job at Valtec.

My first job at Valtec was in the tool room. It was a regimented working environment. I was looking to get out of there and away from all the unnecessary rules and regulations when I came over to the maintenance department. That was 11 years ago. But working for Sari is becoming almost as bad as it was in the tool room. But for different reasons. He doesn't give clear instructions. He talks around the subject and gets angry when you say you don't understand what he wants you to do. He blames you for things that go wrong. It's hard working for him because you can't tell him anything. He won't listen. His first reaction is to rant.

He doesn't let me think for myself. In his eyes, everything I do is a mistake. For example, last month I had to leave early because of an important meeting at the commission. There were changes in government regulations we had to discuss. When I got home after the meeting there was a message waiting for me that someone from the plant had called. I suspected something was up. I went back to the plant and checked things out. I found nothing, so I turned around and went home to my cold supper.

As soon as I got home I received another call from the plant—this time one of the men had noticed smoke coming from one of the shop lights. I told them to shut down the power and I called Dipak immediately and told him what was happening. He scolded me for not being on the job and for not calling him sooner.

THE CURRENT CONFLICT

Jim Hnatyshyn thought over the situation, as it had been described by Sari, Sather, and some other men involved. Earlier in the week, Gil Graham, a production supervisor, had some maintenance work that he wanted done in his department and asked Dwayne Sather to do it for him. Sather said he had standing orders from Sari not to touch anything that wasn't in the schedule. He said his hands were tied. Sather told Graham that if he wanted anything done he would have to go to Sari for approval.

For his part, Sari was pleasant and cooperative with Graham and told him he would have the job done immediately. Then Sari went to Sather and reprimanded him for not taking the time or responsibility to look after the matter promptly himself. Sather then went to Hnatyshyn and lodged a formal complaint of harassment against Sari.

POINTS TO CONSIDER

Both sides in this scenario are blaming each other, rather than trying to understand behavior as a means of planning more effective action. The problem seems to be rooted in the lack of job satisfaction, which encourages both parties to get the personal challenge they need from outside the organization. (Sari is at university, while Sather is on the commission.)

Whatever Hnatyshyn does, he must address the advantages and disadvantages of each alternative. Also, a distinction must be drawn between choosing an alternative and implementing it. Each alternative has its cost in terms of the time, skills, stress, and energy it will require.

●　—　●　—　●　—　●　—　●　—　●　—　●　—　●　—　●　—　●

ENDNOTES

1　Gordon Lippitt, "Managing Conflict In Today's Organizations," in *Training and Development Journal*, July 1982, pages 67-68. Reprinted with permission of The Gordon Lippitt Foundation, Bethesda, Maryland.

2　Reported by Nicholas Regush in *Saturday Night* magazine, April 1991, p. 9.

3　The discussion of conflict resolving strategies on pages 218 to 221 has been adapted from Kenneth Thomas, "Conflict and Conflict Management," in *Handbook of Industrial and Organizational Psychology*, edited by M.D. Dunette (Chicago: Rand McNally, 1976).

4　Jim Cooze, "Conflict Resolution Strategies," *Canadian School Executive*, February 1990, pp. 22-24.

5　The material contained in the Management of Difficulties Exercise on pages 221 to 229 has been adapted from Kenneth Thomas and Ralph Kilmann, *Thomas-Kilmann Conflict Mode Instrument* (New York: Xicom Inc., 1988).

6　Elmer E. Schattschneider, *The Semisovereign People: A Realist's View of Democracy in America* (New York: Henry Holt and Co., 1975).

7　Kenwyn Smith, "The Movement of Conflict in Organizations," in *Administrative Science Quarterly* 34 (1989), pp. 1-20.

8　Gerald Clarke, *Capote* (New York: Simon & Schuster, 1988), pp.302-03. Reprinted by permission of Simon & Schuster.

9　Ronald B. Adler, Lawrence B. Rosenfeld, and Neil Towne, *Interplay: The Process of Interpersonal Communication*, Fifth Edition (New York: Holt, Rinehart and Winston, 1992), pp. 298-300.

10　From *Of Human Interaction* by Joseph Luft, (Palo Alto, Calif.: Mayfield Publshing, 1969). By permission of Mayfield Publishing Company. Copyright © 1969 by the National Press.

11　Reprinted from Jane Whitney Gibson and Richard M. Hodgetts, *Organizational Communication: A Managerial Perspective* (Toronto: Academic Press Inc., 1986), p.121.

CHAPTER 6

Towards Higher Performance

Section 1 **Performance Planning and Appraisal Interviews**

◆ Before we get started . . . ◆ Objectives ◆ Why Should We Do Appraisal Interviews? ◆ Maier's Appproaches to Appraisal ◆ The Nuts and Bolts of Appraisal: Formats ◆ Prepare for Planning and Appraisal ◆ What Next? ◆ Let's Get Personal ◆ Don't Quit Now ◆ Here Are the Pitfalls ◆ **And finally . .**

Section 2 **Coaching for Higher Performance**

◆ Before we get started . . . ◆ Objectives ◆ *Interpersonal Skills Clinic: Coaching Profiles* ◆ Breaking the Four-Minute Mile ◆ The Miracle Mile: A Lesson in Competitiveness ◆ Antecedents of the Manager-as-Coach Metaphor ◆ The Meaning of Empowerment and Support ◆ Coaching for Higher Performance ◆ Coaching Communication an an Ongoing Basis ◆ Coaching Reflective Action ◆ Coaching Through Delegation ◆ A Dozen Guidelines for Giving Feedback to High Performers ◆ *Interpersonal Skills Clinic: Discovering High-Performance Patterns* ◆ **And finally . . .**

Chapter Review Questions

Interpersonal Communication Scenario:
Martinvale Market Gardens

— — — — — — — — — — — —

WORTH REPEATING

Whether you believe you can, or believe you can't, you are probably right.

—Henry Ford

In every field of human endeavour where performance is crucial, coaching is an integral part.

—Roger Evered and James Selman, "Coaching and the Art of Management"

We have only to look beyond our shores to see how countries with few of our natural resources have succeeded in converting human capital into financial capital.

—Brian McGourty, President and CEO of Honeywell Limited

Performance Planning and Appraisal Interviews

Before we get started . . .

In this section, we turn to a discussion of appraisal interviews, where employers and employees reflect on past performance in the context of a consideration of the future. A good appraisal interview should help employees to clarify their responsibilities on the job. It can also function as a source of motivation for higher performance. But perhaps most importantly, it can provide an opportunity for a manager to help and support an employee. The performance planning interview is a time for thinking about how the employee's personal and workplace goals may converge in the coming year.

We will discuss the most common types of performance appraisal being used in organizations and suggest ways that managers can improve their communication in such interviews. However, our treatment of the topic of appraisals is far from complete. Our purpose is to provide a base from which we can discuss the communication skills and strategies that may be usefully employed in performance planning and appraisal interviews.

Our view is that performance planning and appraisal interviews are more than an organizational control process or a means of allocating work fairly among employees; they also constitute an exercise in human relations that helps ensure the personal development of employees. A benefit of appraisal interviews that a manager may not always consider is that they provide a review of his or her management from the employee's perspective. The performance planning interview and the appraisal interview should usually be held as part of the same meeting; however, if this is done, the interviewer must be sure to distinguish the two functions.

Thus, performance planning and appraisal interviews are about more than just the performance of the organization's employees. They are also about the performance of the organization. This is because performance planning and appraisal interviews are a particularly important expression of an organization's *culture*. They reflect the kind of cultural patterns the organization is seeking to establish and provide a basis for sharing values and assumptions about the nature and purpose of the organization. Appraisals are predictable events in the organization; as such, we may consider them as organizational *rituals*. And rituals can reveal a great deal about the social structures of the people who engage in them. As rituals, performance planning and appraisal interviews also lead to the creation of *artifacts*. (One such artifact, for example, would be the written summary of the interview). Artifacts are also useful pieces of evidence about the social structures of the people who create them.

Objectives

After you complete this section, you should be able to:

1. Describe the following approaches to performance appraisal, noting the main advantage associated with each: tell and sell, tell and listen, mutual problem solving.

2. List the three steps for altering the use of the graphic rating scale, in order to measure performance rather than traits.

3. Explain the use of narrative essays, including two variations on their use.

4. Discuss the four main steps of Management by Objectives and explain the strength of MBO as a performance appraisal format.

5. List the documents that should be reviewed by the manager and the employee before the performance planning and appraisal interview.

6. Name the three communication features that are likely to be used during a performance planning and appraisal interview.

7. Describe the five communication control variables for use during a performance planning and appraisal interview.

8. Discuss the three steps to be carried out after the performance planning and appraisal interview.

9. Discuss the importance of creating a written record of the appraisal session.

10. Discuss the five pitfalls of performance planning and appraisal interviews.

Why Should We Do Appraisal Interviews?

In the introduction, we suggested that performance planning and appraisal interviews could be considered organizational rituals. In common parlance, a ritual is sometimes considered "bad" because it is done for no other reason than habit. However, as we consider the culture of an organization, we find that rituals are very important; they are used by employees to invest their work with meaning and to help them define the nature of their membership in the organization.

Let's consider the organizational ritual of conducting an orientation interview for new employees. As we noted in Chapter 4, this event is particularly significant because it is the first formal occasion on which a person learns about the organization as an employee. Suppose the new employee has a question about some of the specifics of the benefits plan offered by the organization. The interaction might go like this:

Manager: That concludes the portion of our interview devoted to discussing the benefits provided by the organization. Do you have any questions or comments about your benefits package?

Employee: Well, I did have one question. As you know, my wife works and I was wondering whether she would be covered under the organization's dental plan.

Manager: Well, you would have to check your benefits manual.

Employee: I can do that. I was wondering whether you had come across a situation similar to mine in the past.

Manager: I haven't, although I'm sure someone in the human resources office might have. Anything else before we end the meeting?

This kind of interaction might well suggest to the employee that the manager does not consider employees' personal situations (as they relate to the organization's financial commitments) to be particularly important. This impression may be confirmed in future interactions.

Similarly, at a performance planning and appraisal interview, the employee will regard the process as an indication of what is expected of him or her and what kinds of assumptions are made in the organization. In such an interview, the employee will expect to learn about job responsibilities, the opportunities for promotion and training, salary increases, and so on. Therefore, managers who view the performance planning and appraisal interview as an occasion simply to find fault with the employee will miss an important opportunity for development—of the employee, the manager, and the organization. Instead of focusing solely on past failures and future objectives, managers should also concentrate on interpreting and building the organization's culture.

Pay and other rewards for good performance are used by an organization to help keep its best employees. However, because performance evaluation can be a somewhat subjective and nonrational process, organizations often try to measure an employee's performance against an objective standard. The problem with this technique is that objective standards usually measure behaviors or accomplishments that are easy to find and measure—not necessarily those that are most valued. Furthermore, the assessment sometimes ends up measuring quantity rather than quality, since quantity is so much easier to measure.

As you might expect, appraisals are easier to do in some occupational fields than in others. For a salesperson, many companies consider the only important criterion to be gross sales produced per year. (Even here, the matter is not as simple as it may seem, since some consideration will usually be given to customer satisfaction and service.) For other occupations—teachers, the public service, health care—objective standards may be difficult to establish. It will, therefore, be more difficult in those occupations to appraise the performance of incumbents.

Maier's Approaches to Appraisal

Norman R.F. Maier has devised three approaches to appraisal interviews, which have become generally accepted by writers and researchers. The approaches are *tell and sell, tell and listen,* and *mutual problem solving.* Maier's approaches correspond to three of the models of communication that we discussed in Chapter 1: linear, interactive, and transactive, respectively. They also correspond to three levels of influence that the manager might have: much power, less power, least power.

As its name suggests, in the **tell and sell** interview, the manager does all the talking. The procedure begins with a review of the previous appraisal period. The manager then informs the employee of the appropriate goals and behaviors for this appraisal interview. He or she tries to persuade the employee to follow the direction being offered. For Maier, the objectives of this approach are simple: to let employees know how they are doing, to inform them of a plan for improvement, and to persuade them to accept this plan.

You might want to think of the relationship that exists in such an interview as being similar to that between a car owner and a mechanic. In such a situation, the mechanic finds out what's wrong with the car and what can be done about the problem, and then informs the car owner of the problem and persuades him or her to accept both the assessment of the problem and the solution. The tell and sell interview saves time and appears to be a simple process. However, the communication in such an interview is, of course, one-sided. One person is in control, the other is not. Not surprisingly, employees—and even managers—find the absence of an opportunity for feedback and dialogue to be constricting. The employee may resent being told what to do, and the manager may not want to shoulder the responsibility of deciding what's best for someone else.

With the **tell and listen** interview, on the other hand, the two participants provide feedback to each other. Dialogue may occur. The manager begins by offering impressions and suggestions concerning the previous appraisal period, and may also offer a suggested plan for the coming appraisal period. However, the manager also encourages the employee to ask questions, make comments, and express concerns. The structure is formal, but interactive. Both participants have an opportunity to try out their ideas and to express their feelings.

For an organization or situation in which power does not play a significant part in the relationship between manager and employee, the **mutual problem solving** approach, in which both parties are more or less equal partners in the discussion, may be the most appropriate. Here, problems and concerns are discussed with as much freedom as possible—the manager is less a mechanic than a counsellor. Both participants take responsibility for ensuring that the employee performs well and that his or her personal and workplace needs are taken into consideration in the setting of goals and objectives for the coming appraisal period.

The Nuts and Bolts of Appraisal: Formats

The performance planning and appraisal interview always involves some paper work, but you should try to keep it to a minimum. In order to plan, carry out, and summarize the interview, you may wish to develop or use a standardized form—the most common device used in appraisal sessions. These forms are especially useful for appraising employees in jobs that entail routine or repetitive duties. For higher level jobs, no single form will be able to cover all aspects of the appraisal process. In fact, as a general rule, the higher one's position in the organizational hierarchy, the more personalized the interview planning and recording mechanism should be. We will discuss the following formats for planning, conducting, and following up on a performance planning and appraisal interview: graphic rating scales, narrative essays, and management-by-objectives (MBO). The interview strategies we suggested in Chapter 3 can be used for all three formats.

Graphic Rating Scales

A **graphic rating scale** is a simple means of assessing performance and is based on a highly structured approach to the performance planning and appraisal interview. It involves assigning a number, from one to five, to a particular trait of the employee, such as punctuality or willingness to learn. Some graphic rating scales list aspects of the job, rather than employee traits, but the use of either of these types of scale is essentially the same.

The graphic rating scale is still perhaps the most commonly used technique for appraising performance. The disadvantage of this method is that, by itself, the scale does not incorporate the employee's responses or comments. Furthermore, some employee traits, such as integrity or perseverance, simply cannot be measured meaningfully. To ensure that the appraisal session remains an opportunity for two-way communication, you may wish to use the scale in combination with some other format or method. While we acknowledge the usefulness of the graphic rating scale in the right context, others are more critical of it: Thomas H. Patten, Jr., an expert in the area of performance appraisal has said, simply, "measure or appraise performance as behavior; forget about personality traits."[1]

Figure 6.1 shows what a graphic rating scale might look like.

If your organization uses a graphic rating scale, you may want to try altering it to reflect performance, rather than traits, by carrying out the following three steps. First, allow the employee to complete the scale first; this can be the basis for a discussion of your own rating and of issues that need discussion and clarification. Second, state the traits in terms of actual tasks or behaviors. For example, if one of the traits that is covered in a text-entry clerk's scale is "Accuracy," you may wish to change it, or expand it, to indicate how accuracy can be attained. For example, you could mention specific behaviors such as keeping below a certain maximum number of errors per page in text entry, or successfully reviewing the

Figure 6.1: Graphic Rating Scale

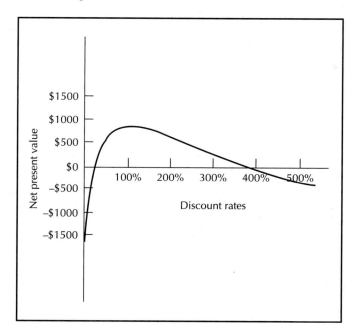

office procedures manual to ensure that the employee knows how to request the services of a temporary worker. Third, agree with the employee on informal performance objectives. Though the written record of the appraisal session would consist of the graphic rating scale, the appraisal process itself would include a meaningful discussion of *how* the employee will improve his or her performance over the coming appraisal period.

Narrative Essays

The graphic rating scale is at the highly structured end of the continuum of appraisal formats. The **narrative essay** is at the other end—it simply calls for the manager to write a description of how the employee did during the appraisal period and how he or she might improve in the coming period. After the employee has seen the description, objectives may be set for the coming period. The narrative essay requires no special forms or training to set up or administer, and it allows both parties to reflect privately on the comments being made. Two variations on this process may also be adopted.

First, the manager may focus on significant incidents or objectives in the essay, rather than trying to deal with all of them. That way, the manager and the employee can deal with a few issues that are of mutual concern, without spending too much time and energy on matters that both agree do not require attention during the appraisal session in question. If you decide to deal only with significant incidents, you will have to keep an ongoing record throughout the appraisal period. You would record incidents (either positive or negative) as they occur, jotting down comments on how the incident came to your attention, what happened, and what your treatment of the incident might be during the appraisal session.

Alternatively, or in combination with the first variation, the employee may take control of the initial stage of the process by writing a *self-appraisal* in the form of a narrative essay. In the essay, the employee would review the results of the previous appraisal session, describe how he or she was able to achieve the objectives, and suggest a framework for planning the next appraisal period. The manager would then meet with the employee and discuss the self-appraisal, after which objectives would be discussed, agreed upon, and recorded.

Management by Objectives (MBO)

Peter Drucker, a management theorist, first described the MBO method in 1954 in a book entitled *The Practice of Management*. The method was based on his study of management practices in General Motors. It was an effort to move the emphasis in appraisal from the employee's traits to his or her performance on the job. It was also intended to change the role of the manager in the appraisal process from that of "judge" to that of "helper." Since its inception MBO has become a popular means of appraisal.

MBO calls for employees to focus on the mission of their organization and to plan their work in a way that helps the organization accomplish that mission. In addition, it can help employees think of the appraisal process as a part of their effort to chart a career. Managers and employees set mutually agreeable performance objectives aimed at contributing to the accomplishment of the organization's mission, and then try to determine, at the next session, whether the employee was able to meet those objectives. Mid-session review points may also be established.

The stages of the MBO cycle are as follows.

Step 1: Develop or identify the objectives of the organization, department, or unit.

Step 2: Identify the responsibilities of employees in terms of reaching the objectives stated in step 1.

Step 3: In consultation with each employee, set goals for the appraisal period, and agree on how the employee will reach those goals. Also, decide on when the goals will be reviewed, and if necessary revised, before the next appraisal session. Review issues to ensure that there will be no surprises at appraisal time.

Step 4: At the end of the appraisal period, assess whether the employee has reached the goals and return to step 1.

The system is simple enough to explain or understand, and, in some applications, it can be a comprehensive appraisal system: At the beginning of the MBO cycle, the organizational unit determines its goals; at the end of the cycle, the manager checks the employee's performance against an expression of these goals. The employee and the manager then set goals for the next appraisal period. In addition to focusing on the goals of the organization, MBO takes into account the needs of the employees in achieving these goals. All employees are thought to need:

◆ knowledge of what is expected of them
◆ appropriate resources, support, and training and development
◆ feedback
◆ opportunities for personal and career growth

When the MBO system works, it is probably because employees have considered the objectives and agreed to them, and the number of objectives is manageable (five or fewer). It makes sense; if people understand and think about their goals often during an appraisal period, they are more likely to able to achieve those goals. The disadvantages of the system are just as obvious. An employee and manager may agree on objectives that cannot be checked because they are vague or difficult to measure. Still, MBO is used in many companies, if only because it is easy to implement and understand. A variation on MBO is the *gain planning appraisal,* which rewards those employees who achieve a level of performance beyond that stated in their objectives. The rewards might include pay increments, bonuses, or days off.

Prepare for Planning and Appraisal

As we have done with the interviews discussed in Chapters 3 and 4, we will suggest how to structure a performance planning and appraisal interview in terms of what to do before, during, and after the interview. And once again, we suggest that nothing can replace preparation and planning.

An appraisal interview is concerned with evaluating what someone has done. In this way, it is more intensive than the other interviews discussed in this book. Even in a recruitment interview, for example, while the interview may be of great personal significance (especially for the candidate), the interview does not cover in detail what a person has accomplished, or perhaps not accomplished, during the last year. Appraisal interviews require a high level of interpersonal skill, especially for the interviewer—often a higher level of skills than is required in the other interviews we discuss. The appraisal interview often calls for the interviewer to act as a helper or counsellor.

One way of considering a performance planning and appraisal interview is to think about what an employee wants to achieve through the session. It is useful for managers to consider the following series of questions, to which they should want an employee to answer "yes" after leaving the interview:

Does my manager challenge me, keeping in mind my abilities and aptitudes?

In the assignments I receive, is he fair?

Does she provide feedback clearly and fairly?

Does he take an interest in me personally?

Is she a good listener and does she accept constructive criticism?

Does he mention my strengths, in addition to my weaknesses?

During the interview, the manager's task is, in part, to help the employee answer those questions with a "yes."

With this kind of a checklist in mind, the manager should begin preparing by reviewing the purpose of the interview and considering its significance for both manager and employee. To do this, both participants will need time to review what happened at the last appraisal. Therefore, you will have to gather the relevant documents well ahead of the interview, say two weeks in advance of the meeting, and provide a copy of them to the employee, if necessary. These documents will include the job description, a record of last year's session (including the objectives to which both of you agreed), memos, letters, and notes you may have kept relating to the employee's performance this year or plan for the coming year, and, if applicable, the collective agreement and other documents that bear on salary, advancement, or employee development.

For your part, you will have to review these same documents and decide on the general structure and content of the interview. Try to imagine what the employee's experience is like. A complaint that is commonly made by employees is that managers do not know (or cannot remember) what it is like to actually do the job in question. Ask yourself the following questions:

What did I feel when I used to do this job?

How did I want to change the job at that time?

What did I think my boss did that was right, or that was not right?

How has the job changed since I was the incumbent?

What can I do for the employee to help him or her do the job?

There are many other techniques for familiarizing yourself with the job that would be particularly useful if you'd never been in the employee's position. These include carrying out some of the tasks related to the job (if this is possible), observing informal conversations among employees, and determining the differences in approach taken by new employees and experienced ones. The results of the performance planning and appraisal interview will be worth the effort. If you feel at all anxious about the appraisal session, you might consider consulting with your own manager. You might role-play the interview that you have planned, or discuss some of the important issues beforehand. Such a pre-interview activity may help you carry out the interview more successfully.

What Next?

Because we have already suggested specific strategies for conducting interviews, we will offer only some general suggestions for structuring the appraisal interview. We hope that during the performance planning and appraisal interview you will apply some of the interviewing techniques discussed in Chapters 3 and 4.

Three Sets of Skills

The following three sets of skills can be used during an appraisal interview: behavior shaping, communication features, and climate setting. We will discuss each of these in turn, although as you will see, the three are interconnected.

Behavior shaping is based on the notion that if you display a certain kind of behavior, it will encourage the person you are interviewing to display the same kind of behavior. To give a negative example of this notion, if you are anxious about the interview and express your anxiety through verbal and nonverbal means, the person being appraised will be more likely to become anxious as well. On the other hand, if you express goodwill—the attitude that you are happy to work with the employee to help him or her reach mutually acceptable goals—the employee will also express goodwill. Having considered the purpose and function of the appraisal interview beforehand, then, you should try to convey them through your behavior and words.

This set of skills may be used to convey an attitude of seriousness or to encourage informality and free expression. For example, if you have to inform the employee that his or her work has been unsatisfactory for the second or third consecutive appraisal period, you may wish to convey your attitude through the tone of your voice or through appropriately serious postures or gestures. The intent would not be to threaten or frighten the employee but to indicate that the matters you will be discussing must be taken seriously, since your previous attempts to deal with them seem to have failed. Only you can determine what behaviors might be appropriate in given situations. We suggest, however, that you consider them carefully before the interview and that you rehearse them, perhaps in front of a mirror in the manner described in Chapter 4.

The conscious use of *communication features*, such as probe questions, reflective listening, and supportive statements, conveys the belief that the questions asked in an interview are perhaps the most important determinant of the success of that interview. If you use too many closed questions, the person being appraised might not have the opportunity to discuss some of the issues that are relevant to his or her performance. Effective appraisal interviews typically employ the three communication features of probe questions, reflective listening, and supporting statements. We have discussed the first two features in Chapter 3, in which we covered the principles of active listening. You may want to review these. At this point, we will discuss the third feature, supporting statements.

Supporting statements are expressions of interest and engagement. The manager would use them to help assure the employee that the purpose of the appraisal process is to attain a mutually beneficial result. Supporting statements can occur in the opening comments, in which the interviewer mentions that the purpose of appraisal is to help the employee to do the job better and to provide opportunities for growth:

> ❝I hope you'll see this performance planning and appraisal interview as I do. It is an opportunity to discuss where you've been and where you're going, but it is also an occasion for me to find out whether I've been of service to you this year as I should have been. I want to incorporate into any plan that we might devise during this interview an understanding of what my role will be in your work and how I can best help you achieve your goals. ❞

Similarly, supporting statements may be incorporated into the form of certain questions. For example, prefaced probes may be used as an opportunity to comment on the employee's accomplishments:

> **❝**You have completed all your assignments on time and on budget this year. All of us in the department are grateful for your work. What kinds of projects do you hope to take on this year?**❞**

The use of supporting statements should be kept in mind from the planning of the interview to the drafting of the final document. Like behavior shaping and the other two communication features, supporting statements are less a device or set of actions than an expression of an attitude.

We can identify six qualities or characteristics that contribute to an attitude of support. During a performance planning and appraisal interview, the manager should be:

Tentative

Improvisational

Empathetic

Problem-oriented

Descriptive

Collegial

Let's deal with each of these in turn.

To provide a supportive atmosphere of communication during the appraisal session, you must make the employee feel that matters are not being decided arbitrarily or summarily. You, the manager, should avoid making quick judgments or coming to conclusions that close off discussion. This is what we mean by being *tentative*. Related to tentativeness is the quality of being *improvisational*. If the employee seems to be taking the interview in a direction that you had not expected—and you sense there is good reason for it—see where the new direction leads and try to make the best of it. To be *empathetic* is to see matters from another's point of view. In an appraisal session, as in other interviews, you should consider not only what the other person is saying but why, from their perspective, they may be saying it.

Being *problem-oriented* means focusing on the matter at hand, not on the person. If the employees feel that their performance—not their character—is being evaluated, they will be more motivated to set out to solve a problem. Similarly, if you provide *descriptive* accounts of the employee's performance, rather than judgmental ones, the employee will be more likely to work with you to find a way of improving his or her performance. Consider the following statements that a manager might make during an appraisal session. The first statement does not exhibit a problem-oriented, descriptive approach, while the second one does:

Statement: In the past six months, you've been over budget and late on three out of the five projects you've been working on. Would you explain why this has been the case?

Improved statement: Before our meeting, I gave you a copy of the project reports for our department. I wanted to look at the projects you've been working on. In three out of five of the projects, you didn't seem able to follow the budget or the schedule we had agreed on. Let's see, yes, the projects you did for our branch office were all over budget and late, although they accomplished their objectives. I think we ought to look at the problem and decide why this happened and what we can do to avoid a similar situation in the next six months.

Finally, you should have a collegial relationship with the employee during the appraisal session. It is true that in most organizational contexts you will have to make some kind of evaluation of the employee's work that implies a relationship of accountability. However, during the session, you should be trying to solve problems as equals, colleagues. If the employee knows that you are both "in it together," he or she will be more likely to work towards the goals set.

Climate control is a technique used to create an appropriate atmosphere for the appraisal. It draws on all the points discussed thus far. Part of the climate control process involves letting the employee know that his or her skills and abilities are valued in the organization. The climate should also make the employee feel that conflicts and disagreements may be discussed openly and that appropriate disclosure can take place. A climate in which empathy and trust prevail will be more likely to result in the setting of mutually agreed-upon objectives and goals.

Five Communication Control Variables

Having mastered the sets of skills we have discussed, you should consider the factors that influence the result of a performance planning and appraisal interview—the communication control variables. These include the proportionate amount of talking done by the participants, the relative degree of freedom allowed to the person being appraised, the extent to which digressions are encouraged during the interview, the "climate" of the interview (is the atmosphere tense or relaxed?), and the pace, or tempo, of the interview. By adjusting these variables, you may ensure that the interview achieves its objectives and that it results in satisfaction for both participants.

For the proportionate amount of talking done by the participants, recall the rule we gave in our discussion of active listening: you should talk forty percent of the time and listen sixty percent of the time. If you find that the employee seems to want to express his or her feelings about a particular situation, event, or interpersonal relationship, you may want to adjust the ratio so that you talk even less.

As for the relative degree of freedom allowed to the person being appraised, this will depend upon whether you have done an appraisal session with the employee previously and whether you believe that allowing him or her more freedom will result in the achievement of the objectives you have agreed upon for the interview. Having the employee begin the appraisal session may be a good idea in some cases; in others, it may cause the employee to feel anxious. Similarly, digressions may be allowed or even encouraged during the interview, as long as some progress is made towards the objectives set for the interview. There is a fine line between "having a free flow of information" and "having an axe to grind."

As we discussed previously, the climate of the interview can contribute greatly to its outcome. The climate may need to be changed as the interview progresses. If the employee begins to indicate that he or she is frustrated about a particular situation you are discussing, but seems unable to express the frustration, you may wish to increase the level of disclosure in the interview (thereby reducing tension) by revealing something about your own views. This may allow the employee to express whatever emotion he or she has felt in connection with the event or situation. The pace of the interview may also be increased or reduced, depending on the context. If you feel that both of you have come to an important point of agreement on the substance of the appraisal, perhaps you will want to bring the interview to a quick conclusion; alternately, if the employee is reluctant to accept the gravity of certain comments you are making, you may wish to slow the interview down and go over the same points again.

Steps to a Successful Performance Planning and Appraisal Interview

You may wish to use the following steps as a guide for carrying out a performance planning and appraisal interview. This guide can also be adapted for use in cases where the interview is structured around an employee's self-appraisal.

1. Review the main objectives of the interview and state what will happen after the interview.

2. State the format of the interview, and agree on a time limit.

3. Ensure that the employee is relaxed and understands that you will listen to his or her comments and concerns with interest.

4. Ask for any questions or concerns before you begin discussing the main subject of the interview. An alternative here is to have the employee speak first, especially if you and the employee know each other well and have done an appraisal together before. However, be ready to step in if he or she seems unwilling to go first.

5. Begin with a discussion of the work that the employee is now doing: current projects, tasks, and activities.

6. Discuss the employee's job description and determine whether it needs changing. Discuss any tasks that will or could be delegated to the employee in the upcoming period.

7. State the employee's strengths, offering congratulations for any particularly significant accomplishments.

8. Ask whether you have missed any of the employee's accomplishments from the past year or appraisal period.

9. Review areas for improvement. Usually, these areas will already have been mentioned during the appraisal period, especially if they are significant. The performance planning and appraisal interview is not a time for surprises.

10. Ask if the employee understands your suggestions for improvement and ask whether he or she wishes to rebut any of them.

11. Summarize the discussion so far. Indicate that the part of the interview dealing with this year's accomplishments and failures is closing, although you may wish to emphasize that revisiting certain points is always possible. Ask for comments or concerns.

12. Ask the employee if there are any ways that you could provide better service to the employee in the coming appraisal period. Make a note of any suggestions.

13. Review the employee's career goals, interests, and training requirements. Ask the employee if there are significant personal projects or activities, away from the workplace, that he or she has been undertaking. Offer your congratulations, support, encouragement, or advice.

14. Discuss, and try to agree upon, the employee's work and personal growth objectives for the coming appraisal period.

15. State what will happen as a result of this interview, including when and how the documents associated with the appraisal will be drafted or revised.

This list must be adapted, of course, depending on the kind of organization you work for and individuals involved. Of particular importance in the process of revising the list is the culture of the organization, especially the means used to control communication. In an organization typified by a person culture, for example, communication, and the direction of the interview, will be shared more than it would be in an organization typified by a task culture. In a task culture, the setting of tangible goals and objectives may be the most important outcome of the interview; in a person culture, establishing and maintaining relationships—which, in turn, will contribute to the achievement of goals during the appraisal period—may be the most important outcome.

A final comment about carrying out the interview. You should keep in mind that as you incorporate the employee's feedback, comments, and questions into the structure of the appraisal interview, you will have to allow more time for the process. If you have done appraisals before without such communication, count on spending more time in preparation and carrying out the interview than you did previously. It is one of the disadvantages of an interactive appraisal, but we suggest that it is worth the cost in time. The employee will appreciate having some "ownership" of the process and will tend to perform better as a result.

Let's Get Personal

As we have mentioned, in order for an organization to attract and keep employees who perform their jobs effectively and consistently, it must consider the whole employee. Managers who consider their employees' personal lives to be completely separate from their work lives are making a mistake. If employees are kept from becoming more satisfied, productive, and fulfilled in the personal sphere because of restraints in their work sphere, they will become less satisfied, productive, and fulfilled in both spheres. That is why we suggest that managers try to find ways of allowing the employee to grow *as a human being*, rather than simply as a member of the organization. The communication that occurs during a performance planning and appraisal interview can be a means of accomplishing that goal.

Let's consider an example. Cindy is the administrative manager for a department in a middle-sized accounting firm. Her main job is to supervise the clerical staff and to coordinate the work of the accounting partners. After six years on the job, she wants to take a year of maternity leave. However, the firm has never allowed more than nine months of maternity leave, unpaid. During the appraisal interview, Cindy brings up the matter with her manager, Deborah, because she wants to begin the leave in three months. If Deborah were to consider the importance of personal growth (which is represented by Cindy's desire to have a full year at home with her new son or daughter), the conversation might turn out as follows.

Deborah: I think you know that the firm's policy is to grant nine months of unpaid leave to women who want to take some time off after having a baby. In fact, I took nine months off for that purpose just before you started with the firm. I sympathize with your desire to have just a little bit more time.

Cindy: I really would like to have a year off, because there's a whole cycle of learning to be with a child that I think a mother needs a year to experience. On the other hand, I don't think that I can afford a year off, even with the unemployment insurance benefits I would collect for some of the that time. Those benefits are much less than my salary.

Deborah: The other complicating factor is that we need you back immediately after the nine months—actually after six months, but we'll wait—to be trained on the new automated accounting system for the office and to train the clerical workers. I just don't know how we can put that off for another three months, especially since it would actually be a delay of six months.

Cindy: So if I insisted on the year, I may not have a job to come back to.

Deborah: It looks that way.

Cindy: I can't give up my job. I'm not sure I'd find one as quickly as I'd need to.

Deborah: We don't want to lose you. But you're not much good to us sitting at home!

Cindy: Say, I wonder if that would be an option. Staying at home. I could learn the new system as soon as it's delivered, six months into my leave.

Deborah: That sounds like a good idea. I don't think you'd have to work full time at it. Perhaps two or three afternoons a week. Would you be able to attend a weekly training session?

Cindy: Yes, because it would be so much more preferable than having to end my leave after nine months. After two or three months, I could come in for an afternoon a week and begin to train the others. Would that work?

Deborah: I don't see why not. Why don't we check with the software manufacturer and see what the training program looks like? Then we'll decide how we can finish planning your work—and your maternity leave—for the next year or so.

Of course, it may not always be possible to make the organization's needs blend with those of the employee to the extent suggested here. However, creative solutions to employee concerns will never be discussed unless the performance planning and appraisal interview is seen as an opportunity for combining personal and workplace goals and objectives. It is the manager's responsibility to ask how the organization can help the employee self-actualize, on the job and off.

Don't Quit Now

The end of the appraisal interview does not constitute the end of the appraisal process. You must *follow up* on the interview by carrying out the following steps.

1. Draft a written summary of the interview and provide a copy to the employee for comment. Include in the summary any points that need to be monitored either shortly after the interview or during the following appraisal period. Remember to discuss matters related to the employee's personal growth and objectives. Commit to helping him or her reach these objectives in whatever way you can.

2. After the employee has had an opportunity to read the summary, speak to him or her about any matter of particular controversy or importance. Confirm

that you and the employee agree on what happened at the interview and what you expect to happen next.

3. During the appraisal period, informally discuss any consequences or implications of the appraisal session.

We emphasize that no matter how well the appraisal has gone, you should prepare a *written* record of the proceedings. This allows interested third parties—such as the human resources office or your successor—to review the progress and performance of the employee. It also provides a cue for you to use in reviewing for the next appraisal session.

Here Are the Pitfalls

We suggest that you watch for the following communication problems as you carry out performance planning and appraisal interiews. You may wish to keep a log of such difficulties from year to year. As we suggest in the next section, the appraisal is an important ritual in the culture of the organization; it is therefore a good idea to remove any chronic barriers to communication and effectiveness.

The climate of the interview is mechanical. Even if the collective agreement, or perhaps the human resources department, requires an annual appraisal session for each employee, you may still treat it as an opportunity for creativity and growth. If the employee senses that the interview has no meaning for you, he or she will tend to feel the same way.

The manager does not get to the specifics. Objectives must be stated specifically; otherwise, it may be impossible to determine whether they have been reached. Similarly, to be effective, feedback (either positive or negative) should be made with concrete and direct statements.

Too little time. We suggested that you discuss a time limit with the employee, but ensure that enough time is allowed and that more time is available if needed. The process of preparing the interview takes time, so don't try to arrange for the session on too little notice.

The manager talks too much and too often. It's up to you to provide the framework, and often the direction, for the appraisal interview. However, the employee needs to have input. Feedback from the employee is an essential component of all successful appraisal sessions. Are you listening?

The manager assumes too much. If you've been working in the organization for a while, or if you have learned about appraisal sessions through a formal channel, the purposes and dynamics of the appraisal interview may be clear enough. However, such things may not be at all clear to your employee, who may be inexperienced in the workplace. Alternately, an employee who has worked in a different organizational culture for a long time may be anxious, believing this will be a disciplinary session. Go through the introductory portion of the interview carefully, especially for the first session between you and the employee.

And finally . . .

We suggest that a well-conducted performance planning and appraisal interview will accomplish the following:

◆ provide an occasion for the manager and employee to consider the past and the future

◆ provide feedback to the employee

◆ help to determine training and development needs for the employee, including personal growth needs

◆ result in an accurate, written record of the employee's performance

◆ reveal the basis for the award of salary increments and promotions

◆ encourage an ongoing dialogue between manager and employee

Also, the performance planning and appraisal interview should be simply one part of a broader process of performance review, a cycle of mutually beneficial, on-going assessment and planning.

Section 2 Coaching For Higher Performance[2]

Before we get started . . .

Doing what was done yesterday, or doing it five percent better is no longer a formula for success. To compete successfully in the new international marketplace, individuals and organizations must commit to more extensive change and development. As early as 1985 North American automakers were being challenged to exceed the performance of their Asian rivals—not by five or ten percent—but by one hundred percent improvement in quality or production.

Such dramatic change is likely to encounter considerable opposition along the way toward higher performance. Overcoming the barriers to change of any kind demands extraordinary energy, commitment, and focus. Anything less than highly motivated performance is almost certain to fail under any competitive circumstances. Such a high level of motivation can best be accomplished, we believe, by **coaching**—the process of two or more people combining their strengths to assist one of them in attaining an elevation in performance.

If the performance planning and appraisal interview is carried out effectively, it will contribute to a relationship between manager and employee in which the manager does everything possible to encourage the employee to reach higher levels of performance on the job. One way of thinking about the idea of coaching for higher performance is to view coaching as an ongoing day-by-day development of the human resources in an organization. In an organization, the challenge for the coach is to align the personal goals and visions of the individual with those of the organization as a whole. The increasing competitiveness of the global economy depends primarily upon improved human performance. We believe that such performance can arise through the development of high-performance coaching strategies and styles designed to lead people to develop greater self-confidence and a commitment to excellence in the work that they do.

Ordinary performance is not going to help anyone improve performance or increase the productivity of an organization. Significant results in performance and productivity require higher levels of response than ordinary performance can provide. Ordinary people in a superior organizational structure can't outperform superior people in an ordinary organization who have the appropriate coaching.

The metaphor that we use in this section for the coaching activities in an organization is sport, especially track and field. We use examples from sport to illustrate how coaching can be used to encourage high performance in the organization. The most fundamental similarity between athletics coaches and business managers is that their success is determined by how well *someone else* performs.

Objectives

After you complete this section, you should be able to:

1. Describe three or four different coaching styles, and explain which one you think is best suited to competitive business circumstances.
2. Discuss the approaches to the manager-as-coach metaphor as stated by Mace, Fournies, and Peters and Austin.
3. Define empowerment in the context of coaching for higher performance.
4. List six ways that high-performance leaders relate to those who follow them.
5. Explain "reflective action" as a means of evaluating or improving one's performance.
6. Discuss the use of delegation in the coaching process.
7. List 12 guidelines for giving feedback to high performers.
8. Identify your own high performance pattern—as well as the high performance pattern of someone seeking your help to improve.

COACHING PROFILES

We can learn a lot from the personality profiles of great generals, athletes, coaches, and other leaders. As an example, consider the following four brief profiles of successful track and field coaches—Brutus Hamilton, Michaly Igloi, Percy Cerutty, and Bud Winter. After you have read them all, ask yourself:

1. Which one of these coaches you most admire, and why.
2. Which one you most identify with, and what it is that you have in common.
3. Which personal coaching style you find most useful for management in the 1990s, and why.

BRUTUS HAMILTON, UNIVERSITY OF CALIFORNIA, BERKELEY—PERSON-CENTRED APPROACH

Brutus Hamilton was an impressive coach and educator. He had a way of inspiring his Olympic and world champions to perform at the peak of their potential. Hamilton was best known for getting things done by encouraging others to help themselves. Without depending solely on him to solve their problems, his athletes learned what it took to regulate their own training and performance. Hamilton's strongest admonition was "Look within yourselves for the answers." A kind of Socrates with a stopwatch, Brutus Hamilton let his performers discover the way to success for themselves; with his help and guidance, of course, but without defining the way for them.

Hamilton seldom urged his point of view on others. He never dictated that others do things his way. He coached not so much by command but by suggestion—by asking questions in such a way that the right answers became evident, and by presenting himself as a resource expert to whom others could come for help in their efforts to help themselves. Above all, Brutus Hamilton believed in urging others to believe in themselves.

MICHALY IGLOI, HUNGARY AND THE U.S.— AUTHORITARIAN APPROACH

Although any simplification is unfair to the wide range of his coaching talents, Michaly Igloi exemplified the authoritarian coach in concentrating on removing all his performers' inner distractions, such as the doubts and anxieties about planning the details of training and competition. When asked what system of training Igloi followed, his athletes would answer that they didn't know. They hadn't thought about it. The coach did all of the planning and thinking for them.

Igloi held complete authority and control over the inner person of his performers. He told them when, how, and what to run—both during training and when racing. Since his knowledge, experience, and personal absorption in running were of the highest degree, his decisions were invariably sound. And so his men placed themselves in his hands without reservation. Although opposed in practice to the person-centred approach, Igloi, like Hamilton, was an extremely successful and respected coach in his day.

PERCY CERUTTY, AUSTRALIA—RADICAL ENDURANCE APPROACH

Percy Cerutty was as colorful as he was unique—some called him "a primitive sorcerer." Cerutty taught that free and uninhibited running could come only from a free and uninhibited person. He had no interest in the popular method of interval training, with its measured and timed distances. He thought such planned effort only magnified the awareness of exertion and fatigue, and therefore limited the spontaneous output and sacrifice necessary for breakthrough performances.

Cerutty offended many other coaches the world over with his remarks about their general inability to demonstrate what it was they were trying to teach. Cerutty was known to witness a runner's unwillingness to make sacrifices, get up onto the track himself, and demonstrate how it should be done—by running himself into complete exhaustion. Despite his eccentricities, he was one of the great coaches of endurance running. He was, for a time, miler John Landy's coach.

BUD WINTER, SAN JOSE STATE—TOTAL COMMITMENT APPROACH

On those aspects of track which he considered important, Bud Winter was totally committed and obsessed. "If purple vitamin milk will make them run faster, then we give it to them," he said. "But open communication remains the most important element in our coaching. The greatest technician won't be more than a fair coach if he can't impart his knowledge and feelings."

Winter was at his best in a one-to-one personal relationship. It was his intense personal interest in individuals—and his desire to be appreciated—that led him to coach 15 Olympic participants, including three gold medallists and a half-dozen world record holders with about 25 world records. However, even though he did eventually get the job done, Winter always spread himself thin in the process. He simply could not delegate responsibility.

WHICH COACHING STYLE IS MOST APPROPRIATE FOR MANAGEMENT IN THE 1990S?

Obviously there is no one best system, formula, or perfect personality for successful coaching in any sport. Nor in any business for that matter. Coaching is as much an art as it is a science, regardless of the field of endeavor. What distinguishes coaching for higher performance from ordinary coaching is that it is meant for competitive circumstances—where success can only be achieved by giving one's best.

In our view, of the four coaching profiles we have shown you, Brutus Hamilton's is the best style to adopt for management in the 1990s. Igloi, Cerutty, and Winter were all successful in their time, but each of them took on a great burden of responsibility for their athletes. Today's managers cannot do all the thinking for their performers the way Igloi would. Nor should they be competing with their charges to see who can suffer the most—as Percy Cerutty was known to do. And the time has passed for people like Bud Winter, who find it impossible to delegate responsibility to others, and who end up grinding themselves or their programs to a halt.

A model coaching profile for the 1990s must be one that recognizes that in highly competitive circumstances, the coach is just another spectator. By allowing his athletes to take charge of their own destinies, Brutus Hamilton empowered them to achieve their highest levels of performance—on their own—with his encouragement and support. Whether in business or on the playing field, it is the performers who must do the task; the manager or coach's task is to empower the performers to do the best possible job they can.

You don't need high-performance coaches working for your organization if you are in a large, standardized, long-run company. But as contemporary organizations continue to downsize, management will be challenged to get increases in quality and productivity from fewer and fewer human resources. Those who remain will have to perform beyond all previous expectations; to do this they will require high-performance coaching.

• — • — • — • — • — • — • — • — • — • — • — • — •

Breaking the Four-Minute Mile

A month before their historic attempt to break the four-minute mile barrier in 1954, British runners Roger Bannister, Chris Chataway, and Chris Brasher found themselves bogged down in training. They were running a series of 10 consecutive quarter-miles in 61 seconds, with a short recovery interval between each. Their target had been 60 seconds. "We were stuck," wrote Bannister. "The training had ceased to do us any good and we needed a change."

At the suggestion of their coach, Franz Stampfl, the runners drove up to Scotland for a few days of exercise, running, and rock-climbing. When they returned and tried running 10 consecutive quarter-miles as before, the time came down to 59 seconds. And so it stayed for the three weeks they had remaining before their assault on the four-minute mile barrier—on a windswept and soggy May 6, 1954, at Oxford University.

On the day of the race, Bannister decided to travel up to Oxford alone, so he could think quietly. By chance, Stampfl was inside the train carriage when Bannister opened the door. The two men talked about the problem Bannister faced that day. He felt he had reached his peak both physically and psychologically. In his mind he had set this as the day when he would attempt to drive himself to the limit. However, if he tried and failed, he would lose confidence and his chances in any later attempt would be destroyed.

There was a gale-force wind that blustery day at Oxford, and Bannister thought it might make a sub-four minute mile impossible. The previous world record of 4 minutes 1.4 seconds, had stood for nearly a decade. In order to succeed, he knew he must run the equivalent of a 3 minute 56 second mile in calm conditions. Stampfl told Bannister he thought he was capable of running a mile in 3 minutes 56 seconds, so he could convincingly argue that it was worth the attempt. It had never been done. It had been said many times that it could never be done. Yet these two men on a train to Oxford were, together, confident that it would be done.

At the beginning of the race Brasher went into the lead, as planned, and Bannister slipped in effortlessly behind him. At one and a half laps Bannister heard a voice shouting "relax" which penetrated above the noise of the crowd. He learnt afterwards that it was Stampfl's. Unconsciously Bannister obeyed. He passed the half-mile in 1 minute 58 seconds. Round the next bend, Chataway went into the lead and at three-quarters of a mile his time was 3 minutes 0.7 seconds. And by now the crowd was roaring.

Somehow, Bannister had to run the last lap in 59 seconds. Chataway led round the next bend and then Bannister pounced past him at the beginning of the back straight. "Those last few seconds seemed never-ending," wrote Bannister. "The faint line of the finishing tape stood ahead as a haven of peace, after the struggle. . . . I leapt at the tape like a man taking his last spring to save himself from the chasm that threatens to engulf him." The stopwatches held the answer: 3 minutes 59.4 seconds! Bannister grabbed Brasher and Chataway, and together they ran a spontaneous victory lap. "We had done it—the three of us!" wrote Bannister.[3]

Bannister's experience is similar to what occurs in all high-performance activities. When there is a commitment to excellence and a challenge to achieve a worthy goal, the best we have to offer can be realized. It took 10 years to get beyond the four-minute threshold. Yet within months of that day at Oxford—several more athletes around the world began running sub-four-minute miles.

And where is the high performance coach in all of this? Casting his mind back to the moment of doubt when he became hesitant, Bannister acknowledged the assistance of his coach, Franz Stampfl, in supporting his self-confidence at a crucial moment. "Confidence that has been supreme until the final moment," said Bannister, "can be lost quite suddenly." But with the help of his coach, Roger Bannister rose to the occasion and established a record of human performance.

Bannister said that, "Franz Stampfl's greatness as a coach rested on his adaptability and patience. He watches and waits for the moment when the athlete really needs him." And this is what all high-performance coaches must do—empower those in their charge to take control for themselves. They must adapt each lesson to each new challenge they experience along the way—all the while supporting the effort to improve competitive performance.

The Miracle Mile: A Lesson in Competitiveness

On June 22, 1954, only 46 days after Bannister had broken the four-minute barrier for the mile at Oxford, Australian John Landy lowered the record to 3 minutes 58 seconds. And less than two months after that, these same two men competed head-to-head at the British Empire Games in Vancouver. This event became known as "the miracle mile."

The day before Bannister left for Vancouver, he had another long talk with Franz Stampfl about how Bannister should prepare for the race. Landy was a stronger and tougher opponent, but Stampfl explained that if Bannister's mental approach was right, he could use his fabulous finishing kick and win the race by inches. The plan was to let Landy set a fast pace, to hang on, to hold enough energy in reserve and then to wrest the lead from Landy at the foot of the final straight—overtaking him with less than 70 yards to go.

At the gun, Bill Baille of New Zealand took the early lead and Bannister tucked himself in to third place, behind Landy. The Australian took over the lead and completed the first lap seven yards ahead of Bannister. Landy remained ahead at the half and three-quarter marks. At one point in the second lap, Landy was ahead by 15 yards, and Bannister recalls thinking Landy would break the world record again. Quickening his stride, Bannister fought back to reel Landy in on the final lap.

"It was incredible that in a race at this speed he should start a finishing burst 300 yards from the tape," Bannister said. He knew if Landy did not slacken soon, he would be beaten. Bannister flung himself past Landy just before the end of the final bend. "As I did so," he said, "I saw him glance inwards over his opposite shoulder. This tiny act of his held great significance. The moment he looked around he was unprotected against me and so lost a valuable fraction of a second in his response to my challenge. It was my tremendous luck that these two happenings—his turning around and my final spurt—came absolutely simultaneously."

Roger Bannister won the gold medal in a time of 3 minutes 58.8 seconds—one tenth of a second ahead of John Landy. Praising Landy lavishly, Bannister called the last lap of the race the most exciting and intense moment of his life. "Landy had shown me what a race can really be at its greatest. His boldness forced me to abandon my own time schedule and lose myself quite completely in the struggle itself. After this experience I felt I could never again be interested in record-breaking without the thrill of competitive struggle."

Antecedents of the Manager-as-Coach Metaphor

The first use of the word *coach* in English referred to a particular kind of carriage. In a sense, the word still means the same as it did in the sixteenth century—"to coach" is to carry a person from where they are, to where they want to be.

Among the first texts to talk about "on-the-job coaching" as a function of management, was the work of Myles Mace in the 1950s. Mace's *The Growth and Development of Executives* (Harvard, 1959) inspired a series of books and articles stressing the value of coaching in executive training.

Throughout the 1960s and 1970s, much of the literature on coaching sought to transpose the models and methods of professional sports coaching onto the management of human resources in organizations. Another book, Ferdinand Fournies' *Coaching for Improved Work Performance* (1978), stimulated renewed interest from a great many marketing, sales, and personnel managers who were drawn to his notion of face-to-face coaching procedures and stringent problem-solving techniques for working with "subordinates."

Perhaps the best-known work on the subject is the chapter on coaching in Tom Peters' and Nancy Austin's *A Passion for Excellence* (1985). Peters and Austin define coaching as follows:

> 66 face-to-face leadership that pulls together people with diverse backgrounds, talents, experiences, and interests, encourages them to step up to responsibility and continued achievement, and treats them as full-scale partners and contributors. 99

This represents a remarkable advance from Fournies' approach, which was concerned with "correcting" unsatisfactory subordinate performance rather than enhancing high performance, and with regaining managerial authority and control, rather than achieving the highest possibilities.

The Meaning of Empowerment and Support

Different people mean different things by the term empowerment. Most of the management literature refers to some sort of participatory management, a flatter organizational structure, fewer rules, or more handing over of decision-making authority to those responsible for doing the work. In each case, **empowerment** is largely the experience of being able to determine one's own objectives and solve one's own problems. Who knows better how to do the job than those who have to do it? And if that's the case, then what role remains for the manager-as-coach?

In his article, "The Boss as Coach," Walter Kiechel III asks bosses to reflect how the notion of coaching is changing the nature of management and requiring new skills from managers.[4] A manager-as-coach can no longer run the job or make decisions for the employee. Instead, he or she must empower the employee to do the job, and support the progress along the way. In the same way, says Kiechel, teachers don't do the algebra for students, they help students learn to do it for themselves.

F. Dean Carrotte, a management consultant who has his own computer services firm, tells us a not uncommon story of how one computer company handled a highly competitive challenge and overcame a potential crisis of confidence:

> 66 The company was developing a new product with a two year development cycle. Senior management estimated that if the firm could produce the new product and bring it to market on time, it would be slightly ahead of the competition.
>
> A couple of months into the development process, some unanticipated problems arose. A lot of the engineers and technicians thought that if they really wanted to do the thing right, it would take longer than two years. They were a group of high-achievers, and they wanted to do it right. They were saying, "We're going to take a stand here; we're not going to let this thing go out unless we get it done right." That presented a major problem to the head of the division. But instead of laying down the law and ordering them to get in line or else, he told them the truth. He sat down with them and said: "Look, here's the situation we're dealing with. If you can't make the deadline, we aren't even going to be in business in two years. That's how stiff the competition is." He laid out all the marketing data he had. The engineers and technicians didn't feel controlled or put down by the confrontation. In fact, they felt challenged, empowered, and supported in their efforts to become more competitive.[5] 99

Empowered people do not have to be held by the hand as they do things. They can be talked to and communicated with. Because they are empowered and supported in what they do, they will know what they need to do without being pushed or controlled. They will act with the organization's best interests in mind because their own best interests are the same; they will work with others as a team because they understand that their self-interest and the interests of the team are inextricably bound together. The better a manager or coach becomes at empowering others to manage themselves and their own activities, the less need there will be for struggling to regulate behavior. Attempts to control others by obedience to any sort of managerial imperative actually hinder the development of self-confidence and commitment, and thus impede competitive performance.

Coaching for Higher Performance

Bernard Bass, Distinguished Professor of Management and Director of the Center for Leadership Studies at the State University of New York, Binghamton, has conducted research on high-performance leaders and their relationship to those in their charge. The research shows the qualities found in high-performance coaches in sport (and their relationship to those they coach) to be very similar. Bass states that high-performance leaders:

◆ give followers a sense of autonomy and foster their self- development

◆ treat followers in a friendly, informed, and accessible way

◆ provide a model of integrity, fairness, and high standards, while being capable of firmness or correcting as appropriate

◆ encourage followers with support, recognition, and openness, while sharing knowledge and expertise

◆ promote trust, loyalty, enthusiasm, pride, and respect

◆ mobilize followers toward more meaningful and comprehensive values.[6]

There is also evidence that a coach's expectations influence the development of the performer. First of all a coach must communicate the belief that a performer can indeed accomplish a task. "Positive regard" for those performing expresses—nonverbally as well as verbally—the coach's confidence in the other person's ability to succeed.

Coaches get things done by communicating with others. But a high-performance coach is more than simply a source of information or technical expertise. He or she must also be able to communicate in such a way that enables or empowers others to actualize their fullest potential. There is a saying in track and field coaching that "You can't put in what God left out." We don't suppose you can. But the coach can and does inspire or trigger an inherent commitment to achieving excellence. And we believe that that commitment exists in all self-actualizing human beings.

As we saw in the chapter on the theoretical antecedents of organizational communication, one of the most helpful contributions for understanding human motivation originated with the work of humanistic psychologist Abraham Maslow. Maslow's *hierarchy of needs* implies that once lower needs such as safety and survival have been provided for, human beings are able to focus on higher-order concerns—to meet the need for self confidence and a sense of belonging. Finally, at the pinnacle of the hierarchy of human needs, is the drive for self-fulfilment or self-actualization. This is the drive which propels our striving for excellence— the effort to become the very best we can be.

Whereas the prevailing management paradigm focuses on control and compliance to management rule, coaching, on the other hand, focuses on empowering people to get more out of themselves and for themselves. In traditional management it is the manager's job to motivate and control. In high-performance coaching motivation is ultimately the performer's own responsibility. In the prevailing management paradigm, "human resources" are used to perform all sorts of impersonal, mechanical functions, whereas the coaching paradigm views people and organizations as open systems, capable of higher-level development and independent action. The result is higher performance for its own sake as well as for the sake of the organization.

Coaching Communication on an Ongoing Basis

One of the reasons that performance appraisals in organizations occur so infrequently is that too often managers assume that someone who has been hired at a certain level of ability will improve marginally with time—whether they do anything to help or not. In high-performance coaching, however, it is understood from the very beginning that a commitment is being made to perform beyond the present level of one's ability. The expectation of the coach is that the performer is going to pursue the limit of his or her potential and perform each new task with increasing confidence in their ability to succeed. All of this cannot possibly be conveyed within the formal constraints of a single interview.

Partly because many managers still seem to view performance appraisals as fault-finding sessions, real, useful, high-quality communication occurs far too infrequently in most organizations, if at all. Imagine if an athletics coach criticized a polevaulter for not making a height in competition and then left the athlete alone, without follow-up training, until the beginning of next season. What would be the result? Higher performance? Doubtful. What is more likely is that the same problems would persist for months afterward. But even worse, these same mistakes would have become so ingrained in the performance that they would now be much harder to eradicate.

Coaching must be carried out on a regular and ongoing basis. Coach-performer communication is a part of the daily routine. The coach's role is not to solve one particular problem, but to empower the individual to grow—so that he or she can not only cope with the present problem, but with any future problems that might occur. The coach acknowledges the self-sufficiency of individuals, and increases opportunities for them to confidently manage new challenges and competitive circumstances. At a day-to-day level, the coach asks the same questions any manager might: "What do you like most about this task?" "What would you change and why?" "Is there anything you'd do differently next time?" And when more serious problems are uncovered, the coach may offer encouragement by asking: "What can we make of this?" "How well do you feel you did?" "How can we change the task to make it a more enjoyable process for you?" "What do you need from me?" The coach then lets the performer decide.

Everyone has a gut feeling about what is right or not right about his or her own performance, and a good coach is careful never to overrule this. Overruling, or judging behavior is of little use in high-performance coaching. There is a significant difference between evaluating an experience and judging it. A coach's evaluation is generally descriptive, interpretive, inquisitive, and meaningful. The wise coach uses evaluation to help the performer understand and improve on each action or experience. This is quite different from the kinds of limiting, critical judgments managers sometimes use to punish, threaten, or coerce others into action. In the long run they only undermine confidence—thereby defeating high performance as well.

Coaching Reflective Action

We use the term "reflective action" to describe a special kind of evaluative experience that focuses on each action independently with the aim of increasing the performer's awareness of his or her potential for learning or improvement. This is what high-performance athletics coaches are doing when they pay close attention to details the performer needs to be more aware of, but cannot always see clearly. The coach is there to help identify these "blind spots" in the learning process, and to bring them to light.

The high-performance coach must also involve the performer in his or her own reflective experience of the event by the *way* in which he or she asks questions, as much as by the questions themselves. Most often, the underlying tone will convey confidence in the fact that—together—the coach and the performer can find a way to improve results, and achieve what could not have been achieved by either one alone.

Each reflective action contributes to clearer understanding of what the coach and performer are trying to accomplish together. What takes us to the next level of improvement is the knowledge that every experience has value and is transferable to other circumstances demanding a commitment to excellence.

Coaching Through Delegation

Where the tasks are many and the responsibilities great—no matter how extraordinary your energy level and capacity for work—you will likely have no choice but to delegate, that is, to get work done through other people. The delegation of work to employees is an important way of helping them increase their performance. By learning new tasks which could be—and perhaps are—done by their managers as well, employees begin the process of apprenticing for possible promotion. Delegating work is not the same as assigning work. Assignment usually involves telling someone what to do and how to do it, and when. In contrast, when a manager delegates work, he or she is asking the delegate to be responsible for developing a plan to achieve the desired results. It is the delegate who must decide how to do the assignment. The manager offers support and feedback, but it is the delegate who must be responsible for the final results, and the road that leads to those results.

Effective managers use discussions of objectives, tasks, obstacles, and timetables as opportunities to develop their employees and to foster in them feelings of responsibility. This process should increase the employees' commitment by involving them in making changes and in creating or modifying objectives.

The delegation of duties may form part of the performance planning and appraisal interview. If that is the case, the manager should consider before the interview begins which tasks should be delegated and how the process of delegation will be carried out during the interview.

A Dozen Guidelines for Giving Feedback to High Performers

Here are 12 guidelines for giving feedback that you can add to your repertory of feedback skills:

1. *Focus your feedback on the "here and now," not on the "there and then."* The more immediate the feedback, the more helpful it is.

2. *Do not give people more feedback than they can handle at the time.* If you overload people with feedback, it reduces the chances that they will use it to good advantage.

3. *Give feedback only when the performer has accepted that his or her behavior can improve to a significant degree.* Suggest ways for the performer to adjust performance to a higher standard.

4. *Focus on sharing ideas that have value for the recipient.* Avoid expressing ideas that are simply based on criticism.

5. *Explore alternatives, rather than fixed solutions.* In other words, don't limit yourself to "one best way"—there isn't one.

6. *Be poised and alert when giving feedback.* Avoid nonverbal distractions and use facial expressions and verbal comments that convey interest.

7. *Show empathy for the performer's feelings.* For example, you might say, "You were angry that your proposal wasn't even considered. I can understand how you feel. You don't feel that you are getting a fair opportunity to show what you can do. Is that it?"

8. *Solicit suggestions by encouraging people to give their opinions on how to deal with problems.* Typical lead-ins are as follows: "What do you think?" "What would you like to see happen?" "How would you do that?" "What can I do to help?"

9. *Get in sync with the other person.* When two people are not in synchronization with each other (when both, for example, are trying to talk at the same time, interrupting, or changing the topic) very little can be gained in terms of real communication about performance or development.

10. *Seize the opportunity.* Do not wait for the official performance appraisal interview to do your job. Coaching means continuous feedback coupled with specific goals and realistic deadlines. Prepare yourself for opportunities to coach.

11. *Clarify the extent to which performers will work independently of others, including the coach.* Who does what together, alone, and when?

12. *Persuade the performer to confront his or her own performance through reflective action.* Problems that go unaddressed or victories that go unrewarded undermine confidence. They can demoralize the workplace or lead to patterns of poor performance that can become difficult to break.

INTERPERSONAL SKILLS CLINIC

DISCOVERING HIGH-PERFORMANCE PATTERNS

We tend to spend a lot of time thinking about problems that need to be solved, but put relatively little time into thinking about what has gone right. Everyone has a story to tell of some success or unexpected surge in confidence or competitive performance. If you can get a performer to recognize a pattern of achievement from past experiences, then you can build confidence upon that pattern in future. The coach can often use these past achievements to help the performer gain access to higher levels of confidence necessary for accomplishing more challenging tasks.

Where does the high performance coach begin? The following exercise can be used by coaches as a means of identifying high-performance patterns each of us has at our disposal. Management consultants Jerry Fletcher and Edward Hinkelman of High Performance Dynamics in San Anselmo, California, have conducted research that indicates there are no 10 or 20 "best" patterns for high performance individuals or their organizations. Each one tends to have a high-performance pattern which is as real as it is unique. The trouble is it may be hidden or unknown.

One way to begin the search is to get employees to tell stories about previous times in which they competed well or otherwise contributed to high performance circumstances. Simply finding something out about who they are, what natural abilities they possess, what their needs and dreams are, what they find challenging or feel passionate about, is enough to help the coach get things started. Once a coach knows something about the talents, interests, and desires of others, he or she can create in them a vision of what may be possible, and coach them toward realizing their potential.

Ask a partner to tell a story about a time when he or she performed to an exceptionally high level of ability; when some task or project turned out better than anyone expected.

You, as the coach, can prompt the story along with the following questions aimed at uncovering four different aspects of a person's high-performance pattern: how they get involved, how they keep things going, how they overcome obstacles, and how they celebrate or reward themselves when the high-performance part is over.

◆ How did you get involved?

◆ What were your expectations or the expectations of others?

◆ What resources were available to you?

◆ What made the task important or attractive to you?

◆ How did you get started?

◆ Who else was involved?

◆ How did you use people with different expertise from your own?

◆ What did you do yourself, and what were you willing to let others do?

◆ How did you deal with obstacles?

◆ What was your biggest challenge?

◆ How did you make use of past experiences and obtain information for understanding the situation?

◆ What patterns do you see in the ways you organized and used your time?

◆ What were the rewards?

◆ How did the high-performance part end?

◆ What did you do when it was over?

◆ What did you learn from the experience that can help you in the future?

After you have heard one or two stories, record aspects of any patterns you uncover. You will probably need to have heard at least two or three stories before you can properly detect a high-performance pattern. The following examples demonstrate how two very different stories can contain similar patterns. Two anecdotes from a high performer, let's call him Dylan Michaels, are followed by a statement of the patterns of his high performance.

"I'm Not Supposed To Win This Race"

66 What drew me in was that my coach had arranged a dual meet with St. Michael's track team. Our coach knew me primarily as a running-back in football, but this was Spring and I guess he thought it would do me good to stay in shape over the summer. So he asked me to come out for track despite the fact that I didn't have a lot of experience at that time.

St. Mike's had this fabulous middle-distance runner who was well known around the city in those days. To my surprise the coach entered me in the 800 metres against this guy. What little experience I had in track was limited to 200 metres. I don't remember how I prepared myself for the 800 other than what the coach said to me just before the gun. Why I remember it so well is because I didn't do any of it! He told me to stay as close to the competition as I felt comfortable with until the last 150-200 metres (since that was the only distance I could recognize). "Then," he said, "kick past this guy and make yourself think that you've got the ball and he's the only man left to stop you. And don't look back."

"But I'm not supposed to win this race," I said to myself. The coach looked at me as though he could hear what I was thinking. Then he looked me straight in the eye and said: "I know you can do it and you know you want to do it. So just do it."

Once the gun went off and the race was on I suddenly felt this unexpected surge of confidence and energy; so I just naturally took the lead and held it comfortably all the way around to the 600 metre mark where the coach was standing. That's when I felt this guy coming after me. No one else around us. Just the two of us barrelling toward the tape. As I got fully into my kick I could sense his response and his confidence in his own ability to pass me. I dug deeper. I could hear his footsteps, but I didn't dare to look around. I could feel his pulse and hear my own pulse throbbing in the engine room of my heart and mind. I dug deep for a way to hang on and broke the tape just inches ahead of my opponent. He had pushed me to my absolute limit. I must have fainted—not from exhaustion—but from the thrill of having run absolutely as hard and as fast as I was capable of at the time.

I had a long talk with the coach afterward on the bus ride back to my school. I told him that this experience had taught me not to underestimate my own ability to compete in unfamiliar territory. Now I'm generally no longer afraid to compete at something new. Just tell me what to do and I won't do it. **"**

"The Only Tourist in Sturgeon Falls Turns His Thoughts to Paper"

"I had just finished my graduate studies that summer and was invited to visit an old school chum of mine, Marc, who had been teaching law in Ottawa. We took off for a week to his parents' cottage near Sturgeon Falls, with the intention of relaxing, and maybe doing a bit of work on Marc's new curriculum plan for the university. I know absolutely nothing about the law of course, but I was confident in what

I knew about teaching and curriculum design. I was also flattered that Marc wanted my help with this assignment.

The cottage was on Lake Nippissing—a beautiful spot—lots of hard rock and tall trees. We would go for long walks first thing each morning after coffee. That was usually when we generated our best ideas. Breakfast was at 8 a.m. We would usually spend the rest of the morning at the picnic table they had on a deck facing the water—and hammer out ideas in rough notes and extended conversations. We rarely ate lunch, but we would usually take breaks every two to three hours.

Marc was impressed with what I knew about adult education and I was equally impressed with his ability to think out loud. We got a lot done that week. On the last two evenings we were at the cottage I took it upon myself to stay up late and enter our rough notes onto a disk in my laptop computer. Both Marc and I took shots at editing the text off-screen, and that draft became the basis for Marc's proposal—which was subsequently submitted, approved, and successfully implemented in the first-year law program at Marc's university.

When we got together again last month we each had a riot retelling the events of that week in Sturgeon Falls to our friends in Toronto. I took a lot of pleasure in that. We exaggerated our problems—things I hardly noticed at the time. When we were in the thick of it, all seemed well. When we laughed about it later I realized how hard I must have been trying to impress Marc at the time. I learned a lesson about taking myself too seriously—and I took as much pleasure from seeing that, as I did in the fact that we managed to accomplish something of value. Everyone there that night understood. We all had fun. And I, for one, learned something more about myself and my friendships with others. **99**

Dylan Michaels' Pattern of High Performance

Whenever Dylan Michaels is confronted with a challenge he displays similar behavior patterns in terms of the way he:

◆ *Gets involved.* When those he trusts and respects express confidence in his ability to take on new challenges, Dylan makes the effort to learn something new in order to accomplish the tasks.

◆ *Gets started.* By associating the task with patterns from past accomplishments, and by eliminating distractions, he sets aside sufficient time to make real headway.

◆ *Gets over hurdles.* By recognizing an opportunity to surpass the expectations of others, and by working as a team, he gets a sense of satisfaction.

◆ *Gets rewarded.* By sharing his accomplishments with those who can appreciate the thrill of having given the best possible effort, Dylan receives a personal sense of accomplishment.

Considering the Patterns

After a while the coach and performer can compare different stories for their unique or common themes or patterns, and work with these. Aspects of a pattern may arise to form new visions or new possibilities for the individual or the organization to reflect and build upon. Once you recognize an opportunity to surpass expectations—and work toward it—anything is possible.

And finally . . .

In order to get a real commitment to excellence from individuals and from the institutions for which they work, managers need to think more like coaches and less like bosses. Higher performance is never accomplished by some organizational imperative or by taking responsibility for the performance of others. Ever-higher performances can only be achieved by increasing self-confidence and the commitment to excellence by empowering others to take responsibility for managing themselves.

We believe that if organizational leaders and managers act as coaches, they can empower and support others to expand their capabilities and improve their organization's performance. Coaching is about creating environments and opportunities in which people can become more fully engaged in the process of challenging their own limits, and in so doing discover greater success for themselves and for their organizations.

CHAPTER REVIEW QUESTIONS

1. How can the performance planning and appraisal interview indicate to the employee what the culture of the organization is like?
   a. The artifacts of the organization will be revealed.
   b. The employee will regard the nature of the process as an indication of what is expected of him or her and what kinds of assumptions are made in the organization.
   c. The employee will examine the artifacts and rituals of the organization by using information interviews.
   d. The artifacts and rituals of the organization will be constructed during a tell and sell interview.
2. Name three occupational fields in which it may be difficult to carry out performance appraisals meaningfully.

3. Which of the following approaches to appraisal saves time?
   a. tell and sell
   b. tell and listen
   c. mutual problem solving
   d. tell and query

4. Which of the following approaches may be used in situations in which power plays the least significant part in the relationship between manager and employee?
   a. tell and sell
   b. tell and listen
   c. mutual problem solving
   d. tell and query

5. Which of the following three approaches is formal, but interactive?
   a. tell and sell
   b. tell and listen
   c. mutual problem solving
   d. tell and query

6. What is the main weakness of the graphic rating scale?
   a. Used by itself, it does not allow for the use of verbal communciation.
   b. It is not suitable for employees who do not have artistic tendencies.
   c. It is expensive to implement.
   d. Used by itself, the graphic rating scale does not allow for much feedback from the employee.

7. How might you overcome the main weakness of the graphic rating scale?

8. What is a significant incident?

9. Discuss briefly the four basic steps to be carried out during the MBO cycle.

10. Three of the suggested techniques for familiarizing yourself with an employee's job are as follows:
    Carrying out some of the _____ related to the employee's job (if this is possible).
    Observing informal _____ among employees.
    Determining the _____ in approach taken by new employees.

11. Why might behavior shaping be used during a performance planning and appraisal interview?

12. Which terms describe the qualities or characteristics that contribute to an attitude of support during a performance planning and appraisal interview?
    a. communication features, climate setting, open probes
    b. tentative, improvisational, empathetic, problem-oriented, descriptive, collegial
    c. informal, informational, infrequent
    d. tell and sell, tell and listen, mutual problem solving3

13. Name the five communication control variables.

14. The following is a hypothetical situation in an organization. Discuss a means of encouraging the convergence of the employee's personal goals with the goals of the organization.

    Ross is a computer programmer who has been working at an organization for four years. He wants to finish his undergraduate degree. Without it, he feels he will never really be able to advance in his field. He needs only two courses and was working on them when he took up his full-time job as a programmer. He is thinking of quitting in order to take the courses at the local university this fall. At the performance planning and appraisal session, he mentions this to his boss.

15. Describe the three steps to be taken after the appraisal interview.

16. The results of Bernard Bass' research on the high performance leaders' relationships to those in their charge show that they do all of the following EXCEPT:
    a. use constructive feedback
    b. give followers a sense of autonomy
    c. treat followers in a friendly way
    d. provide a model of integrity

17. Empowerment is the experience of _____ to solve one's own _____ and to _____ to the best of one's ability.

18. Identify four different, yet effective coaching styles taken from the history of track and field, and relate at least one of these styles to your own.

19. Identify five of the 12 guidelines for giving feedback to high performers.

SUGGESTED ANSWERS

1. b.
2. teaching, public service, management
3. a.
4. c.
5. b.
6. d.
7. One of the three alterations that can be made to the use of the graphic rating scale is to allow the employee to complete the scale first, using his or her assessment as a basis for discussion.
8. It is an event in which the employee has been involved during the past appraisal period that may be used as the focus for an appraisal session. It is "significant" because it has had particularly positive or negative implications for the employee's performance.
9. Step 1: Develop or identify the objectives of the organization, department, or unit. Step 2: Identify the responsibilities of employees in terms of reaching the objectives stated in step 1.

Step 3: In consultation with each employee, set goals for the appraisal period, and agree on how the employee will reach those goals. Also, decide on when the goals will be reviewed, and if necessary revised, before the next appraisal session. Review points between appraisal sessions to ensure that there are no surprises at appraisal time.

Step 4: At the end of the appraisal period, assess whether the employee has reached the goals and return to step 1.

10. tasks; conversations; differences

11. Behavior shaping may be used to encourage the employee to display behaviors that are consistent with the purpose and climate of the interview.

12. b.

13. The proportionate amount of talking done by the participants; the relative degree of freedom allowed to the person being appraised; the extent to which digressions are encouraged; the climate of the interview; the pace, or tempo, of the interview.

14. Ross's boss might suggest that the organization could, if operations allow, grant leave without pay so that Ross could take the courses without quitting. Alternately, Ross could arrange for a flexible schedule so that he attended the courses and made up for the time on Saturday or in the evening.

15. Draft a written summary of the interview and give it to the employee.
Speak to the employee about any outstanding issues.
Follow up during the appraisal period.

16. a.

17. power; problems; perform

18. person-centred, authoritarian, radical endurance, flexible commitment.

19. Any five of the following will provide an appropriate response to this question:
    1. *Focus your feedback on the "here and now," not on the "there and then."* The more immediate the feedback, the more helpful it is.
    2. *Do not give people more feedback than they can handle at the time.* If you overload people with feedback, it reduces the chances that they will use it to good advantage.
    3. *Give feedback only when the performer has accepted that his or her behavior can improve to a significant degree.* Suggest ways for the performer to adjust performance to a higher standard.
    4. *Focus on sharing ideas that have value for the recipient.* Avoid expressing ideas that are simply based on criticism.
    5. *Explore alternatives, rather than fixed solutions.* In other words, don't limit yourselves to "one best way"—there isn't one.
    6. *Be poised and alert when giving feedback.* Avoid nonverbal distractions and use facial expressions and verbal comments that convey interest.

7. *Show empathy for the performer's feelings.* For example, you might say, "You were angry that your proposal wasn't even considered. I can understand how you feel. You don't feel that you are getting a fair opportunity to show what you can do. Is that it?"

8. *Solicit suggestions by encouraging people to give their opinions on how to deal with problems.* Typical lead-ins are as follows: "What do you think?" "What would you like to see happen?" "How would you do that?" "What can I do to help?"

9. *Get in sync with the other person.* When two people are not in synchronization with each other (when both, for example, are trying to talk at the same time, interrupting, or changing the topic, very little can be gained in terms of real communication about performance or development.

10. *Seize the opportunity.* Do not wait for the official performance appraisal interview to do your job. Coaching means continuous feedback coupled with specific goals and realistic deadlines. Prepare yourself for opportunities to coach.

11. *Clarify the extent to which performers will work independently of others, including the coach.* Who does what together, alone, and when?

12. *Persuade the performer to confront his or her own performance through reflective action.* Problems that go unaddressed or victories that go unrewarded undermine confidence. They can demoralize the organization or lead to patterns of poor performance that can become difficult to break.

INTERPERSONAL COMMUNICATION SCENARIO

MARTINVALE MARKET GARDENS

OVERVIEW AND ASSIGNMENT QUESTIONS

In the following scenario, which is based on a situation that could well occur in an organization, you will have the opportunity to apply the principles and skills you have learned in this chapter. The scenario can be used as the basis for a written or oral analysis or for role-play.

This scenario describes the institution of a job enrichment program at Martinvale Market Gardens—a combination multi-market retail, landscape services, and garden supply company on the outskirts of Sydney, Nova Scotia. In a performance planning and appraisal interview between the general manager and the Crafts Shop supervisor, the following issues are raised: (1) enhanced autonomy and group cohesion among the employees of the subunit; (2) greater profit generation and reduced costs for the company accompanying job enrichment; and (3) requests for greater financial compensation for the area supervisor and her staff.

1. Assume you are Ralph Riley, general manager of Martinvale Market Gardens. How will you respond to Mavis Johnson's success as the Crafts Shop supervisor and her request for greater financial compensation.

2. How do you plan to provide Johnson with greater challenges in her job?

3. What facts or materials will you need to acquire prior to the interview?

4. How will you outline the structure of the interview?

5. How do you plan to record the outcomes and follow-up?

INTRODUCTION

Expanding into the 1990s, Martinvale Market Gardens has begun using job enrichment as a means of improving the productivity of its employees and the quality of their work life. It has been especially important to Ralph Riley that the company provide meaningful employment and opportunities for growth, participation, and fulfillment through greater individual autonomy and responsibility.

Mavis Johnson has been an outspoken advocate of these new freedoms in the Crafts Shop segment of the business. In her annual performance review, Johnson reaffirmed her enthusiasm for the job enrichment program and emphasized the remarkable cost savings and profit generation the company enjoyed as a result of her implementation of the program in the Crafts Shop. Not only had she created an opportunity for everyone in the shop to learn new skills such as purchasing, each of her seven co-workers had become better performers in all their responsibilities. The

Crafts Shop had a thirty-five percent improvement in sales, cost reductions, and attendance. The total value of these changes has amounted to nearly $80 000 in total revenues since the job enrichment program began one year ago. Johnson feels that her pay raise should reflect the value of these gains for the organization. Therefore, she is requesting an additional $15 000 per annum for herself, and another $15 000 in increased wages for her staff.

MAVIS JOHNSON AND THE CRAFTS SHOP

Since all 11 business subunits of Martinvale Market Gardens are wholly owned and operated through a central administration, the Crafts Shop supervisor reports directly to the general manager who handles all operations from stock to personnel. When the job enrichment program began, Mavis Johnson interviewed all seven of her staff to solicit suggestions from them as to how their jobs could be enhanced and the operations of the Crafts Shop improved. Each of the Crafts Shop staff suggested that they would prefer greater autonomy and responsibility for such things as product buying, pricing, and work scheduling.

Johnson set up procedures in the Crafts Shop whereby everyone had a say in what products to purchase and sell, pricing on occasional over-stocked seasonal items such as summer sundries and Christmas ornaments, and more flexible and informally negotiated time tables and work schedules. Encouraged by the results in cost savings, increased profits, and reduced absenteeism, Johnson made reference to these facts and figures in her written performance review for Riley. In it she states that, under the job enrichment program, she views her role as "less one of control than of persuasion, empowerment, and staff support."

Johnson had also instituted weekly Wednesday meetings with each shift to discuss any problems in the smooth running of the shop. Since the staff rotates shifts, each individual meets with Johnson and others on their shift at least once every three weeks. These meetings have become the vehicle by which future changes and new decisions are made. The tone of the meetings is invariably informal. There is rarely a set agenda. The staff are encouraged to discuss any matter that concerns them individually or as a group. Since the situation is more fragile and less rigid than it was in the past, a great deal depends on maintaining mutual trust in the group.

"I let all my staff members make their own decisions," Johnson states with pride. "There is no one who is constantly pushing at them. The increased sense of responsibility achieved from the weekly meetings has promoted a more cooperative atmosphere in the shop. No one likes to be pushed around by a jailer with a key. I encourage everyone to contribute to the successful operation of the business. That way they take greater pride in their work and everyone benefits."

A REQUEST FOR FINANCIAL COMPENSATION

"I take more pride in my job, too." Johnson added to her report. "I feel I'm accomplishing more by helping others accomplish more for themselves. It gives me an incentive to come to work. Everyone in the Crafts Shop appears to be satisfied with both the new freedom and the new responsibilities. This increased responsibility justifies an increase in pay. I believe that job enrichment can be made to work in all areas of Martinvale Market Gardens as well as it has in the Crafts Shop."

Even though Ralph Riley sympathizes with the demands for higher financial rewards for Mavis Johnson and employees of the Crafts Shop, he also recognizes that the current two-year employment contract still has a year to run. On the other hand, he also knows that the current improvements in the Crafts Shop depend on the goodwill of all parties involved. Not only has the company already made substantial gains through job enrichment, Martinvale stands to gain more in the future if this success continues. With this in mind, Riley begins to plan his strategy for the meeting with Johnson. He especially wants to consider carefully how he will respond to the request for an adjustment in financial compensation.

POINTS TO CONSIDER

When assessing an employee's past work performance, we are also charged with clarifying what is expected of them in the future. The performance planning and appraisal interview is a vital opportunity for strengthening the relationship between the organization, the manager, the individual, and the work group involved. As a manager faced with this situation, be sure to give the respondent an opportunity to express his or her feelings about performance-related matters, and use this information to help identify potential for future development and advancement, including financial incentives. Furthermore, an effective manager will use the appraisal process as a means for building the culture he or she is seeking for the organization.

ENDNOTES

1 Thomas H. Patten, Jr., *A Manager's Guide to Performance Appraisal: Pride, Prejudice, and the Law of Equal Opportunity* (New York: The Free Press, 1982), p. 5.

2 We gratefully acknowledge the contributions of Andy Higgins and Daniel Zwicker to this section.

3 Roger Bannister, *The Four Minute Mile* (New York: Lyons & Burford Publishers, 1981), pp. 212-15.

4 Walter Kiechel III, "The Boss as Coach," *Fortune Magazine*, November 1991.

5 Adapted from an interview between P. Chiaramonte and F. Dean Carrotte, Toronto, circa 1990.

6 Bernard Bass, "Leadership: Good, Better, Best," in *Organizational Dynamics* 13, no. 2 (Winter 1985), 26-40. Reprinted with the permission of The Free Press, a Division of Macmillan, Inc. from *Leadership and Performance Beyond Expectations* by Bernard M. Bass. Copyright © 1985 by The Free Press.

CHAPTER 7

Oral Presentations, Meetings, and the Media

WORTH REPEATING

Don't read to people! Don't stand up in front of four people or 400 and read to them. It's insulting. Have notes—don't get lost but whatever you do—don't read to me! I know how to read. Talk to me.

—John De Shano

I want to do something where I know there's a chance of failing. . . . I'm not going to put out stuff that comes from a bored mind.

—Neil Young, songwriter

Journalists…are sometimes tough on business because business hides from them, and they figure there must be something to hide. Business tells me that the reason they don't talk to the press is that reporters always print the negative … never the positive. There is some truth to both arguments.

—Roger Ailes, presidential media consultant

Section 1 Oral Presentations and Meetings Management

Before we get started . . .

Without the ability to communicate it, technical brilliance is worth little in any business enterprise. Oral presentations are an integral part of business. And yet while people spend years developing knowledge and skills in their professional specialty, they usually spend very little time studying or practising how to communicate this knowledge. The most brilliant idea is worthless until it is expressed; how well it is communicated can be as significant to its acceptance and implementation as the idea itself. The more complex the business, the greater the need for communication of those complexities—in concise terms that a broader audience can follow and understand.

There is no shortage of published rules, laws, or guidelines for good presentations, but none are as universally accepted as this one: stick to topics you care deeply about, or ideas you have a real passion for. Nothing is as important as the speaker's enthusiasm for his or her subject. Less than ten percent of our impressions of oral presentations are made by the actual words the speaker uses. The rest is based on the energy and enthusiasm for the topic, conveyed by voice inflections, intonation, facial expression and body language.

The ability to use oral communication effectively does not occur naturally, despite the impression of effortlessness given by outstanding presenters. One of ancient Greece's greatest and most persuasive orators was Demosthenes whose first public speech was so feebly delivered and tortuous that his audience laughed him out of the Greek assembly. As he walked home disheartened and resigned to his inability to speak, Satyrus—a friend and actor—caught up with him and gave him a lesson in how to deliver a speech. Demosthenes then made himself an underground study where he stayed for weeks at a time. He shaved one side of his head (which, although fashionable today, would then have made him unpresentable) in order to keep away from the distractions of the world. He cured a stammer by speaking with pebbles in his mouth, and shortness of breath by shouting out Homer's poetry while running uphill. With these efforts, he eventually acquired the confidence and ability to hold an Athenian audience spellbound. After one of his speeches to the assembly he displayed his newly developed way with words when an enemy shouted out, "One of these days Athenians will kill you when they are in a rage." "And you too," he responded, "when they are in their *right* minds."

The organization provides opportunities daily for people to communicate with one another in various ways. Whereas the interview provides an opportunity for the members of an organization to communicate one-on-one, the presentation or meeting is an occasion for one person to talk to a group. While the dynamics for such interactions can be very different from those in an interview, we deal with them together in this chapter.

A consideration of the following four dimensions of an oral presentation or meeting will determine how you plan and carry out the presentation or meeting.

◆ *purpose* (to be expressed in a thesis, or purpose, statement)

◆ *method* (to be carried out through one of four rhetorical modes)

◆ *audience* (especially its number, demography, understanding, and familiarity)

◆ *environment* (to be considered in terms of proxemic design)

After you have considered the expression of these components in your presentation or meeting, you can go on to draft your notes. Your notes, which will serve as a plan beforehand and a prompt during the presentation or meeting, should be short. They do not constitute a manuscript to be read but rather an outline with appropriate cues. We will also offer suggestions for how to deliver your presentation.

The sections on planning and delivering a presentation may also be applied to planning and holding a meeting. In the last two sections, however, we discuss some specific aspects of planning, calling, and holding a meeting.

Objectives

After you complete this section you should be able to:

1. Define purpose statement.
2. Given a sample statement, discuss whether or not it is arguable; that is, whether or not it is a purpose statement.
3. List and discuss the Aristotelian topics of chronology, comparison and contrast, definition, and cause and effect.
4. List and discuss the rhetorical modes of narration, description, exposition, and argumentation, as they correspond to the Aristotelian topics.
5. Describe the traditional comparison and contrast formula.
6. Describe the structure of the formal definition.
7. Discuss the four aspects of an audience to be considered in planning an oral presentation: number, demography, understanding, and familiarity.
8. Given a description of an oral presentation, design the proxemics for the presentation.
9. State the three purposes and six steps of drafting a set of notes for an oral presentation.
10. Describe the importance of beginning a meeting with a statement of purpose and the setting of a time limit.
11. Discuss the four ways a chair of a meeting may influence or enhance the proceedings of a meeting: encourage discussion, focus the discussion, cue others, end or postpone further discussion.

The Bard on Public Speaking

As you may recall from the third act in Shakespeare's *Julius Caesar*, Brutus—fresh from plunging the knife into Caesar's heart—manages to persuade many in the mob to see the assassination as a "sacrifice," rather than a butchery. He did what was best for them and for the greater glory or Rome—or so he would have them believe. And then he turns the platform over to Marc Antony, who is supposed to say the same thing—more or less.

> "Friends, Romans, countrymen, lend me your ears!
> I come to bury Caesar, not to praise him.
> The evil that men do lives after them,
> The good is oft interred with their bones:
> So let it be with Caesar. The noble Brutus
> Hath told you Caesar was ambitious;
> If it were so, it was a grievous fault,

And grievously hath Caesar answered it . . .
He was my friend, faithful and just to me,
But Brutus says he was ambitious,
And Brutus is an honourable man.
He hath brought many captives home to Rome,
Whose ransoms did the general coffers fill;
Did this in Caesar seem ambitious?
When that the poor have cried, Caesar hath wept:
Ambition should be made of sterner stuff;
Yet Brutus says he was ambitious,
And Brutus is an honourable man.
You all did see that on the Lupercal
I thrice presented him a kingly crown,
Which he did thrice refuse. Was this ambition?
Yet Brutus says he was ambitious,
And sure he is an honourable man.[1] **99**

Careful attention to the organization and intonation of his speech allowed Marc Antony to conceal his true objective of condemning the murder of Caesar until after he had conditioned his audience to hear it. Marc Antony realized he'd first have to give the crowd the impression that he felt the same way they did—even before he spoke he heard rumblings from the mob: "Best speak no harm of Brutus here." And even though Antony's real intent was the opposite of Brutus's, Antony managed to express his view without contradicting Brutus outright. Marc Antony won the mob over to his opinion by doing the following:

◆ Treating the crowd with respect ("Friends, Romans, countrymen . . .")

◆ *Reminding them of their right to their own opinions and demonstrating his understanding of their point of view* ("The noble Brutus hath told you Caesar was ambitious. If it were so, it was a grievous fault.")

◆ *Stating his own opinion, and presenting the evidence for it* ("He was my friend, faithful and just to me. . . . [Caesar] brought many captives home to Rome, whose ransoms did the general coffers fill. . . . I thrice presented him a kingly crown, which he did thrice refuse. . . .")

Then Marc Antony produces Caesar's will—in which the slain ruler leaves most of his wealth to the citizens of Rome. After readying the crowd for the facts as he saw them, Antony drives them over the edge with feelings of remorse and vengeance. The sight of Caesar's body raises the mob to a frenzy and they soon drive the assassins out of Rome, as Antony intends. By presenting his ideas in this order to conceal his true feelings until he has conditioned the audience, Marc Antony is able to achieve his objective.

Advertisers and other people who sell for a living use a similar approach when they want to persuade an audience to buy a product or service. Because persuasion is such an important part of any oral presentation or meeting, you should keep in mind some of the principles and practices of persuasion covered in Chapter 2 as you proceed in this chapter.

What's Your Purpose?

The first step in making a persuasive presentation is to create a purpose statement. The **purpose statement** is a brief expression of the main idea that you will be conveying in your presentation. A purpose statement is not simply a sentence describing your topic or subject. It is an *arguable assertion*, which you will try to persuade your audience to accept. The following are purpose statements that could be the basis for an oral presentation.

◆ Our market share will continue to shrink unless we lower our price.

◆ The drop in productivity in our organization is a result of the increased rate of employee turnover we have experienced in the last two years.

◆ We should not appoint a task force for this project, because the task forces that have been appointed for similar projects have usually avoided making recommendations.

◆ Using a microcomputer for preparing documents is an efficient use of time.

◆ Our long-term costs in cash and other resources will be lower if we lease our vehicle fleet rather than purchase it.

The following statements, on the other hand, are not purpose statements, because they are not arguable. In each case we suggest how an inarguable assertion can become a purpose statement.

Statement: Our sales have increased by ten percent this year.

Comment: This fact may be interesting, but once stated it cannot be argued, only contested.

Revised Statement: Our sales have increased by ten percent this year because we improved the training program taken by our new sales representatives.

Statement: Our competitor's publication is much more attractive than their old one.

Comment: This is a matter of taste and cannot be argued.

Revised Statement: We should redesign our publication because our competitor has increased their sales by investing in a new look.

Statement: You will never regret buying this insurance policy.

Comment:	This is an unverifiable statement.
Revised Statement:	You will find this insurance policy attractive, because it has important features and benefits.
Statement:	I have completed the most comprehensive project in this organization's history.
Comment:	It is likely that insufficient information is available to verify it.
Revised Statement:	The results of this project are important, because the topic is timely and my research was comprehensive and painstaking.
Statement:	We chose a man for this position because the job called for long hours of negotiating.
Comment:	This statement is based on the assumption that men are "tougher" than women.
Revised Statement:	Of all the people considered, this candidate seemed to fill the requirements best.

Note that none of our purpose statements are longer than one sentence. The shorter, the better. If you are having trouble writing your purpose statement, ask yourself the following: What do I want my audience to learn from this presentation? Then, ask yourself whether what you have stated is arguable, fair-minded, clear and concise. If it isn't, revise.

In the Mode

After you have written your purpose statement, you should consider the rhetorical mode that suits it best. The rhetorical mode is the method of discussion that you will use to convey your main idea or purpose.

As in our discussion of persuasion, we turn to Aristotle for the beginnings of rhetorical theory and practice. The rhetorical modes are based on the *Aristotelian topics*, which are categories used for exploring a subject. The *topics* are chronology, comparison and contrast, definition, and cause and effect. We consider these topics to be the fundamental means of carrying out oral presentations. We will use the topics' corresponding rhetorical modes in our discussion. The rhetorical modes are *narration, description, exposition,* and *argumentation.*

Narration is the mode in which the speaker tells others about something that has happened to him or her or to someone else. As suggested by its corresponding Aristotelian topic, chronology, the most important part of narration is the notion of when an event occurred in relation to some other event. Narration can help keep your audience interested, because narration is one of the most appealing and widely used methods of communicating. Children in all cultures first hear the stories of their clan and society, and most people, when offered a description of "what happened," want to know "what happened next." In an oral presentation in which you explain the mandate for the members of a task force, you might use narration to discuss when the group will begin its work and when the mid-term and final reports must be completed.

With **description**—and its corresponding topic of comparison and contrast—the speaker talks about something by stating what it is and by suggesting what it is like and what it is not like. A description may be highly technical, using specialized terms with spatial and temporal precision or it may be poetic, employing metaphors and other literary devices.

You may want to consider as a guide for structuring a description the traditional comparison and contrast formula used in literature. It is as follows:

1. Say what the thing is not.
2. Then say what it is.
3. Say what the thing is like.
4. Finally, say what is not like.

If you used this formula in an oral sales presentation to describe a new product, for example, you might say something like the following.
Say what the thing is not: This is not the product you have been using for many years.

Then say what it iΪs:	It is a completely redesigned product.
Say what the thing is like:	It is similar to the ones that you may have seen described in your technical journal.
Finally, say what is not like:	It is much better than the one being sold by my competitor.

Exposition, like the Aristotelian topic of definition, is an attempt by a speaker to inform an audience. You are in the expository mode if you are orienting a new employee to the procedures to be followed to request vacation leave. Similarly, if you are reporting to a colleague on the status and progress of a project on which you are working, you will likely choose the expository mode. Because exposition often involves simply defining, you may wish to use the formal method of definition. A formal definition is a statement of what a thing is and what it is not like. You will recognize these as the second and fourth steps of the descriptive mode (or formal comparison and contrast) listed earlier. In technical terms, a formal definition identifies the genus, or larger category, to which the subject belongs, and then it differentiates the subject from other members of the genus. In the example we considered for the descriptive mode, the genus for the product would be the group of products now being described in technical journals; the differentiation is that this particular product is sold only by your company. The following are two more examples:

Subject:	pencil
Genus:	writing implement
Differentiation:	lead
Definition:	A pencil is a writing implement whose marking substance is lead.
Subject:	pen
Genus:	writing implement
Differentiation:	ink
Definition:	A pen is a writing implement whose marking substance is ink.

Argumentation, like Aristotle's cause and effect, is the mode in which an appeal is made to logic. It involves forming reasons, making inferences, and drawing conclusions with the aim of persuading an audience. It is thus distinguished from description, narration and exposition. For a fuller discussion of argumentation, you may wish to review the material on persuasion presented in Chapter 2.

For any oral presentation, you will likely find that you must engage in more than one mode. For example, even if your purpose is primarily to inform, you may find that you also must persuade. You may also find that in many cases you must appeal, as Marc Antony did, to your audience's emotions as well as to their logic and goodwill. However, deciding on your primary rhetorical mode will help you focus your presentation.

Playing to the Audience

After you have decided on the primary purpose and mode for your presentation, you must consider the nature of your audience. In this section, we identify the characteristics of your audience that you should think about, along with a few corresponding suggestions.

Number. How many people will be listening to you? Can you categorize the size of the audience to help you tailor your presentation? Your presentation may need to be revised based on the number of people.

There are no strict guidelines relating presentation style to the size of the audience. For example, some oral presentations may be just as informal for 100 people as they are for two or three. On the other hand, consider the case of a businessman who has never addressed an audience of more than 20 people. He enjoys speaking to others and usually ends his presentation with a lively discussion among everyone present. He uses questions for the audience and personal anecdotes to maintain rapport. One day he gets up to speak at a banquet and sees 100 faces looking back at him. And no one responds to his questions or talks to him during the presentation. He finds that his presentation was just not suited for a large group. As you rehearse your presentation, try to imagine what the room will look like, including how many people are likely to be attending your presentation.

Demography. As you consider your audience, you should try to identify the demographic characteristics that may affect the way they will regard your presentation. Age, sex, ethnic or cultural background, and social class would be the most important factors to consider for most audiences. You may need to tailor your language level and style according to these factors. For sales presentations especially, the demographic make-up of the audience will directly determine what qualities of the product you will emphasize or what product from a range of products you will focus on.

Understanding. As you plan your presentation, you should take into account how much the audience knows about your topic, as well as their education level. For people who are familiar with the project you are going to discuss, you will not have to provide much background information. Similarly, if your audience is familiar with projects similar to the one you are discussing, you may be able to assume that they will not need to be given the details of certain aspects of your project. People with advanced degrees or specialized training are often able to grasp a concept or idea quickly, simply because they deal with concepts and ideas daily. Try to determine the most probable educational profile for your audience, as well as a profile of their "understanding," and tailor your presentation accordingly.

Familiarity. You should also consider the personal and professional relationship you have with your audience. By focusing your presentation on the things you have (and do not have) in common with your audience, you will improve the efficiency and effectiveness of your presentation. Ask yourself questions such as the following.

◆ Have you met the person, or people, previously?

◆ Can you discuss experiences common to you and the audience?

◆ As part of your presentation, do you need to acknowledge disagreements you have had with your audience in the past?

◆ Might the humor that you have shared with the audience in the past be appropriate in this context?

◆ Will the relationship you have with members of the audience influence the relative degree of formality you adopt for the presentation? Will it influence your ability to ask for feedback or encourage questions during or after the presentation?

◆ Can you build on the knowledge that the audience possesses about the topic you will be discussing during your presentation?

In summary, in planning an oral presentation or meeting, a consideration of the audience is just as important as a consideration of your purpose. As we have suggested, you should take into account the audience's needs and disposition according to its number, demography, understanding, and familiarity.

INTERPERSONAL SKILLS CLINIC

BRAINSTORMING

Classical "brainstorming" is the forerunner of many group problem-solving methods in use today. This widely-used technique was developed in the 1930s by Alex Osborn[2] and has spurred many related idea-generation techniques. As Osborn conceived of the process, there are three major activities involved in brainstorming: (1) fact-finding, (2) idea-finding, and (3) solution-finding. The first two steps involve the generation and refinement of ideas through free association, modification, and combination. Solution-finding involves the evaluation and selection of ideas for further development or implementation.

There are six basic rules used to guide a brainstorming session:

1. Judgment is initially deferred. (The failure of a group to abide by this rule is often a major reason why some brainstorming sessions do not produce the expected results.)

2. Freewheeling is welcomed and encouraged. (This rule is intended to relax inhibitions and to enhance the creative process.)

3. Only one idea is suggested at a time and a time limit of 20-30 minutes for generating ideas should be strictly enforced. (This prevents sidetracking and confusion.)

4. Quantity is encouraged because it breeds quality. (The greater the number of ideas generated, the greater the possibility that one of them will provide a suitable solution.)

5. Combination and improvement are sought. (Better ideas are often built upon others.)

6. Negative and traditional thinking are ruled out. (Because no time is devoted to criticism, a great many more good ideas can be expressed.)

When determining the specific steps to follow for a brainstorming session, we encourage you to adapt the following general guidelines to suit your own particular circumstances and requirements:

PART I

1. Select a group leader to determine the problem to be dealt with and to distribute a one-page memorandum to the participants—usually a group of between five and twelve people—at least a day before the meeting. The memo should contain: (1) the statement of the problem, (2) the general background, (3) examples of possible solutions, (4) the six brainstorming rules, and (5) the time and place for the meeting. The first element, the problem statement is usually phrased as: "How can we . . . ?" or "How to . . . " In some cases the memo can be supplemented with a file folder containing pictures, symbols, or photographs that are *unrelated* to the problem. The pictures can be used to help participants overcome inhibitions often found during the face-to-face idea generation phase by stimulating free association.

2. Ask all participants to write down their initial ideas and bring them to the meeting.

3. Begin the brainstorming session by writing the problem on a chalkboard or chart visible to the entire group. Appoint a recording secretary to write down *all* the ideas generated by the group and restate the brainstorming rules.

4. After 20-30 minutes of generating ideas, take a break of at least one hour before beginning Part II.

PART II

1. Present the group with a list of the ideas generated in Part 1 and instruct them to select and cluster the best ideas for evaluation. At this stage no further generation of ideas is permitted.

2. Present the selected ideas to the persons responsible for implementing the solutions and request that they submit any additional ideas.

3. Evaluate the best solution(s) to the problem. The ideas are then edited by the recording secretary to make sure they are expressed clearly and concisely.

4. Select the ideas most likely to produce the best solution to the problem.

An optional extra activity is *reverse brainstorming*, in which you think of all the possible limitations or shortcomings of an idea. These new problems are then made the focus of the next round of creative problem solving.

Brainstorming was designed primarily to find new ideas, not to judge existing ones. Therefore general brainstorming sessions are most useful for relatively simple problems which don't require separate problem-solving sessions for each part of the overall process.

● ● ● ● ● ● ● ● ● ● ● ● ● ●

The Proxemics of Oral Presentations and Meetings

In Chapter 4, we discussed the ways managers can use their understanding of proxemics (the study of physical closeness) to improve their interviews. The importance of proxemics is illustrated by the emphasis given to it by those in the helping professions. Conscious of the importance of seating and the physical environment of human interaction, psychotherapists have, over the decades, changed their seating arrangements to reflect new approaches to their practice. In a Freudian session, for example, the patient lies on a couch in front of the therapist, facing away. The objective here is to allow the patient to "associate" without any distractions; the therapist, conceptually and physically, tries to stay out of the way. In a Gestalt session, on the other hand, an experimental approach is taken, in which the patient and therapist may try different seating arrangements as required. The idea here is that the patient must be "open to the moment." A fluid seating plan is a simple expression of this notion. There are many other situations that demonstrate the importance of seating, including religious services, the theatre, and university classes,[3]—that illustrate the important relationship between the purpose of an interpersonal interaction and the way people arrange themselves in a room.

For an oral presentation or meeting, seating and physical environment will determine the way the presenter and the audience regard one another and the presentation. The proxemics may also determine the outcome of the interaction to some extent. When you are planning for an oral presentation or meeting, you should consider the structure and nature of the interpersonal relationships that will be at play. You should design the proxemics by carefully arranging the leader, audience, intervening space, and props (lights, tables, chairs, plants, and so on). Let's consider three hypothetical situations and how the proxemics for each might be designed.

Situation 1: Dinner Meeting

Tim has written a final report on a year-long research project he has just completed. You are Tim's manager and the sponsor for the project. Although your input to the project was limited to advice and suggestions to Tim during the course of the project, you support him fully and believe that the report is significant for the company.

Your colleagues—other managers and supervisors at your level in the organization—disagree. They believe the project represents a waste of resources. They state that although there is nothing wrong with what Tim has done, they don't want to spend more money on similar projects in the future. A dinner meeting has been called to sort out the issues. Tim is to present his report formally and to respond to any questions, comments or concerns. In addition to Tim, the people attending will be you and six other managers and supervisors. You have called the meeting. Although Tim will be making the presentation, you will introduce him and you have ultimate responsibility for his work. How will you design the proxemics for the presentation and meeting?

Three relationships should be made clear in the meeting through the design of the proxemics:

1. the relationship between you (the sponsor for the project) and Tim;
2. the relationship between you and your colleagues; and
3. the relationship between Tim and your colleagues

Furthermore, you must provide a buffer between your colleagues and Tim, since he has worked under your direction. We would suggest the use of a long dinner table, with you and Tim facing one another in the middle, as shown in Figure 7.1.

This design makes clear the three relationships we listed. You and Tim are together at the center of the meeting, where you will address the others. Any questions or comments from the managers and supervisors must therefore be directed not only at Tim but at you as well. It is an open, yet secure arrangement that evokes that of the queen or king at table with the nobles.

Situation 2: Caucus

You are a member of a team that has been chosen to negotiate the terms for a collective agreement for your professional association. The employer has offered what it calls a final offer. If the association does not accept this offer, the em-

Figure 7.1: Dinner Meeting

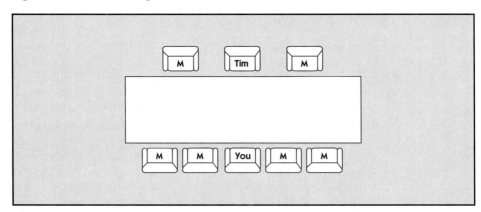

ployer has threatened to break off negotiations, and the association will likely go on strike as a result. Because there is no opportunity to consult the members of the association, the negotiating team will meet late this evening to decide whether to accept or reject this final offer.

Seven people will attend the meeting; four members of the executive of the association and three members who have been negotiating. Linda is the chair of the negotiating team, and she is the one who will briefly present the details of the employer's offer and ultimatum. Linda was chosen as chair partly because there have been criticisms from the association's membership that women have not had a strong enough voice in association matters. Besides Linda, only one other person in the group is a woman. Because the offer is unprecedented and sudden, no agenda has been set for the meeting. You have been chosen to organize the meeting, including the preparation of the meeting room. How should you proceed?

The factors to be considered in the proxemic design for the meeting are the following:

1. The comments of all the participants are needed.
2. Any decision made must be supported by all or almost all the participants.
3. All participants will have to accept responsibility for the decision made.
4. The proceedings will be flexible, since they are unprecedented.

We would suggest the following layout of chairs, without the aid of a table (Figure 7.2).

Figure 7.2: Caucus

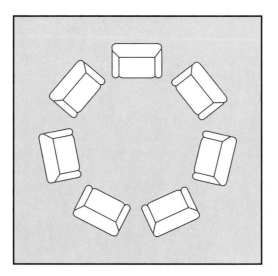

The matter of where Linda, the presenter, will sit is of no consequence, since she is only a messenger. The layout encourages all to participate, with no physical barriers to communication. This is particularly important, given the history of gender inequity in the organization and given that the women are outnumbered in the group. The tighter the circle, the better. The design suggests that of an evangelical "prayer meeting," which calls on all to participate and for which the "sense of the meeting" (its general direction) is the most important characteristic of the meeting's outcome.

Situation 3: Colloquium

You are to teach a senior university course on interpersonal communication in management. The class is small, you have six students. The course will require each student to undertake a major research paper. Each week, you want to have a student present his or her research findings to date and receive feedback from you and from the other students. How will you design the proxemics for these weekly oral presentations? Figure 7.3 shows one way of designing the proxemics for such a meeting.

The oval shape of the table allows for a "head," where you may choose to sit, offering advice and guidance to the presenting student. The shape also allows for a sense of collegiality; it may well encourage dialogue and spontaneous comment. For that reason it is the traditional university seminar design.

Designing the proxemics for an oral presentation or meeting takes practice. Observe the way people arrange themselves in various situations: working, eating, relaxing, and so on. In considering the way people seat themselves try to determine the purpose they are trying to accomplish. As well, try to think of ways of improving their seating patterns, given the purpose of their interaction.

Figure 7.3: Colloquium

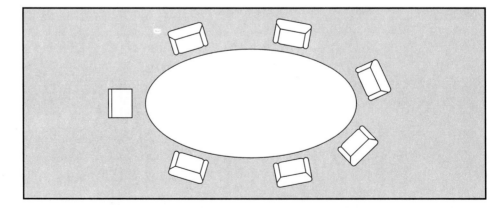

Is There a Draft in Here?

No matter how short your presentation, it's wise to prepare some notes for reference. These notes will accomplish three objectives. First, they will allow you to decide in advance whether you should add or drop topics or issues; the notes will thus act as a *planning* device. Second, they will provide a focal point for your thoughts as the time of the presentation draws near; as a result, they may help you to *build confidence*. Third, even if you don't actually look at them as you speak, your notes will be available for *reference* during the presentation.

Step 1: Identify the Dimensions

After considering the proxemics, you should identify the four dimensions of your presentation, as we have discussed previously: purpose, rhetorical mode (method), audience, and proxemics (environment). Your plan at this point might look like the following.

Purpose: We should request an increase in the budget allocated to training our clerical staff.

Rhetorical mode: argumentation

Audience: Four other middle managers in the organization, all with whom I have worked for four years and all of whom, like me, have eight or nine clerical staff members.

Proxemics: I have decided to use a small conference room in the office that can accommodate eight or 10 people. The room has an oval table surrounded by chairs, as shown in Figure 7.4. I will sit or stand at the head of the table. I will have an overhead projector focused to the left of the audience, at the front of the room to be used for projecting some facts and figures.

Step 2: Gather Your Information

The work you do at this stage is determined mainly by the rhetorical mode you have chosen. If, for example, you are going to use argumentation or exposition, you will have to gather more information, and perhaps do more research, than if you were to use narration or description. On the other hand, any oral presentation or meeting requires some research, even if that research involves as simple a task as consulting the minutes of a previous meeting.

In the case of the training budget we discussed in Step 1, you will need to gather at least the following information:

◆ training budgets for the past two or three years
◆ a statement of what the budget has been used for
◆ information indicating whether the money has been well spent

Figure 7.4: Proposal Meeting

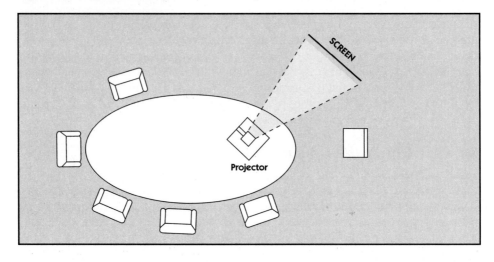

The following information, while not essential to the presentation, might be helpful in arguing your case:

♦ comparable training budgets for other companies
♦ a detailed example of how the money has been spent (perhaps an anecdote about how the budget has benefited the organization with reference to the training completed by a particular clerical employee)
♦ information, if appropriate, as to where the "new" money might come from
♦ a description of the negative consequences encountered by organizations that have not provided sufficient resources for training their workers

At this point, you need not spend too much time organizing or editing the information you are gathering. That step is next. Instead, you should try to ensure that you have a reasonably complete body of relevant and useful information. You will never be able to gather *all* the information that exists on a given topic, therefore your goal should be to ensure that you haven't neglected an important aspect or area of your topic.

Step 3: Organize Your Ideas

The purpose of this step is to develop the body of your presentation. We will work on the introduction and conclusion in the next step. For the training budget presentation, let's assume that you have been able to gather most of the information that we listed in the previous step. You will now try to determine how the information could best be presented, whether some of it needs to be omitted, and whether you have neglected to gather important information. From this process, you will structure the body of your presentation, which is your argument to the other managers.

1. The training budgets for the past three years have remained unchanged at $7500. This works out to approximately $190 per clerical staff member per year.

2. Over the three years, half of the budget has been used mainly for training clerical staff on the use of microcomputers. Another twenty percent has been used to pay for workshops and courses in interpersonal communication and writing skills. The remaining money, some $2250, has been used for the staff Christmas party one year and for gifts for long-time staff who retired.

3. The organization has an evaluation form to be used by staff who attend education programs using the training budget. All staff who attended courses, along with their managers, have stated that the training was well worth the investment. You have been able to determine, for example, that the clerical staff's productivity in producing documents has increased by twelve percent over the past three years.

4. Two comparable branches of your organization also spend $7500 per year on training clerical staff. However, their clerical staff complement in every case is smaller by at least a half. The amount the branches spend per clerical staff member is $290.

5. You have a two-page description from one of the staff on her experience in taking a course in writing skills. The paper discusses how the employee came to recognize the need for the course, how she applied for and received funding, and how she did in the course. The paper is especially impressive because it illustrates, through its prose, the skills taught in the course.

6. You have not been able to determine where "new" money might come from: Your memo to the organization's budget officer is, as yet, unanswered.

7. You have clipped an article from *The Globe and Mail* that offers anecdotal evidence of the effectiveness of investing in employee training.

It appears that you can make a strong case for increasing the budget. From the information you have gathered, write an outline of the body of your presentation. Because your presentation is in the mode of argumentation, you could use the structure for persuasion we presented in Chapter 3.

◆ *State the issue:* The issue is whether the training program, and in particular the budget, is adequate for the needs of the clerical workers.

◆ *State your point of view, with evidence:* Your point of view is expressed in the purpose statement. The evidence may be summarized by the following points:

—Compared to two other branches, we don't spend enough.

—Clerical staff and their managers are making effective use of the funds available: Productivity is up by twelve percent.

—The two-page report by one of the clerical staff members provides the best evidence of the need for training.

◆ *Acknowledge your opponent's point of view and its merits:* The fact that not all the money is being used for training might indicate that there is enough in the budget already.

◆ *State the shortcomings of your opponent's point of view:* This is the one component of your argument you will have to gather more information on, because you have not yet considered why some of the budget has been spent on a Christmas party and gifts.

◆ *Resolve the issue:* Assuming you will be able to find evidence of demand for the funds, you will recommend that the entire budget this year be used for training and that next year, if the funds are used up, the budget be increased. However, you have not determined how much of an increase you will recommend.

At this point, suppose you find that there has indeed been a great deal of demand for funds. The human resources department has provided you with several applications for funding, legitimate in your view, that were turned down because of lack of funds.

The question of how much of an increase to the budget you will recommend is resolved simply by using the guideline of the other branches. You will recommend that the organization adopt a "per staff member" system with a target of $300 per staff member. Since you have approximately 40 clerical staff members, you would increase the budget from $7500 to $12 000. This would represent a budget increase of sixty percent. This is a large percentage increase, but its size can provide evidence of the need; in recommending a figure of $12 000, you are simply advising that the organization "catch up" with the branches.

Step 4: Write an Introduction and a Conclusion

Although the body is the most important part of your presentation, the introduction and the conclusion are what will stay with your audience. During the introduction, the audience forms its impressions of you and your topic; during the conclusion, the audience makes the decision as to whether your presentation has been successful or not. Therefore, both of these sections should "frame" the body by accomplishing the following:

◆ appealing to the audience's interests;

◆ providing a source of curiosity;

- establishing and maintaining the atmosphere of the presentation;
- introducing, and then summarizing, the purpose statement

In the case of the training budget, you could use your clipping from *The Globe and Mail* as an introductory item. The clipping is on topic, current, and credible. You could provide copies of it to the other managers or perhaps summarize and discuss it. At the end of the introduction, you would introduce the purpose, perhaps with a statement such as, "The organizations described in this article are not very different from ours. We need to improve our training program, too." Then you would present the body of your argument.

The conclusion could include the two-page report by the clerical staff member who took the writing skills course. You might describe the report briefly and then provide copies for the managers to read later. Again, the report would be effective as a conclusion because it provides anecdotal and personal evidence to complement the facts and figures you present in the body of your argument. At the end of the conclusion, restate your purpose.

Step 5: Rewrite

After you have all the elements of your presentation together, rewrite it. At this point, you should ensure that the transitions between the parts of the presentation (introduction, body, conclusion) and between the main points in the body are clear and smooth. As well, you should try to anticipate any objections from the audience. Because we do not recommend reading a presentation word for word, we suggest that this stage should result in one or two pages of notes that contain the following:

- the major headings for the sections of your presentation
- any quotations, dollar figures, or statistics that you will use
- cues for prompting you to tell an anecdote or to elaborate on a point

In Figure 7-5, on page 324, we provide an example of the notes that could be used for the training budget example.

Step 6: Rehearse

When your speaking notes are in hand, rehearse your presentation. This will help you master the material, estimate a time length, and find and eliminate any problem areas in the presentation. If you can, you should try delivering the presentation in front of someone else. If this is not possible, use a tape recorder and mirror. Better still, videotape your presentation and criticize your own performance. It is at this point that you should try to eliminate or reduce the use of vocalisms such as *uh*, *er*, and *mmm*. When we described the use of similar vocalisms in chapter 3, we called them "nonverbal cues" because they were used con-

Figure 7.5

NOTES FOR A PRESENTATION ON INCREASING THE TRAINING BUDGET FOR CLERICAL STAFF MEMBERS

INTRODUCTION

—Hold up Globe article and discuss,

—Mention the Standard Telephone company in particular (approximately same size and business as us).

—Transition: "We have a good base for training our workers, but we need to do more."

BODY

—We allocate $190 per year per employee on training, spend some of the money for non-training purposes.

—Calgary and Winnipeg spend $100 more than we do per employee.

—Usage and demand are up. (Figures on overhead projector.)

—More training means more efficiency, savings. (Figures on overhead projector.)

—Transition: "We should make sure all of our budget is spent only on training this year. Next year, let's plan to increase the budget to $12 000."

CONCLUSION

—Summarize Marion's paper, hand it out.

—Ask for questions.

—(I am recommending a 60% increase, but the extra $4 500 is only 1/2% of our annual budget.)

sciously as a means of eliciting information. In an oral presentation, they will likely distract the audience from the message and should therefore be avoided. You may also wish to consider whether phrases such as *Well, you see?*, and *You know?* are being used appropriately. We will offer some specific suggestions for the delivery of your presentation in the next section of this chapter.

Business Is a Team Sport

Oral presentations in business are often given by a team of presenters. Therefore they require good planning and coordination. Team presentations are a good predictor of future performance. They allow an audience to see the ability of the team to work together. Oral presentations have long been a standard part of an organization's pursuit of new business. Think of a salesperson trying to get a new account or a contractor making a bid for a tendered project. Presentations also play an increasingly significant role *after* the business is won. A series of presentations can explain the progress of planned courses of action. The following elements distinguish effective team presentations from ineffective ones.

- well-organized content (each segment clearly tied together) supporting one overall message or theme
- looking and acting like a team and supporting one another (the audience is probably a team too!)
- each presenter identifying, during the design phase, what he or she perceives as the key points to be made in the body of the presentation
- strict adherence to the time allotted—being attentive and alert to the needs of others
- use of simple visuals and interpretive concepts and titles
- compatibility of formats and visuals that contribute to the image of a harmonious team.

Passion and Presentation

Use the following suggestions to improve the delivery of your presentation.

Maintain eye contact. This is an important part of any interpersonal communication. Especially at the beginning of your presentation, look up from your notes often to let the members of the audience know that you are there for them.

Stick to your plan. During rehearsals, try to test how far you can depart from the outline. While you may wish to elaborate on certain points in further detail than you might have expected, don't try to change the outline of your presentation at the last moment. It will likely cause you to go over your time allotment and to get into areas for which you are not prepared.

Emphasize transitions. When you drafted your notes, you incorporated transitions into your plan—between the introduction and the body, between points in the body, and between the body and the conclusion. There are two ways of emphasizing these transitions. The first is to use transitional words, such as *first, next, finally, then, similarly, in contrast*, and so on. The other way of emphasizing transition, which should be used to complement the first, is to use vocal gradations. You might raise the pitch and volume of your voice somewhat to begin a new, important point. Similarly, you might slow the pace of your speech as you enunciate the most important point of your presentation. Lowering the pitch and volume of your voice might signal that you are coming to the end of a section. And two or three seconds of silence can be used before moving to the next section. Try out these transitional devices in your rehearsal.

A caution. Many speakers "fade out" at the end of a sentence, so be sure you can still be heard if you are using the technique of lowering pitch and volume at the end of a section.

Determine whether you are being heard. By checking the audience's reactions to certain points, you may be able to find out if you are speaking loudly enough. Try to watch the people at the back of the room in particular. Of course, for a very large audience, you will be using a public address system. In rehearsal, try to test the public address system beforehand to check that it is loud and clear.

Ensure that the audience can see and hear your audio-visual aids. In the case of overhead projectors, the best position for the screen is off to the side, assuming you will be speaking in the middle. That provides the best sight lines for most of the audience. As part of your rehearsal, try out any audio-visual material to ensure that it will be heard and seen by everyone in the audience.

Use hand-out material with care. If you intend to hand out material for reference, try to have an assistant do this for you at a specified point in your presentation. It's best to say all you have to say about a hand-out first, because after people have reading material in their hands they are likely to focus their attention on reading, rather than on listening to you. If possible, provide hand-outs after the presentation.

Today's audiences have become quite accustomed to the use of a great variety of sophisticated audio and visual resources—everything from overhead projections, slide shows, and film clips to dramatic song and dance interludes. Whatever you choose, keep in mind that back-up or supplementary material can never replace a dynamic or enthusiastic speaker. A good general rule is to make sure that you spend most of your time designing and practising a clear, coherent, thoughtful speech. Then, if you feel your delivery would be *enhanced* by audiovisual support, use it. Materials that are poorly produced, difficult to see, or used as fillers rather than reinforcement, can detract from your overall presentation. Use the following criteria when deciding on the use of an audiovisual aid:

◆ Is it necessary?

◆ Is it big enough and clear enough?

◆ Is it interesting or dramatic?

◆ Does it clarify the material?

◆ Does it provide necessary or entertaining variety?

◆ Does it usefully take the focus off the speaker?

◆ Do all visuals have the same style?

◆ Are fonts or art quality consistent?

Don't emphasize mistakes. If you have given a number or fact that is incorrect, give the correct one with a brief introductory phrase. If the mistake was not significant, avoid correcting it at all; the correction will call undue attention to the mistake. If possible, work the correction into the structure of the presentation. For example, in the transition from the introduction to the body, you might say, "I mentioned that we have already spent approximately $60 000 to register a patent for this idea—actually, it's closer to $80 000—and now I will turn to some of the problems we encountered in doing so."

End on time. Before the presentation, determine whether there is a time limit. If there is none, set one for yourself and then stick to it.

Meetings Management

A meeting is very much like an oral presentation. In both the meeting and the oral presentation, planning and preparation are required. Also, in both cases, one person (the speaker, in the case of the presentation; the chair, in the case of the meeting) has the primary responsibility to "present." We may distinguish a meeting from oral presentations by the fact that in a meeting, the audience becomes the speaker for much of the session; that is, while the chair will do much of the preparation and planning for the meeting, the other participants also have a responsibility to prepare and participate. Therefore, much of what we have discussed concerning oral presentations will also apply to meetings. In the rest of this section we discuss the special steps involved in holding an effective meeting.

Most meetings in an organization are for the purpose of providing and gathering information or deciding on a course of action or solving a problem. The approach to planning either an information or decision meeting can be the same. The steps are as follows:

1. State the purpose of the meeting.
2. Choose the participants and inform them of the time and place for the meeting.
3. Draft, circulate, and finalize the agenda.
4. Hold the meeting.
5. Follow up.

We will discuss each of these steps in turn.

State the purpose of the meeting. This step is the same as that of writing the purpose statement for an oral presentation. The purpose of the meeting should be expressed in one sentence and should be as clear as possible. This purpose statement is what will guide your actions in the rest of the planning process, especially in drafting the agenda, and in holding the meeting. Therefore, you should spend some time to make sure you get it right. The following are some flawed purpose statements for meetings, along with a short comment and rewrite for each.

Purpose: To talk about some of the ideas Kerry has for next week's trade show.

Comment: No decision is implied here. Unless the meeting is purely for information (which is unlikely, given that the show is next week), the decision should be made explicit.

Rewrite: To choose one of Kerry's ideas for next week's trade show and to plan how we will carry it out.

Purpose: To hear the report on the progress of the Lakeview Project.

Comment: This will evidently be an information meeting. However, the details and context for the presentation of the information should be stated.

Rewrite: To have Jeremy report to the other members of the department on the progress of the Lakeview Project as of January 1, with a short question and answer session to follow.

Purpose: To hold our monthly meeting.

Comment: Some meetings are held regularly for no other reason than to provide an opportunity for planning, discussion, and information. However, the purpose can still be made more explicit.

Rewrite: To plan next month's special activities, to hear a report from all department members on current issues, and to table any important documents produced by other departments that may affect our department's operations.

Choose the participants and then inform them of the time and place for the meeting. Not everyone needs or wants to attend every meeting. Unless the meeting is a departmental or organizational one, in which anyone interested may attend, you will have to decide who should be invited. The categories of people you should consider include the following: those affected by any decisions made in the meeting; those who have special expertise or a particular interest in the topics to be discussed; those who must be kept informed about the status of certain issues or projects, especially those who act in a liaison capacity for other departments or organizations; and those who may have a symbolic or political function, such as visiting guests or observers, government officials, or benefactors. That's a long list. Ideally, you should keep the number of people in a meeting to a minimum, while soliciting the participation of everyone who should be included.

Draft, circulate, and finalize the agenda. Your agenda should be circulated before the meeting so that participants have an opportunity to prepare themselves and to bring along any relevant material such as background documents or statistics bearing on a particular issue. If possible, ask people to comment on or approve the agenda. Even if you do not have a chance to create and circulate a revised agenda, having heard comments in advance will help you to adapt the agenda during the meeting. An agenda should include the following components:

1. the date, time, and place (including the room) of the meeting
2. the purpose of the meeting
3. a mention of introductory or background material or documents
4. the topics to be discussed

5. a brief comment about the context of the topic (for example, how the topic came up, who has been involved in developing it, what has been discussed or decided to date).

Except in the case of an annual general meeting or some other extraordinary meeting, the agenda should be no longer than one or two pages. If it is longer than that, you may be trying to cover too much in one meeting.

A good agenda is the "blueprint" for a meeting. In drafting your agenda and running the meeting, be sure to do the following:

◆ Provide adequate lead time
◆ Order the items on the agenda
◆ Code agenda items with appropriate tags or headings
◆ Begin the meeting with minutes, announcements, and modest decision items
◆ Move to moderately important decision items before addressing the most difficult ones which will require a lot of discussion
◆ End the meeting when the group has achieved the objectives it set out to accomplish.

Hold It!

Two steps are essential at the beginning of any meeting. After greeting the participants, the first thing to do is to state verbally the purpose of the meeting that you formulated in the planning stages. This statement provides an overview of what will be covered in the meeting. The second thing to do is to inform the group of when the meeting will end. This will already have been done during the agenda-setting process, and now is no time to revise the time limits. If people find that the time you allocate to meetings is "as long as it takes," they may avoid such meetings in the future.

Even if you have someone taking formal minutes of the meeting, you should keep your own notes of what issues need to be followed up in future meetings or outside the context of a meeting. Others may be responsible for carrying out the duties assigned during a meeting, but it is up to the chair to ensure that all issues and problems have been followed up.

You will have determined what background information is needed before the meeting begins. You may refer to this information in introducing each item on the agenda. As you introduce each item, be sure to indicate what action (voting, debating, etc.) is required. For items that require discussion, set a time limit. And for those that require the group to make a decision, try to ensure that everyone agrees on the process to be used in making that decision. Will it be by majority vote or consensus? Or will one person be making the decision based in part on the group's deliberations? If the decision-making process can be changed, try to come to an agreement on it. If the process cannot be changed, simply inform the group of how the process will work.

As the group discusses each item, it may become necessary for you to influence or enhance the progress of the meeting. We suggest four ways of doing this.

First, you may need to *encourage discussion*. If the purpose of a meeting is to gather information or to come to a decision, people will have to participate. One way to get a discussion started is to offer a suggestion. For example, if a decision is to be made, you may offer your opinion, and ask the group to comment. As the discussion continues, you will have to decide whether you wish to continue to act as an advocate for your own suggestion. Another way to encourage discussion is to ask one person for comments or suggestions.

Once the discussion is under way, you may need to help *focus the discussion*. This may be accomplished through summarizing what one person or a group of people have said. Or, if the discussion has gone off topic, it may be accomplished by reminding the group of the purpose of the discussion and of the meeting. Yet another way of focusing the discussion is to remind the group of the time limits for the meeting. Mentioning the time is not done to rush the group or to cut off relevant discussion; rather, it is a means of reminding the group that all its energy should not be expended on a single agenda item.

You may also wish to *cue* others. If, for example, you are aware that someone in the group has expertise in a particular area, you may want to suggest to the group that the expert's views be heard. Similarly, you might arrange beforehand for someone to give a short presentation on an aspect of the topic being discussed. This mini-presentation may be for background, but it need not occur at the outset of the discussion. To encourage a fresh exchange of ideas, you could plan to introduce the mini-presentation during the discussion.

And finally, it may be helpful for you to *end or postpone further discussion* on a particular topic. If the discussion seems to have accomplished its purpose, move on to the next matter. If, on the other hand, it seems that further discussion is necessary, but will only be fruitful on another occasion (for example, after more information is gathered), suggest to the group that the discussion be continued later. Sometimes, a break may be called in order to allow participants to reconsider their arguments or to encourage them to think of ways of breaking a stalemate.

When the time limit for the meeting is up, or when the agenda has been covered (whichever comes first), bring the meeting to an end. If you have not been able to cover the agenda, ask the participants how and when it should be completed. A possible consequence of a meeting may be having to call another meeting. Other consequences include: informing people who were not in attendance of the proceedings or decisions taken, finding more information on a topic or issue, asking for the input of others in the organization, and forming a committee or task force to work on recommending solutions or approaches to certain problems or issues.

Points to Ponder for Those Who Manage Meetings

1. Keeping Your Purpose in Mind

◆ How do you want the audience to respond?

◆ Do you want them to change their minds, learn something new, demonstrate a new technique, or is your purpose simply to entertain the troops?

2. Scouting Report and Reading the Defence

◆ Who are the key decision makers?

◆ Has this idea been tried before? With what result?

◆ What knowledge does the audience already possess?

◆ Can you anticipate attitudes, prejudices, affiliations?

3. Portrait of the Audience as Safety Net

When you can't find the words you are looking for, or the next idea you want to move toward, it may be because you are nervous. No amount of searching your notes or cue cards will help that nervousness go away. In fact, it usually only makes you more nervous. Our advice is that you relax as best you can, look up, and find a few friendly faces with which you can make eye contact. The right words will come on their own.

One of the best things that can happen to you—and you may find this hard to believe until it actually happens—is to *forget* a part of your presentation. When you forget a part of what you intend to say, your listeners will sense the gap. And very often this will elicit a question from them. Your idea, given in response to a question from the audience, is often more powerful and convincing than if it were given as a part of your initial presentation.

4. Riding the Wave

If you show respect for your audience through solid preparation, you will be ready for one of the great thrills in life—surfing the currents of audience energy and positive response. How do you ride the wave without wiping out?

◆ Watch your audience closely

◆ Prepare extra material but don't use it unless you have to.

◆ Have faith in yourself.

◆ Stick to the game plan, but leave room for thinking on your feet.

◆ Finish strong and finish on time.

5. No Panaceas

The degree to which your audience will share your ideas and commitments will depend on the degree to which you compel them to participate in the ideas or solutions you put forth. To inspire an enthusiastic response, you must challenge your audience—at least symbolically. Consider the following techniques for accomplishing this:

◆ Ask a rhetorical question, such as "Suppose we were to . . . ?"

◆ Follow up with an imperative, such as "Let us . . . !"

The rhetorical question sets up an emotional agreement. You can assume a rational agreement; this type of question ensures that the heart follows the head. The imperative opens the floodgates of passion and action. After asking a question or making an exclamation, you should pause slightly to allow the audience to answer silently—to agree with you before you move on to your next point.

The 10 Most Common Problems in Meetings

Forewarned is forearmed. If you are able to recognize the most common pitfalls of meetings in organizations, you will be better able to avoid them in the first place.

1. No clear goals or agenda
2. No pre-meeting orientation
3. Starting late
4. Poor or inadequate preparation
5. Lack of participation by some
6. Ineffective leadership
7. Wasted time
8. Too many interruptions or emotional outbursts
9. Rambling, digressive discussions
10. No published results or follow-up actions.

And finally . . .

Perhaps the reason that some people feel anxious about making a presentation or chairing a meeting is that the feedback they receive in such a situation is difficult to control. In an interaction with only one other person (as is the case in an interview), negative or hostile comments can be dealt with more easily, if necessary simply by ending the interaction. When presenting to a group of people, on the other hand, it is more difficult to mediate or end the interaction.

The suggestions we have made in this chapter will help you to establish control in a presentation or a meeting. However, you should keep in mind that any feedback you receive from others can help you learn. We hope that with practice you will come to encourage, not discourage, the process of having a group of people offer their opinions about what you have to say.

Section 2 · Business Communications with the Media

Before we get started . . .

When a manager, or anyone else responsible for company-media relations, gets involved in a media situation, we tend to expect the outcome to be the result of a kind of information tug-of-war. But it needn't be. Business and the media need one another. The media need to know what is driving the business world, while business needs to understand the way the media work. One should not be out to defeat the other.

The most important kind of information gathered in reporting the economic life of a country or community is that which reaches below the surface of events, and brings forth some understanding of underlying trends and their significance. Stock-market figures, commodity prices, car sales, and unemployment data are not meaningful in and of themselves. It is the meaning they have in terms of their relevance to people that determines their social value as well as their newsworthiness.

Even poorly trained journalists or novice columnists cannot afford to restrict their questions to just the obvious facts. They must go deeper. For example, in reaction to a local plant closing, they might ask: "Are you planning to close any more factories in the province?" and immediately follow up with: "What, then, will be its effect upon the unions, on the unemployment rate, housing, taxes, and so on?" What does business mean in the lives of local people? That's what we want to know.

Journalists are often poorly educated about business, but business should be prepared to accept some of the responsibility for properly informing them. To that end, business must begin to be more open and to tell even the bad news as accurately and honestly as it can. Companies and organizations need to help the media learn more about their missions, strategies, products, services—and their value to the community or society as a whole—as well as the problems they face. The less that is known or understood about an organization, the more vulnerable it will be to suspicion or attack from the public or the press.

Objectives

After you complete this section you should be able to:

1. Define *news*.
2. Discuss the notions of intensity and extensity with regard to newsworthiness.
3. List the three ways reporters use news.
4. Describe some of the questioning tactics used by reporters.
5. Discuss the four stages in the development of a news story: facts, perceptions, implications, call to action.
6. Discuss the *inverted pyramid* style of news story.
7. Demonstrate the use of the *NEWS* acronym for testing a lead.
8. Discuss the function of crisis response groups in an organization.
9. Describe the three-step approach to responding to reporters' questions.
10. Discuss 10 guidelines for dealing with reporters.
11. Discuss 10 common problems in communicating with the media.

What Has the News Got to Do with Business?

"The news" is an account of an event, fact, or opinion that interests or excites people. Most often, what's in the news is an account of the changing relationships between people, and between people and their environment or circumstances. Change, or the potential for change, is the essential element in the news. Thus, the extent of *disruption* or *community consequence* of some event is how we usually measure the importance of the news and its audience appeal.

Good reporters or editors with a "nose for the news" know a good story when they see it. Are there any reliable scales by which to determine the importance of a story? Two useful assessments that we can make are intensity and extensity. **Intensity** refers to the degree of disruption, while **extensity** denotes the scope or number of persons affected.

It is also true in the media that big names make big news. In political journalism, for example, the big name is important because of that individual's capacity for disrupting the status quo. The same potential exists in business, science and the arts.

For business, the most valuable information the media can provide relates to personnel changes. Why? Because one of the best times to sell to someone is when the person is joining a new company, or when someone has just been promoted. That's when people are most eager to make an impact. Of course, someone leaving a company or industry can also have some real potential for disruption, but the effect may not extend to anyone other than that one individual.

It is a goal of most businesses and organizations to increase the number of people who know about the good work they do. Media can help or hinder the achievement of this goal. Therefore, it helps to understand something about how the media operate and how news stories are made. It benefits both to know more about the other.

The Making of a News Story

The usual progression of a news story begins with the basic *facts* of the event:

What happened? Who was involved? When did it happen? Where did it take place? How did it happen? Why did it happen?

The next phase deals with *perceptions* of the events in the story:

What was your reaction?

It is generally at this stage that an opposing opinion will be quoted. This alternate view will be used to add a sense of balance to the discussion. The third phase deals with the direct or indirect *implications* of the issue, and links these to other events already in the public's attention. Finally, the story may end with a *call to action*—to make things right if they are wrong. A call to action will be more likely to appear in a column or editorial than in a front-page news story.

News reporting is quite different from other forms of writing or storytelling. The facts or events in a novel or short story can often be told in a straightforward chronological order, whereas those in a news story must be arranged in order of their newsworthiness, from the most to least important. The most newsworthy event in any story is its climax. In ordinary prose, the climax usually comes after the bulk of the story has been told. In the news story, the climax is given right up front, usually in the first sentence or in a short paragraph right at the start. That is why the name used for this form of writing is the *inverted pyramid*. If faced with restricted space, editors cut "from the bottom up." An example of an inverted pyramid form would be as follows:

> "Three people were injured Tuesday afternoon when a train derailed in the town of Oaks, Saskatchewan. The train was heading east through the town of 100 residents when three of the train's 21 cars tipped, spilling sulfur and sand onto a road and adjoining field. Public safety officials have been assessing the situation since the derailment occurred."

The lead is the first sentence or two of any story.

In this example, an editor could remove the second and third sentences without losing the core of the "story." In a longer story, entire paragraphs could be cut, without affecting the story's viability as a publishable item. The lead is where all the important details are contained. The rest of the story provides clarification or elaboration.

There are other differences as well. The news story strives to omit all insignificant details. The lead should reveal the whole story, or at least its most newsworthy aspects. What follows the lead is a logical development of the evidence used to support it. Hence, the relationship of a lead to the rest of the story is similar to that of the topic sentence to the rest of a paragraph.

Testing a Lead

> N = Newsworthiness. Does the lead say anything worthy of note?
> E = Emphasis. Does the lead emphasize the most interesting facts?
> W = W5. Does the lead answer who, what, where, when, and why?
> S = Sources. Does the lead indicate the sources of information?

Crises Are Inevitable

Neither businesspeople nor bureaucrats like unpleasant surprises such as crises or disasters. But then again, who does? When calamity occurs, peacetime managers must sometimes stand aside and be replaced by crisis leaders or expert trouble shooters. The formal organizational structure may or may not be changed, but certainly the politics of power and influence may be transformed forever.

No one likes to think of a crisis coming too close to home or to the workplace. Nevertheless, accidents, layoffs, chemical leaks, criminal acts, war, and death do occur. And when they do, even if handled well, they are expensive for business and government in terms of money, time, and reputation. During scandals, for example, the company's communications network must function like a medical triage on the battlefield, sorting out priorities under pressures of time, stress, and scarcity of resources. Preparation is everything. Disasters happen and the consequences are often swift and deadly. Business crises are inevitable events with the potential to damage a company and the individual careers within it. Is there anything you can do to protect yourself? Yes, you can *prepare* for crisis scenarios before they arrive.

Communicating Disasters[4]

Most airlines have accepted the possibility of a terrible crash occurring someday and, therefore, have developed *crisis response groups* and contingency plans to implement in the case of disaster. Managers in other industries can benefit greatly from having the same type of routine communications planning. As a minimum, you and your company should:

◆ Identify potential problems from past incidents that may recur in the future.

◆ Identify affected audiences (customers, communities, employees, stakeholders, government, and media), and determine specific plans for each group.

◆ Prepare and develop appropriate spokespeople, messages, and actions for different contingencies.

◆ Since most accidents seem to happen, perversely, at the most inconvenient times (nights, weekends, and during vacation), managers and duty officers should have available the names, phone numbers, standby numbers, and alternate numbers of all key personnel in charge of functional priorities.

◆ Have background information and statistics on hand that will help to position the company positively despite the accident (airlines keep data on the type of plane, its safety record, number of passengers, number of passenger miles flown without fatality, names of the crew, and other relevant details).

◆ Tell it all and tell it fast. Get as much information out as quickly as possible. Quick release expedites coverage of the event, minimizing drawn out follow-ups and quelling rumours which are usually more horrible than the truth. The less people know, the more they will fear the consequences.

◆ Agree on one voice for the company, someone who is confident, articulate, cool-headed, and decisive. Good luck.

Some Pointed Media Tactics

Whether they are gathering specific data for a story or simply "fishing" for new information, most journalists will say that the information you provide them will be used in one of three ways:

1. Material they will use with your name attributed.
2. Material they will use as background, without attribution.
3. Material they will just use for their own personal understanding of the issue—"off the record".

Whatever journalists say about how they will use the information you provide, once the piece has gone to press, distinctions that may have existed in earlier drafts are now often blurred. For example, what you intended to be background information only, may end up as a quote attributed directly to you.

Some of the more obvious, and legitimate, tactics journalists use to search out information for news material are hypothetical questions, closed questions, and prefaced probes. **Hypothetical**, or "what if?," *questions* can be helpful in identifying attitudes a person has that may make him or her prone toward certain decisions. The following are examples of hypothetical questions:

If you were promoted to vice-president of this company, what new projects would you implement?

Let's assume you were in charge of this sales campaign; what approaches would you use?

Answers to these kinds of questions can say a lot about how a person will react in various situations.

Whereas hypothetical questions give the respondent the freedom to elaborate on an answer, **closed questions** often force a "yes" or "no" response, on issues that really demand more explanation. Closed questions can be used as a tactic to stir controversy or to enliven an interview.

Prefaced probes are another device used to set up a question. These are similar to "set-for-spike" plays in volleyball. The reporter tosses up a brief statement or two as a setup, before driving home the main question. For example:

> "CEOs of corporations in 1994 are paying themselves outrageous salaries, and have been for some time. Mr. Whitworth, you were quoted in *Newsweek* as saying that the only real restraint, in terms of CEO compensation, is the amount of gall the CEO possesses. Why all the sudden indignation?"

Another ploy or strategy journalists use is to offer a choice between options A or B, when what you may really believe is that C or D is the best option. If you are confronted with this tactic, the best response is simply to *point out the fallacy gently*, and rephrase the question to suit yourself. Some politicians have absolutely perfected this method of making their point simply by rephrasing a question to their own liking before answering it. Here is an example of a question asked by a reporter and the same question rephrased by a respondent:

Reporter:	Your committee has spent six months preparing this legislation, twice the amount of time you stated would be needed. Why the delay?
Committee chair:	Legislation in a difficult area like this has been a long time coming. I agree that no one should be rushing the process. Why have we taken more time than we said would be needed? Well, in an area like this, decisions have to be made . . .

Setting Your Own Agenda

Bearing in mind that the media viewpoint may differ from your personal or the corporate perspective, managers can prepare themselves for media interviews by setting their own agenda and linking it to the reporter's agenda whenever possible.

You can start by anticipating questions and thinking through your replies. There is no substitute for thorough planning and preparation. If you were the journalist, what issues or questions would you want addressed? Ask yourself what you want the audience to do or remember as a result of your comments. Why should they listen to you?

Have an agenda of at least three major points you want to discuss in the interview, and plan to work them into the conversation whenever the opportunity arises. In the press there will be room for you to clarify your point, but the average radio or television remark is usually edited down to 10 to 20 seconds. You should keep a stash of six or seven intriguing 15-second quotes on hand, and use them as a bridge between the reporter's agenda and your own.

A Three-Step Approach to Dealing with the Media

In their book, *You Are the Message*,[5] Roger Ailes and Jon Kraushar introduce the following three-step approach to answering questions on the spot from reporters:

1st Step: Give a one- or two-sentence summary of your position.

2nd Step: Supply a concrete example to back it up.

3rd Step: Provide further elaboration in support of your original statement.

When asked a question, answer briefly and directly. Then, if it helps, add a point or two to elaborate, preferably from your own agenda. Only if pressed should you go to the third step. For example, imagine that a reporter has asked the following of a Member of Parliament:

> 66You were pressured by the large, multinational chemical companies to block new environmental legislation, weren't you?99

The MP's answer might be, "I met or heard from everyone involved in the issue, including environmentalists, consumer groups, and the companies." Then he or she might add: "Based on these discussions, all parties agreed that the industry would set its own standards, rather than us having to pass another law through the legislature."

Here is another example of the three-step strategy for handling a particular encounter with the media:

Reporter (to CEO):	Your salary and bonuses seem exorbitant when compared to what your employees are paid.
CEO (1st step reply):	My pay is in line with the compensation generally awarded the chairman of any similarly outstanding company.
(2nd step):	As you know, I do not set my own pay. It gets set by a group of professionals who have a great many factors to consider in determining who gets paid what amount.
Reporter:	But isn't that a lot like extorting the shareholders? I mean, you make better than $20.2 million a year—and your company *lost* money the first quarter of this year!
CEO (2nd step):	My compensation is based on long-term rates of return. Our average rate of return on common stock during my seven years as chairman is 22 percent—double the seven-year average for the industry as a whole.
Reporter:	But don't you think that $20 million is a bit much compared to, say, your secretary—who earns less than 0.25 percent of what you do?
CEO (3rd step):	I'm paid based on my proven, long-term ability to manage the company and find new challenges in my work. Look, the world's Formula One racing champion earns as much as I do. More, in fact. So far this year he has won the first four of five Grand Prix. And he has won the world's championship twice in the last three years. He gets compensated according to the standards of his profession—and so do I—according to the standards of mine.
Reporter:	But you haven't answered my question. Don't you think that you and other corporate CEOs in this country are being overpaid? And don't you think the public has a right to be upset about it?
CEO (looping back to the 1st step—be brief and to the point—and smile):	Well, as I said before, this is what people in my position get paid for our results.

There Are No Rules, But Here Are Some of Them

Each media situation is unique. There are no "rules" for every situation, but there are some general guidelines that you might apply to help you determine the appropriate course of action to take in each case.

◆ Find out, if you can, what the press article or media show is all about. Ask what you will be expected to say, and who else will be interviewed.

◆ Never go into a media interview unprepared. Discuss the interview in advance with a trusted advisor, coach, or public relations consultant.

◆ Be brief, be friendly, and be positive.

◆ Never argue with the press. Remain composed at all times. The more inflammatory the journalist or the remarks, the cooler you should be in contrast.

◆ Generally the tougher the questions, the shorter your answers should be. Don't get sucked in, or foul yourself up, by ranting and raving. Whether it is for TV, radio, or the press, say what you have to say and then stop. It is the reporter's job to come up with the next question.

◆ Whenever you can, frame your answers in the context of "the public interest", which most journalists would like to believe they serve and protect. For example, rather than focusing on the "return-on-investment" of a new product (as you would at a board of directors meeting), focus on ways this product will save consumers' time, or otherwise improve the quality of their lives.

◆ If you find yourself in the midst of a crowded and confusing hallway (or the courthouse steps, perhaps) with 20 reporters and blinding lights—and 20 more crew pushing microphones into your face—you can usually maintain control by selecting a *single question* to which you want to respond. Look directly at the reporter who asked it, and give that person your reply.

◆ When appearing on television, don't worry about which camera to look into. That's the job of the studio crew or other production staff. Moreover, always bear in mind that, even when you are not speaking, you may still be on the air.

◆ Avoid jargon. Roger Ailes (George Bush's media consultant) provides us with the following interpretations of quotes as examples of "deadly versions of lively thoughts":

DULL: The two leading ways to achieve success are improving upon existing technology and finding a means of evading a larger obligation.

INTERESTING: The two leading recipes for success are building a better mousetrap and finding a bigger loophole.

—Edgar A. Schoaff

DULL: To construct an amalgam, you have to be willing to split open its component parts.

               INTERESTING: To make an omelette, you have to be willing to break a few eggs.

                       —Robert Penn Warren

DULL: Capital will not produce great pleasure, but it will remunerate a large research staff to examine the questions proposed for a solution.

INTERESTING: Money won't buy happiness, but it will pay the salaries of a large research staff to study the problem.

                       —Bill Vaughan

The Big Ten

According to Roger Ailes (*You Are the Message*, 1988), the ten most common problems in communications are:

1. Lack of rapport with the audience.
2. Overall lack of energy or spark.
3. Rigid body language.
4. Overly intellectual versus emotional orientation.
5. Obvious fear of failure and discomfort.
6. Poor eye contact and facial expression.
7. Lack of humor.
8. Unclear presentation/obviously unprepared.
9. No use of silence for impact.
10. Boring language and/or subject matter.

Self-Evaluation Form

In the following Interpersonal Skills Clinic you will be asked to role-play a business-media interaction. You can use this self-evaluation form to determine how you would respond to questions from the media. Use a tape-recorder or video camera to provide a record of your responses for analysis.

Voice and Delivery:

◆ Did I sound confident?
◆ Was my voice under control?

- Was I aware of my breathing?
- Did I manage to avoid using too many "ums" and "ahs"?
- Did I sound interesting and interested?

Body Language:

- How did it feel?
- Was my posture natural and appropriate?
- Did I make good eye contact with others?
- Was I aware of my facial expressions and hand gestures?
- Were there any distracting mannerisms that I was aware of?
- Was there a good exchange of energy with my audience?

Content and Design:

- Was I clear and concise enough?
- Was I well enough prepared?
- How well did the introduction and conclusion work?
- Was there a unifying framework for what I was saying?
- Was there a natural progression from point to point?
- What worked well?
- What would I change next time if I were to do it again?

Overall Effectiveness:

- Did I achieve what I wanted to achieve?
- Did I have good rapport with my audience?
- What do I remember most of all?
- What was unexpected?
- What am I most pleased about?
- What lessons can I take away with me from this experience?

INTERPERSONAL SKILLS CLINIC

THREE MEDIA SITUATIONS

This exercise is intended to give you practice in handling business-related media interviews. The purpose of these interviews is to give you another opportunity to develop your oral presentation skills as well as to coach others to communicate effectively in a public forum. Try to arrange to meet with a group of five or six people. Each member of each group should take the role of an executive being interviewed by a small group of enquiring reporters (played by the others in each group). The interviews may be videotaped and played back for discussion later.

A brief description of the roles of "executives" and "reporters" is provided, as well as three media situations. You can make whatever assumptions you must to flesh-out the story. Each group should read over the assigned scenario and discuss appropriate communication strategies among themselves (prior to the presentation).

The Executive's Role

1. Give a brief (one minute) statement to the press. It should be typed, copied, and handed out to members of the media corps either simultaneously with or in advance of the interview.

2. For the next three minutes, be prepared to respond to any or all of the reporters' questions.

   Here are some general suggestions:

◆ Focus on two or three points, each of which you can articulate in short sentences or 10-second "sound bites."

◆ In reinforcing your points, try to be colorful, quotable, and concrete. Interesting images, metaphors, analogies, facts and figures are more newsworthy than clichés or vague generalities.

◆ Keep to your agenda and return, when appropriate, to the major points you want to make.

◆ Avoid repeating reporters' negative terms, such as "disaster," "illegal," "bankrupt," "collapse," "kickbacks," and "corruption." Be cautious of words that may get you into legal trouble.

◆ Avoid speculation or seductive hypothetical questions.

◆ Avoid defensive, hostile, punishing, or sarcastic remarks.

◆ If uncertain about facts, say so. And promise to get back with an answer later. Avoid saying things you might later have to correct.

◆ Avoid a brusque "no comment"—which may suggest that you have something to hide. If you can't respond, say why not. Remember that the reporter needs a story. He or she will either get it from you—or from other sources whose interests may not be the same as yours.

The Reporter's Role

1. Consider, in consultation with your media colleagues, possible angles for a news story based on the scenario you have been assigned to cover.

2. Prepare an interview guide of at least 10 questions and probes. (It is always best

to have more questions on hand than you will need to use.) Each questioner should ask two or three short questions in rotation. Since there will be five or six reporters in each set of interviews, assign one to handle the videotape machine and another to keep strict time. The other three or four reporters should ask the questions.

SITUATION 1: CAPITAL INVESTMENTS INC.

You are CEO of one of the most powerful and aggressive Bay Street investment firms, Capital Investments Inc. Your firm does fifteen to twenty percent of all trading on the Toronto Stock Exchange (TSE). In 1991 Capital traded $22-billion worth of stock on the TSE—more than any other brokerage. However, the Ontario Securities Commission (OSC) had occasion to fine the company over $100 000 for a variety of trading violations during that year.

The OSC rules require investors to publicly disclose holdings of ten percent or more of a share-class stock. Last week, one of Capital's senior floor traders, James Bond, was discovered to have bought almost forty percent of ACE Industries share-class stock without publicly disclosing the holdings. When challenged by the OSC, Bond said it was simply an "inadvertent mistake." A great fuss has been made about this in the press since then.

Yesterday, the OSC announced that it will be imposing a 10-day trading ban on both Capital Investments and Mr. James Bond. The ban from trading on the TSE is to take effect in three weeks. Your PR chief has arranged today's press conference with representatives of the *Financial Post, The Globe and Mail*, and CBC News. The media corps are anxious to hear your reaction to yesterday's OSC announcement.

What the Media Already Know

◆ The OSC ban is a rare event. It has happened only twice in the past 10 years.

◆ If public shareholders had known of James Bond's acquisition (a takeover is triggered when a company buys more than twenty percent of a class of equity shares in a company), they would have been entitled to bid up the share price of ACE Industries' share-class stock.

What Only You Know for Sure

◆ Capital's corporate finance department estimates that a 10-day trading suspension would cut Capital's profits by eighty to ninety percent.

◆ Although prepared at first to launch an appeal of the OSC ban in the Supreme Court of Ontario, James Bond and his lawyer have now decided definitely *not* to appeal the personal suspension.

SITUATION 2: SAUNDERS AND MILLS PHARMACEUTICALS

You are the CEO of Saunders and Mills, one of the largest multinational chemical and pharmaceutical companies in the world. In 1991, your company spent over $200 million on cardiovascular research in Canada alone. In early January 1992, word leaked out that researchers at the University of Montreal (U of M) had evidence that a Saunders and Mills cholesterol-reducer, Vasodor, had the side-effect of halting hardening of the arteries and could even shrink arterial plaque deposits that lead to heart attacks.

The Health Protection Branch (HPB) of Health and Welfare Canada, and the FDA in the United States, do not permit drugmakers to publicize that their drugs might have potentially beneficial uses other than those that have gone all the way through the rigors of the HPB and FDA approval processes.

Yesterday morning *The Globe and Mail* published a report that researchers at the U of M have confirmed that "Vasodor acts as a powerful weapon against heart attacks." Yesterday afternoon you received a telephone call from HPB Chief Dr. Peter Gray. Dr. Gray called to remind you that your company faces discipline and possibly federal prosecution if any further claims are made for Vasodor as preventive treatment for heart attack *before the drug has been approved for that purpose*. You have called a press conference for today to respond to yesterday's story in the *Globe*.

What the Media Already Know

◆ Many drugs are used routinely by patients for other than strictly approved treatments.

◆ Another Saunders and Mills drug, the antihypertensive Mertec, (which was designed and approved to help people suffering from chronic congestive heart failure) has also proved to curb heart failure among patients with damaged hearts. Approval for that purpose has recently been granted by the American FDA.

What Only You Know for Sure

◆ Vasodor may prove to cause adverse side effects such as drowsiness, blurred vision, nausea, or tremors in some patients.

◆ HPB Chief Dr. Peter Gray has warned you that your company faces discipline and possibly federal prosecution if further claims for Vasodor as preventive treatment for heart attacks are publicized.

SITUATION 3: EXCEL SOFTWARE DEVELOPMENT CORPORATION

You are CEO and president of Excel Software Development Corp. You are a former journalist and marketing consultant for IBM. Since taking over the helm at

Excel in 1986 you have led the company from a twenty percent share of a specialized computer software market in North America, to over thirty-five percent in 1990. However, in 1991 Excel saw an erosion of its market share (now at twenty-two percent) down five percent in the last two quarters alone.

The newest version of Excel's *Vanguard Spreadsheet*, one of the first designed for Microsoft Corp's hot-selling Windows graphics system, appeared in March 1991—rife with bugs. A month later, the company had to replace it. Five months after that, Senior VP Frank Mann quit the company after eight years at his position. By the end of the year, six other Excel executives left the company—many of them publicly blaming you for their departure.

This morning, Anne Wilson, Excel's VP of research and development also announced she was leaving the company. In a statement to the press, Ms. Wilson said, "At the end of the day, the issue at Excel is one of leadership or, more properly, the lack of it!"

Since hearing this remark broadcast in all the media, you have decided to fight back. You have granted a media interview so that you might make a statement in your own defence, and counter any negative media coverage that has already taken place.

What the Media Already Know

◆ In addition to being CEO and president, you are also chair of Excel's four-person board of directors.

◆ Market researcher International Data Corp. estimates that only about 250 000 copies of Vanguard for Windows have been sold to date—one fourth of the volume analysts had projected. Excel stock is down to $20 from approximately $42 in August 1991.

What Only You Know for Sure

◆ Despite flat sales and falling stock prices, Excel still has support from some prominent Bay Street analysts. James Bond at Capital Investments recommends Excel as a "bargain," in terms of its projected 1992 earnings.

◆ Excel's projected twenty percent revenue growth, to $800 million this year, will actually lag behind the industry's thirty percent growth. You expect earnings of $1.03 a share—less than in 1986, when you started.

●　　●　　●　　●　　●　　●　　●　　●　　●　　●　　●　　●

And finally . . .

Unfortunately, at present there continue to be, against all practical considerations, some business executives who categorically refuse to be interviewed by the media. Although they undoubtedly have their reasons, they risk having their company's story told poorly, adversely, or not at all, by those less informed about or less favorably disposed towards the firm. Managers today, and in future, will be expected to play a central role in establishing and maintaining effective media relationships. "No comment" just won't be acceptable anymore. Management must make a commitment to providing more open communications and cooperation with all of its public constituencies.

What journalists want most from the business world are cooperative relations with bright, pleasant people. They expect business to make some moves in the direction of establishing trust and rapport with the editors and reporters most likely to be involved in a company story. Most of all, they want candid, accurate information, and some respectful consideration in such matters as returning phone calls. This is not a lot to ask. In return, business obtains useful information and, sometimes, favorable press or publicity. Enhanced relations with the media will ultimately benefit any firm's reputation, sales, success, and profits.

CHAPTER REVIEW QUESTIONS

1. What is a purpose statement?
   a. A purpose statement is an extended essay describing your full intentions on a given action item.
   b. A purpose statement is a brief expression of the main idea that you will be conveying in your presentation.
   c. A purpose statement is the introduction to a graduate-level discussion group.
   d. A purpose statement is a record, usually in audiotape form, of a meeting.

2. Why is setting the purpose statement an important part of planning an oral presentation in an organization?

3. Comment on and revise the following purpose statement.
   Statement: This hospital is spending too much money.

4. The following is the traditional formula used for comparison and contrast:
   1. Say what the thing is _____.
   2. Then say what it is.
   3. Say what the thing is _____.
   4. Finally, say what it is _____.

5. What is the structure for a formal definition?
   a. Say what the thing is like, then say what it is not like (steps 3 and 4 of a formal comparison and contrast)
   b. Say what the thing is *not*, then say what it is (steps 1 and 2 of a formal comparison and contrast)
   c. Say what a thing is (step 2 of a formal comparison and contrast)
   d. Say what the thing is, then say what it is not like (steps 2 and 4 of a formal comparison and contrast)

6. What are the four characteristics of an audience to consider for an oral presentation?

7. For the following situation, state the interpersonal relationships to be made clear and suggest a design for the proxemics.
   You are the new supervisor of a small graphic design company. Every week, the three designers meet with you to discuss current projects. The meetings are for information and consultation, and they have always been informal and collegial.

8. Why should you draft a set of notes as you plan an oral presentation or meeting?

9 Briefly state and discuss the six steps for drafting a set of notes for an oral presentation or meeting.

10. What are the suggestions we offer for delivering a presentation?

11. What are the five steps for planning and calling a meeting?

12. How may the chair of a meeting influence or enhance the proceedings of a meeting?
    a. Cue the discussion, focus others' attention.
    b. Postpone discussion, focus all cues.
    c. Cue further discussion, focus on cues, and pay attention.
    d. Focus the discussion, cue others, and end or postpone further discussion.

13. Define news.

14. Intensity refers to the _____ of disruption present, while extensity denotes the _____ or number of persons affected.

15. Most journalists will say that the information you provide them will be used in one of three ways:
    a. Material they will use unedited; material they will use copy-edited; material they will use substantially edited.
    b. On radio, on television, in the newspaper.
    c. Material they will use with your name attributed; material they will use as background; material they will use for personal understanding.
    d. Material for their notes; material for their assignment; material for their editor.

16. What is the best response when you are given only two alternatives, neither of which suits your view of the situation?

17. What are the stages of progression in a news story?
    a. introduction, body, summary, conclusion
    b. facts, perceptions, implications, call to action
    c. facts, interpretation, implication, speculation
    d. narration, description, definition, argumentation

18. The lead should reveal the _____ story, or at least its most _____ aspects.

19. What should a company do to establish good media communications following a crisis or an accident?

20. What is the three-step technique for dealing with reporters' questions?

SUGGESTED ANSWERS

1. b.

2. The purpose statement is particularly important in the plan of an oral presentation in an organization because the intention of the presenter is usually to persuade, and to persuade requires a clear statement of the speaker's purpose.

3. *Comment:* It would be difficult to verify this statement, since a point of comparison is not stated for the spending.

Revised Statement: Last year, this hospital spent X percent more for certain comparable procedures than any other hospital in the province.

4. not; not

5. d.

6. The four characteristics of the audience to consider are number, demography, understanding, and familiarity.

7. The interpersonal relationship to be made clear is the fact that the group works as a team and that the purpose of the meeting is the generation of ideas and the provision of support for one another. You might use a small round table, or you might have the meeting in the designers' work space, perhaps around one of their drafting tables.

8. Notes can act as an aid to planning; they can help you build confidence by providing a focal point for your thoughts; and they will be your reference during the presentation or meeting.

9. *Step 1: Identify the Dimensions.* List the four dimensions of your presentation: purpose, rhetorical mode, audience, and proxemics.
Step 2: Gather Your Information. Based on the rhetorical mode you have chosen, carry out the research required.
Step 3: Organize Your Ideas. Develop the body of your presentation by determining how the information can best be presented, whether some of it needs to be deleted, and whether you have neglected to gather important information.
Step 4: Write an Introduction and a Conclusion. Write the "frame" for the body, which will appeal to the audience's interests, provide a source of curiosity, establish and maintain the atmosphere of the presentation, and suggest the purpose statement.
Step 5: Rewrite. Ensure that the transitions between the three parts of the presentation (introduction, body, conclusion) and between the main points in the body are clear and smooth. Anticipate any objections to your presentation.
Step 6: Rehearse. Try your presentation in front of someone else, or with the aid of a mirror or video camera.

10. Maintain eye contact.
Stick to your plan.
Emphasize transitions.

Determine whether you are being heard.
Ensure that the audience can see and hear your audio-visual aids.
Use hand-out material with care.
Don't emphasize mistakes.
End on time.

11. 1. State the purpose of the meeting.
    2. Choose the participants and inform them of the time and place for the meeting.
    3. Draft, circulate, and finalize the agenda.
    4. Hold the meeting.
    5. Follow up.

12. d.

13. "The news" is an account of an event, fact, or opinion that interests people and excites their comment. Most often, what's in the news is an account of the changing relationships between people, and between people and their environment or circumstances. Change, or the potential for change, is the essential element in the news.

14. degree; scope

15. c.

16. The best response is simply to *point out the fallacy gently*, and rephrase the question to suit yourself.

17. b.

18. whole; newsworthy

19. ◆ Identify potential problems from past incidents that may recur again in the future.
    ◆ Identify affected audiences (customers, communities, employees, stakeholders, government, and media), and determine specific plans for each group.
    ◆ Prepare and develop appropriate spokespeople, messages, and actions for different contingencies.
    ◆ Have available the names, phone numbers, standby numbers, and alternate numbers of all key personnel in charge of functional priorities.
    ◆ Have background information and statistics on hand that will help to position the company positively despite the accident. Tell it all and tell it fast. Get as much information out as quickly as possible.
    ◆ Agree on one voice for the company, someone who is confident, articulate, cool-headed, and decisive. Good luck.

20. When asked a question, answer briefly and directly. Then, if it helps, add a point or two to elaborate, preferably from your own agenda. Only if pressed should you go to the third step of providing further elaboration in support of your original statement.

PIONEER PET FOODS

OVERVIEW AND ASSIGNMENT QUESTIONS

In the following scenario, which is based on a situation that could well occur in an organization, you will have the opportunity to apply the principles and skills you have learned in this chapter. The scenario can be used as the basis for a written or oral analysis or for role-play.

The director of public affairs for Pioneer Pet Foods will be meeting with a senior executive to discuss the development of a new employee communication program. Among the considerations for the director is the success of the first part of the new program, which is now complete.

1. Assume you are Robert Laidlaw, director of public relations at Pioneer Pet Foods. Develop a plan for the upcoming meeting with the senior executive group to discuss the new employee communication program.

2. How will the plan for passing the president's message down through the organization be structured? How will employee suggestions be passed back up through the organization to the executive? How much deviation from the suggested format will be tolerated?

3. How will feedback from the employees be solicited and recorded? What will the employees' role be?

4. How will suggestions and recommendations be monitored or responded to? Who will be responsible for implementing those action plans?

INTRODUCTION

Robert Laidlaw, director of public affairs for Pioneer Pet Foods glances at his calendar. Less than one week to go before his meeting with company president Elizabeth Robbins and 10 senior managers, to discuss the future of Pioneer's new employee communication program. The first activity in the program—an employee survey—is complete. It is now time to plan a follow-up program and present it to the executive.

As Laidlaw thinks about the plan's progress to date, he feels uncertain as to which direction to take next. The employee survey has indicated the following:

◆ a slim majority of employees are not entirely satisfied with the degree to which they are involved in decisions affecting their work;

◆ an even greater number is dissatisfied with the way supervisors handle work plans and development; and

◆ an overwhelming number believe that overall productivity could be significantly improved if better management communication practices were in place, so that their voices could be heard on matters affecting the company.

MANDATE OF THE PUBLIC AFFAIRS DEPARTMENT

The public affairs department at Pioneer came into existence four years earlier and was headed by a task force run by Elizabeth Robbins, who turned the department over to Robert Laidlaw when Robbins became company president six months later. The mandate of the department is as follows:

> ❝To assist the company in improving the communication and public relations aspects of its two primary functions—to produce the highest quality pet foods and distribute it to customers for a profit. ❞

Overall responsibilities of the department are to produce a company newsletter (*The Pioneer*) for employees and to implement programs and communications that address customer relations matters, including everything from bill inserts to collection notices. Any communication which falls in the area of advertising to promote sales remains the responsibility of the marketing department.

The employee survey had been Elizabeth Robbins' idea as well. Three months earlier she asked Laidlaw to conduct a survey and to report back on the communication needs of Pioneer employees. As the president said, "We need to tell people where we have been, where we are now, and where we are going!" The first phase of the program is complete. Laidlaw's next concern is how to follow up the survey with a series of small group meetings centred on a videotaped presentation by Robbins. According to the guidelines set out by Robbins for the next phase of the plan, each employee will attend a meeting conducted by his or her immediate supervisor. At the meeting, an information exchange will occur, all suggestions will be recorded, and feedback will later be given to employees concerning subsequent phases of the program.

THE PRESIDENT'S VIDEOTAPED MESSAGE

A professionally produced videotape with commentary by Elizabeth Robbins has been made to illustrate Pioneer's successes and strengths, customer expectations, and an action plan for dealing with company policies and objectives according to a new corporate strategy of open two-way communications. The forty-minute videotape contains many graphs and charts as well as visual scenes of employees, customers, and their pets. At the close of the videotape presentation, Elizabeth Robbins states the following:

> "We've all seen that our corporate environment is rapidly changing—most significantly with regard to increasing competition from other companies in the marketplace. We are facing many challenges in the decade ahead and we need these new corporate strategies just to keep our present customers and continue our growth. I believe, as I am sure you do too, there is no better demonstration of our competitive edge than the quality of our product and the efficiency of its distribution. This meeting today will unlock the door to a strong future for Pioneer. As part of this process, I want to hear from each of you. Together we can plan a strategy that not only deals with today's issues, but also opens up greater opportunities for tomorrow. "

MANAGEMENT'S REPONSE SO FAR

Judging from informal conversations Laidlaw has had with managers and supervisors who have been shown a preview of the videotape, not everyone agrees on the ultimate goals of the program. Robbins thinks of it as a vehicle for improving customer service through employee awareness and sensitivity to new customer demands. Others on the senior executive team view the program primarily as a means of establishing more open communication within the working environment at Pioneer Pet Foods. Some senior managers have voiced their opinion that a company-wide program would be "too unwieldy" and difficult to manage. One vice-president has asked Laidlaw if the next phase of the program could be restricted to functional areas—concentrating on ideas the individual departments would be able to implement on their own.

Besides differences in individual motivation, agendas, and formats, presiding managers display a wide range of leadership styles, attitudes, and degrees of expertise in conducting small group meetings. Some appear judgmental in their comments about the plan—terming some suggestions made in the videotape as "useless" or "ridiculous." The following is a sample of these responses:

"Here we go again with another useless exercise."

"As an executive, I feel undermined when the president communicates directly with my troops."

"It'll just turn into another gripe session. I doubt anything substantial will come of it."

On the other hand, there are others who indicate their support for the plan. They state the following:

"Some of our people will finally get to see what the president looks like."

"Information *should* come from the top level as much as possible—it loses authority when I give it to my middle managers to carry out."

"I think the idea is an excellent one! This will give us a chance to talk about how our department has been pushed to the limit for the last three years. This will give me the opportunity to explain why."

FUTURE CONSIDERATIONS

Thinking about his upcoming meeting with the senior executives and Elizabeth Robbins, Robert Laidlaw wonders, "How are we going to get this program in gear? Where do we go from here? What should I suggest to the executive when they ask for my recommendations? What guidelines should there be for presenting the videotape and conducting feedback sessions?"

POINTS TO CONSIDER

As well as serving an information-giving function, the employee survey and communications plan has the potential for establishing an ongoing communications climate and culture for the organization and its employees. How the plan is presented to the senior executive and Pioneer employees will likely impact the future of the company. Therefore it is imperative that the company indicate a common perspective regarding the exchange of ideas for improving performance, and act on it.

ENDNOTES

1   William Shakespeare, *Julius Caesar* (Cambridge: University of Cambridge), Act 3, Scene 2, lines 65-91.

2   Alex Osborn, *Applied Imagination,* 3rd edition (New York: Scribner, 1963).

3   See Paul Goodman, *Utopian Essays and Practical Proposals* (New York: Vintage Books, 1962), especially the chapter entitled, "Seating Arrangements: An Elementary Lecture in Functional Planning."

4   Adapted with the permission of Lexington Books, an imprint of Macmillan, Inc. from *Communicating When Your Company Is Under Siege* by Marion Pinsdorf. Copyright © 1986 by Lexington Books.

5   Roger Ailes, with Jon Kraushar, You Are the Message: The Master Commmunicators (Homewood, Illinois: Dow Jones-Irwin), 1988.

CHAPTER 8

The Harmony of Self, Organization, and Society

Chapter Review Questions

Interpersonal Communication Scenario:
Dionysos Kazantzakis, PhD

● ● ● ● ● ● ● ● ● ● ● ● ● ●

WORTH REPEATING

To venture causes anxiety, but not to venture is to lose one's self. . . . And to venture in the highest sense is precisely to become conscious of one's self.

—Soren Kierkegaard

We have been taught to strive to get ahead of the next man, but actually today one's success depends much more on how well one learns to work with one's fellow workers.

—Rollo May, *Man's Search For Meaning*

Better to write for yourself and have no public, than write for the public and have no self.

—Cyril Connolly

Self-Management and Understanding

Before we get started . . .

According to psychologist Rollo May,[1] one of the central values of the modern period (since the Renaissance) has been the belief in the importance of individual competitiveness. This value is based on the notion that the more an individual works to further his or her own economic self-interest, the more he or she will have to contribute to society. This belief was seen, until recently, as a boon to industry and commerce.

However, today, with gigantic corporations and the ever-present threat of monopoly capitalism, not many people have the luxury of being their own bosses or masters of their own destinies. In order to survive, most workers, professionals, and businesspeople must fit into broad groups or conform to large, impersonal systems. In such a milieu, individuals are hard-pressed to discover and contribute their own unique powers and initiative to the good of the community or society at large.

The professional and scientific literature on organization and administration as taught in business schools through lectures, reading, seminars, workshops, and case discussions are all used successfully to extend students' range of knowledge. But there are types of professional knowledge that are quite inaccessible through any of these methods. There are levels of knowledge which can only be attained through direct personal experience coupled with different kinds of reflection on that experience.

In this chapter we examine some of the means by which individuals may retrieve the ability to reflect before acting. Reflection must touch on the self, and so this chapter discusses methods of considering and nurturing the self.

Objectives

After you complete this section, you should be able to:

1. Describe, using an example, the importance of self-reflection for organizational leaders.
2. Describe briefly Freud's conception of the id, ego, and superego.
3. Describe briefly Berne's conception of the ego states.
4. Discuss the notion of subselves.
5. Define the following transactions: complementary, crossed, ulterior.
6. Discuss Rogers' three conditions for individual change.

Why Reflect on the Self?

When management theorists Warren Bennis and B. Nanus asked 90 prominent leaders about the personal qualities they needed to run their organizations:

> 66 They never mentioned charisma, or dressing for success, or time management, or any of the other glib formulas that pass for wisdom in the popular press. Instead, they talked about persistence and self-knowledge; about commitment, consistency, and challenge. But, above all, they talked about learning. 99 [2]

We gain self-knowledge (this learning about the self) through the process of self-reflection in which we observe and analyze our own actions.

Lee Iacocca, the CEO of Chrysler Corporation, serves as a very positive example of the value of self-reflection for business leaders. He was born in the early 1920s to Italian parents, and went on to become a leading U.S. businessman, and in the early 1980s he was being pressed to stand as a U.S. presidential candidate.

Iacocca has always appeared to be someone who knew where he was going. He was always seeking to understand himself as well as encouraging others in his organization to do the same. This effort can be glimpsed in his autobiography (itself a potent form of self-reflection) in which he talks about "the key to management":

> 66 Over the years, I've regularly asked my key people…"What are your objectives for the next ninety days? …. And how do you intend to go about achieving them?" 99

This approach is valuable because the quarterly review system makes employees accountable to *themselves..*[3]

Although self-reflection is a process primarily directed at change and development in the personal sphere, there are many self-reflective strategies and techniques that business leaders can use to learn more about themselves, their roles in the workplace, and ways of increasing the effectiveness of those teams for which they are responsible. *Journalling*, which we will discuss in Section 2, is one of them.

Encouraging self-reflection among organizational leaders is one way to encourage people in the organization to think over their collective experiences, analyze assumptions and beliefs about work, and gain insights that are personally satisfying, while at the same time contributing to the organizational development of various work groups and management teams. By facilitating self-reflective learning, we can achieve both the goals of self-knowledge and organizational learning—the process by which companies develop cumulative knowledge.

The Self in an Age of Conformity

A lot of what is written and taught about interpersonal communication (including much of the material presented in this book) has to do with helping individuals understand and take responsibility for their relationships with others. How we relate to others shapes both ourselves and our messages to others. The self is almost always focused on the other, through our involvement in the exchange of information, influence, instruction, and so on. But no self is created entirely by the social context around it. We are, to an equal extent, created by ourselves and by our relationships to others. Evaluation by others should not be our only guide to how we see ourselves. Despite the light others' opinions may cast on who we are and what we have to say, there are truths about ourselves that no one other than our *selves* can uncover or authenticate.

Intrapersonal Communication

Intrapersonal communication is the name usually given to the processing of internal messages, or communication within the self. We define **intrapersonal communication** as the process of understanding and creating meaning within the self. Such meaning occurs when we evaluate the interactions between ourselves and others. Many theories about effective intrapersonal communication presume that before we can contact another person, we must first know ourselves.

And in order to know ourselves, the theorists contend, we must recognize that we are all made up of 'subselves'.

The idea that the self is composed of elements began—as did so many ideas—with ancient Greek philosophy. Plato speaks of three parts to the psyche (the self). He likens the psyche to a charioteer and two sterling steeds which represent an impulsive self, a restrained self, and a governing self. Sigmund Freud also saw the psyche as composed of three parts: the *id*, *ego*, and *superego*. The id he saw as a chaos of instincts and blind, irrational impulses. The ego is a kind of executive chairperson whose task is to permit outlets for the id forces. The super-ego, Freud believed, is a split-off of the ego, roughly synonymous with the voice of conscience. The ego's task then, is to mediate between the id, the outside world, and superego. According to Freud, healthy psychic functioning involves the harmonizing of the three psychic elements so that no single one becomes too powerful and submerges the others.

Transactional Analysis

Another important contribution to our understanding of intrapersonal communication has been the field of transactional analysis as first described by Eric Berne in *Games People Play*[4] . The central principle of transactional analysis (TA) is that each person has three separate, internal ego states (selves) that serve as sources for our thoughts and actions. These three are the parent, the child, and the adult. According to Berne, one can tell which ego state a person is in by noting his or her posture, facial expression, tone of voice, choice of words, and other cues. The child ego state represents the input of internal events during the first five years of childhood. The adult ego state is characterized by rational, logical thinking and analytic behavior. The parent ego state is one in which you think, feel, and act as a typical parent would.

One of Berne's followers, Stewart Shapiro, has further divided these subselves by function. For example, the parent part can be divided into a nurturing parent and an evaluative parent. The *nurturing parent selves* provide support, love, care, positive reinforcement, attention, and praise. The *evaluative parent selves* are sometimes referred to as "critics" or the "voice of authority"; they reflect the values and norms of society and may be masculine or feminine. The *central organizing selves* are those voices that help coordinate the others. This coordination may be strong or weak, depending on the person. The child can be divided into a compliant child or a free, natural child. The *compliant, socialized, adapted child subselves* are the obedient, conforming child selves who try to please authorities. These selves are necessary for socialization, but too much may lead to over-conformity or a lack of creativity. Finally, the *natural child selves* may be rebellious while carrying much of the playfulness of the original child. A sense of humor often comes with this subself. The grand total of ego states found by Berne's followers appears to have no fixed number. Transactional analysis is concerned with helping the person identify his or her ego states and controlling them so that they do not "contaminate" each other. The "transactions" of transactional analysis are those that occur between the various ego states. There are three types of these: complementary, crossed, and ulterior transactions.

Complementary transactions occur when the speaker's message is received by the intended ego state of the listener and is responded to appropriately. **Crossed transactions** occur when the communicator receives a response from an ego state other than the intended one. Finally, **ulterior transactions** are implied or hidden messages given in addition to what is openly stated.

Here's an example of a complementary transaction. (See also Figure 8.1)

X: "Robin, I'd like you to analyze these data, and tell me which investment offers the best return."

Y: "I'll get on it right away, Dean. I'll have the results for you first thing in the morning."

In this case, an adult-to-adult comment was followed by an adult-to-adult response.

A diagram of a crossed transaction is shown in Figure 8.2.

Here's an example of a crossed transaction

X: "Hey Mike, it's your turn to write the monthly progress report for our group."

Figure 8.1: Complementary Transaction

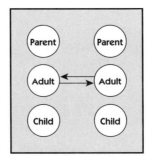

Figure 8.2: Crossed Transaction

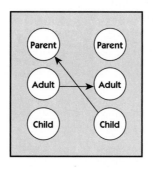

Y: "Why me? It's been my turn twice this year already. Why don't you get Alice to do this one?"

This transaction illustrates an obstacle to effective communication—a child-to-parent response.

Figure 8.3 shows an ulterior transaction. An example of such a transaction follows the figure.

X: "Pete, we're recommending you to head up our new operations in Spitsbergen." (*It's about time you got out of the home office and started assuming some real responsibility.*)

Y: "Thanks just the same Cass, but I really think I can make a greater contribution here in my current position." (*If you think I'm going to move my family above the Arctic Circle, you have another think coming!*)

When there is more than one stimulus and response transaction, communication breakdown can occur because true feelings are not being expressed or acknowledged.

Figure 8.3: Ulterior Transaction

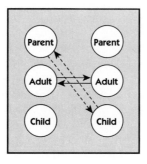

Three Climatic Conditions for Constructive Change

According to Carl Rogers,[5] there are three conditions for a psychological climate that promotes the individual's capacity for self-management and constructive change:

The first has to do with authenticity—realness, genuineness, and congruence. The more a person is himself or herself, the less need there is for putting up a false front or facade when dealing with others. And the greater the likelihood that constructive change and growth will occur.

The second attitude in creating a climate for change is acceptance, caring, or prizing—unconditional positive regard. It is a nonpossessive caring—total rather than conditional.

The third facilitative aspect is empathic understanding. This means that as individuals communicate with one another, they accurately sense the feelings and personal meanings that are being experienced by the other—and communicate this understanding.

In such growth-promoting climates, learning comes about because the direction is self-determined and managed. Self-management moves us toward an actualization of our potentialities.

And Finally...

Organizations are made up of individuals who work and think independently, but in concert with others with whom they share a part of their organizational or collective identity. Norwegian explorer Roald Amundsen (the first human being to set foot at the South Pole, in 1911) had a saying: "We are all captains; we are all crew." Amundsen's words serve to remind us that being treated like a cog in a machine isn't likely to inspire self-knowledge or voluntary discipline. The will to work is greater when people know who they are and have the feeling of being independent and responsible within their own spheres. It also serves as a reminder that we are, as a team, culture or society, working towards a common goal of identity.

Section 2 Journalling Techniques for Self-Reflection

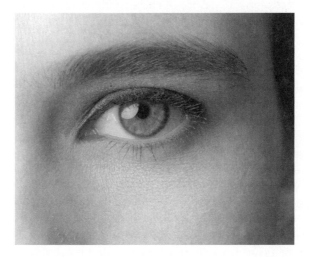

Before we get started . . .

Most studies of interpersonal communication in the workplace focus upon individual style or behavior, as well as on the development of skills for understanding the *organization*. However, the development of skills for understanding the *self* has, until recently, received much less attention. As the more traditional approaches fail to explain fully the dynamics of interpersonal and organizational communication, there has been a recent, notable shift in focus toward the significance of intrapersonal communication and self-reflection in the literature.[6]

In this section we briefly explore the *what, why,* and *how* of journalling techniques as instruments of organizational learning. Journalling is the term given to writing whose primary purpose is to record the journey of the self as it travels from one place and time to another. Learning about the self is an essential aspect of leadership. Leaders must know themselves well if they are to guide the process of self-discovery for the organization as a whole.

The section ends with an extended set of techniques that may be used for beginning and developing the process of self-reflection through journalling.

Objectives

After you complete this section, you should be able to:

1. Define *epistemic writing*.

2. Discuss the four modes of expression, which may be used in journalling.

3. Explain the notion of a "writer's workshop," and demonstrate some of the techniques that may be used in such an exercise.

Epistemic Writing

Writing enables us to find out what we know—and don't know—about whatever subject we are exploring, including ourselves. With each stroke of the pen an idea takes shape and becomes clearer. Mark Strand, a Canadian poet, describes the act of writing poetry as one of self-discovery: "What I want to do in a poem is discover what it is that I have to say."[7]

Epistemology is the theory of the methods of knowledge. Therefore, **epistemic writing** is writing that aids in thinking, learning, and self-knowledge. This approach considers writing to be a form of thinking. We suggest that writing is an important means not only of expressing thought, but of discovering new ideas and reformulating them. In this sense, then, writing *is* thinking and thinking *is* writing.

Keeping a Journal

Many people keep journals, for many reasons. A university student, for example, may keep a journal to digest and integrate what her professors teach and what she is learning in her day-to-day life. A novelist, on the other hand, might accumulate material for his novel by posing questions to himself, and writing down descriptions, bits of conversation overheard or imagined, and snatches of dreams or surfaced memories. We each have our reasons for writing—self-guidance, personal growth, the realization of our creative and leadership potential. Journalling can "help you to understand your past, discover joy in the present, and create your own future".[8]

Journalist Tristine Rainer describes four natural modes of expression, which may overlap or lead into one another. The modes are catharsis, description, free-intuitive writing, and reflection. *Catharsis* may be used to release the pressure of intense emotion that calls for some immediate expression. Writing may be used to unleash strong emotions safely. *Description* can include any narrative or story-telling account of events, feelings, dreams, places, or anything else that derives from conscious experience. It also preserves certain "unforgettable" perceptions against the annihilation of time. *Free-intuitive* writing comes from the inner consciousness. This is the realm of free association, stream of consciousness, and automatic writing. The writer simply writes down whatever comes into the mind, without worrying about whether it makes any immediate sense. *Reflection* is the observation of the process of our life and our writing. It may allow us to make new connections or realize significance where we had noticed none before. Reflection is characterized by the perspective it provides, and by the light or illumination it casts on our minds.

INTERPERSONAL SKILLS CLINIC

A WRITER'S WORKSHOP

One way to become good at anything—playing hockey, making pizza, making money, or simply fixing a bicycle tire—is to do a lot of it! We suggest that good self-reflective writing and learning require practice, some of which must be intensive for a period of time. If you are serious enough about self-reflective learning to devote a weekend—or perhaps only a day or afternoon—to the practice of these techniques and exercises, you will not only improve your communication skills, you will also learn something about yourself in the process. Guaranteed.

A writer's workshop involves two stages. The first stage involves structured and semi-structured freewriting—an oxymoron of sorts. At this stage, you do not try to edit, review, rewrite, or revise. The following techniques help to provide a focus for your writing: *unsent letters*, in which you write (but don't send) a letter to some famous, or not so famous, person—living or dead; *altered states*, in which you examine a topic from someone else's point of view; *scenes and portraits*, in which you use words to portray some person, thing, or situation. During the first stage, you do not make a conscious effort to focus on your topic. Instead, you try to mine for ideas that may be of use in the next stage.

During the second stage you must take notes on your notes. Reflect on what you've written. Go over your previous notes, and review, reflect, select, expand, reorganize, and revise what you have already created. What new ideas come to mind? What interesting combinations of thoughts can you make to progress your ideas further? Ask yourself: What are the implications of what I've written? What do I make of this? What is it connected to? How can I find out?

By taking notes on our notes we can begin to see patterns and draw inferences between disparate subjects or items of interest. This allows certain unexpected connections to arise out of the synthesis of new ideas spun out of older ones. Use the following section as a means of initiating and developing your notetaking.

A REPERTORY OF JOURNAL EXERCISES[9]

As part of the writer's workshop clinic, or simply for an experiment in journalling, you may wish to try some of the techniques and tactics listed below. Do the exercises that appeal to you, or adapt your own exercises from these basic outlines. These descriptions are deliberately sparse. There is not much to them. After all, their real value lies in what you yourself make of them.

Turn Off the Monitor/Put Down Your Pen

Many writers need a rather unstructured period during the planning phases of their work—generally "free-writing" techniques for generating and joining ideas. One way to begin is to free associate—to write without stopping or trying to compose structured sentences. Brainstorm without involving your built-in mental censor. Turn your internal editor off. Just nail down thoughts as they come to you. This might take the form of a list, a series of random notes, some key words or images—whatever will help you recall your ideas later on. If you get stalled or blocked along the way, try unsent letters, altered states, or scenes and portraits to break the impasse.

Beginning With Ourselves

Discovering what is right for us often comes from recognizing what options are not right for us.

- ◆ How do you explore the world and your options in it? Do you travel? Take mind-expanding drugs? Do you read or study? Do you interview others? Cast yourself into new experiences?

- ◆ What are you truly seeking to learn and get out of life? Where, when, and from whom do you hide or deemphasize what your true interests are?

- ◆ What are you hesitant or afraid of letting others know about you? What are your best-kept secrets? What are you afraid of?

- ◆ Are there people and situations in your life *right now* that you should leave in order to be true to who you are?

The Mythology of the Self

Myths are the interlocking stories and themes that give our lives and experiences meaning. A personal mythology is like an organizing plotline that runs through life experiences and through the critical thresholds that shape our character and behavior. For example, a business leader might discover some themes in answering the following questions:

> ❝Why are we here in this business to begin with? What are we really trying to accomplish? What quest are we (am I) on? What are my duties and obligations? What vision do I have of the future? Whom

should I aspire to become? What stage am I at in life? What must I do to prepare for the next stage? 99

Scrapbook Research

Research is an activity we all conduct daily—it is also a skill that no leader can do without. And it can be *fun* as well as important.

Research involves more than simply discovering information. It must include organization, analysis, synthesis, and application. The researcher must identify a purpose, locate sources of information, provide insights, and apply them to new settings and situations. One way to keep track of your interests—out of the mass of multi-media influences—is to put certain items of interest in a scrapbook. A well-kept scrapbook can serve as a useful "trigger" for other forms of self-reflective learning. Suggested items to load into a scrapbook: new words and definitions, interesting quotes, fortune cookie aphorisms, newspaper articles, horoscopes, pictures out of magazines, subway transfers, runes, movie stubs, photos, medicine labels, weather reports, song lyrics, pressed flowers. You name it—anything that activates your memories or imagination can be added to your scrapbook.

With a Little Help From My Friends

◆ Make a list of people and things you can trust or depend on.

◆ Where and when do you feel safest?

◆ Where and when do you feel the most dependable and trustworthy yourself?

◆ What has been the most exciting time in your life and with whom did you share it?

Walls and Bridges

Imagine you are strolling casually down a country lane in summer. Suddenly, you turn a forested corner and come upon a huge granite wall as high and as wide as the eye can see. Be as focused as you can on every detail of this situation. Now, let yourself continue to explore the situation—imagine what happens next . . .

Sometimes the way we deal with imaginary walls tells us something about the ways we deal with other walls in our lives. Do you build walls or bridges? Did you (in your fantasy) call in an air strike, tunnel your way under with the help of Steve McQueen and the cast from *The Great Escape*? Did you retreat? Pole Vault? Picnic? Or ignore the barriers you encountered?

Synchronicity

What fortunate accidents, coincidences, synchronicities, or lucky breaks have you experienced? What events seemed prearranged? What premonitions have you had of future events? Who appears in your dreams? What symbols and themes appear in your journals? When? Why? Why now?

Utopian Daydreams

◆ Imagine a utopian society in an ideal world.

◆ How is this society to be governed? Who works? When? What for?

◆ How and by whom are children raised and educated?

◆ What are the most essential features of your ideal world?

Return from the Stars

Imagine that you have been away from planet earth for 10 years space-time. But that is 127 earth years—a long, long way from home—and a lot of things have changed since you've been gone. When you return to earth you begin to travel the globe—taking whatever form of transportation appeals to you—allowing yourself to notice your strange new surroundings.

Take a few minutes to see if you are alone or with others. What do you see (in fantasy)? What sounds are there? How does the world feel and smell? When you are ready to leave, travel back the way you came. See if anything else has changed.

Portrait of a Home

◆ Draw a floor plan of a house in which you would like to be living in 10 years' time. Who lives with you? What are the physical surroundings like? What is the mood of the place? Music?

◆ Do the same for your office. What work do you do there 10 years from now? What's the view of? How do you spend your time there? And with whom? What for?

Cut! Print It!

◆ Go back to some incident in your life during which you felt very disappointed. This time stay a bit distant, if you can, and treat it as though you were watching a movie—a film in which you are the leading character, a tragic hero or protagonist.

◆ When you get to the sad part of the story yell "Cut!" Now, go back and reshoot the end of the movie. Shoot the disappointment scene *the way you wish* it had turned out. Throw away the earlier "rushes"—scrap them!—and set about "printing" a better end.

According to psychologist Carol Pearson[10], by shooting a new version of the film of your life you are creating alternative mental circuitry, and hence "printing" new beliefs about the world and what the future might hold for you.

Celebrating Victories

As decision-makers, we spend a lot of time thinking about problems that need to be solved; but we also need to put some time into thinking about the things that have gone right for us in the past. We need to recognize our own unique "high-performance patterns", so that we can call upon them again when we need to.

◆ Think of two or three times in the past when you performed to the very best of your ability—times when some task or project you were working on turned out a whole lot better than you first expected.

◆ Prompt the story along with the following probes:

How did you get involved?

What were your expectations and the expectations of others?

How did you prepare?

How did you deal with obstacles?

What was the high point of the performance?

What were the rewards?

What did you do when it was over?

What did the experience teach you?

◆ Compare these stories for their common themes and features. Look for aspects of a pattern in (1) the way you got involved, (2) the way you dealt with obstacles, (3) the feelings you had when things came to a climax, and (4) your reflections on the lessons you learned.

◆ Discuss ways in which you can build these patterns into a vision of what is possible for you in future.

Telling Tales

Being a skilled storyteller is an important organizational skill. Stories are used to make sense of what is going on, to effect change, to register information and to interpret the dramatic events that encompass the lives of every individual in every workplace.

Recalling stories about your favorite teachers, coaches, or mentors is a good way of priming your own personal journal entries. Telling someone else's story—especially someone you admire—requires a great deal of interpersonal skill: active listening, analysis, interpretation, persuasion, mutual trust, and reciprocal self-disclosure. It's good practice.

And finally . . .

Self-reflection leads to self-knowledge. And authentic communication must be based on self-knowledge. In this section we have offered suggestions for beginning or developing the process of self-reflection through journalling. We encourage you to use the techniques described to find your own path to authentic interpersonal communication.

CHAPTER REVIEW QUESTIONS

1. According to psychologist Rollo May, one of the central values of the modern period has been the belief in the importance of _____ competitiveness. This value is based on the notion that the more an individual works to further his or her own economic _____ , the more he or she will have to _____ to society.

2. By facilitating self-reflective learning, we can achieve the following:
   a. self-knowledge and organizational learning
   b. increased employee interest and improved performance
   c. little tangible but much intangible
   d. a measurable increase in employee satisfaction

3. Theories about effective _____ communication presume that before we can contact another person, we must first know _____ .

4. A sense of humor often comes with the following subself:
   a. playful child
   b. natural child
   c. original child
   d. laughing child

5. Freud's conception of the self was based on his notion of the following:
   a. psyche, natural self, and ego
   b. sex, violence, and id impulses
   c. ego, superego, and psyche
   d. id, ego, and superego

6. State whether the following is a(n) complementary, crossed, or ulterior transaction.

   Sharma: "The work you did on the audit this year was done very quickly. Good job!"

   Ellie: "Don't patronize me. Just because I work fast doesn't mean I sacrifice accuracy in the process."

7. The three key words in Rogers' conditions for change are:
   a. authenticity, acceptance, and understanding
   b. alertness, alacrity, and acceptance
   c. caring, empathy, and understanding
   d. authenticity, empathy, and analysis

8. What is epistemic writing?

9. What are the four modes of written expression?

SUGGESTED ANSWERS

1. individual; self-interest; contribute
2. a.
3. intrapersonal; ourselves
4. b.
5. d.
6. crossed
7. a.
8. *Epistemic writing* is writing that aids in thinking, learning, and self-knowledge.
9. The modes are catharsis, description, free-intuititive writing, and reflection.

INTERPERSONAL COMMUNICATION SCENARIO

DIONYSOS KAZANTZAKIS, PHD

OVERVIEW AND ASSIGNMENT QUESTIONS

In the following scenario, which is based on a situation that could well occur in an organization, you will have the opportunity to apply the principles and skills you have learned in this chapter. The scenario can be used as the basis for a written or oral analysis or for role-play.

A PhD graduate's career history and first six months on the job as Director of Staff Development in a county hospital is described. Dr. Kazantzakis is at the end of his probationary period of employment with the hospital and is told that his contract will not be extended. He and his wife are about to discuss what went wrong and what they should do now.

1. Assume you are Dionysos Kazantzakis. Talk about your career and what you want most from the future. What are your most immediate plans? What are your longer term goals?

2. As you discuss your long-term strategy, what lessons can you take with you from your experience at Bethesda County Hospital?

3. What might you have done differently, and why?

4. What can you do to plan a better fit for yourself with the next organization you join?

INTRODUCTION

Stunned at being "let go," Dionysos Kazantzakis ponders the incomprehensible events which characterized his last six months at Bethesda County Hospital in the Muskoka region of Southern Ontario. What started out as the promise of a bright future has suddenly run aground, and Dionysos wonders what he will do next. His short time at Bethesda had been one of ravaging anxiety and utter turmoil, and he was determined to find a better "fit" for himself in another organization—far away from this one. "It is our future that lays down the law of our today," he thinks to himself. But today, Dionysos wonders how he will explain things to his pregnant wife—and closest friend—Marisa.

BEGINNINGS

Dion Kazantzakis was born in 1965 near the Yorkville district of Toronto. Unlike his father—a one-time welterweight prize fighter turned real estate broker—Dion wanted to go to university and learn to be a teacher. Ever since his freshman year at Michigan Tech, he has had dreams and ambitions of becoming a professor of philosophy. Dion had attended Michigan Tech on an athletic scholarship for track and field. Although he had always prided himself on being a "well-rounded" person, there was a part of himself that held serious reservations as to whether this was true.

Dion earned his B.A. and M.A. in education at Michigan Tech. But he chose to pursue his PhD at UCLA's graduate school of philosophy. He chose UCLA for the opportunity to work with professors he had studied and admired while at Michigan Tech. It was while living in Los Angeles that Dion met and married his wife Marisa.

LATER

As he drives the 20 minutes it takes for him to go from the Hospital to his brown cedar house on the edge of Island Lake, Dion thinks to himself:

I've gained six months' experience—but I don't know if that's a plus or not. Having *some* actual hands-on experience is better than none from my own point of view. But how will it be viewed by others? I still have my training and degrees to emphasize. But without any practical experience I may be painting myself into a corner. Employers might consider me too expensive and inexperienced. University degrees are rarely enough on their own. But six months is not a lot. Prospective employers will want to know why my stay at Bethesda has been so abrupt. Marisa knows why. But knowing why won't help her to cope with the burden of being tossed out of her home again. With no security. With a baby on the way. With our new house for sale and our new life—temporarily—in shambles.

THE ROAD TO BETHESDA COUNTY

After he graduated from UCLA with a PhD, Dion, together with Marisa, moved from Los Angeles to Toronto. When he read the advertisement for the job at Bethesda County Hospital in *The Globe and Mail*, he applied and got it. The job paid well and Dion and Marisa immediately bought a spacious cedar cottage on Island Lake—20 minutes by car from the Hospital.

Although Dion hoped to ultimately become an academic philosopher in a well-regarded university, at this stage of his career he was anxious to broaden his professional experience and leadership skills in whatever way he could. The position of Director of Staff Development at Bethesda County Hospital seemed like the perfect opportunity. The current economic recessions in Canada and the United States, and current government policy regarding reductions in the transfer of payments in support of higher education, meant that there would not likely to be any immediate openings in university faculties of philosophy.

Not only was Dion's job well paid, Marisa was able to pursue her own career in art by making ceramic artwork and pottery at home, which she sold throughout the region with the help of a very successful travelling retail agent. The couple's home on Island Lake had cost them a modest amount, and their combined incomes left them relatively affluent. They decided to put fifty percent of their net income toward the mortgage. Now they would have to worry about selling the house in a depressed market. They would also have to sell many of their furnishings as well and move in with Dion's mother in Toronto.

ORIENTATION AT BETHESDA COUNTY HOSPITAL

When Dion had been hired by the president of the hospital, Dr. Kurt Vetter, he was most impressed. Dr. Vetter explained that the hospital was ripe for change and that he was intent on doing something about it. He wanted Dion to lead the newly-formed Department of Staff Development and Education as a part of this action for change. Vetter went on to explain that the job would involve a six-month trial period, after which a mutual assessment would be made with respect to longer term prospects. Dion and Marisa were both confident that this was going to turn out to be an excellent opportunity for them and their children—and for the hospital.

As president, Dr. Vetter would not be involved in the day-to-day planning of the new department of Staff Development and Education. He told Dion that he would leave the planning and budgetary matters to him and his vice-president of finance and administration, Jackie Slater, to work out. Slater was away on sabbatical leave at the time Vetter brought Dion on. She arrived within the first month of Dion's appointment. Slater soon made it known that, according to the official chain of command at Bethesda County Hospital, she would be Dion's supervisor.

In the course of their planning and work together, it became evident to all parties concerned that Dion and Jackie Slater would never get along with one another. Both people had very different personal styles as well as goals and visions for the organization and its department of Staff Development and Education. When Slater had him re-assigned to a dark and distant office in the far reaches of the hospital, Dion moved himself into a vacant office adjacent to the administrative corridor of the hospital. When Slater proposed he restrict his program planning to kitchen, maintenance, and cafeteria staff, Dion submitted his proposal to include the training of more senior-level nurses, doctors, and administrative staff.

Slater and Kazantzakis were at odds on every topic and technique. Once Slater had returned from sabbatical, Vetter left to take an administrative leave of his own. He was gone for the middle four months of Dion's tenure. Slater was "in charge" while Vetter was away, of course, and this made daily work a living hell for Kazantzakis. He and Marisa kept telling each other that things would be better once Dr. Vetter was back from Fort Lauderdale, Florida. Slater got her version of events to Vetter sooner than later. But the *coup de grace* was Slater's declaration: "Either Kazantzakis goes when his contract expires," she said, "or I resign." Slater had been with Bethesda County Hospital for more than 10 years—two years longer than Vetter had been president.

"GOOD LUCK IN YOUR JOB SEARCH!"

These words of Dr. Vetter's were still echoing in Dion's mind as he entered the kitchen, where Marisa was standing and waiting for him to speak first. His words were not bitter so much as resigned: "They said 'no' to any severance package, but told me, if I wanted to use them for a reference or recommendation, not to hesitate to ask."

"What did you say when they told you your contract wouldn't be extended?" Marisa asked.

"I said, 'What a coincidence, I was thinking of leaving, myself. I'm glad to see that we are finally on the same wave length.'"

POINTS TO BE CONSIDERED

This scenario may be more difficult to role-play than some of the others in this text. Try to work your way through different issues and levels of analysis. For instance, you can begin with a dialogue about the extrapersonal or organizational matters involved in the story, and then move on to interpersonal conflicts between Dion Kazantzakis and Jackie Slater or Kurt Vetter. What about the relationship between Dion and Marisa? Immediate survival issues involve the new arrival, the sale of the house, Marisa's business, and the move to Toronto. And what about intrapersonal issues regarding one's personal development, or one's calling to a marriage or a profession? You can go as far or deep with this—by reflecting on your own career and life experiences—as you are comfortable to do. *Amor fati*

● ─ ● ─ ● ─ ● ─ ● ─ ● ─ ● ─ ● ─ ● ─ ● ─ ● ─ ●

ENDNOTES

[1] Rollo May, *Man's Search For Meaning* (New York: W.W. Norton, 1953), p. 42.

[2] Warren Bennis and B. Nanus, *Leaders* (New York: Harper and Row, 1985), p. 187.

[3] Lee Iacocca, *Iacocca: An Autobiography* (New York: Bantam, 1987) p. 47.

[4] Eric Berne, *Games People Play* (New York: Ballantine, 1957).

[5] Carl Rogers, *On Personal Power* (New York: Delacorte Press, 1977).

[6] Peter Chiaramonte and Albert Mills, "Self Reflection Counselling as an Instrument in Organizational Learning," *British Journal of Guidance and Counseling*, Volume 21, No. 2, May 1993.

[7] Personal interview with Mark Strand, Athens, Ohio, October 19, 1971.

[8] Tristine Rainer, *The New Diary* (Los Angeles: J.P. Tarcher, 1978), p.18.

[9] Adapted from Carol Pearson *The Hero Within* (San Francisco: Harper & Row, 1989); Sam Keen and Valley-Fox, *Your Mythic Journey* (Los Angeles: Tarcher Inc., 1989); and David Boje "Learning Storytelling" *Sage Journal of Management Education* 15, no. 3 (August 1991).

[10] Carol Pearson, *The Hero Within* (San Francisco: Harper & Row, 1989).

Index

specific format, 162
strategy, 163-64
"In front of," 129-30
"Inside the House of Stairs," 34-36
Integration, 218-20
Intensity, 336
Interaction, 9
Interactive model of communication, 9
Intercultural communication, 195-97
Internal competitions, 145
Interpersonal communication, xvi, xvii
Interpersonal vs. intrapersonal
    communication, 6
"Interview, An," 177-80
Interviews, vii, 92
        appraisal, 260-61
        climate control, 104
        combined approach, 97
        directive and nondirective format
            of, 147
        disciplinary, 95
        "Dos and Don'ts of," 113-15
        employment, 94-95
        exit, 174
        highly structured strategy, 97
        inadequate responses, 108
        information, 121
        irrelevant responses, 109
        nondirective strategy, 97
        notetaking, 112-13
        organizational, 94
        orientation, 160-61
        orientation statement, 106
        performance planning and
            appraisal, 94-95
        persuasive, 52, 94
        prominent or famous respondents,
            109
        purpose statements, 96
        regulating, 107
        stages of, 104-12
        transitions, 108
        turn-denying, 107
        turn-maintaining, 108
        turn-requesting, 107
        turn-taking, 107
        turn-yielding, 107

Invention, 7
Inverted pyramid, 337
ITT, 33

Jackson, Don, 12
Job postings, 145
Johari Window, 240-42
Journalling, 362, 367
Julius Caesar, 306-07

Kahn, Robert, 22
Katz, Daniel, 22
Kennedy, Allan, 27
Kiechel, Walter III, 284
Kilmann, Ralph, 218
Kincaid, Laurence, 12
Kinesics, 186-87
King, Larry, 106
Knapp, Mark, 184

Labelling, 181
Laing, R.D., xv
Lasswell, Harold, 9
Lead, 337
Leading questions, 100
Lewin, Kurt, 24
Likert, Rensis, 24, 27
Linear model of communication, 6
Listening
        active, 128
        attending skills, 122
        clusters of skills, 122
        dialogic, 128-29
        following skills, 123-24
        reflecting skills, 125
"Listening Journal," 118-20
"Listening to an Interview," 120
Loaded questions, 101

Mace, Myles, 284
Machiavelli, Nicolo, 50
MacLean, Malcolm, 11
Maier, Norman R.F., 261
"Making Eye Contact," 123
"Management of Difficulties, The," 221-26
Manager-as-coach metaphor, xix, 283-84
"Managing by wandering around," 30
"Mapping" organizational communication, 16
MARCS, 56-57

Photo Credits

Avon Canada Inc.: 367
Angelika Baur: 189(2), 195
Cathy Bellesisles: 30, 50, 277, 299
Peter Chiaramonte: 188(1)
Peter Croydon: 136
Warren Evans CSP: 304
Jeremy Jones: 142
John McNeill: 251, 353, 360
Glenna Salsbury of Salsbury Enterprises: 334
Marco Shark: 116
David Starrett: 4, 14, 60, 85(Courtesy of Alive and Well), 92, 166, 175, 187, 188(2),
        189(1), 190, 204, 210, 234, 258, 376
Karen Taylor: 41